Max Müller

Lectures on the Science of Language

Max Müller

Lectures on the Science of Language

ISBN/EAN: 9783337385545

Printed in Europe, USA, Canada, Australia, Japan

Cover: Foto ©Andreas Hilbeck / pixelio.de

More available books at **www.hansebooks.com**

LECTURES

ON

THE SCIENCE OF LANGUAGE

DELIVERED AT THE

ROYAL INSTITUTION OF GREAT BRITAIN

IN

APRIL, MAY, & JUNE, 1861

BY MAX MÜLLER, M.A.

Correspondent de l'Institut de France; Foreign Member of the Royal Bavarian Academy; Honorary
Member of the Royal Society of Literature, of the Royal Asiatic Society, of the Asiatic Society of
Bengal, and of the Société d'Ethnographie de France; Corresponding Member of the Royal
Institute Academy, of the Royal Society of Göttingen, of the Royal Irish Academy, of
the American Philosophical Society, and of the American Oriental Society; Member
of the Asiatic Society of Paris, and of the German Oriental Society; Taylorian
Professor in the University of Oxford, Fellow of All Souls College,
&c. &c.

'Opera naturale è ch' uom favella;
Ma, così o così, natura lascia
Poi fare a voi, secondo che v' abbella.'
DANTE, Paradiso, 26. 130.

FOURTH EDITION.

LONDON:
LONGMAN, GREEN, LONGMAN, ROBERTS, & GREEN.
1864.

PREFACE.

MY LECTURES on the Science of Language are here printed as I had prepared them in manuscript for the Royal Institution. When I came to deliver them, a considerable portion of what I had written had to be omitted, and, in now placing them before the public in a more complete form, I have gladly complied with a wish expressed by many of my hearers. As they are, they form only a short abstract of several Courses delivered from time to time in Oxford, and they do not pretend to be more than an introduction to a science far too comprehensive to be treated successfully in so small a compass.

My object, however, will have been attained, if I should succeed in attracting the attention, not only of the scholar, but of the philosopher, the historian, and the theologian, to a science which concerns them all, and which, though it professes to treat of words only, teaches us that there is more in words than is dreamt of in our philosophy. I quote from Bacon: 'Men believe that their reason is lord over their words, but it happens, too, that words exercise a reciprocal and reactionary power over our intellect.' 'Words, as a Tartar's bow, shoot back upon the understanding of the wisest, and mightily entangle and pervert the judgement.'

MAX MÜLLER.

OXFORD: *June* 11, 1861.

DEDICATED

TO

THE MEMBERS OF THE UNIVERSITY OF OXFORD,

BOTH RESIDENT AND NON-RESIDENT,

TO WHOM I AM INDEBTED

FOR NUMEROUS PROOFS OF SYMPATHY AND KINDNESS

DURING THE LAST TWELVE YEARS,

IN GRATEFUL ACKNOWLEDGMENT OF THEIR GENEROUS SUPPORT

ON THE

7TH OF DECEMBER 1864.

CONTENTS.

LECTURE I.
THE SCIENCE OF LANGUAGE ONE OF THE PHYSICAL SCIENCES . 1

LECTURE II.
THE GROWTH OF LANGUAGE IN CONTRADISTINCTION TO THE HISTORY OF LANGUAGE . . . 29

LECTURE III.
THE EMPIRICAL STAGE IN THE SCIENCE OF LANGUAGE . 62

LECTURE IV.
THE CLASSIFICATORY STAGE IN THE SCIENCE OF LANGUAGE . 113

LECTURE V.
THE GENEALOGICAL CLASSIFICATION OF LANGUAGES . 170

LECTURE VI.
COMPARATIVE GRAMMAR 222

LECTURE VII.

THE CONSTITUENT ELEMENTS OF LANGUAGE . . . 260

LECTURE VIII.

THE MORPHOLOGICAL CLASSIFICATION OF LANGUAGES . 286

LECTURE IX.

THE PRESENT STAGE OF THE SCIENCE OF LANGUAGE.
ORIGIN OF LANGUAGE 335

APPENDIX

. . . . 411

. . . . 415

LECTURES.

LECTURE I.

THE SCIENCE OF LANGUAGE ONE OF THE PHYSICAL SCIENCES.

WHEN I was asked some time ago to deliver a course of lectures on Comparative Philology in this Institution, I at once expressed my readiness to do so. I had lived long enough in England to know that the peculiar difficulties arising from my imperfect knowledge of the language would be more than balanced by the forbearance of an English audience, and I had such perfect faith in my subject that I thought it might be trusted even in the hands of a less skilful expositor. I felt convinced that the researches into the history of languages and into the nature of human speech, which have been carried on during the last fifty years in England, France, and Germany, deserved a larger share of public sympathy than they had hitherto received; and it seemed to me, as far as I could judge, that the discoveries in this newly-opened mine of scientific inquiry were not inferior, whether in novelty or importance, to the most brilliant discoveries of our age.

It was not till I began to write my lectures that I became aware of the difficulties of the task I had undertaken. The dimensions of the science of language are so vast that it is impossible in a course of nine lectures to give more than a very general survey of it; and as one of the greatest charms of this science consists in the minuteness of the analysis by which each language, each dialect, each word, each grammatical form is tested, I felt that it was almost impossible to do full justice to my subject, or to place the achievements of those who founded and fostered the science of language in their true light. Another difficulty arises from the dryness of many of the problems which I shall have to discuss. Declensions and conjugations cannot be made amusing, nor can I avail myself of the advantages possessed by most lecturers, who enliven their discussions by experiments and diagrams. If, with all these difficulties and drawbacks, I do not shrink from opening to-day this course of lectures on mere words, on nouns and verbs and particles—if I venture to address an audience accustomed to listen, in this place, to the wonderful tales of the natural historian, the chemist, and geologist, and wont to see the novel results of inductive reasoning invested by native eloquence with all the charms of poetry and romance—it is because, though mistrusting myself, I cannot mistrust my subject. The study of words may be tedious to the school-boy, as breaking of stones is to the wayside labourer, but to the thoughtful eye of the geologist these stones are full of interest—he sees miracles on the high road, and reads chronicles in every ditch. Language, too, has marvels of her own, which she unveils to the inquiring glance of the patient student. There are chronicles below her surface, there are sermons in every word. Language has been called sacred ground, because it is the deposit of thought. We cannot tell as yet what language is. It may be a production of nature, a work of human art, or a divine gift. But to whatever sphere it belongs, it would seem to stand unsurpassed—nay, unequalled in it—by anything else. If it be a production of nature, it is her last and crowning production, which she reserved for man alone. If it be a work of human art, it would seem to lift the human artist almost to the level of a divine creator. If it be the gift of God, it is God's greatest gift; for through it God spake to man and man speaks to God in worship, prayer, and meditation.

Although the way which is before us may be long and tedious, the point to which it tends will be full of interest; and I believe I may promise that the view opened before our eyes from the summit of our science, will fully repay the patient travellers, and perhaps secure a free pardon to their venturous guide.

THE SCIENCE OF LANGUAGE is a science of very modern date. We cannot trace its lineage much beyond the beginning of our century, and it is scarcely received as yet on a footing of equality by the elder branches of learning. Its very name is still unsettled, and the various titles that have been given to it in England, France, and Germany are so vague and varying that they have led to the most confused ideas among the public at large as to the real objects of this new science. We hear it spoken of as Comparative Philology, Scientific Etymology, Phonology, and

Glossology. In France it has received the convenient, but somewhat barbarous, name of *Linguistique*. If we must have a Greek title for our science, we might derive it either from *mythos*, word, or from *logos*, speech. But the title of *Mythology* is already occupied, and *Logology* would jar too much on classical ears. We need not waste our time in criticising these names, as none of them has as yet received that universal sanction which belongs to the titles of other modern sciences, such as Geology or Comparative Anatomy; nor will there be much difficulty in christening our young science after we have once ascertained its birth, its parentage, and its character. I myself prefer the simple designation of the Science of Language, though in these days of high-sounding titles, this plain name will hardly meet with general acceptance.

From the name we now turn to the meaning of our science. But before we enter upon a definition of its subject-matter, and determine the method which ought to be followed in our researches, it will be useful to cast a glance at the history of the other sciences, among which the science of language now, for the first time, claims her place; and examine their origin, their gradual progress, and definite settlement. The history of a science is, as it were, its biography, and as we buy experience cheapest in studying the lives of others, we may, perhaps, guard our young science from some of the follies and extravagances inherent in youth by learning a lesson for which other branches of human knowledge have had to pay more dearly.

There is a certain uniformity in the history of most sciences. If we read such works as Whewell's

History of the Inductive Sciences or Humboldt's *Kosmos*, we find that the origin, the progress, the causes of failure and success have been the same for almost every branch of human knowledge. There are three marked periods or stages in the history of every one of them, which we may call the *Empirical*, the *Classificatory*, and the *Theoretical*. However humiliating it may sound, every one of our sciences, however grand their present titles, can be traced back to the most humble and homely occupations of half-savage tribes. It was not the true, the good, and the beautiful which spurred the early philosophers to deep researches and bold discoveries. The foundation-stone of the most glorious structures of human ingenuity in ages to come was supplied by the pressing wants of a patriarchal and semi-barbarous society. The names of some of the most ancient departments of human knowledge tell their own tale. Geometry, which at present declares itself free from all sensuous impressions, and treats of its points and lines and planes as purely ideal conceptions, not to be confounded with the coarse and imperfect representations as they appear on paper to the human eye, geometry, as its very name declares, began with measuring a garden or a field. It is derived from the Greek *gê*, land, ground, earth, and *metron*, measure. Botany, the science of plants, was originally the science of *botanê*, which in Greek does not mean a plant in general, but fodder, from *boskein*, to feed. The science of plants would have been called Phytology, from the Greek *phyton*, a plant.[*] The founders of Astronomy were not the poet or the philosopher,

---

[*] See Jessen, *Was heisst Botanik?* 1861.

but the sailor and the farmer. The early poet may have admired the 'mazy dance of planets,' and the philosopher may have speculated on the heavenly harmonies; but it was to the sailor alone that a knowledge of the glittering guides of heaven became a question of life and death. It was he who calculated their risings and settings with the accuracy of a merchant and the shrewdness of an adventurer; and the names that were given to single stars or constellations clearly show that they were invented by the ploughers of the sea and of the land. The moon, for instance, the golden hand on the dark dial of heaven, was called by them the Measurer—the measurer of time; for time was measured by nights, and moons, and winters, long before it was reckoned by days, and suns, and years. Moon* is a very old word. It was *mâna* in Anglo-Saxon, and was used there, not as a feminine, but as a masculine; for the moon was a masculine in all Teutonic languages, and it is only through the influence of classical models that in English moon has been changed into a feminine, and sun into a masculine. It was a most unlucky assertion which Mr. Harris made in his *Hermes*, that all nations ascribe to the sun a masculine, and to the moon a feminine gender.† In Gothic moon is *mena*, which is a masculine. For month we have in A.-S. *mônâdh*, in Gothic *menoth*, both masculine. In Greek we find *mēn*, a masculine, for month, and *mēnē*, a feminine, for moon. In Latin we have the derivative

---

* Kuhn's *Zeitschrift für vergleichende Sprachforschung*, b. ix. s. 104. A Bask name for moon is *argi-izari*, light-measure. See *Dissertation Critique et Apologétique sur la langue Basque*, p. 28.

† Horne Tooke, p. 27, note.

mensis, month, and in Sanskrit we find *mâs* for moon, and *mâsa* for month, both masculine.* This *mâs* in Sanskrit is clearly derived from a root *mâ*, to measure, to mete. In Sanskrit, I measure is *mâ-mi*; thou measurest, *mâ-si*; he measures, *mâ-ti* (or *mimî-te*). An instrument of measuring is called in Sanskrit *mâ-tram*, the Greek *metron*, our metre. Now if the moon was originally called by the farmer the measurer, the ruler of days and weeks and seasons, the regulator of the tides, the lord of their festivals, and the herald of their public assemblies, it is but natural that he should have been conceived as a man, and not as the love-sick maiden which our modern sentimental poetry has put in his place.

It was the sailor who, before entrusting his life and goods to the winds and the waves of the ocean, watched for the rising of those stars which he called the Sailing-stars or *Pleiades*, from *plein*, to sail. Navigation in the Greek waters was considered safe after the return of the Pleiades; and it closed when they disappeared. The Latin name for the *Pleiades* is *Vergiliæ*, from *virga*, a' sprout or twig. This name was given to them by the Italian husbandmen, because in Italy, where they became visible about May, they marked the return of summer.† Another constellation, the seven stars in the head of Taurus, received the name of *Hyades* or *Pluviæ* in Latin,

---

* See Curtius, *Griechische Etymologie*, s. 297.

† Ideler, *Handbuch der Chronologie*, b. 1. s. 241, 243. In the Oscan Inscription of Agnone a Jupiter Virgarius (djovei verehasiof, dat. sing.) occurs, a name which Professor Aufrecht compares with that of Jupiter Viminius, Jupiter who fosters the growth of twigs (Kuhn's *Zeitschrift*, 1. s. 89).—See, however, on Jupiter Viminius and his altars near the Porta Viminalis, Hartung, *Religion der Römer*, ii. 61.

because at the time when they rose with the sun they were supposed to announce rain. The astronomer retains these and many other names; he still speaks of the pole of heaven, of wandering and fixed stars,* but he is apt to forget that these terms were not the result of scientific observation and classification, but were borrowed from the language of those who were themselves wanderers on the sea or in the desert, and to whom the fixed stars were in full reality what their name implies, stars driven in and fixed, by which they might hold fast on the deep, as by heavenly anchors.

But although historically we are justified in saying that the first geometrician was a ploughman, the first botanist a gardener, the first mineralogist a miner, it may reasonably be objected that in this early stage a science is hardly a science yet: that measuring a field is not geometry, that growing cabbages is very far from botany, and that a butcher has no claim to the title of comparative anatomist. This is perfectly true, yet it is but right that each science should be reminded of these its more humble beginnings, and of the practical requirements which it was originally intended to answer. A science, as Bacon says, should be a rich storehouse for the glory of God, and the relief of man's estate. Now, although it may seem as if in the present high state of our society students were enabled to devote their time

---

* As early as the times of Anaximenes of the Ionic, and Alcmæon of the Pythagorean, schools, the stars had been divided into travelling (ἄστρα πλανώμενα or πλανητά), and non-travelling stars (ἀπλανεῖς ἀστέρες, or ἀπλανῆ ἄστρα). Aristotle first used ἄστρα ἐνδεδεμένα, or fixed stars. (See Humboldt, Kosmos, vol. iii. p. 28.) Πόλος, the pivot, hinge, or the pole of heaven.

to the investigation of the facts and laws of nature, or to the contemplation of the mysteries of the world of thought, without any side-glance at the practical results of their labours, no science and no art have long prospered and flourished among us, unless they were in some way subservient to the practical interests of society. It is true that a Lyell collects and arranges, a Faraday weighs and analyses, an Owen dissects and compares, a Herschel observes and calculates, without any thought of the immediate marketable results of their labours. But there is a general interest which supports and enlivens their researches, and that interest depends on the practical advantages which society at large derives from these scientific studies. Let it be known that the successive strata of the geologist are a deception to the miner, that the astronomical tables are useless to the navigator, that chemistry is nothing but an expensive amusement, of no use to the manufacturer and the farmer—and astronomy, chemistry, and geology would soon share the fate of alchemy and astrology. As long as the Egyptian science excited the hopes of the invalid by mysterious prescriptions (I may observe by the way that the hieroglyphic signs of our modern prescriptions have been traced back by Champollion to the real hieroglyphics of Egypt*)—and as long as it instigated the avarice of its patrons by the promise of the discovery of gold, it enjoyed a liberal support at the courts of princes, and under the roofs of monasteries. Though alchemy did not lead to the discovery of gold, it prepared the way to discoveries more valuable. The same with astrology. Astrology

---

* Bunsen's *Egypt*, vol. iv. p. 108.

was not such mere imposition as it is generally supposed to have been. It is counted a science by so sound and sober a scholar as Melancthon, and even Bacon allows it a place among the sciences, though admitting that 'it had better intelligence and confederacy with the imagination of man than with his reason.' In spite of the strong condemnation which Luther pronounced against it, astrology continued to sway the destinies of Europe; and a hundred years after Luther, the astrologer was the counsellor of princes and generals, while the founder of modern astronomy died in poverty and despair. In our time the very rudiments of astrology are lost and forgotten.* Even real and useful arts, as soon as they cease to be useful, die away, and their secrets are sometimes lost beyond the hope of recovery. When after the Reformation our churches and chapels were divested of their artistic ornaments, in order to restore, in outward appearance also, the simplicity and purity of the Christian church, the colours of the painted windows began to fade away, and have never regained their former depth and harmony. The invention of printing gave the death-blow to the art of ornamental writing and of miniature-painting employed in the illumination of manuscripts; and the best artists of the present day despair of rivalling the

---

* According to a writer in *Notes and Queries* (2nd Series, vol. x. p. 500), astrology is not so entirely extinct as we suppose. 'One of our principal writers,' he states, 'one of our leading barristers, and several members of the various antiquarian societies, are practised astrologers at this hour. But no one cares to let his studies be known, so great is the prejudice that confounds an art requiring the highest education with the jargon of the gipsy fortune-teller.'

minuteness, softness, and brilliancy combined by the humble manufacturer of the mediæval missal.

I speak somewhat feelingly on the necessity that every science should answer some practical purpose, because I am aware that the Science of language has but little to offer to the utilitarian spirit of our age. It does not profess to help us in learning languages more expeditiously, nor does it hold out any hope of ever realising the dream of one universal language. It simply professes to teach what language is, and this would hardly seem sufficient to secure for a new science the sympathy and support of the public at large. There are problems, however, which, though apparently of an abstruse and merely speculative character, have exercised a powerful influence for good or evil in the history of mankind. Men before now have fought for an idea, and have laid down their lives for a word; and many of the problems which have agitated the world from the earliest to our own times, belong properly to the science of language.

Mythology, which was the bane of the ancient world, is in truth a disease of language. A mythe means a word, but a word which, from being a name or an attribute, has been allowed to assume a more substantial existence. Most of the Greek, the Roman, the Indian, and other heathen gods are nothing but poetical names, which were gradually allowed to assume a divine personality never contemplated by their original inventors. *Eos* was a name of the dawn before she became a goddess, the wife of *Tithonos*, or the dying day. *Fatum*, or fate, meant originally what had been spoken; and before Fate became a power, even greater than Jupiter, it meant that which had once been spoken by Jupiter, and could never be changed—not even by Jupiter himself. *Zeus* originally meant the bright heaven, in Sanskrit *Dyaus*; and many of the stories told of him as the supreme god, had a meaning only as told originally of the bright heaven, whose rays, like golden rain, descend on the lap of the earth, the *Danae* of old, kept by her father in the dark prison of winter. No one doubts that *Luna* was simply a name of the moon; but so was likewise *Lucina*, both derived from *lucere*, to shine. *Hecate*, too, was an old name of the moon, the feminine of *Hekatos* and *Hekatebolos*, the far-darting sun; and *Pyrrha*, the Eve of the Greeks, was nothing but a name of the red earth, and in particular of Thessaly. This mythological disease, though less virulent in modern languages, is by no means extinct.

During the middle ages the controversy between Nominalism and Realism, which agitated the church for centuries, and finally prepared the way for the Reformation, was again, as its very name shows, a controversy on names, on the nature of language, and on the relation of words to our conceptions on one side, and to the realities of the outer world on the other. Men were called heretics for believing that words such as *justice* or *truth* expressed only conceptions of our mind, not real things walking about in broad daylight.

In modern times the science of language has been called in to settle some of the most perplexing political and social questions. 'Nations and languages against dynasties and treaties,' this is what has remodelled, and will remodel still more, the map of Europe; and in America comparative philologists have been encouraged to prove the impossibility of a common origin of languages and races, in order to justify, by scientific arguments, the unhallowed theory of slavery. Never do I remember to have seen science more degraded than on the title-page of an American publication in which, among the profiles of the different races of man, the profile of the ape was made to look more human than that of the negro.

Lastly, the problem of the position of man on the threshold between the worlds of matter and spirit has of late assumed a very marked prominence among the problems of the physical and mental sciences. It has absorbed the thoughts of men who, after a long life spent in collecting, observing, and analysing, have brought to its solution qualifications unrivalled in any previous age; and if we may judge from the greater warmth displayed in discussions ordinarily conducted with the calmness of judges and not with the passion of pleaders, it might seem, after all, as if the great problems of our being, of the true nobility of our blood, of our descent from heaven or earth, though unconnected with anything that is commonly called practical, have still retained a charm of their own—a charm that will never lose its power on the mind and on the heart of man. Now, however much the frontiers of the animal kingdom have been pushed forward, so that at one time the line of demarcation between animal and man seemed to depend on a mere fold in the brain, there is *one* barrier which no one has yet ventured to touch—the barrier of language. Even those philosophers with whom *penser c'est sentir,*[*] who

---

[*] 'Man has two faculties, or two passive powers, the existence of which is generally acknowledged: 1, the faculty of receiving the different impressions caused by external objects, physical

reduce all thought to feeling, and maintain that we share the faculties which are the productive causes of thought in common with beasts, are bound to confess that *as yet* no race of animals has produced a language. Lord Monboddo, for instance, admits that *as yet* no animal has been discovered in the possession of language, 'not even the beaver, who of all the animals we know, that are not, like the orang-outangs, of our own species, comes nearest to us in sagacity.'

Locke, who is generally classed together with these materialistic philosophers, and who certainly vindicated a large share of what had been claimed for the intellect as the property of the senses, recognized most fully the barrier which language, as such, placed between man and brutes. 'This I may be positive in,' he writes, 'that the power of abstracting is not at all in brutes, and that the having of general ideas is that which puts a perfect distinction between man and brutes. For it is evident we observe no footsteps in these of making use of general signs for universal ideas; from which we have reason to imagine that they have not the faculty of abstracting or making general ideas, since they have no use of *words* or any other general signs.'

If, therefore, the science of language gives us an insight into that which, by common consent, distinguishes man from all other living beings; if it establishes a frontier between man and the brute,

---

sensibility; and 2, the faculty of preserving the impressions caused by these objects, called memory, or weakened sensation. These faculties, the productive causes of thought, we have in common with beasts..... Everything is reducible to feeling.'—*Helvetius*.

which can never be removed, it would seem to possess at the present moment peculiar claims on the attention of all who, while watching with sincere admiration the progress of comparative physiology, yet consider it their duty to enter their manly protest against a revival of the shallow theories of Lord Monboddo.

But to return to our survey of the history of the physical sciences. We had examined the empirical stage through which every science has to pass. We saw that, for instance, in botany, a man who has travelled through distant countries, who has collected a vast number of plants, who knows their names, their peculiarities, and their medicinal qualities, is not yet a botanist, but only a herbalist, a lover of plants, or what the Italians call a *dilettante*, from *dilettare*, to delight. The real science of plants, like every other science, begins with the work of classification. An empirical acquaintance with facts rises to a scientific knowledge of facts as soon as the mind discovers beneath the multiplicity of single productions the unity of an organic system. This discovery is made by means of comparison and classification. We cease to study each flower for its own sake; and by continually enlarging the sphere of our observation, we try to discover what is common to many and offers those essential points on which groups or natural classes may be established. These classes again, in their more general features, are mutually compared; new points of difference, or of similarity of a more general and higher character, spring to view, and enable us to discover classes of classes, or families. And when the whole kingdom of plants has thus been surveyed, and a simple tissue of names been thrown over the garden of nature; when we can lift it up, as it were, and view it in our mind, as a whole, as a system well defined and complete, we then speak of the science of plants, or botany. We have entered into altogether a new sphere of knowledge where the individual is subject to the general, fact to law; we discover thought, order, and purpose pervading the whole realm of nature, and we perceive the dark chaos of matter lighted up by the reflection of a divine mind. Such views may be right or wrong. Too hasty comparisons, or too narrow distinctions, may have prevented the eye of the observer from discovering the broad outlines of nature's plan. Yet every system, however insufficient it may prove hereafter, is a step in advance. If the mind of man is once impressed with the conviction that there must be order and law everywhere, it never rests again until all that seems irregular has been eliminated, until the full beauty and harmony of nature has been perceived, and the eye of man has caught the eye of God beaming out from the midst of all His works. The failures of the past prepare the triumphs of the future.

Thus, to recur to our former illustration, the systematic arrangement of plants which bears the name of Linnæus, and which is founded on the number and character of the reproductive organs, failed to bring out the natural order which pervades all that grows and blossoms. Broad lines of demarcation which unite or divide large tribes and families of plants were invisible from his point of view. But in spite of this, his work was not in vain. The fact that plants in every part of the world

belonged to one great system was established once
for all; and even in later systems most of his classes
and divisions have been preserved, because the con-
formation of the reproductive organs of plants happened to run parallel with other more characteristic
marks of true affinity.* It is the same in the
history of astronomy. Although the Ptolemæan
system was a wrong one, yet even from its eccentric
point of view, laws were discovered determining the
true movements of the heavenly bodies. The conviction that there remains something unexplained is
sure to lead to the discovery of our error. There
can be no error in nature; the error must be with
us. This conviction lived in the heart of Aristotle
when, in spite of his imperfect knowledge of nature,
he declared 'that there is in nature nothing interpolated or without connection, as in a bad tragedy;'
and from his time forward every new fact and every
new system have confirmed his faith.

The object of classification is clear. We understand things if we can comprehend them; that is
to say, if we can grasp and hold together single
facts, connect isolated impressions, distinguish between what is essential and what is merely acci-
dental, and thus predicate the general of the
individual, and class the individual under the general. This is the secret of all scientific knowledge.
Many sciences, while passing through this second or
classificatory stage, assume the title of comparative.
When the anatomist has finished the dissection of

* 'The generative organs being those which are most remotely
related to the habits and food of an animal, I have always regarded
as affording very clear indications of its true affinities.'—Owen,
as quoted by Darwin, *Origin of Species*, p. 414.

C

numerous bodies, when he has given names to each organ, and discovered the distinctive functions of each, he is led to perceive similarity where at first he saw dissimilarity only. He discovers in the lower animals rudimentary indications of the more perfect organisation of the higher; and he becomes impressed with the conviction that there is in the animal kingdom the same order and purpose which pervades the endless variety of plants or any other realm of nature. He learns, if he did not know it before, that things were not created at random or in a lump, but that there is a scale which leads, by imperceptible degrees, from the lowest infusoria to the crowning work of nature—man; that all is the manifestation of one and the same unbroken chain of creative thought, the work of one and the same all-wise Creator.

In this way the second or classificatory leads us naturally to the third or final stage—the theoretical, or metaphysical. If the work of classification is properly carried out, it teaches us that nothing exists in nature by accident; that each individual belongs to a species, each species to a genus; and that there are laws which underlie the apparent freedom and variety of all created things. These laws indicate to us the presence of a purpose in the mind of the Creator; and whereas the material world was looked upon by ancient philosophers as a mere illusion, as an agglomerate of atoms, or as the work of an evil principle, we now read and interpret its pages as the revelation of a divine power, and wisdom, and love. This has given to the study of nature a new character. After the observer has collected his facts, and after the classifier has placed

them in order, the student asks what is the origin
and what is the meaning of all this? and he tries to
soar, by means of induction, or sometimes even of
divination, into regions not accessible to the mere
collector. In this attempt the mind of man no doubt
has frequently met with the fate of Phaeton; but,
undismayed by failure, he asks again and again for
his father's steeds. It has been said that this so-
called philosophy of nature has never achieved anything; that it has done nothing but prove that things
must be exactly as they had been found to be by the
observer and collector. Physical science, however,
would never have been what it is without the impulses which it received from the philosopher, nay
even from the poet. 'At the limits of exact knowledge,' (I quote the words of Humboldt) 'as from a
lofty island-shore, the eye loves to glance towards
distant regions. The images which it sees may be
illusive; but like the illusive images which people
imagined they had seen from the Canaries or the
Azores, long before the time of Columbus, they may
lead to the discovery of a new world.'

Copernicus, in the dedication of his work to
Pope Paul III. (it was commenced in 1517, finished
1530, published 1543), confesses that he was brought
to the discovery of the sun's central position, and of
the diurnal motion of the earth, not by observation
or analysis, but by what he calls the feeling of a
want of symmetry in the Ptolemaic system. But
who had told him that there *must* be symmetry in
all the movements of the celestial bodies, or that
complication was not more sublime than simplicity?
Symmetry and simplicity, before they were discovered by the observer, were postulated by the phi-

losopher. The first idea of revolutionising the heavens was suggested to Copernicus, as he tells us himself, by an ancient Greek philosopher, by Philolaus, the Pythagorean. No doubt with Philolaus the motion of the earth was only a guess, or, if you like, a happy intuition, not, as it was with Tycho de Brahe and his friend Kepler, the result of wearisome observations of the orbits of the planet Mars. Nevertheless, if we may trust the words of Copernicus, it is quite possible that without that guess we should never have heard of the Copernican system. Truth is not found by addition and multiplication only. When speaking of Kepler, whose method of reasoning has been considered as unsafe and fantastic by his contemporaries as well as by later astronomers, Sir David Brewster remarks very truly, 'that, as an instrument of research, the influence of imagination has been much overlooked by those who have ventured to give laws to philosophy.' The torch of imagination is as necessary to him who looks for truth, as the lamp of study. Kepler held both, and more than that, he had the star of faith to guide him in all things from darkness to light.

In the history of the physical sciences, the three stages which we have just described as the empirical, the classificatory, and the theoretical, appear generally in chronological order. I say, generally, for there have been instances, as in the case just quoted of Philolaus, where the results properly belonging to the third have been anticipated in the first stage. To the quick eye of genius one case may be like a thousand, and one experiment, well chosen, may lead to the discovery of an absolute law. Besides, there are great chasms in the history of science.

The tradition of generations is broken by political or ethnic earthquakes, and the work that was nearly finished has frequently had to be done again from the beginning, when a new surface had been formed for the growth of a new civilisation. The succession, however, of these three stages is no doubt the natural one, and it is very properly observed in the study of every science. The student of botany begins as a collector of plants. Taking each plant by itself, he observes its peculiar character, its habitat, its proper season, its popular or unscientific name. He learns to distinguish between the roots, the stem, the leaves, the flower, the calyx, the stamina, and pistils. He learns, so to say, the practical grammar of the plant before he can begin to compare, to arrange, and classify. Again, no one can enter with advantage on the third stage of any physical science without having passed through the second. No one can study *the* plant, no one can understand the bearing of such a work as, for instance, Professor Schleiden's *Life of the Plant*,[*] who has not studied the life of plants in the wonderful variety, and in the still more wonderful order, of nature. These last and highest achievements of inductive philosophy are possible only after the way has been cleared by previous classification. The philosopher must command his classes like regiments which obey the order of their general. Thus alone can the battle be fought and truth be conquered.

After this rapid glance at the history of the other physical sciences, we now return to our own,

---

[*] *Die Pflanze und ihr Leben*, von M. T. Schleiden, Leipzig, 1858.

the science of language, in order to see whether it really is a science, and whether it can be brought back to the standard of the inductive sciences. We want to know whether it has passed, or is still passing, through the three phases of physical research; whether its progress has been systematic or desultory, whether its method has been appropriate or not. But before we do this, we shall, I think, have to do something else. You may have observed that I always took it for granted that the science of language, which is best known in this country by the name of comparative philology, is one of the physical sciences, and that therefore its method ought to be the same as that which has been followed with so much success in botany, geology, anatomy, and other branches of the study of nature. In the history of the physical sciences, however, we look in vain for a place assigned to comparative philology, and its very name would seem to show that it belongs to quite a different sphere of human knowledge. There are two great divisions of human knowledge, which, according to their subject-matter, may be called *physical* and *historical*. Physical science deals with the works of God, historical science with the works of man.* Now if we were to judge by its name, comparative philology, like classical philology, would seem to take rank, not as a physical, but as an historical science, and the proper method to be applied to it would be that which is followed in the

---

* 'Thus the science of optics, including all the laws of light and colour, is a physical science, whereas the science of painting, with all its laws of manipulation and colouring, being that of a man-created art, is a purely historical science.'—*Intellectual Repository*, June 2, 1862, p. 247.

history of art, of law, of politics, and religion. However, the title of comparative philology must not be allowed to mislead us. It is difficult to say by whom that title was invented; but all that can be said in defence of it is, that the founders of the science of language were chiefly scholars or philologists, and that they based their inquiries into the nature and laws of language on a comparison of as many facts as they could collect within their own special spheres of study. Neither in Germany, which may well be called the birth-place of this science, nor in France, where it has been cultivated with brilliant success, has that title been adopted. It will not be difficult to show that, although the science of language owes much to the classical scholar, and though in return it has proved of great use to him, yet comparative philology has really nothing whatever in common with philology in the usual meaning of the word. Philology, whether classical or oriental, whether treating of ancient or modern, of cultivated or barbarous languages, is an historical science. Language is here treated simply as a means. The classical scholar uses Greek or Latin, the oriental scholar Hebrew or Sanskrit, or any other language, as a key to an understanding of the literary monuments which bygone ages have bequeathed to us, as a spell to raise from the tomb of time the thoughts of great men in different ages and different countries, and as a means ultimately to trace the social, moral, intellectual, and religious progress of the human race. In the same manner, if we study living languages, it is not for their own sake that we acquire grammars and vocabularies. We do so on account of their practical usefulness.

We use them as letters of introduction to the best society or to the best literature of the leading nations of Europe. In comparative philology the case is totally different. In the science of language, languages are not treated as a means; language itself becomes the sole object of scientific inquiry. Dialects which have never produced any literature at all, the jargons of savage tribes, the clicks of the Hottentots, and the vocal modulations of the Indo-Chinese are as important, nay, for the solution of some of our problems, more important, than the poetry of Homer, or the prose of Cicero. We do not want to know languages, we want to know language; what language is, how it can form a vehicle or an organ of thought; we want to know its origin, its nature, its laws; and it is only in order to arrive at that knowledge that we collect, arrange, and classify all the facts of language that are within our reach.

And here I must protest, at the very outset of these lectures, against the supposition that the student of language must necessarily be a great linguist. I shall have to speak to you in the course of these lectures of hundreds of languages, some of which, perhaps, you may never have heard mentioned even by name. Do not suppose that I know these languages as you know Greek or Latin, French or German. In that sense I know indeed very few languages, and I never aspired to the fame of a Mithridates or a Mezzofanti. It is impossible for a student of language to acquire a practical knowledge of all the tongues with which he has to deal. He does not wish to speak the Kachikal language, of which a professorship was lately founded in the University of

Guntemala,* or to acquire the elegancies of the idiom of the Tcheremissians; nor is it his ambition to explore the literature of the Samoyedes, or the New-Zealanders. It is the grammar and the dictionary which form the subject of his inquiries. These he consults and subjects to a careful analysis, but he does not encumber his memory with paradigms of nouns and verbs, or with long lists of words which have never been used in any work of literature. It is true, no doubt, that no language will unveil the whole of its wonderful structure except to the scholar who has studied it thoroughly and critically in a number of literary works representing the various periods of its growth. Nevertheless, short lists of vocables, and imperfect sketches of a grammar, are in many instances all that the student can expect to obtain, or can hope to master and to use for the purposes he has in view. He must learn to make the best of this fragmentary information, like the comparative anatomist, who frequently learns his lessons from the smallest fragments of fossil bones, or the vague pictures of animals brought home by unscientific travellers. If it were necessary for the comparative philologist to acquire a critical or practical acquaintance with all the languages which form the subject of his inquiries, the science of language would simply be an impossibility. But we do not expect the botanist to be an experienced gardener, or the geologist a miner, or the ichthyologist a practical fisherman. Nor would it be reasonable to object in the science of language to the same division of labour which is necessary for the successful cultivation of

* Sir J. Stoddart, *Glossology*, p. 22.

subjects much less comprehensive. Though much of what we might call the realm of language is lost to us for ever, though whole periods in the history of language are by necessity withdrawn from our observation, yet the mass of human speech that lies before us, whether in the petrified strata of ancient literature or in the countless variety of living languages and dialects, offers a field as large, if not larger, than any other branch of physical research. It is impossible to fix the exact number of known languages, but their number can hardly be less than nine hundred.* That this vast field should never have excited the curiosity of the natural philosopher before the beginning of our century may seem surprising, more surprising even than the indifference with which former generations treated the lessons which even the stones seemed to teach of the life still throbbing in the veins and on the very surface of the earth. The saying that 'familiarity breeds contempt,' would seem applicable to the subjects of both these sciences. The gravel of our walks hardly seemed to deserve a scientific treatment, and the language which every ploughboy can speak could not be raised without an effort to the dignity of a scientific problem. Man had studied every part of nature, the mineral treasures in the bowels of the earth, the flowers of each season, the animals of every continent, the laws of storms, and the movements of the heavenly bodies; he had analysed every substance, dissected every organism, he knew every bone and muscle, every nerve and fibre of his own body to the ultimate elements which compose his flesh and blood;

* Balbi in his *Atlas* counts 860. Cf. Pott, *Rassen*, p. 230; *Etymologische Forschungen*, ii. 83. (Second Edition.)

he had meditated on the nature of his soul, on the laws of his mind, and tried to penetrate into the last causes of all being—and yet language, without the aid of which not even the first step in this glorious career could have been made, remained unnoticed. Like a veil that hung too close over the eye of the human mind, it was hardly perceived. In an age when the study of antiquity attracted the most energetic minds, when the ashes of Pompeii were sifted for the playthings of Roman life; when parchments were made to disclose, by chemical means, the erased thoughts of Grecian thinkers; when the tombs of Egypt were ransacked for their sacred contents, and the palaces of Babylon and Nineveh forced to surrender the clay diaries of Nebuchadnezzar; when everything, in fact, that seemed to contain a vestige of the early life of man was anxiously searched for and carefully preserved in our libraries and museums —language, which in itself carries us back far beyond the cuneiform literature of Assyria and Babylonia and the hieroglyphic documents of Egypt; which connects ourselves, through an unbroken chain of speech, with the very ancestors of our race, and still draws its life from the first utterances of the human mind—language, the living and speaking witness of the whole history of our race, was never cross-examined by the student of history, was never made to disclose its secrets until questioned, and, so to say, brought back to itself within the last fifty years, by the genius of a Humboldt, Bopp, Grimm, Bunsen, and others. If you consider that, whatever view we take of the origin and dispersion of language, nothing new has ever been added to the substance of language,*

* Pott, *Etym. Forsch.*, ii. 230.

that all its changes have been changes of form, that no new root or radical has ever been invented by later generations, as little as one single element has ever been added to the material world in which we live; if you bear in mind that in one sense, and in a very just sense, we may be said to handle the very words which issued from the mouth of the son of God, when he gave names to 'all cattle, and to the fowl of the air, and to every beast of the field,' you will see, I believe, that the science of language has claims on your attention, such as few sciences can rival or excel.

Having thus explained the manner in which I intend to treat the science of language, I hope in my next lecture to examine the objections of those philosophers who see in language nothing but a contrivance devised by human skill for the more expeditious communication of our thoughts, and who would wish to see it treated, not as a production of nature, but as a work of human art.

LECTURE II.

THE GROWTH OF LANGUAGE IN CONTRADISTINCTION TO THE HISTORY OF LANGUAGE.

IN claiming for the science of language a place among the physical sciences, I was prepared to meet with many objections. The circle of the physical sciences seemed closed, and it was not likely that a new claimant should at once be welcomed among the established branches and scions of the ancient aristocracy of learning.*

---
* Dr. Whewell classes the science of language as one of the palaitiological sciences; but he makes a distinction between palaitiological sciences treating of material things, for instance, geology, and others respecting the products which result from man's imaginative and social endowments, for instance, comparative philology. He excludes the latter from the circle of the physical sciences, properly so called, but he adds: "We began our inquiry with the trust that any sound views which we should be able to obtain respecting the nature of truth in the physical sciences, and the mode of discovering it, must also tend to throw light upon the nature and prospects of knowledge of all other kinds—must be useful to us in moral, political, and philological researches. We stated this as a confident anticipation; and the evidence of the justice of our belief already begins to appear. We have seen that biology leads us to psychology, if we choose to follow the path; and thus the passage from the material to the immaterial has already unfolded itself at one point; and we now perceive that there are several large provinces of speculation which concern subjects belonging to man's immaterial nature, and which are governed by the same laws as sciences altogether physical. It is not our business to dwell on the prospects which our philosophy thus opens to our contemplation; but we may

The first objection which was sure to be raised on the part of such sciences as botany, geology, or physiology is this:—Language is the work of man; it was invented by man as a means of communicating his thoughts, when mere looks and gestures proved inefficient; and it was gradually, by the combined efforts of succeeding generations, brought to that perfection which we admire in the idiom of the Bible, the Vedas, the Koran, and in the poetry of Homer, Virgil, Dante, and Shakespeare. Now it is perfectly true that if language be the work of man, in the same sense in which a statue, or a temple, or a poem, or a law are properly called the works of man, the science of language would have to be classed as an historical science. We should have a history of language as we have a history of art, of poetry, and of jurisprudence, but we could not claim for it a place side by side with the various branches of Natural History. It is true, also, that if you consult the works of the most distinguished modern philosophers you will find that whenever they speak of language, they take it for granted that language is a human invention, that words are artificial signs, and that the varieties of human speech arose from different nations agreeing on different sounds as the most appropriate signs of their different ideas. This view of the origin of language was so powerfully advocated by the leading philosophers of the last century, that it has retained an undisputed currency even among those who,

allow ourselves, in this last stage of our pilgrimage among the foundations of the physical sciences, to be cheered and animated by the ray that thus beams upon us, however dimly, from a higher and brighter region.'—*Indications of the Creator*, p. 146.

on almost every other point, are strongly opposed to the teaching of that school. A few voices, indeed, have been raised to protest against the theory of language being originally invented by man. But they, in their zeal to vindicate the divine origin of language, seem to have been carried away so far as to run counter to the express statements of the Bible. For in the Bible it is not the Creator who gives names to all things, but Adam. 'Out of the ground,' we read, 'the Lord God formed every beast of the field, and every fowl of the air; and brought them unto Adam to see what he would call them: and whatsoever Adam called every living creature that was the name thereof.'* But with the exception of this small class of philosophers, more orthodox even than the Bible,† the generally received opinion on the origin of language is that which was held by Locke, which was powerfully advocated by Adam Smith in his *Essay on the Origin of Language*, appended to his *Treatise on Moral Sentiments*, and which was adopted

---

* *Gen.* ii. 19.

† St. Basil was accused by Eunomius of denying Divine Providence, because he would not admit that God had created the names of all things, but ascribed the invention of language to the faculties which God had implanted in man. St. Gregory, bishop of Nyssa in Cappadocia (331–396), defended St. Basil. 'Though God has given to human nature its faculties,' he writes, 'it does not follow that therefore He produces all the actions which we perform. He has given us the faculty of building a house and doing any other work; but we, surely, are the builders, and not He. In the same manner our faculty of speaking is the work of Him who has so framed our nature; but the invention of words for naming each object is the work of our mind.' See Ladevi-Roche, *De l'Origine du Langage*, Bordeaux, 1860, p. 14; Also Horne Tooke, *Diversions of Purley*, p. 19.

with slight modifications by Dugald Stewart. According to them, man must have lived for a time in a state of mutism, his only means of communication consisting in gestures of the body, and in the changes of countenance, till at last, when ideas multiplied that could no longer be pointed at with the fingers, 'they found it necessary to invent artificial signs of which the meaning was fixed by mutual agreement.' We need not dwell on minor differences of opinion as to the exact process by which this artificial language is supposed to have been formed. Adam Smith would wish us to believe that the first artificial words were *verbs*. Nouns, he thinks, were of less urgent necessity because things could be pointed at or imitated, whereas mere actions, such as are expressed by verbs, could not. He therefore supposes that when people saw a wolf coming, they pointed at him, and simply cried out, 'He comes.' Dugald Stewart, on the contrary, thinks that the first artificial words were nouns, and that the verbs were supplied by gesture; that, therefore, when people saw a wolf coming, they did not cry 'He comes,' but 'Wolf, Wolf,' leaving the rest to be imagined.*

But whether the verb or the noun was the first to be invented is of little importance; nor is it possible for us, at the very beginning of our inquiry into the nature of language, to enter upon a minute examination of a theory which represents language as a work of human art, and as established by mutual agreement as a medium of communication. While fully admitting that if this theory were true, the science of language would not come within the pale of the physical sciences, I must content myself for the pre-

* D. Stewart, *Works*, vol. iii. p. 27.

sent with pointing out that no one has yet explained how, without language, a discussion on the merits of each word, such as must necessarily have preceded a mutual agreement, could have been carried on. But as it is the object of these lectures to prove that language is not a work of human art, in the same sense as painting, or building, or writing, or printing, I must ask to be allowed, in this preliminary stage, simply to enter my protest against a theory, which, though still taught in the schools, is, nevertheless, I believe, without a single fact to support its truth.

But there are other objections besides this which would seem to bar the admission of the science of language to the circle of the physical sciences. Whatever the origin of language may have been, it has been remarked with a strong appearance of truth, that language has a history of its own, like art, like law, like religion; and that, therefore, the science of language belongs to the circle of the *historical*, or, as they used to be called, the *moral*, in contradistinction to the *physical* sciences. It is a well-known fact, which recent researches have not shaken, that nature is incapable of progress or improvement. The flower which the botanist observes to-day was as perfect from the beginning. Animals which are endowed with what is called an artistic instinct, have never brought that instinct to a higher degree of perfection. The hexagonal cells of the bee are not more regular in the 19th century than at any earlier period, and the gift of song has never, as far as we know, been brought to a higher perfection by our nightingale than by the Philomele of the Greeks. 'Natural History,' to quote Dr. Whewell's words,* 'when

---

* *History of Inductive Sciences*, vol. iii. p. 531.

systematically treated, excludes all that is historical, for it classes objects by their permanent and universal properties, and has nothing to do with the narration of particular or casual facts.' Now, if we consider the large number of tongues spoken in different parts of the world with all their dialectic and provincial varieties, if we observe the great changes which each of these tongues has undergone in the course of centuries, how Latin was changed into Italian, Spanish, Portuguese, Provençal, French, Wallachian, and Roumansch; how Latin again, together with Greek, and the Celtic, the Teutonic, and Slavonic languages, together likewise with the ancient dialects of India and Persia, must have sprung from an earlier language, the mother of the whole Indo-European or Aryan family of speech; if we see how Hebrew, Arabic, and Syriac, with several minor dialects, are but different impressions of one and the same common type, and must all have flowed from the same source, the original language of the Semitic race; and if we add to these two, the Aryan and Semitic, at least one more well-established class of languages, the Turanian, comprising the dialects of the nomad races scattered over Central and Northern Asia, the Tungusic, Mongolic, Turkic,* Samoyedic, and Finnic, all radii from one common centre of speech: if we watch this stream of language rolling on through centuries in these three mighty arms, which, before they disappear from our sight in the far distance, clearly show a convergence towards one common source: it would seem, indeed, as if there were an historical life inherent in language,

* Names in *ic* are names of classes as distinct from the names of single languages.

and as if both the will of man and the power of time could tell, if not on its substance, at least on its form. And even if the mere local varieties of speech were not considered sufficient ground for excluding language from the domain of natural science, there would still remain the greater difficulty of reconciling with the recognised principles of physical science the historical changes affecting every one of these varieties. Every part of nature, whether mineral, plant, or animal, is the same in kind from the beginning to the end of its existence, whereas few languages could be recognised as the same after the lapse of but a thousand years. The language of Alfred is so different from the English of the present day that we have to study it in the same manner as we study Greek and Latin. We can read Milton and Bacon, Shakespeare and Hooker; we can make out Wycliffe and Chaucer; but when we come to the English of the thirteenth century, we can but guess its meaning, and we fail even in this with works previous to the Ormulum and Layamon. The historical changes of language may be more or less rapid, but they take place at all times and in all countries. They have reduced the rich and powerful idiom of the poets of the Veda to the meagre and impure jargon of the modern Sepoy. They have transformed the language of the Zend-Avesta and of the mountain records of Behistun into that of Firdusi and the modern Persians; the language of Virgil into that of Dante, the language of Ulfilas into that of Charlemagne, the language of Charlemagne into that of Goethe. We have reason to believe that the same changes take place with even greater violence and rapidity in the dialects of savage tribes, although, in the absence of a written literature, it is extremely difficult to obtain trustworthy information. But in the few instances where careful observations have been made on this interesting subject, it has been found that among the wild and illiterate tribes of Siberia, Africa, and Siam, two or three generations are sufficient to change the whole aspect of their dialects. The languages of highly civilised nations, on the contrary, become more and more stationary, and sometimes seem almost to lose their power of change. Where there is a classical literature, and where its language has spread to every town and village, it seems almost impossible that any further changes should take place. Nevertheless, the language of Rome, for so many centuries the queen of the whole civilised world, was deposed by the modern Romance dialects, and the ancient Greek was supplanted in the end by the modern Romaic. And though the art of printing and the wide diffusion of Bibles and Prayer-books and newspapers have acted as still more powerful barriers to arrest the constant flow of human speech, we may see that the language of the authorised version of the Bible, though perfectly intelligible, is no longer the spoken language of England. In Booker's Scripture and Prayer-book Glossary* the number of words or senses of words which have become obsolete since 1611, amount to 388, or nearly one fifteenth part of the

* *Lectures on the English Language*, by G. P. Marsh: New York, 1860, pp. 363 and 630. These lectures embody the result of much careful research, and are full of valuable observations. They have lately been published in England, with useful omissions and additions by Dr. Smith, under the title of *Handbook of the English Language*.

whole number of words used in the Bible. Smaller changes, changes of accent and meaning, the reception of new, and the dropping of old words, we may watch as taking place under our own eyes. Rogers* said that '*cóntemplate* is bad enough, but *bálcony* makes me sick,' whereas at present no one is startled by *cóntemplate* instead of *contémplate*, and *bálcony* has become more usual than *balcóny*. Thus *Roome* and *chaney*, *layloc* and *goold*, have but lately been driven from the stage by *Rome*, *china*, *lilac* and *gold*, and some courteous gentlemen of the old school still continue to be *obleeged* instead of being *obliged*.† *Force*,‡ in the sense of a waterfall, and *gill*, in the sense of a rocky ravine, were not used in classical English before Wordsworth. *Handbook*,§ though an old Anglo-Saxon word, has but lately taken the place of *manual*, and a number of words such as *cab* for cabriolet, *bus* for omnibus, and even a verb such as *to shunt* tremble still on the boundary line between the vulgar and the literary idioms. Though the grammatical changes that have taken place since the publication of the authorised version are yet fewer in number, still we may point out some. The termination of the third person singular in *th* is now entirely replaced by *s*. No one now says *he liveth*, but only *he lives*. Several of the irregular imperfects and participles have assumed a new form. No one now uses *he spake*, and *he drave*, instead of *he spoke*, and *he drove*; *holpen* is replaced

* Marsh, p. 532, *note*.
† Trench, *English Past and Present*, p. 210, mentions *great*, which was pronounced *graet* in Johnson's time, and *tea*, which Pope rhymes with *obey*.
‡ Marsh, p. 589.
§ Sir J. Stoddart, *Glossology*, p. 60.

by *helped*; *holden* by *held*; *shapen* by *shaped*. The distinction between *ye* and *you*, the former being reserved for the nominative, the latter for all the other cases, is given up in modern English; and what is apparently a new grammatical form, the possessive pronoun *its*, has sprung into life since the beginning of the seventeenth century. It never occurs in the Bible; and though it is used three or four times by Shakespeare, Ben Jonson does not recognise it as yet in his English Grammar.*

It is argued, therefore, that as language, differing thereby from all other productions of nature, is liable to historical alterations, it is not fit to be treated in the same manner as the subject-matter of all the other physical sciences.

There is something very plausible in this objection, but if we examine it more carefully, we shall find that it rests entirely on a confusion of terms. We must distinguish between historical change and natural growth. Art, science, philosophy, and religion all have a history; language, or any other production of nature, admits only of growth.

Let us consider, first, that although there is a continuous change in language, it is not in the power of man either to produce or to prevent it. We might think as well of changing the laws which control the circulation of our blood, or of adding an inch to our height, as of altering the laws of speech, or inventing new words according to our own pleasure. As man is the lord of nature only if he knows her laws and submits to them, the poet and the philosopher become the lords of language only if they know its laws and obey them.

* Trench, *English Past and Present*, p. 114; Marsh, p. 397.

When the Emperor Tiberius had made a mistake and was reproved for it by Marcellus, another grammarian of the name of Capito, who happened to be present, remarked that what the emperor said was good Latin, or, if it were not, it would soon be so. Marcellus, more of a grammarian than a courtier, replied, 'Capito is a liar; for, Cæsar, thou canst give the Roman citizenship to men, but not to words.' A similar anecdote is told of the German Emperor Sigismund. When presiding at the Council of Constance, he addressed the assembly in a Latin speech, exhorting them to eradicate the schism of the Hussites. 'Videte Patres,' he said, 'ut eradicetis schismam Hussitarum.' He was very unceremoniously called to order by a monk, who called out, 'Serenissime Rex, schisma est generis neutri.'* The emperor, however, without losing his presence of mind, asked the impertinent monk, 'How do you know it?' The old Bohemian schoolmaster replied, 'Alexander Gallus says so.' 'And who is Alexander Gallus?' the emperor rejoined. The monk replied, 'He was a monk.' 'Well,' said the emperor, 'and I am emperor of Rome; and my word, I trust, will be as good as the word of any monk.' No doubt the laughers were with the emperor; but for all that, *schisma* remained a neuter, and not even an emperor could change its gender or termination.

The idea that language can be changed and

---

* As several of my reviewers have found fault with the monk for using the genitive *neutri*, instead of *neutrius*, I beg to refer to Priscianus, l. vi. c. l. and c. vii. The expression *generis neutrius*, though frequently used by modern editors, has no authority, I believe, in ancient Latin.

improved by man is by no means a new one. We
know that Protagoras, an ancient Greek philosopher,
after laying down some laws on gender, actually began
to find fault with the text of Homer, because it did
not agree with his rules. But here, as in every
other instance, the attempt proved unavailing. Try
to alter the smallest rule of English, and you will
find that it is physically impossible. There is
apparently a very small difference between *much* and
very, but you can hardly ever put one in the place of
the other. You can say, 'I am very happy,' but
not, 'I am much happy,' though you may say 'I am
most happy.' On the contrary, you can say 'I am
much misunderstood,' but not 'I am very misunderstood.' Thus the western Romance dialects,
Spanish and Portuguese, together with Wallachian,
can only employ the Latin word *magis* for forming
comparatives :— Sp. *mas dulce* ; Port. *mais doce* ;
Wall. *mai dulce* : while French, Provençal, and
Italian only allow of *plus* for the same purpose :
Ital. *più dolce* ; Prov. *plus dous* ; Fr. *plus doux*.
It is by no means impossible, however, that this
distinction between *very*, which is now used with
adjectives only, and *much*, which precedes participles, should disappear in time. In fact, 'very
pleased' and 'very delighted' are expressions which
may be heard in many drawing-rooms. But if
that change take place, it will not be by *the will* of
any individual, nor by *the mutual agreement* of any
large number of men, but rather in spite of the
exertions of grammarians and academics. And
here you perceive the first difference between history
and growth. An emperor may change the laws of
society, the forms of religion, the rules of art: it

is in the power of one generation, or even of one individual, to raise an art to the highest pitch of perfection, while the next may allow it to lapse, till a new genius takes it up again with renewed ardour. In all this we have to deal with the conscious and intentional acts of individuals, and we therefore move on historical ground. If we compare the creations of Michael Angelo or Raphael with the statues and frescoes of ancient Rome, we can speak of a history of art. We can connect two periods separated by thousands of years through the works of those who handed on the traditions of art from century to century; but we shall never meet here with the same continuous and unconscious growth which connects the language of Plautus with that of Dante. The process through which language is settled and unsettled combines in one the two opposite elements of necessity and free will. Though the individual seems to be the prime agent in producing new words and new grammatical forms, he is so only after his individuality has been merged in the common action of the family, tribe or nation to which he belongs. He can do nothing by himself, and the first impulse to a new formation in language, though given by an individual, is mostly, if not always, given without premeditation, nay, unconsciously. The individual, as such, is powerless, and the results apparently produced by him depend on laws beyond his control, and on the co-operation of all those who form together with him one class, one body, or one organic whole.

But, though it is easy to show, as we have just done, that language cannot be changed or moulded by the taste, the fancy, or genius of man, it is very difficult to explain what causes the growth of language. Ever since Horace it has been usual to compare the growth of languages with the growth of trees. But comparisons are treacherous things. What do we know of the real causes of the growth of a tree, and what can we gain by comparing things which we do not quite understand with things which we understand even less? Many people speak, for instance, of the terminations of the verb, as if they sprouted out from the root as from their parent stock.* But what ideas can they connect with such expressions? If we must compare language with a tree, there is one point which may be illustrated by this comparison, and this is that neither language nor the tree can exist or grow by itself. Without the soil, without air and light, the tree could not live; it could not even be conceived to live. It is the same with language. Language cannot exist by itself; it requires a soil on which to grow, and that soil is the human soul. To speak of language as a thing by itself, as living a life of its own, as growing to maturity, producing offspring, and dying away, is sheer mythology; and though we cannot help using metaphorical expressions, we should always be on our guard, when engaged in inquiries like the present, against being carried away by the very words which we are using.

Now, what we call the growth of language comprises two processes which should be carefully distinguished, though they may be at work simultaneously. These two processes I call

1. *Dialectic Regeneration.*
2. *Phonetic Decay.*

* Castelvetro, in Horne Tooke, p. 629, *note.*

I begin with the second as the more obvious, though in reality its operations are mostly subsequent to the operations of dialectic regeneration. I must ask you at present to take it for granted that everything in language had originally a meaning. As language can have no other object but to express our meaning, it might seem to follow almost by necessity that language should contain neither more nor less than what is required for that purpose. It would also seem to follow that if language contains no more than what is necessary for conveying a certain meaning, it would be impossible to modify any part of it without defeating its very purpose. This is really the case in some languages. In Chinese, for instance, *ten* is expressed by *shī*. It would be impossible to change *shī* in the slightest way without making it unfit to express *ten*. If instead of *shī* we pronounced *tsī*, this would mean *seven*, but not *ten*. But now, suppose we wished to express double the quantity of ten, twice ten, or twenty. We should in Chinese take *eúl*, which is two, put it before *shī*, and say *eúl-shī*, twenty. The same caution which applied to *shī*, applies again to *eúl-shī*. As soon as you change it, by adding or dropping a single letter, it is no longer twenty, but either something else or nothing. We find exactly the same in other languages which, like Chinese, are called monosyllabic. In Tibetan, *chu* is ten, *nyi* two; *nyi-chu*, twenty. In Burmese *she* is ten, *nhit* two; *nhit-she*, twenty.

But how is it in English, or in Gothic, or in Greek and Latin, or in Sanskrit? We do not say *two-ten* in English, nor *duo-decem* in Latin, nor *dvi-daśa* in Sanskrit.

We find* in

Sanskrit	Greek	Latin	English
vinśati	eikati	viginti	twenty.

Now here we see, first, that the Sanskrit, Greek and Latin, are only local modifications of one and the same original word; whereas the English *twenty* is a new compound, the Gothic *twai tigjus* (two decads), the Anglo-Saxon *tuëntig*, framed from Teutonic materials; a product, as we shall see, of dialectic regeneration.

We next observe that the first part of the Latin *viginti* and of the Sanskrit *vinśati* contains the same number, which from *dvi* has been reduced to *vi*. This is not very extraordinary; for the Latin *bis*, twice, which you still hear at concerts, likewise stands for an original *dvis*, the English *twice*, the Greek *dis*. This *dis* appears again as a Latin preposition, meaning *a-two*; so that, for instance, *discussion* means, originally, striking a-two, different from *percussion*, which means striking through and through. *Discussion* is, in fact, the cracking of a nut in order to get at its kernel. Well, the same word, *dvi* or *vi*, we have in the Latin word for twenty, which is *vi-ginti*, the Sanskrit *vinśati*.

It can likewise be proved that the second part of *viginti* is a corruption of the old word for ten. Ten, in Sanskrit, is *daśan*; from it is derived *daśati*, a decad; and this *daśati* was again reduced to *śati*; thus giving us with vi for *dvi*, two, the Sanskrit *viśati* or *vinśati*, twenty. The Latin *viginti*, the Greek *eikati*, owe their origin to the same process.

* Bopp, *Comparative Grammar*, § 320. Schleicher, *Deutsche Sprache*, s. 233.

Now consider the immense difference—I do not mean in sound, but in character—between two such words as the Chinese *eúl-shí*, two-ten, or twenty, and those mere cripples of words which we meet with in Sanskrit, Greek, and Latin. In Chinese there is neither too much, nor too little. The word speaks for itself, and requires no commentary. In Sanskrit, on the contrary, the most essential parts of the two component elements are gone, and what remains is a kind of metamorphic agglomerate which cannot be understood without a most minute microscopic analysis. Here, then, we have an instance of what is meant by *phonetic corruption*; and you will perceive how, not only the form, but the whole nature of language is destroyed by it. As soon as phonetic corruption shows itself in a language, that language has lost what we considered to be the most essential character of all human speech, namely, that every part of it should have a meaning. The people who spoke Sanskrit were as little aware that *vinśati* meant *twice ten* as a Frenchman is that *vingt* contains the remains of *deux* and *dix*. Language, therefore, has entered into a new stage as soon as it submits to the attacks of phonetic change. The life of language has become benumbed and extinct in those words or portions of words which show the first traces of this phonetic mould. Henceforth those words or portions of words can be kept up only artificially or by tradition; and, what is important, a distinction is henceforth established between what is substantial or radical, and what is merely formal or grammatical in words.

For let us now take another instance, which will make it clearer how phonetic corruption leads to the first appearance of so-called grammatical forms. We are not in the habit of looking on *twenty* as the plural or dual of *ten*. But how was a plural originally formed? In Chinese, which from the first has guarded most carefully against the taint of phonetic corruption, the plural is formed in the most sensible manner. Thus, man in Chinese is *jin*; *kiai* means the whole or totality. This added to *gin* gives *jin-kiai*, which is the plural of man. There are other words which are used for the same purpose in Chinese; for instance, *péi*, which means a class. Hence *ï*, a stranger, followed by *péi*, class, gives *ï-péi*, strangers. We have similar plurals in English, but we do not reckon them as grammatical forms. Thus, *man-kind* is formed exactly like *ï-péi*, stranger-kind; *Christendom* is the same as all Christians, and *clergy* is synonymous with *clerici*. The same process is followed in other cognate languages. In Tibetan the plural is formed by the addition of such words as *kun*, all, and *t'sogs*, multitude.* Even the numerals, *nine* and *hundred*, are used for the same purpose. And here again, as long as these words are fully understood and kept alive, they resist phonetic corruption; but the moment they lose, so to say, their presence of mind, phonetic corruption sets in, and as soon as phonetic corruption has commenced its ravages, those portions of a word which it affects retain a merely artificial or conventional existence and dwindle down to grammatical terminations.

I am afraid I should tax your patience too much were I to enter here on an analysis of the grammatical terminations in Sanskrit, Greek, or Latin, in order to show how these terminations arose out of

* Foucaux, *Grammaire Tibétaine*, p. 27, and Preface, p. x.

independent words which were slowly reduced to
mere dust by the constant wear and tear of speech.
But in order to explain how the principle of phonetic
decay leads to the formation of grammatical terminations, let us look to languages with which we are
more familiar. Let us take the French adverb. We
are told by French grammarians* that in order to
form adverbs we have to add the termination *ment*.
Thus from *bon*, good, we form *bonnement*, from *vrai*,
true, *vraiment*. This termination does not exist in
Latin. But we meet in Latin† with expressions
such as *bonâ mente*, in good faith. We read in Ovid,
'Insistam forti mente,' I shall insist with a strong
mind or will, I shall insist strongly; in French,
'J'insisterai fortement.' Therefore, what has happened in the growth of Latin, or in the change of
Latin into French, is simply this: in phrases such as
forti mente, the last word was no longer felt as a
distinct word, and it lost at the same time its distinct pronunciation. *Mente*, the ablative of *mens*,
was changed into *ment*, and was preserved as a
merely formal element, as the termination of adverbs,
even in cases where a recollection of the original
meaning of *mente* (with a mind), would have rendered its employment perfectly impossible. If we
say in French that a hammer falls *lourdement*, we
little suspect that we ascribe to a piece of iron a
heavy mind. In Italian, though the adverbial termination *mente* in *chiaramente* is no longer felt as a
distinct word, it has not as yet been affected by
phonetic corruption; and in Spanish it is sometimes

---

* Fuchs, *Romanische Sprachen*, s. 355.
† Quint. v. 10, 52. 'Bonâ mente factum, ideo palam; malâ, ideo ex insidiis.'

used as a distinct word, though even then it cannot be said to have retained its distinct meaning. Thus, instead of saying, 'claramente, concisamente y elegantemente,' it is more elegant to say in Spanish, 'clara, concisa y elegante mente.'

It is difficult to form any conception of the extent to which the whole surface of a language may be altered by what we have just described as phonetic change. Think that in the French *vingt* you have the same elements as in *deux* and *dix*; that the second part of the French *douze*, twelve, represents the Latin *decim* in *duodecim*; that the final *te* of *trente* was originally the Latin *ginta* in *triginta*, which *ginta* was again a derivation and abbreviation of the Sanskrit *daśa* or *daśati*, ten. Then consider how early this phonetic disease must have broken out. For in the same manner as *vingt* in French, *veinte* in Spanish, and *venti* in Italian presuppose the more primitive *viginti* which we find in Latin, so this Latin *viginti*, together with the Greek *eikati*, and the Sanskrit *vinśati* presuppose an earlier language from which they are in turn derived, and in which, previous to *viginti*, there must have been a more primitive form *dvi-ginti*, and previous to this again, another compound as clear and intelligible as the Chinese *eul-shi*, consisting of the ancient Aryan names for two, *dvi*, and ten, *daśati*. Such is the virulence of this phonetic change, that it will sometimes eat away the whole body of a word, and leave nothing behind but decayed fragments. Thus, *sister*, which in Sanskrit is *svasar*,* appears in Pehlvi and

---

* Sanskrit *s* = Persian *h*; therefore *svasar* = *hvahar*. This becomes *chahar*, *char*, and *cha*. Zend, *qanha*, acc. *qanharem*, Persian, *khâher*. Bopp, *Comp. Gram.*, § 35.

in Ossetian as *cho*. *Daughter*, which in Sanskrit is *duhitar*, has dwindled down in Bohemian to *dci* (pronounced *tsi*).* Who would believe that *tear* and *larme* are derived from the same source; that the French *même* contains the Latin *semetipsissimus*; that in *aujourd'hui* we have the Latin word *dies* twice?† Who would recognise the Latin *pater* in the Armenian *hayr*? Yet we make no difficulty about identifying *père* and *pater*; and as several initial h's in Armenian correspond to an original p (*het* = *pes*, *pedis*; *hing* = Greek *pente*, five; *hour* = Greek *pyr*, fire), it follows that *hayr* is *pater*.‡

We are accustomed to call these changes the growth of language, but it would be more appropriate to call this process of phonetic change decay, and thus to distinguish it from the second, or dialectic process, which we must now examine, and which involves, as you will see, a more real principle of growth.

In order to understand the meaning of *dialectic regeneration* we must first see clearly what we mean by dialect. We saw before that language has no independent substantial existence. Language exists in man, it lives in being spoken, it dies with each word that is pronounced, and is no longer heard. It is a mere accident that language should ever have been reduced to writing, and have been made the vehicle of a written literature. Even now

---

* Schleicher, *Beiträge*, b. ii. s. 392: *dei* = *dägte*; gen. *deere* = *dägtere*.

† *Hui* = *hodie*, Ital. *oggi* and *oggidi*; *jour* = *diurnum*, from *diet*.

‡ See M. M.'s *Letter to Chevalier Bunsen*, On the Turanian Languages, p. 67.

the largest number of languages are unwritten, and have produced no literature. Among the numerous tribes of Central Asia, Africa, America, and Polynesia, language still lives in its natural state, in a state of continual combustion; and it is there that we must go if we wish to gain an insight into the growth of human speech previous to its being arrested by any literary interference. What we are accustomed to call languages, the literary idioms of Greece, and Rome, and India, of Italy, France, and Spain, must be considered as artificial, rather than as natural forms of speech. The real and natural life of language is in its dialects, and in spite of the tyranny exercised by the classical or literary idioms, the day is still very far off which is to see the dialects, even of such classical languages as Italian and French, entirely eradicated. About twenty of the Italian dialects have been reduced to writing, and made known by the press.* Champollion-Figeac reckons the most distinguishable dialects of France at fourteen.† The number of modern Greek dialects‡ is carried by some as high as seventy, and though many of these are hardly more than local varieties, yet some, like the Tzaconic, differ from the literary language as much as Doric differed from Attic. In the island of Lesbos, villages distant from each other not more than two or three hours have frequently peculiar words of their own, and their own peculiar pronunciation.§ But let us take a language which, though not with-

---

* See Marsh, p. 678; Sir John Stoddart's *Glossology*, s. 31.
† *Glossology*, p. 33.
‡ *Ibid.* p. 29.
§ *Nea Pandora*, 1859, Nos. 227, 229; *Zeitschrift für vergleichende Sprachforschung*, x. s. 190.

out a literature, has been less under the influence of classical writers than Italian or French, and we shall then see at once how abundant the growth of dialects. The Friesian, which is spoken on a small area on the north-western coast of Germany, between the Scheldt and Jutland, and on the islands near the shore, which has been spoken there for at least two thousand years,* and which possesses literary documents as old as the twelfth century, is broken up into endless local dialects. I quote from Kohl's *Travels*. 'The commonest things,' he writes, 'which are named almost alike all over Europe, receive quite different names in the different Friesian Islands. Thus, in Amrum, *father* is called *aatj*; on the Halligs, *baba* or *babe*; in Sylt, *foster* or *vaar*; in many districts on the mainland, *täte*; in the eastern part of Föhr, *oti* or *ohitj*. Although these people live within a couple of German miles from each other, these words differ more than the Italian *padre* and the English *father*. Even the names of their districts and islands are totally different in different dialects. The island of *Sylt* is called *Söl*, *Sol*, and *Sal*.' Each of these dialects, though it might be made out by a Friesian scholar, is unintelligible except to the peasants of each narrow district in which it prevails. What is therefore generally called the Friesian language, and described as such in Friesian grammars, is in reality but one out of many dialects, though, no doubt, the most important; and the same holds good with regard to all so-called literary languages.

It is a mistake to imagine that dialects are every-

---

* Grimm, *Geschichte der Deutschen Sprache*, s. 668; Marsh, p. 379.

where corruptions of the literary language. Even in England,* the local patois have many forms which are more primitive than the language of Shakespeare, and the richness of their vocabulary surpasses, on many points, that of the classical writers of any period. Dialects have always been the feeders rather than the channels of a literary language; anyhow, they are parallel streams which existed long before one of them was raised to that temporary eminence which is the result of literary cultivation.

What Grimm says of the origin of dialects in general applies only to such as are produced by phonetic corruption. 'Dialects,' he writes,† 'develop themselves progressively, and the more we look backward in the history of language the smaller is their number, and the less definite their features. All multiplicity arises gradually from an original unity.' So it seems, indeed, if we build our theories of language exclusively on the materials supplied by literary idioms, such as Sanskrit, Greek, Latin, and Gothic. No doubt these are the royal heads in the history of language. But as political history ought

---

* 'Some people, who may have been taught to consider the Dorset dialect as having originated from corruption of the written English, may not be prepared to hear that it is not only a separate offspring from the Anglo-Saxon tongue, but purer, and in some cases richer, than the dialect which is chosen as the national speech.'—Barnes, *Poems in Dorset Dialect*, Preface, p. xiv.

'En général, l'hébreu a beaucoup plus de rapports avec l'arabe vulgaire qu'avec l'arabe littéral, comme j'aurai peut-être l'occasion de le montrer ailleurs, et il en résulte que ce que nous appellons l'arabe vulgaire est également un dialecte fort ancien.'—Munk, *Journal Asiatique*, 1850, p. 229, note.

† *Geschichte der Deutschen Sprache*, s. 833.

to be more than a chronicle of royal dynasties, so the historian of language ought never to lose sight of those lower and popular strata of speech from which these dynasties originally sprang, and by which alone they are supported.

Here, however, lies the difficulty. How are we to trace the history of dialects? In the ancient history of language, literary dialects alone supply us with materials, whereas the very existence of spoken dialects is hardly noticed by ancient writers.

We are told, indeed, by Pliny,* that in Colchis there were more than three hundred tribes speaking different dialects; and that the Romans, in order to carry on any intercourse with the natives, had to employ a hundred and thirty interpreters. This is probably an exaggeration; but we have no reason to doubt the statement of Strabo,† who speaks of seventy tribes living together in that country, which, even now, is called 'the mountain of languages.' In modern times, again, when missionaries have devoted themselves to the study of the languages of savage and illiterate tribes, they have seldom been able to do more than to acquire one out of many dialects; and, when their exertions have been at all successful, that dialect which they had reduced to writing, and made the medium of their civilising influence, soon assumed a kind of literary supremacy, so as to leave the rest behind as bar-

* Pliny, vi. 5; Hervas, *Catalogo*, i. 118.
† Pliny depends on Timosthenes, whom Strabo declares untrustworthy (ii. p. 93, ed. Casaub.) Strabo himself says of Dioscurias, συνέρχεσθαι ἐς αὐτὴν ἑβδομήκοντα, οἱ δὲ καὶ τριακόσια ἔθνη φασὶν οἷς οὐδὲν τῶν ὄντων μέλει (x. p. 498). The last words refer probably to Timosthenes.

barous jargons. Yet, whatever is known of the dialects of savage tribes is chiefly or entirely due to missionaries; and it is much to be desired that their attention should again and again be directed to this interesting problem of the dialectic life of language which they alone have the means of elucidating. Gabriel Sagard, who was sent as a missionary to the Hurons in 1626, and published his *Grand Voyage du Pays des Hurons*, at Paris, in 1631, states that among these North American tribes hardly one village speaks the same language as another; nay, that two families of the same village do not speak exactly the same language. And he adds what is important, that their language is changing every day, and is already so much changed that the ancient Huron language is almost entirely different from the present. During the last two hundred years, on the contrary, the languages of the Hurons and Iroquois are said not to have changed at all.* We read of missionaries† in Central America

---

* *Du Ponceau*, p. 110.

† S. F. Waldeck, *Lettre à M. Jomard des Environs de Palenqué, Amérique Centrale*. ('Il ne pourrait se servir, en 1833, d'un vocabulaire composé avec beaucoup de soin dix ans auparavant.') 'But such is the tendency of languages, amongst nations in the hunter state, rapidly to diverge from each other, that, apart from those primitive words, a much greater diversity is found in Indian languages, well known to have sprung from a common source, than in kindred European tongues. Thus, although the Minsi were only a tribe of the Delawares, and adjacent to them, even some of their numerals differed.'—*Archæologia Americana*, vol. ii. p. 160.

* Most men of mark have a style of their own. If the community be large, and there be many who have made language their study, it is only such innovations as have real merit that become permanent. If it be small, a single eminent man, especially where writing

who attempted to write down the language of savage tribes, and who compiled with great care a dictionary of all the words they could lay hold of. Returning to the same tribe after the lapse of only ten years, they found that this dictionary had become antiquated and useless. Old words had sunk to the ground, and new ones had risen to the surface; and to all outward appearance the language was completely changed.

Nothing surprised the Jesuit missionaries so much as the immense number of languages spoken by the natives of America. But this, far from being a proof of a high state of civilisation, rather showed that the various races of America had never submitted, for any length of time, to a powerful political concentration, and that they had never succeeded in founding great national empires. Hervas reduces,

is unknown, may make great changes. There being no one to challenge the propriety of his innovations, they become first fashionable and then lasting. The old and better vocabulary drops. If, for instance, England had been a small country, and scarce a writer of distinction in it but Carlyle, he without doubt would have much altered the language. As it is, though he has his imitators, it is little probable that he will have a perceptible influence over the common diction. Hence, where writing is unknown, if the community be broken up into small tribes, the language very rapidly changes, and for the worse. An offset from an Indian tribe in a few generations has a language unintelligible to the parent stock. Hence the vast number of languages among the small hunting tribes of Indians in North and South America, which yet are all evidently of a common origin, for their principles are identical. The larger, therefore, the community, the more permanent the language; the smaller, the less it is permanent, and the greater the degeneracy. The smaller the community, the more confined the range of ideas, consequently the smaller the vocabulary necessary, and the falling into abeyance of many words.'—Dr. Rae, *The Polynesian*, No. 23. 1862.

indeed, all the dialects of America to eleven families[*]—four for the south, and seven for the north; but this could be done only by the same careful and minute comparison which enables us to class the idioms spoken in Iceland and Ceylon as cognate dialects. For practical purposes the dialects of America are distinct dialects, and the people who speak them are mutually unintelligible.

We hear the same observations everywhere where the rank growth of dialects has been watched by intelligent observers. If we turn our eyes to Burmah, we find that there the Burmese has produced a considerable literature, and is the recognised medium of communication not only in Burmah, but likewise in Pegu and Arakan. But the intricate mountain ranges of the peninsula of the Irawaddy[†] afford a safe refuge to many independent tribes, speaking their own independent dialects; and in the neighbourhood of Manipura alone Captain Gordon collected no less than twelve dialects. 'Some of them,' he says, 'are spoken by no more than thirty or forty families, yet so different from the rest as to be unintelligible to the nearest neighbourhood.' Brown, the excellent American missionary, who has spent his whole life in preaching the Gospel in that part of the world, tells us that some tribes who left their native village to settle in another valley, became unintelligible to their forefathers in two or three generations.[‡]

In the North of Asia the Ostiakes, as Messerschmidt informs us, though really speaking the same

---

[*] *Catalogo*, i. 893.
[†] *Turanian Languages*, p. 114.
[‡] *Ibid.* p. 233.

language everywhere, have produced so many words and forms peculiar to each tribe, that even within the limits of twelve or twenty German miles, communication among them becomes extremely difficult. Castrén, the heroic explorer of the languages of northern and central Asia,[*] assures us that some of the Mongolian dialects are actually entering into a new phase of grammatical life; and that while the literary language of the Mongolians has no terminations for the persons of the verb, that characteristic feature of Turanian speech had lately broken out in the spoken dialects of the Buriates and in the Tungusic idioms near Njertschinsk in Siberia.

One more observation of the same character from the pen of Robert Moffat, in his *Missionary Scenes and Labours in Southern Africa*. 'The purity and harmony of language,' he writes, 'is kept up by their pitchos, or public meetings, by their festivals and ceremonies, as well as by their songs and their constant intercourse. With the isolated villagers of the desert it is far otherwise; they have no such meetings; they are compelled to traverse the wilds, often to a great distance from their native village. On such occasions fathers and mothers, and all who can bear a burden, often set out for weeks at a time, and leave their children to the care of two or three infirm old people. The infant progeny, some of whom are beginning to lisp, while others can just master a whole sentence, and those still further advanced, romping and playing together, the children of nature, through their live-long day, *become habituated to a language of their own*. The more

---

[*] *Turanian Languages*, p. 30.

voluble condescend to the less precocious; and thus, from this infant Babel, proceeds a dialect of a host of mongrel words and phrases, joined together without rule, and *in the course of one generation the entire character of the language is changed*.

Such is the life of language in a state of nature; and in a similar manner, we have a right to conclude, languages grew up which we only know after the bit and bridle of literature were thrown over their necks. It need not be a written or classical literature to give an ascendency to one out of many dialects, and to impart to its peculiarities an undisputed legitimacy. Speeches at pitchos or public meetings, popular ballads, national laws, religious oracles, exercise, though to a smaller extent, the same influence. They will arrest the natural flow of language in the countless rivulets of its dialects, and give a permanency to certain formations of speech which, without these external influences, could have enjoyed but an ephemeral existence. Though we cannot fully enter, at present, on the problem of the origin of language, yet this we can clearly see, that whatever the origin of language, its first tendency must have been towards an unbounded variety. To this there was, however, a natural check, which prepared from the very beginning the growth of national and literary languages. The language of the father became the language of a family; the language of a family that of a clan. In one and the same clan different families would preserve among themselves their own familiar forms and expressions. They would add new words, some so fanciful and quaint as to be hardly intelligible to other members of the same clan. Such expressions would naturally be suppressed, as we suppress provincial peculiarities and pet words of our own, at large assemblies where all clansmen meet and are expected to take part in general discussions. But they would be cherished all the more round the fire of each tent, in proportion as the general dialect of the clan assumed a more formal character. Class dialects, too, would spring up; the dialects of servants, grooms, shepherds, and soldiers. Women would have their own household words; and the rising generation would not be long without a more racy phraseology of their own. Even we, in this literary age, and at a distance of thousands of years from those early fathers of language, do not speak at home as we speak in public. The same circumstances which give rise to the formal language of a clan, as distinguished from the dialects of families, produce, on a larger scale, the languages of a confederation of clans, of nascent colonies, of rising nationalities. Before there is a national language, there have always been hundreds of dialects in districts, towns, villages, clans, and families; and though the progress of civilisation and centralisation tends to reduce their number and to soften their features, it has not as yet annihilated them, even in our own time.

Let us now look again at what is commonly called the history, but what ought to be called, the natural growth, of language, and we shall easily see that it consists chiefly in the play of the two principles which we have just examined, *phonetic decay* and *dialectic regeneration* or *growth*. Let us take the six Romance languages. It is usual to call these the daughters of Latin. I do not object to the names of parent and daughter as applied to languages; only we must not allow such apparently clear and simple terms to cover obscure and vague conceptions. Now if we call Italian the daughter of Latin, we do not mean to ascribe to Italian a new vital principle. Not a single radical element was newly created for the formation of Italian. Italian is Latin in a new form. Italian is modern Latin, or Latin ancient Italian. The names *mother* and *daughter* only mark different periods in the growth of a language substantially the same. To speak of Latin dying in giving birth to her offspring is again pure mythology, and it would be easy to prove that Latin was a living language long after Italian had learnt to run alone. Only let us clearly see what we mean by Latin. The classical Latin is one out of many dialects spoken by the Aryan inhabitants of Italy. It was the dialect of Latium, in Latium the dialect of Rome, at Rome the dialect of the patricians. It was fixed by Livius Andronicus, Ennius, Nævius, Cato, and Lucretius, polished by the Scipios, Hortensius, and Cicero. It was the language of a restricted class, of a political party, of a literary set. Before their time, the language of Rome must have changed and fluctuated considerably. Polybius tells us (iii. 22), that the best-informed Romans could not make out without difficulty the language of the ancient treaties between Rome and Carthage. Horace admits (*Ep.* ii. 1, 86), that he could not understand the old Salian poems, and he hints that no one else could. Quintilian (i. 6, 40) says that the Salian priests themselves could hardly understand their sacred hymns. If the plebeians had obtained the upperhand instead of the patricians, Latin would have been very different from what it is in Cicero, and we know that even Cicero, having been brought up at Arpinum, had to give up some of his provincial peculiarities, such as the dropping of the final *s*, when he began to mix in fashionable society, and had to write for his new patrician friends.* After having been established as the language of legislation, religion, literature, and general civilisation, the classical Latin dialect became stationary and stagnant. It could not grow, because it was not allowed to change or to deviate from its classical correctness. It was haunted by its own ghost. Literary dialects, or what are commonly called classical languages, pay for their temporary greatness by inevitable decay. They are like stagnant lakes at the side of great rivers. They form reservoirs of what was once living and running speech, but they are no longer carried on by the main current. At times it may seem as if the whole stream of language was absorbed by these lakes, and we can hardly trace the small rivulets which run on in the main bed. But if lower down, that is to say, later in history, we meet again with a new body of stationary language, forming or formed, we may be sure that its tributaries were those very rivulets which for a time were almost lost from our sight. Or it may be more accurate to compare a classical or literary idiom with the frozen surface of a river, brilliant and smooth, but stiff and cold. It is mostly by political commotions that this surface of the more polite and cultivated speech is broken and carried away by the waters rising underneath. It is during times when

* Quintilian, ix. 4. 'Nam neque Lucilium patiar uti eadem (s) ultima, cum dicit Serenu fuit, et Dignu loco. Quin etiam Cicero in Oratore plures antiquorum tradit sic locutos.' In some phrases the final *s* was omitted in conversation; e. g. *abin* for *ablisne, viden* for *videsne, opu'st* for *opus est, conubere* for *conuberis.*

the higher classes are either crushed in religious and social struggles, or mix again with the lower classes to repel foreign invasion; when literary occupations are discouraged, palaces burnt, monasteries pillaged, and seats of learning destroyed—it is then that the popular, or, as they are called, the vulgar dialects, which had formed a kind of undercurrent, rise beneath the crystal surface of the literary language, and sweep away, like the waters in spring, the cumbrous formations of a bygone age. In more peaceful times, a new and popular literature springs up in a language which *seems* to have been formed by conquests or revolutions, but which, in reality, had been growing up long before, and was only brought out, ready made, by historical events. From this point of view we can see that no literary language can ever be said to have been the mother of another language. As soon as a language loses its unbounded capability of change, its carelessness about what it throws away, and its readiness in always supplying instantaneously the wants of mind and heart, its natural life is changed into a merely artificial existence. It may still live on for a long time, but while it seems to be the leading shoot, it is in reality but a broken and withering branch, slowly falling from the stock from which it sprang. The sources of Italian are not to be found in the classical literature of Rome, but in the popular dialects of Italy. English did not spring from the Anglo-Saxon of Wessex only, but from the dialects spoken in every part of Great Britain, distinguished by local peculiarities and modified at different times by the influence of Latin, Danish, Norman, French, and other foreign elements. Some of the local dialects of English, as spoken at the present day, are of great importance for a critical study of English, and a French prince, now living in this country, deserves great credit for collecting what can still be saved of English dialects. Hindustani is not the daughter of Sanskrit as we find it in the Vedas, or in the later literature of the Brahmans; it is a branch of the living speech of India, springing from the same stem from which Sanskrit sprang, when it first assumed its literary independence.

While thus endeavouring to place the character of dialects, as the feeders of language, in a clear light, I may appear to some of my hearers to have exaggerated their importance. No doubt, if my object had been different, I might easily have shown that, without literary cultivation, language would never have acquired that settled character which is essential for the communication of thought; that it would never have fulfilled its highest purpose, but have remained the mere jargon of shy troglodytes. But as the importance of literary languages is not likely to be overlooked, whereas the importance of dialects, as far as they sustain the growth of language, had never been pointed out, I thought it better to dwell on the advantages which literary languages derive from dialects, rather than on the benefits which dialects owe to literary languages. Besides, our chief object to-day was to explain the growth of language, and for that purpose it is impossible to exaggerate the importance of the constant undergrowth of dialects. Remove a language from its native soil, tear it away from the dialects which are its feeders, and you arrest at once its natural growth. There will still be the progress of phonetic corruption, but no longer the restoring influence of dialectic regeneration. The language which the Norwegian refugees brought to Iceland has remained almost the same for seven centuries, whereas on its native soil, and surrounded by local dialects, it has grown into two distinct languages, the Swedish and Danish. In the eleventh century, the languages of Sweden, Denmark, and Iceland are supposed* to have been identical, nor can we appeal to foreign conquest, or to the admixture of foreign with native blood, in order to account for the changes which the language underwent in Sweden and Denmark, but not in Iceland.†

We can hardly form an idea of the unbounded resources of dialects. When literary languages have stereotyped one general term, their dialects will supply fifty, though each with its own special shade of meaning. If new combinations of thought are evolved in the progress of society, dialects will readily supply the required names from the store of their so-called superfluous words. There are not only local and provincial, but also class dialects. There is a dialect of shepherds, of sportsmen, of soldiers, of farmers. I suppose there are few persons here present who could tell the exact meaning of a horse's poll, crest, withers, dock, hamstring, cannon, pastern, coronet, arm, jowl, and muzzle. Where the literary language speaks of the young of all sorts of animals, farmers, shepherds, and sportsmen would be ashamed to use so general a term.

* Marsh, *Lectures*, pp. 133, 368.
† 'There are fewer local peculiarities of form and articulation in our vast extent of territory (U.S.), than on the comparatively narrow soil of Great Britain.'—*Marsh*, p. 667.

'The idiom of nomads,' as Grimm says, 'contains an abundant wealth of manifold expressions for sword and weapons, and for the different stages in the life of their cattle. In a more highly cultivated language these expressions become burthensome and superfluous. But in a peasant's mouth, the bearing, calving, falling, and killing of almost every animal has its own peculiar term, as the sportsman delights in calling the gait and members of game by different names. The eye of these shepherds, who live in the free air, sees further, their ear hears more sharply— why should their speech not have gained that living truth and variety?'*

Thus Juliana Berners, lady prioress of the nunnery of Sopwell in the fifteenth century, the reputed author of the *Book of St. Albans*, informs us that we must not use names of multitudes promiscuously, but we are to say, 'a congregacyon of people, a hoost of men, a felyshyppynge of yomen, and a bevy of ladies; we must speak of a herde of dere, swannys, cranys, or wrenys, a sege of herons or bytourys, a muster of pecockes, a watche of nyghtyngales, a flyghte of doves, a claterynge of choughes, a pryde of lyons, a slewthe of beeres, a gagle of geys, a skulke of foxes, a sculle of frerys, a pontificality of prestys, a bonnynable syght of monkes, and a superfluyte of nonnes,' and so of other human and brute assemblages. In

---

* Many instances are given in Pott's *Etym. Forsch.*, p. 128– 169. Grimm, *Geschichte der Deutschen Sprache*, p. 25. 'Wir sagen: die stute fohlt, die kuh kalbt, das schaf lammt, die griss sickelt, die sau frischt (von frisching, frischling), die hündin welft (mhd. erwirfet das wolf); nicht anders heisst es französisch la chèvre chèvrote, la brebis agnele, la truie porcele, la louve louvete, &c.'

like manner, in dividing game for the table, the animals were not carved, but 'a dere was broken, a goose reryd, chekyn frusshed, a cony unlaced, a crane dysplayed, a curlewe unioynted, a quayle wynggyd, a swanne lyfte, a lambe sholdered, a heron dysmembryd, a pecocke dysfygured, a samon chynyd, a hadoke sydyd, a sole loynyd, and a breme splayed.'*

What, however, I wanted particularly to point out in this lecture is this, that neither of the causes which produce the growth, or, according to others, constitute the history of language, is under the control of man. The phonetic decay of language is not the result of mere accident; it is governed by definite laws, as we shall see when we come to consider the principles of comparative grammar. But these laws were not made by man; on the contrary, man had to obey them without knowing of their existence.

In the growth of the modern Romance languages out of Latin, we can perceive not only a general tendency to simplification, not only a natural disposition to avoid the exertion which the pronunciation of certain consonants, and still more, of groups of consonants, entails on the speaker: but we can see distinct laws for each of the Romance dialects, which enable us to say, that in French the Latin *patrem* would naturally grow into the modern *père*. The final *m* is always dropped in the Romance dialects, and it was dropped even in Latin. Thus we get *patre* instead of *patrem*. Now, a Latin *t* between two vowels in such words as *pater* is invariably sup-

---

* Marsh, *Lectures*, pp. 161, 590.

pressed in French. This is a law, and by means of it we can discover at once that *catena* must become *chaîne*; *fata*, a later feminine representation of the old neuter *fatum*, *fée*; *pratum* a meadow, *pré*. From *pratum* we derive *prataria*, which in French becomes *prairie*; from *fatum*, *fataria*, the English *fairy*. Thus every Latin participle in *atus*, like *amatus*, loved, must end in French in *é*. The same law then changed *patre* (pronounced *patere*) into *paere*, or *père*; it changed *matrem* into *mère*, *fratrem* into *frère*. These changes take place gradually but irresistibly, and, what is most important, they are completely beyond the reach or control of the free will of man.

Dialectical growth again is still more beyond the control of individuals. For although a poet may knowingly and intentionally invent a new word, its acceptance depends on circumstances which defy individual interference. There are some changes in the grammar which at first sight might seem to be mainly attributable to the caprice of the speaker. Granted, for instance, that the loss of the Latin terminations was the natural result of a more careless pronunciation; granted that the modern sign of the French genitive *du* is a natural corruption of the Latin *de illo*—yet the choice of *de*, instead of any other word, to express the genitive, the choice of *illo*, instead of any other pronoun, to express the article, might seem to prove that man acted as a free agent in the formation of language. But it is not so. No single individual could deliberately have set to work in order to abolish the old Latin genitive, and to replace it by the periphrastic compound *de illo*. It was necessary that the inconvenience of having no distinct or distinguishable sign of the genitive should have been felt by the people who spoke a vulgar Latin dialect. It was necessary that the same people should have used the preposition *de* in such a manner as to lose sight of its original local meaning altogether (for instance, *una de multis*, in Horace, i. e. one out of many). It was necessary, again, that the same people should have felt the want of an article, and should have used *illo* in numerous expressions, where it seemed to have lost its original pronominal power. It was necessary that all these conditions should be given, before one individual, and after him another, and after him hundreds and thousands and millions, could use *de illo* as the exponent of the genitive; and change it into the Italian *dello*, *del*, and the French *du*.

The attempts of single grammarians and purists to improve language are perfectly bootless; and we shall probably hear no more of schemes to prune languages of their irregularities. It is very likely, however, that the gradual disappearance of irregular declensions and conjugations is due, in literary as well as in illiterate languages, to the dialect of children. The language of children is more regular than our own. I have heard children say *badder* and *baddest*, instead of *worse* and *worst*. In Urdú the old sign of the possessive was *rá*, *re*, *rí*. Now it is *ká*, *ke*, *kí*, except in *hamárá*, my, our, *tumhárá*, your, and a few other words, all pronouns. My learned friend, Dr. Fitz-Edward Hall, informs me that he heard children in India use *hamká* and *tumká*. Children will say, *I gaed*, *I coomd*, *I catched*; and it is this sense of grammatical justice, this generous feeling

of what ought to be, which in the course of centuries
has eliminated many so-called irregular forms. Thus
the auxiliary verb in Latin was very irregular. If
sumus is *we are*, and *sunt*, *they are*, the second
person, *you are*, ought to have been, at least according to the strict logic of children, *sutis*. This, no
doubt, sounds very barbarous to a classical ear
accustomed to *estis*. And we see how French, for
instance, has strictly preserved the Latin forms in
nous sommes, vous êtes, ils sont. But in Spanish we
find *somos, sois, son*; and this *sois* stands for *sutis*.
We find similar traces of grammatical levelling in
the Italian *siamo, siete, sono*, formed in analogy of
regular verbs such as *crediamo, credete, credono*.
The second person, *sei*, instead of *es*, is likewise
infantine grammar. So are the Wallachian *súntemu*,
we are, *súnteti*, you are, which owe their origin to
the third person plural *súnt*, they are. And what
shall we say of such monsters as *essendo*, a gerund
derived on principles of strict justice from an infinitive *essere*, like *credendo* from *credere*! However,
we need not be surprised, for we find similar bar-
barisms in English. Even in Anglo-Saxon, the third
person plural, *sind*, had by a false analogy been
transferred to the first and second persons; and
instead of the modern English,

		In Old Norse.	In Gothic.
we are		ër-um	sijum*
you are	we find	ër-udh	sijuth
they are†		ër-u.	sind.

* The Gothic forms *sijum, sijuth*, are not organic. They are
either derived by false analogy from the third person plural *sind*,
or a new base *sij* was derived from the subjunctive *sijau*, Sanskrit
syâm.

† The Scandinavian origin of these English forms has been

Dialectically we hear *I be*, instead of *I am*; and if Chartism should ever gain the upper hand, we must be prepared for newspapers adopting such forms as *I says, I knows*.

These various influences and conditions, under which language grows and changes, are like the waves and winds which carry deposits to the bottom of the sea, where they accumulate and rise, and grow, and at last appear on the surface of the earth as a stratum, perfectly intelligible in all its component parts, not produced by an inward principle of growth, nor regulated by invariable laws of nature; yet, on the other hand, by no means the result of mere accident, or the production of lawless and uncontrolled agencies. We cannot be careful enough in the use of our words. Strictly speaking, neither *history* nor *growth* is applicable to the changes of the shifting surface of the earth. *History* applies to the actions of free agents; *growth* to the natural unfolding of organic beings. We speak, however, of the growth of the crust of the earth, and we know what we mean by it; and it is in this sense, but not in the sense of growth as applied to a tree, that we have a right to speak of the growth of language. If that modification which takes place in time by continually new combinations of given elements, which withdraws itself from the

---

well explained by Dr. Lottner, *Transactions of the Philological Society*, 1861, p. 63. The third person plural *arun* is found in Kemble's *Codex Diplomaticus Ævi Saxonici*, vol. i. p. 235 (A.D. 803–831). It does not occur in Layamon. It is found in the Ormulum as *ærrn*; but even in Chaucer it has been met with twice only. See Gesenius, *De Ling. Chaucer.* p. 72; Monicke, *On the "Ormulum,"* p. 35.

control of free agents, and can in the end be recognised as the result of natural agencies, may be called growth; and if, so defined, we may apply it to the growth of the crust of the earth; the same word, in the same sense, will be applicable to language, and will justify us in removing the science of language from the pale of the historical to that of the physical sciences.

There is another objection which we have to consider, and the consideration of which will again help us to understand more clearly the real character of language. The great periods in the growth of the earth which have been established by geological research are brought to their close, or very nearly so, when we discover the first vestiges of human life, and when the history of man, in the widest sense of the word, begins. The periods in the growth of language, on the contrary, begin and run parallel with the history of man. It has been said, therefore, that although language may not be merely a work of art, it would, nevertheless, be impossible to understand the life and growth of any language without an historical knowledge of the times in which that language grew up. We ought to know, it is said, whether a language which is to be analysed under the microscope of comparative grammar, has been growing up wild, among wild tribes without a literature, oral or written, in poetry or in prose; or whether it has received the cultivation of poets, priests, and orators, and retained the impress of a classical age. Again, it is only from the annals of political history that we can learn whether one language has come in contact with another, how long this contact has lasted, which of the two nations stood higher in civilisation, which was the conquering and which the conquered, which of the two established the laws, the religion, and the arts of the country, and which produced the greatest number of national teachers, popular poets, and successful demagogues. All these questions are of a purely historical character, and the science which has to borrow so much from historical sources, might well be considered an anomaly in the sphere of the physical sciences.

Now, in answer to this, it cannot be denied that among the physical sciences none is so intimately connected with the history of man as the science of language. But a similar connection, though in a less degree, can be shown to exist between other branches of physical research and the history of man. In zoology, for instance, it is of some importance to know at what particular period of history, in what country, and for what purposes certain animals were tamed and domesticated. In ethnology, a science, we may remark in passing, quite distinct from the science of language, it would be difficult to account for the Caucasian stamp impressed on the Mongolian race in Hungary, or on the Tatar race in Turkey, unless we knew from written documents the migrations and settlements of the Mongolic and Tataric tribes in Europe. A botanist, again, comparing several specimens of rye, would find it difficult to account for their respective peculiarities, unless he knew that in some parts of the world this plant has been cultivated for centuries, whereas in other regions, as, for instance, in Mount Caucasus, it is still allowed to grow wild. Plants have their own countries, like races, and the presence of the cucumber in Greece, the orange and cherry in Italy, the potato in England, and the vine at the Cape, can be fully explained by the historian only. The more intimate relation, therefore, between the history of language and the history of man is not sufficient to exclude the science of language from the circle of the physical sciences.

Nay, it might be shown that, if strictly defined, the science of language can declare itself completely independent of history. If we speak of the language of England, we ought, no doubt, to know something of the political history of the British Isles, in order to understand the present state of that language. Its history begins with the early Britons, who spoke a Celtic dialect; it carries us on to the Saxon conquest, to the Danish invasions, to the Norman conquest: and we see how each of these political events contributed to the formation of the character of the language. The language of England may be said to have been in succession Celtic, Saxon, Norman, and English. But if we speak of the history of the English language, we enter on totally different ground. The English language was never Celtic, the Celtic never grew into Saxon, nor the Saxon into Norman, nor the Norman into English. The history of the Celtic language runs on to the present day. It matters not whether it be spoken by all the inhabitants of the British Isles, or only by a small minority in Wales, Ireland, and Scotland. A language, as long as it is spoken by anybody, lives and has its substantive existence. The last old woman that spoke Cornish, and to whose memory it is now intended to raise a monument, represented by herself alone the ancient language of

Cornwall. A Celt may become an Englishman, Celtic and English blood may be mixed; and who could tell at the present day the exact proportion of Celtic and Saxon blood in the population of England? But languages are never mixed. It is indifferent by what name the language spoken in the British Islands be called, whether English or British or Saxon; to the student of language English is Teutonic, and nothing but Teutonic. The physiologist may protest, and point out that in many instances the skull, or the bodily habitat of the English language, is of a Celtic type; the genealogist may protest and prove that the arms of many an English family are of Norman origin; the student of language must follow his own way. Historical information as to an early substratum of Celtic inhabitants in Britain, as to Saxon, Danish, and Norman invasions, may be useful to him. But though every record were burned, and every skull mouldered, the English language, as spoken by any ploughboy, would reveal its own history, if analysed according to the rules of comparative grammar. Without the help of history, we should see that English is Teutonic, that like Dutch and Friesian it belongs to the Low-German branch; that this branch, together with the High-German, Gothic, and Scandinavian branches, constitute the Teutonic class; that this Teutonic class, together with the Celtic, Slavonic, the Hellenic, Italic, Iranic, and Indic classes, constitute the great Indo-European or Aryan family of speech. In the English dictionary the student of the science of language can detect, by his own tests, Celtic, Norman, Greek, and Latin ingredients, but not a single drop of foreign blood has entered into the organic system of the English language. The grammar, the blood and soul of the language, is as pure and unmixed in English as spoken in the British Isles, as it was when spoken on the shores of the German ocean by the Angles, Saxons, and Juts of the continent.

In thus considering and refuting the objections which have been, or might be, made against the admission of the science of language into the circle of the physical sciences, we have arrived at some results which it may be useful to recapitulate before we proceed further. We saw that whereas philology treats language only as a means, comparative philology chooses language as the object of scientific inquiry. It is not the study of one language, but of many, and in the end of all, which forms the aim of this new science. Nor is the language of Homer of greater interest, in the scientific treatment of human speech, than the dialect of the Hottentots.

We saw, secondly, that after the first practical acquisition and careful analysis of the facts and forms of any language, the next and most important step is the classification of all the varieties of human speech, and that only after this has been accomplished would it be safe to venture on the great questions which underlie all physical research, the questions as to the what, the whence, and the why of language.

We saw, thirdly, that there is a distinction between what is called history and growth. We determined the true meaning of growth, as applied to language, and perceived how it was independent of the caprice of man, and governed by laws that could be discovered by careful observation, and be traced back in the end to higher laws, which govern the organs both of human thought, and of the human voice. Though admitting that the science of language was more intimately connected than any other physical science with what is called the political history of man, we found that, strictly speaking, our science might well dispense with this auxiliary, and that languages can be analysed and classified on their own evidence, particularly on the strength of their grammatical articulation, without any reference to the individuals, families, clans, tribes, nations or races by whom they are or have been spoken.

In the course of these considerations, we had to lay down two axioms, to which we shall frequently have to appeal in the progress of our investigations. The first declares grammar to be the most essential element, and therefore the ground of classification in all languages which have produced a definite grammatical articulation ; the second denies the possibility of a mixed language.

These two axioms are, in reality, but one, as we shall see when we examine them more closely. There is hardly a language which in one sense may not be called a mixed language. No nation or tribe was ever so completely isolated as not to admit the importation of a certain number of foreign words. In some instances these imported words have changed the whole native aspect of the language, and have even acquired a majority over the native element. Thus Turkish is a Turanian dialect; its grammar is purely Tataric or Turanian;—yet at the present moment the Turkish language, as spoken by the higher ranks at Constantinople, is so entirely overgrown with Persian and Arabic words, that a common clod from the country understands but little of the so-called Osmanli, though its grammar is the same as the grammar which he uses in his Tataric utterance. The presence of these Persian and Arabic words in Turkish is to be accounted for by literary and political, even more than by religious influences. Persian civilisation began to tell on the Arabs from the first days of their religious and military conquests, and although the conquered and converted Persians had necessarily to accept a large number of religious and political terms of Arabic, i.e. Semitic, origin, it would appear from a more careful examination of the several Persian words admitted into Arabic, that the ancient Aryan civilisation of Persia, reinvigorated by the Sassanian princes, reacted powerfully, though more silently, on the primitive nomadism of Arabia.* The Koran itself is not free from Persian expressions, and it contains even a denunciation of the Persian romances which circulated among the more educated followers of Mohammed. Now the Turks, though accepting a Semitic religion and with it necessarily a Semitic religious terminology, did not accept that religion till after it had passed through a Persian channel. Hence the large number of Persian words in Turkish, and the clear traces of Persian construction and idiom even in Arabic words as used in Turkish. Such Aryan words as *din*, faith, *gaur*, an infidel, *oruj*, a fast, *namaz*, prayers, used by a Turanian race, worshipping according to the formularies of a Semitic religion, are more instructive as to the history of civilisation than coins, inscriptions, or chronicles.†

---

* Reinaud, *Mémoire sur l'Inde*, p. 310. Renan, *Histoire des Langues Sémitiques*, pp. 292, 379, &c.

† In the earlier editions of these Lectures the influence of Persian civilisation on the language of the Arabs had been much

There is, perhaps, no language so full of words evidently derived from the most distant sources as English. Every country of the globe seems to have brought some of its verbal manufactures to the intellectual market of England. Latin, Greek, Hebrew, Celtic, Saxon, Danish, French, Spanish, Italian, German—nay, even Hindustani, Malay, and Chinese words—lie mixed together in the English dictionary. On the evidence of words alone it would be impossible to classify English with any other of the established stocks and stems of human speech. Leaving out of consideration the smaller ingredients, we find, on comparing the Teutonic with the Latin, or Neo-Latin or Norman-French elements in English, that the latter have a decided majority over the home-grown Saxon terms. This may seem incredible; and if we simply took a page of any English book, and counted therein the words of purely Saxon and Latin origin, the majority would be no doubt on the Saxon side. The articles, pronouns, prepositions, and auxiliary verbs, all of which are of Saxon growth, occur over and over again in one and the same page. Thus, Hickes maintained that nine-tenths of the English dictionary were Saxon, because there were only three words of Latin origin in the Lord's prayer. Sharon Turner, who extended his observations over a larger field, came to the conclusion that the relation of Norman to Saxon was as four to six. Another writer, who estimates the whole number of English words at 38,000, assigns 23,000 to a Saxon, and

overstated, while its influence on the Turkish dictionary had not been estimated sufficiently high. I owe to Viscount Strangford the corrections here introduced.

15,000 to a classical source. On taking, however, a more accurate inventory, and counting every word in the dictionaries of Robertson and Webster, M. Thommerel has established the fact that of the sum total of 43,566 words, 29,853 came from classical, 13,230 from Teutonic, and the rest from miscellaneous sources.* On the evidence of its dictionary, therefore, and treating English as a mixed language, it would have to be classified, together with French, Italian, and Spanish, as one of the Romance or Neo-Latin dialects. Languages, however, though mixed in their dictionary, can never be mixed in their grammar. Hervas was told by missionaries that in the middle of the eighteenth century the Araucans used hardly a single word which was not Spanish, though they preserved both the grammar and the syntax of their own native speech.† This is the reason why grammar is made the criterion of the relationship and the base of the classification in almost all languages; and it follows, therefore, as a matter of course, that in the classification and in the science of language, it is impossible to admit the existence of a mixed idiom. We may form whole

---

* Some excellent statistics on the exact proportion of Saxon and Latin in various English writers, are to be found in Marsh's *Lectures on the English Language*, p. 120 seq. and 181 seq.

† 'En este estado, que es el primer paso que las naciones dan para mudar de lengua, estaba quarenta años ha la araucana en las islas de Chiloue (como he oido á los jesuitas sus misioneros), en donde los araucanos apénas proferian palabra que no fuese española; mas la proferian con el artificio y órden de su lengua nativa, llamada araucana.'—Hervas, *Catalago*, t. i. p. 16. 'Este artificio ha sido en mi observacion el principal modio de que me he valido para conocer la afinidad ó diferencia de las lenguas conocidas, y reducirlas á determinadas clases.'—*Ibid.* p. 23.

sentences in English consisting entirely of Latin or Romance words; yet whatever there is left of grammar in English bears unmistakable traces of Teutonic workmanship. What may now be called grammar in English is little more than the terminations of the genitive singular, and nominative plural of nouns, the degrees of comparison, and a few of the persons, and tenses of the verb. Yet the single *s*, used as the exponent of the third person singular of the indicative present, is irrefragable evidence that in a scientific classification of languages, English, though it did not retain a single word of Saxon origin, would have to be classed as Saxon, and as a branch of the great Teutonic stem of the Aryan family of speech. In ancient and less matured languages, grammar, or the formal part of human speech, is far more abundantly developed than in English; and it is, therefore, a much safer guide for discovering a family likeness in scattered members of the same family. There are languages in which there is no trace of what we are accustomed to call grammar; for instance, ancient Chinese; there are others in which we can still watch the growth of grammar, or, more correctly, the gradual lapse of material into merely formal elements. In these languages new principles of classification will have to be applied, such as are suggested by the study of natural history; and we shall have to be satisfied with the criteria of a morphological affinity, instead of those of a genealogical relationship.

I have thus answered, I hope, some of the objections which threatened to deprive the science of language of that place which she claims in the circle of the physical sciences. We shall see in our next lecture what the history of our science has been from its beginning to the present day, and how far it may be said to have passed through the three stages, the empirical, the classificatory, and the theoretical, which mark the childhood, the youth, and the manhood of every one of the natural sciences.

LECTURE III.

THE EMPIRICAL STAGE.

WE begin to-day to trace the historical progress of the science of language in its three stages, the *Empirical*, the *Classificatory*, and the *Theoretical*. As a general rule each physical science begins with analysis, proceeds to classification, and ends with theory; but, as I pointed out in my first lecture, there are frequent exceptions to this rule, and it is by no means uncommon to find that philosophical speculations, which properly belong to the last or theoretical stage, were attempted in physical sciences long before the necessary evidence had been collected or arranged. Thus, we find that the science of language, in the only two countries where we can watch its origin and history—in India and Greece—rushes at once into theories about the mysterious nature of speech, and cares as little for facts as the man who wrote an account of the camel without ever having seen the animal or the desert. The Brahmans, in the hymns of the Veda, raised language to the rank of a deity, as they did with all things of which they knew not what they were. They addressed hymns to her in which she is said to have been with the gods from the beginning, achieving wondrous things, and never revealed to man except in part. In the Brâhmanas, language is called the cow, breath the bull, and their young is said to be

the mind of man.* Brahman, the highest being, is
said to be known through speech, nay, speech herself
is called the Supreme Brahman. At a very early
period, however, the Brahmans recovered from their
raptures about language, and set to work with wonderful skill dissecting her sacred body. Their achievements in grammatical analysis, which date from the
6th century, B.C., are still unsurpassed in the grammatical literature of any nation. The idea of reducing a whole language to a small number of roots,
which in Europe was not attempted before the sixteenth century by Henry Estienne,† was perfectly
familiar to the Brahmans at least 500 B.C.

The Greeks, though they did not raise language to
the rank of a deity, paid her, nevertheless, the greatest
honours in their ancient schools of philosophy.

* Colebrooke, *Miscellaneous Essays*, i. 32. The following
verses are pronounced by Vâch, the goddess of speech, in the
125th hymn of the 10th book of the Rig-Veda: 'Even I myself
say this (what is) welcome to gods and to men: "Whom I love,
him I make strong, him I make a Brahman, him a great prophet,
him I make wise. For Rudra (the god of thunder) I bend the
bow, to slay the enemy, the hater of the Brahmans. For the
people I make war; I pervade heaven and earth. I bear the
father on the summit of this world; my origin is in the water in
the sea; from thence I go forth among all beings, and touch this
heaven with my height. I myself breathe forth like the wind,
embracing all beings; above this heaven, beyond this earth, such
am I in greatness."' See also *Atharva-Veda*, iv. 30; xix. 9, 3.
Muir, *Sanskrit Texts*, part iii. pp. 108, 150.

† Sir John Stoddart, *Glossology*, p. 276. The first complete
Hebrew Grammar and Dictionary of the Bible were the work of
Rabbi Jonâ, or Abul Walid Merwân ibn Djanâh, in the middle of
the 11th century. The idea of Hebrew roots was explained
even before him by Abu Zacariyya 'Hayyudj, who is called the
First Grammarian by Ibn Ezra. Cf. Munk, *Notice sur Aboul
Walid, Journal Asiatique*, 1850, Avril.

There is hardly one of their representative philosophers who has not left some saying on the nature of language. The world without, or nature, and the world within, or mind, did not excite more wonder and elicit deeper oracles of wisdom from the ancient sages of Greece than language, the image of both, of nature and of mind. 'What is language?' was a question asked quite as early as 'What am I?' and 'What is all this world around me?' The problem of language was in fact a recognised battle-field for the different schools of ancient Greek philosophy, and we shall have to glance at their early guesses on the nature of human speech, when we come to consider the third or theoretical stage in the science of language.

At present, we have to look for the early traces of the first or empirical stage. And here it might seem doubtful what was the real work to be assigned to this stage. What can be meant by the empirical treatment of language? Who were the men that did for language what the sailor did for his stars, the miner for his minerals, the gardener for his flowers? Who was the first to give any thought to language? —to distinguish between its component parts, between nouns and verbs, between articles and pronouns, between the nominative and accusative, the active and passive? Who invented these terms, and for what purpose were they invented?

We must be careful in answering these questions, for, as I said before, the merely empirical analysis of language was preceded in Greece by more general inquiries into the nature of thought and language; and the result has been that many of the technical terms which form the nomenclature of empirical grammar, existed in the schools of philosophy long before they were handed over, ready made, to the grammarian. The distinction of noun and verb, or more correctly, of subject and predicate, was the work of philosophers. Even the technical terms for case, number, and gender, were coined at a very early time for the purpose of entering into the nature of thought; not for the practical purpose of analysing the forms of language. This, their practical application to the spoken language of Greece, was the work of a later generation. It was the teacher of languages who first compared the categories of thought with the realities of the Greek language. It was he who transferred the terminology of Aristotle and the Stoics from thought to speech, from logic to grammar; and thus opened the first roads into the impervious wilderness of spoken speech. In doing this, the grammarian had to alter the strict acceptation of many of the terms which he borrowed from the philosopher, and he had to coin others before he could lay hold of all the facts of language even in the roughest manner. For, indeed, the distinction between noun and verb, between active and passive, between nominative and accusative, does not help us much towards a scientific analysis of language. It is no more than a first grasp, and it can only be compared with the most elementary terminology in other branches of human knowledge. Nevertheless, it was a beginning, a very important beginning; and if we preserve in our histories of the world the names of those who are said to have discovered the physical elements, the names of Thales and Anaximenes and Empedocles, we ought not to forget the names of the discoverers of the elements of language—the founders of one of the most useful and most successful branches of philosophy—the first Grammarians.

Grammar, then, in the usual sense of the word, or the merely formal and empirical analysis of language, owes its origin, like all other sciences, to a very natural and practical want. The first practical grammarian was the first practical teacher of languages, and if we want to know the beginnings of the science of language we must try to find out at what time in the history of the world, and under what circumstances, people first thought of learning any language besides their own. At *that* time we shall find the first practical grammar, and not till then. Much may have been ready at hand through the less interested researches of philosophers, and likewise through the critical studies of the scholars of Alexandria on the ancient forms of their language as preserved in the Homeric poems. But rules of declension and conjunction, paradigms of regular and irregular nouns and verbs, observations on syntax, and the like, these are the work of the teachers of languages, and of no one else.

Now, the teaching of languages, though at present so large a profession, is comparatively a very modern invention. No ancient Greek ever thought of learning a foreign language. Why should he? He divided the whole world into Greeks and Barbarians, and he would have felt himself degraded by adopting either the dress or the manners or the language of his barbarian neighbours. He considered it a privilege to speak Greek, and even dialects closely related to his own, were treated by him as mere jargons. It takes time before people conceive the idea that it is possible to express oneself in any but one's own language. The Poles called their neighbours, the Germans, *Niemiec, niemy* meaning *dumb*;* just as the Greeks called the Barbarians *Aglossoi*, or speechless. The name which the Germans gave to their neighbours, the Celts, *Walh* in old High German, *vealh* in Anglo-Saxon, the modern *Welsh*, is supposed to be the same as the Sanskrit *mlechchha*, and means a person who talks indistinctly.†

Even when the Greeks began to feel the necessity of communicating with foreign nations, when they felt a desire of learning their idioms, the problem was by no means solved. For how was a foreign language to be learnt as long as either party could only speak their own? The problem was almost as difficult as when, as we are told by some persons, the first men, as yet speechless, came together in order to invent speech, and to discuss the most appropriate names that should be given to the perceptions of the senses and the abstractions of the mind. At first, it must be supposed that the Greek learned foreign languages very much as children learn their own. The interpreters mentioned by ancient historians were probably children of parents speaking different

---

* The Turks applied the Polish name *Niemiec* to the Austrians. As early as Constantinus Porphyrogeneta, cap. 30, Νεμίτζοι was used for the German race of the Bavarians (Pott, *Indo-Germ. Sp.* s. 44; Loo, *Zeitschrift für vergleichende Sprachforschung*, b. ii. s. 258). Russian, *njemez*'; Slovenian, *němec*; Bulgarian, *němec*; Polish, *niemiec*; Lusatian, *njemc*, mean German; Russian, *njemo*, indistinct; *njemyi*, dumb; Slovenian, *něm*, dumb; Bulgarian, *něm*, dumb; Polish, *njemy*, dumb; Lusatian, *njemy*, dumb.

† Loo, *Zeitschrift für vergl. Sprachf.* b. ii. s. 252. Baluch, the name given to the tribes on the western borders of India, south of Afghanistán, has likewise been identified with the Sanskrit Mlechchha.

languages. Cyaxares, the King of Media, on the arrival of a tribe of Scythians in his country, sent some children to them that they might learn their language and the art of archery.* The son of a barbarian and a Greek would naturally learn the utterances both of his father and mother, and the lucrative nature of his services would not fail to increase the supply. We are told, though on rather mythical authority, that the Greeks were astonished at the multiplicity of languages which they encountered during the Argonautic expedition, and that they were much inconvenienced by the want of skilful interpreters.† We need not wonder at this, for the English army was hardly better off than the army of Jason; and such is the variety of dialects spoken in the Caucasian Isthmus, that it is still called by the inhabitants 'the Mountain of Languages.' If we turn our eyes from those mythical ages to the historical times of Greece, we find that trade gave the first encouragement to the profession of interpreters. Herodotus tells us (iv. 24), that caravans of Greek merchants, following the course of the Volga upwards to the Oural mountains, were accompanied by seven interpreters, speaking seven different languages. These must have comprised Sclavonic, Tataric and Finnic dialects, spoken in those countries in the time of Herodotus, as they are at the present day. The wars with Persia first familiarised the Greeks with the idea that other nations also possessed real languages. Themistocles studied Persian, and is said to have spoken it fluently. The expedition of Alexander contributed still more powerfully to a

---

* Herod. I. 73.
† Humboldt's *Kosmos*, vol. ii. p. 141.

knowledge of other nations and languages. But when Alexander went to converse with the Brahmans, who were even then considered by the Greeks as the guardians of a most ancient and mysterious wisdom, their answers had to be translated by so many interpreters that one of the Brahmans remarked, they must become like water that had passed through many impure channels.* We hear, indeed, of more ancient Greek travellers, and it is difficult to understand how, in those early times, anybody could have travelled without a certain knowledge of the language of the people through whose camps and villages and towns he had to pass. Many of these travels, however, particularly those which are said to have extended as far as India, are mere inventions of later writers.† Lycurgus may have travelled to Spain and Africa, he certainly did not proceed to India, nor is there any mention of his intercourse with the Indian Gymnosophists before

---

* This shows how difficult it would be to admit that any influence was exercised by Indian on Greek philosophers. Pyrrhon, if we may believe Alexander Polyhistor, seems indeed to have accompanied Alexander on his expedition to India, and one feels tempted to connect the scepticism of Pyrrhon with the system of Buddhist philosophy then current in India. But the ignorance of the language on both sides must have been an almost insurmountable barrier between the Greek and the Indian thinkers. (*Fragmenta Histor. Graec.*, ed. Müller, t. iii. p. 243, b; Lassen, *Indische Alterthumskunde*, b. iii. s. 380.)

† On the supposed travels of Greek philosophers to India, see Lassen, *Indische Alterthumskunde*, b. iii. s. 379: Brandis, *Handbuch der Geschichte der Philosophie*, b. i. s. 425. The opinion of D. Stewart and Niebuhr that the Indian philosophers borrowed from the Greeks, and that of Görres and others that the Greeks borrowed from the Brahmans, are examined in my Essay on Indian Logic, in *Dr. Thomson's Laws of Thought.*

Aristocrates, who lived about 100 B.C. The travels of Pythagoras are equally mythical; they are inventions of Alexandrian writers, who believed that all wisdom must have flowed from the East. There is better authority for believing that Democritus went to Egypt and Babylon, but his more distant travels to India are likewise legendary. Herodotus, though he travelled in Egypt and Persia, never gives us to understand that he was able to converse in any but his own language.

As far as we can tell, the barbarians seem to have possessed a greater facility for acquiring languages than either Greeks or Romans. Soon after the Macedonian conquest we find * Berosus in Babylon, Menander in Tyre, and Manetho in Egypt, compiling, from original sources, the annals of their countries.† Their works were written in Greek, and for the Greeks. The native language of Berosus was Babylonian, of Menander Phenician, of Manetho Egyptian. Berosus was able to read the cuneiform documents of Babylonia with the same ease with

---

* See Niebuhr, *Vorlesungen über alte Geschichte*, b. l. s. 17.

† The translation of Mago's work on agriculture belongs to a later time. There is no proof that Mago, who wrote twenty-eight books on agriculture in the Punic language, lived, as Humboldt supposes (*Kosmos*, vol. ii. p. 184), 500 B.C. Varro *de R. H.* i. 1. says: 'Hos nobilitate Mago Carthaginiensis praeterit Punica lingua, quod res dispersas comprehendit libris xxiix., quos Cassius Dionysius Uticensis vertit libris xx., Graeca lingua, ac Sextilio praetori misit: in quae volumina de Graecis libris eorum quos dixi adjecit non pauca, et de Magonis dempsit instar librorum viii. Hosce ipsos utiliter ad vi. libros redegit Diophanes in Bithynia, et misit Dejotaro regi.' This Cassius Dionysius Uticensis lived about 40 B.C. The translation into Latin was made at the command of the Senate, shortly after the third Punic war.

which Manetho read the papyri of Egypt. The almost contemporaneous appearance of three such men, barbarians by birth and language, who were anxious to save the histories of their countries from total oblivion, by entrusting them to the keeping of their conquerors, the Greeks, is highly significant. But what is likewise significant, and by no means creditable to the Greek or Macedonian conquerors, is the small value which they seem to have set on these works. They have all been lost, and are known to us by fragments only, though there can be little doubt that the work of Berosus would have been an invaluable guide to the student of the cuneiform inscriptions and of Babylonian history, and that Manetho, if preserved complete, would have saved us volumes of controversy on Egyptian chronology. We learn, however, from the almost simultaneous appearance of these works, that soon after the epoch marked by Alexander's conquests in the East, the Greek language was studied and cultivated by literary men of barbarian origin, though we should look in vain for any Greek, learning or employing for literary purposes any but his own tongue. We hear of no intellectual intercourse between Greeks and barbarians before the days of Alexander and Alexandria. At Alexandria, various nations, speaking different languages, and believing in different gods, were brought together. Though primarily engaged in mercantile speculations, it was but natural that in their moments of leisure they should hold discourse on their native countries, their gods, their kings, their law-givers, and poets. Besides, there were Greeks at Alexandria who were engaged in the study of antiquity, and who knew how to ask questions from men coming from any country of the world. The pretension of the Egyptians to a fabulous antiquity, the belief of the Jews in the sacred character of their law, the faith of the Persians in the writing of Zoroaster, all these were fit subjects for discussion in the halls and libraries of Alexandria. We probably owe the translation of the Old Testament, the Septuagint, to this spirit of literary inquiry which was patronised at Alexandria by the Ptolemies.* The writings of Zoroaster also, the Zend-Avesta, would seem to have been rendered into Greek about the same time. For Hermippus, who is said by Pliny to have translated the writings of Zoroaster, was in all probability Hermippus † the Peripatetic philosopher, the pupil of Callimachus, one of the most learned scholars at Alexandria.

* Ptolemæus Philadelphus (287—246 B.C.), on the recommendation of his chief librarian (Demetrius Phalereus), is said to have sent a Jew of the name of Aristeas, to Jerusalem, to ask the high priest for a MS of the Bible, and for seventy interpreters. Others maintain that the Hellenistic Jews who lived at Alexandria, and who had almost forgotten their native language, had this translation made for their own benefit. Certain it is, that about the beginning of the third century B.C. (285), we find large portions of the Hebrew Bible translated into Greek by different hands.

† Plin. xxx. 2. 'Sine dubio illa orta in Perside a Zoroastre, ut inter auctores convenit. Sed unus hic fuerit, an postea et alius, non satis constat. Eudoxus qui inter sapientiæ sectas clarissimam utilissimamque eam intelligi voluit, Zoroastrem hunc sex millibus annorum ante Platonis mortem fuisse prodidit. Sic et Aristoteles. Hermippus qui de tota ea arte diligentissime scripsit, et vicies centum millia versuum a Zoroastre condita, indicibus quoque voluminum ejus positis explanavit, præceptorem a quo institutum disceret, tradidit Azonacem, ipsum vero quinque millibus annorum ante Trojanum bellum fuisse.' See Bunsen's *Egypten*, Va, 101.

But although we find at Alexandria these and similar traces of a general interest having been excited by the literatures of other nations, there is no evidence which would lead us to suppose that their languages also had become the subject of scientific inquiry. It was not through the study of other languages, but through the study of the ancient dialects of their own language, that the Greeks at Alexandria were first led to what we should call critical and philological studies. The critical study of Greek took its origin at Alexandria, and it was chiefly based on the text of Homer. The general outline of grammar existed, as I remarked before, at an earlier period. It grew up in the schools of Greek philosophers.* Plato knew of noun and verb as the two component parts of speech. Aristotle added conjunctions and articles. He likewise observed the distinctions of number and case. But neither Plato nor Aristotle paid much attention to the forms of language which corresponded to these forms of thought, nor had they any inducement to reduce them to any practical rules. With Aristotle the verb or *rhēma* is hardly more than predicate, and in sentences such as 'the snow is white,' he would have called *white* a verb. The first who reduced the actual forms of language to something like order were the scholars of Alexandria. Their chief occupation was to publish correct texts of the Greek classics, and particularly of Homer. They were forced, therefore, to pay attention to the exact forms of Greek grammar. The MSS sent to Alexandria and Pergamus from different parts of Greece varied considerably, and it could only be

---

* M. M.'s *History of Ancient Sanskrit Literature*, p. 163.

determined by careful observation which forms were to be tolerated in Homer and which were not. Their editions of Homer were not only *ekdoseis*, a Greek word literally rendered in Latin by *editio*, i.e. issues of books, but *diorthōseis*, that is to say, critical editions. There were different schools, opposed to each other in their views of the language of Homer. Each reading that was adopted by Zenodotus or Aristarchus had to be defended, and this could only be done by establishing general rules on the grammar of the Homeric poems. Did Homer use the article? Did he use it before proper names? These and similar questions had to be settled, and as one or the other view was adopted by the editors, the text of these ancient poems was changed by more or less violent emendations. New technical terms were required for distinguishing, for instance, the article, if once recognised, from the demonstrative pronoun. *Article* is a literal translation of the Greek word *arthron*. *Arthron* (Lat. artus) means the socket of a joint. The word was first used by Aristotle, and with him it could only mean words which formed, as it were, the sockets in which the members of a sentence moved. In such a sentence as 'Whoever did it, he shall suffer for it,' Greek grammarians would have called the demonstrative pronoun *he* the first socket, and the relative pronoun *who* the second socket;* and before Zenodotus, the first librarian of Alexandria, 250 B.C., all pronouns were simply classed as sockets or articles of speech. He was the first to introduce a distinction between personal pronouns or *antonymiai*, and the mere articles or articulations of

---

* ἄρθρον προτακτικόν, ἄρθρον ὑποτακτικόν.

speech, which henceforth retained the name of *arthra*. This distinction was very necessary, and it was, no doubt, suggested to him by his emendations of the text of Homer, Zenodotus being the first who restored the article before proper names in the Iliad and Odyssey. Who, in speaking now of the definite or indefinite article, thinks of the origin and original meaning of the word, and of the time which it took before it could become what it is now, a technical term familiar to every school-boy?

Again, to take another illustration of the influence which the critical study of Homer at Alexandria exercised on the development of grammatical terminology—we see that the first idea of numbers, of a singular and a plural, was fixed and defined by the philosopher. But Aristotle had no such technical terms as singular and plural; and he does not even allude to the dual. He only speaks of the cases which express one or many, though with him *case* or *ptôsis*, had a very different meaning from what it has in our grammars. The terms singular and plural were not invented till they were wanted, and they were first wanted by the grammarians. Zenodotus, the editor of Homer, was the first to observe the use of the dual in the Homeric poems, and, with the usual zeal of discoverers, he has altered many a plural into a dual when there was no necessity for it.

The scholars of Alexandria, therefore, and of the rival academy of Pergamus, were the first who studied the Greek language critically, that is to say, who analysed the language, arranged it under general categories, distinguished the various parts of speech, invented proper technical terms for the various functions of words, observed the more or less correct usage of certain poets, marked the difference between obsolete and classical forms, and published long and learned treatises on all these subjects. Their works mark a great era in the history of the science of language. But there was still a step to be made before we can expect to meet with a real practical or elementary grammar of the Greek language. Now the first real Greek grammar was that of Dionysius Thrax. It is still in existence, and though its genuineness has been doubted, these doubts have been completely disposed of.

But who was Dionysius Thrax? His father, as we learn from his name, was a Thracian; but Dionysius himself lived at Alexandria, and was a pupil of the famous critic and editor of Homer, Aristarchus.[*] Dionysius afterwards went to Rome, where he taught about the time of Pompey. Now here we see a new feature in the history of mankind. A Greek, a pupil of Aristarchus, settles at Rome, and writes a practical grammar of the Greek language—of course, for the benefit of his young Roman pupils. He was not the inventor of grammatical science. Nearly all the framework of grammar, as we saw, was supplied to him through the labours of his predecessors from Plato to Aristarchus. But he was the first who applied the results of former philosophers and critics to the practical purpose of teaching Greek; and, what is most important, of teaching Greek not to Greeks, who know Greek and only wanted the theory of their language, but to

[*] Suidas, s. v. Διονύσιος. Διονύσιος Ἀλεξανδρεύς, Θρᾷξ δὲ ἀπὸ πατρὸς τοὔνομα ἐλαθείς. Ἀριστάρχου μαθητής, γραμματικὸς ὃς ἐσοφίστευσεν ἐν Ῥώμῃ ἐπὶ Πομπηΐου τοῦ Μεγάλου.

Romans who had to be taught the declensions and conjugations, regular and irregular. His work thus became one of the principal channels through which the grammatical terminology, which had been carried from Athens to Alexandria, flowed back to Rome, to spread from thence over the whole civilized world.

Dionysius, however, though the author of the first practical grammar, was by no means the first ‘*professeur de langue*’ who settled at Rome. At his time Greek was more generally spoken at Rome than French is now spoken in London. The children of gentlemen learnt Greek before they learnt Latin, and though Quintilian in his work on education does not approve of a boy learning nothing but Greek for any length of time, ‘as is now the fashion,’ he says, ‘with most people,’ yet he too recommends that a boy should be taught Greek first, and Latin afterwards.* This may seem strange, but the fact is that as long as we know anything of Italy, the Greek language was as much at home there as Latin. Italy owed almost everything to Greece, not only in later days when the setting sun of Greek civilisation mingled its rays with the dawn of Roman greatness; but ever since the first Greek colonists started Westward Ho! in search of new homes. It was from the Greeks that the Italians received their alphabet; it was by them they were taught to read and to write.† The

---

* Quintilian, i. 1, 12.
† See Mommsen, *Römische Geschichte*, b. i. s. 197. ‘The Latin alphabet is the same as the modern alphabet of Sicily; the Etruscan is the same as the old Attic alphabet. *Epistola*, letter, *charta*, paper, and *stilus* (?), are words borrowed from Greek.’— *Mommsen*, b. i. s. 184.

names for balance, for measuring-rod, for engines in general, for coined money,* many terms connected with sea-faring,† not excepting *nausea* or sea-sickness, are all borrowed from Greek, and show the extent to which the Italians were indebted to the Greeks for the very rudiments of civilisation. The Italians, no doubt, had their own national gods, but they soon became converts to the mythology of the Greeks. Some of the Greek gods they identified with their own; others they admitted as new deities. Thus *Saturnus*, originally an Italian harvest god, was identified with the Greek *Kronos*, and as *Kronos* was the son of *Uranos*, a new deity was invented, and *Saturnus* was fabled to be the son of *Cœlus*. Thus the Italian *Herculus*, the god of hurdles, enclosures, and walls, was merged in the Greek *Heracles*.‡ *Castor* and *Pollux*, both of purely Greek origin, were readily believed in as nautical deities by the Italian sailors, and they were the first Greek gods to whom, after the battle on the Lake Regillus (485), a temple was erected at Rome.§ In 431 another temple was erected at Rome to Apollo, whose oracle at Delphi had been consulted by Italians ever since Greek colonists had settled on their soil. The oracles of

---

* Mommsen, *Römische Geschichte*, b. i. s. 186. *Statera*, the balance, the Greek στατήρ; *machina*, an engine, μηχανή; *nummus*, a silver coin, νόμος, the Sicilian νοῦμμος; *groma*, measuring-rod, the Greek γνώμων or γνῶμα; *clathri*, a trellis, a grate, the Greek κλῇθρον, the native Italian word for lock being *claustra*.

† *Gubernare*, to steer, from κυβερνᾶν; *anchora*, anchor, from ἄγκυρα; *prora*, the forepart, from πρῶρα. *Navis*, *remus*, *velum*, &c., are common Aryan words, not borrowed by the Romans from the Greeks, and show that the Italians were acquainted with navigation before the discovery of Italy by the Phocæans.

‡ Mommsen, i. 154. § Ibid. i. 408.

the famous Sibylla of Cumae were written in Greek,* and the priests (duoviri sacris faciundis) were allowed to keep two Greek slaves for the purpose of translating these oracles.†

When the Romans, in 454 B.C., wanted to establish a code of laws, the first thing they did was to send commissioners to Greece to report on the laws of Solon at Athens and the laws of other Greek towns.‡ As Rome rose in political power, Greek manners, Greek art, Greek language and literature found ready admittance.§ Before the beginning of the Punic wars, many of the Roman statesmen were able to understand, and even to speak Greek. Boys were not only taught the Roman letters by their masters, the *literatores*, but they had to learn at the same time the Greek alphabet. Those who taught Greek at Rome were then called *grammatici*, and they were mostly Greek slaves or *liberti*.

Among the young men whom Cato saw growing up at Rome, to know Greek was the same as to be a gentleman. They read Greek books, they conversed in Greek, they even wrote in Greek. Tiberius Gracchus, consul in 177, made a speech in Greek at Rhodes, which he afterwards published. ‖ Flaminius when addressed by the Greeks in Latin, returned

---

* Mommsen, I. 165.

† *Sibylla*, or *Sibulla*, is a diminutive of an Italian *sabus* or *sabius*, wise; a word which, though not found in classical writers, must have existed in the Italian dialects. The French *sage* presupposes an Italian *sabius*, for it cannot be derived either from *sapiens* or from *sapius*.—Diez, *Lexicon Etymologicum*, p. 300. *Sapius* has been preserved in *nesapius*, foolish. *Sibulla*, therefore, meant a wise old woman.

‡ Mommsen, I. 256.   § Ibid. I. 425, 444.

‖ Ibid. I. 857.

the compliment by writing Greek[*] verses in honour of their gods. The first history of Rome was written at Rome in Greek, by Fabius Pictor,[*] about 200 B.C.; and it was probably in opposition to this work and to those of Lucius Cincius Alimentus, and Publius Scipio, that Cato wrote his own history of Rome in Latin. The example of the higher classes was eagerly followed by the lowest. The plays of Plautus are the best proof; for the affectation of using Greek words is as evident in some of his characters as the foolish display of French in the German writers of the eighteenth century. There was both loss and gain in the inheritance which Rome received from Greece; but what would Rome have been without her Greek masters? The very fathers of Roman literature were Greeks, private teachers, men who made a living by translating school-books and plays. Livius Andronicus, sent as prisoner of war from Tarentum (272 B.C.), established himself at Rome as professor of Greek. His translation of the *Odyssey* into Latin verse, which marks the beginning of Roman literature, was evidently written by him for the use of his private classes. His style, though clumsy and wooden in the extreme, was looked upon as a model of perfection by the rising poets of the capital. Nœvius and Plautus were his contemporaries and immediate successors. All the plays of Plautus were translations and adaptations of Greek originals; and Plautus was not even allowed to transfer the scene from Greece to Rome. The Roman public wanted to see Greek life and Greek

[*] Mommsen, i. 902.

depravity; it would have punished the poet who had ventured to bring on the stage a Roman patrician or a Roman matron. Greek tragedies, also, were translated into Latin. Ennius, the contemporary of Nævius and Plautus, though somewhat younger (239-169), was the first to translate Euripides. Ennius, like Andronicus, was an Italian Greek, who settled at Rome as a teacher of languages and translator of Greek. He was patronised by the liberal party, by Publius Scipio, Titus Flaminius, and Marcus Fulvius Nobilior.* He became a Roman citizen. But Ennius was more than a poet, more than a teacher of languages. He has been called a neologian, and to a certain extent he deserved that name. Two works written in the most hostile spirit against the religion of Greece, and against the very existence of the Greek gods, were translated by him into Latin.† One was the philosophy of Epicharmus (470 B.C., in Megara), who taught that Zeus was nothing but the air, and other gods but names of the powers of nature; the other the work of Euhemerus of Messene (300 B.C.), who proved, in the form of a novel, that the Greek gods had never existed, and that those who were believed in as gods had been men. These two works were not translated without a purpose; and though themselves shallow in the extreme, they proved destructive to the still shallower systems of Roman theology. Greek became synonymous with infidel; and Ennius would

* Mommsen, i. 892.
† Ibid. i. 843, 194. It has been doubted whether the work of Ennius was a translation of Epicharmus. See Ennius, ed. Vahlen, p. xciii. On Epicharmus, see Bernays, *Rheinisches Museum*, viii. p. 280 (1853).

hardly have escaped the punishment inflicted on Nævius for his political satires, had he not enjoyed the patronage and esteem of the most influential statesmen at Rome. Even Cato, the stubborn enemy of Greek philosophy* and rhetoric, was a friend of the dangerous Ennius; and such was the growing influence of Greek at Rome, that Cato himself had to learn it in his old age, in order to teach his boy what he considered, if not useful, at least harmless in Greek literature. It has been the custom to laugh at Cato for his dogged opposition to everything Greek; but there was much truth in his denunciations. We have heard much of young Bengál—young Hindus who read Byron and Voltaire, play at billiards, drive tandems, laugh at their priests, patronise missionaries, and believe nothing. The description which Cato gives of the young idlers at Rome reminds us very much of young Bengál.

When Rome took the torch of knowledge from the dying hands of Greece, that torch was not burning with its brightest light. Plato and Aristotle had been succeeded by Chrysippus and Carneades; Euripides and Menander had taken the place of Æschylus and Aristophanes. In becoming the guardian of the Promethean spark first lighted in Greece, and intended hereafter to illuminate not only Italy, but every country of Europe, Rome lost much of that native virtue to which she owed her greatness. Roman frugality and gravity, Roman citizenship and patriotism, Roman purity and piety, were driven away by Greek luxury and levity, Greek intriguing and self-seeking, Greek vice and infidelity. Re-

* Mommsen, i. 911.

strictions and anathemas were of no avail; and Greek ideas were never so attractive as after they had been reprobated by Cato and his friends. Every new generation became more and more impregnated with Greek. In 131* we hear of a consul (Publius Crassus) who, like another Mezzofanti, was able to converse in the various dialects of Greek. Sulla allowed foreign ambassadors to speak in Greek before the Roman senate.† The Stoic philosopher Panætius ‡ lived in the house of the Scipios, which was for a long time the rendezvous of all the literary celebrities at Rome. Here the Greek historian Polybius, and the philosopher Clitomachus, Lucilius the satirist, Terence the African poet (196-159), and the improvisatore Archias (102 B.C.), were welcome guests.§ In this select circle the masterworks of Greek literature were read and criticised; the problems of Greek philosophy were discussed; and the highest interests of human life became the subject of thoughtful conversation. Though no poet

* Mommsen, ii. 407.
† Ibid. ii. 410. Valerius Maximus, at the time of Tiberius, asks 'Quis ergo huic consuetudini, quâ nunc Græcis actionibus aures curiæ exsurdantur, januam patefecit?' (lib. ii. cap. ii. 3.) Dio Cassius (lib. lvii. cap. 15) relates that Tiberius heard cases argued, and asked questions himself, in Greek. Πολλὰς μὲν δίκας ἐν τῇ διαλέκτῳ ταύτῃ καὶ ἐπὶ λεγομένας ἀκούων, πολλὰς δὲ καὶ αὐτὸς ἐπερωτῶν. Cf. Roberts, *Discussions on the Gospels*, p. 29. Suetonius remarks, however, of Tiberius: 'Sermone Græco, quanquam alias promptus et facilis, non tamen usquequaque usus est, abstinuitque maxime in senatu, adeo quidem, ut "monopolium" nominaturus, prius veniam postulârit, quod sibi verbo peregrino utendum esset.' ' Militem quoque Græco interrogatum, nisi Latine respondere vetuit.'—Suet. *Tib.*, cap. 71.
‡ Ibid. ii. 408.
§ Ibid. ii. 437, note; ii. 430.

of original genius arose from this society, it exercised a most powerful influence on the progress of Roman literature. It formed a tribunal of good taste; and much of the correctness, simplicity, and manliness of the classical Latin is due to that 'Cosmopolitan Club,' which met under the hospitable roof of the Scipios. With every succeeding generation the knowledge of Greek became more general at Rome. Cicero spoke Greek in the senate of Syracuse, Augustus in the town of Alexandria. Boys and girls, as Ovid relates, used to read the plays of Menander—'solet pueris virginibusque legi'—and Juvenal (Sat. vi. 186, seq.) exclaims:—

'Omnia Græce,
Cum sit turpe magis nostris nescire Latine.
Hoc sermone pavent, hoc iram, gaudia, curas,
Hoc cuncta effundunt animi secreta.'

The religious life of Roman society at the close of the Punic wars was more Greek than Roman. All who had learnt to think seriously on religious questions were either Stoics or followers of Epicurus; or they embraced the doctrines of the New Academy, denying the possibility of any knowledge of the Infinite, and putting opinion in the place of truth.* Though the doctrines of Epicurus and the New Academy were always considered dangerous and heretical, the philosophy of the Stoics was tolerated, and a kind of compromise effected between philosophy and religion. There was a state-philosophy as well as a state-religion. The Roman priesthood, though they had succeeded, in 161, in getting all Greek

* Zeno died 263; Epicurus died 270; Arcesilaus died 241; Carneades died 129.

rhetors and philosophers expelled from Rome, perceived that a compromise was necessary. It was openly avowed that in the enlightened classes* philosophy must take the place of religion, but that a belief in miracles and oracles was necessary for keeping the large masses in order. Even Cato,† the leader of the orthodox, national, and conservative party, expressed his surprise that a haruspex, when meeting a colleague, did not burst out laughing. Men like Scipio Æmilianus and Lælius professed to believe in the popular gods; but with them Jupiter was the soul of the universe, the statues of the gods mere works of art.‡ Their gods, as the people complained, had neither body, parts, nor passions. Peace, however, was preserved between the Stoic philosopher and the orthodox priest. Both parties professed to believe in the same gods, but they claimed the liberty to believe in them in their own way.

I have dwelt at some length on the changes in the intellectual atmosphere of Rome at the end of the Punic wars, and I have endeavoured to show how completely it was impregnated with Greek ideas, in order to explain, what otherwise would seem almost inexplicable, the zeal and earnestness with which the study of Greek grammar was taken up at Rome, not only by a few scholars and philosophers, but by the leading statesmen of the time. To our minds, discussions on nouns and verbs, on cases and gender, on regular and irregular conjugation, retain always something of the tedious character which these subjects

* Mommsen, ii. 417, 418.
† Ibid. i. 845. Cicero, *De Divinatione*, ii. 24: 'Mirari se ajebat (Cato) quod non rideret haruspex haruspicem cum vidisset.'
‡ Ibid. ii. 415, 417.

had at school, and we can hardly understand how at Rome, grammar—pure and simple grammar—should have formed a subject of general interest, and a topic of fashionable conversation. Although the grammatical studies of the Romans may have been enlivened by illustrations from the classical authors of Greece,* yet their main object was language as such. When one of the first grammarians of the day, Crates of Pergamus, was sent to Rome as ambassador of King Attalus, he was received with the greatest distinction by all the literary statesmen of the capital. It so happened that when walking one day on the Palatian hill, Crates caught his foot in the grating of a sewer, fell and broke his leg.† Being thereby detained at Rome longer than he intended, he was persuaded to give some public lectures, or *akroaseis*, on grammar; and from these lectures, says Suetonius, dates the study of grammar at Rome. This took place about 159 B.C., between the second and third Punic wars, shortly after the death of Ennius, and two years after the famous expulsion of the Greek rhetors and philosophers (161). Four years later Carneades, likewise sent as ambassador to Rome, was prohibited from lecturing by Cato. After these lectures of Crates, grammatical and philological studies became extremely popular at Rome. We hear of Lucius Ælius Stilo,‡ who lectured on Latin as Crates had

---

* Suetonius, *De illustr. Gramm.* cap. 2.

† Scioppius, in the introduction to his *Grammatica philosophica* (1638), writes: 'Hæc ergo ut legi, minime jam mirandum mihi visum est, tanti flagitii erroribus inquinatam esse veterem Grammaticam, quæ ex cloacæ foramine una cum claudo magistro emerserit.'

‡ Mommsen, ii. 413, 426, 445, 457. Lucius Ælius Stilo wrote

lectured on Greek. Among his pupils were Varro, Lucilius, and Cicero. Varro composed twenty-four books on the Latin language, four of which were dedicated to Cicero. Cicero, himself, is quoted as an authority on grammatical questions, though we know of no special work of his on grammar. Lucilius devoted the ninth book of his satires to the reform of spelling.* But nothing shows more clearly the wide interest which grammatical studies had then excited in the foremost ranks of Roman society than Cæsar's work on Latin grammar. It was composed by him during the Gallic war, and dedicated to Cicero, who might well be proud of the compliment thus paid him by the great general and statesman.† Most of these works are lost to us, and we can judge of them by means of casual quotations only. Thus we learn from a fragment of Cæsar's work, *De Analogia*, that he was the inventor of the term *ablative* in Latin. The word never occurs before, and, of course, could not be borrowed, like the names of the other cases, from Greek grammarians, as no ablative had been admitted in Greek grammar. To think of Cæsar fighting the barbarians of Gaul and Germany, and watching from a distance the political complications at Rome, ready to grasp the sceptre of the world, and at the same time carrying on his philological and grammatical studies together with his secretary, the Greek Didymus,‡ gives us a new view both of that extraordinary man, and of the time in which he lived. After Cæsar had triumphed, one of his favourite plans

a work on etymology, and an index to Plautus.—Lersch, *Die Sprachphilosophie der Alten*, ii. 111.

* Lersch, ii. 113, 114, 143.   † Cicero, *Brut.* cap. 72.
‡ Lersch, iii. 144.

was to found a Greek and Latin library at Rome, and he offered the librarianship to the best scholar of the day, to Varro, though Varro had fought against him on the side of Pompey.*

We have thus arrived at the time when, as we saw in an earlier part of this lecture, Dionysius Thrax published the first elementary grammar of Greek at Rome. Empirical grammar had thus been transplanted to Rome, the Greek grammatical terminology was translated into Latin, and in this new Latin garb it has travelled for nearly two thousand years over the whole civilized world. Even in India, where a different terminology had grown up in the grammatical schools of the Brahmans, a terminology in some respects more perfect than that of Alexandria and Rome, we may now hear such words as *case*, and *gender*, and *active* and *passive*, explained by European teachers to their native pupils. The fates of words are curious indeed, and when I looked the other day at some of the examination papers of the government schools in India, such questions as — 'What is the genitive case of Siva?' seemed to reduce whole volumes of history into a single sentence. How did these words, genitive case, come to India? They came from England, they had come to England from Rome, to Rome from Alexandria, to Alexandria from Athens. At Athens, the term *case*, or *ptôsis*, had a philosophical meaning; at Rome, *casus* was merely a literal translation; the original meaning of *fall* was lost, and the word had dwindled down to a mere technical term. At Athens, the philosophy of language was a counterpart of the philosophy of the mind. The

---

* Mommsen, iii. 557. 48 B.C.

terminology of formal logic and formal grammar was the same. The logic of the Stoics was divided into two parts,* called *rhetoric* and *dialectic*, and the latter treated, first, 'On that which signifies, or language;' secondly, 'On that which is signified, or things.' In their philosophical language *ptôsis*, which the Romans translated by *casus*, really meant fall; that is to say, the inclination or relation of one idea to another, the falling or resting of one word on another. Long and angry discussions were carried on as to whether the name of *ptôsis*, or fall, was applicable to the nominative; and every true Stoic would have scouted the expression of *casus rectus*, because the subject or the nominative, as they argued, did not fall or rest on anything else, but stood erect, the other words of a sentence leaning or depending on it. All this is lost to us when we speak of cases.

And how are the dark scholars in the government schools of India to guess the meaning of *genitive*? The Latin *genitivus* is a mere blunder, for the Greek word *genikē* could never mean *genitivus*. *Genitivus*, if it is meant to express the case of origin or birth, would in Greek have been called *gennētikē*, not *genikē*. Nor does the genitive express the relation of son to father. For though we may say, 'the son of the father,' we may likewise say, 'the father of the son.' *Genikē*, in Greek, had a much wider, a much more philosophical meaning.† It meant *casus generalis*, the general case, or rather,

---

* Lersch, ii. 25. Περὶ σημαινόντων, or περὶ φωνῆς; and περὶ σημαινομένων, or περὶ πραγμάτων.

† *Beiträge zur Geschichte der Grammatik*, von Dr. K. E. A. Schmidt, Halle, 1859. Ueber den Begriff der γενικὴ πτῶσις, S. 320.

the case which expresses the genus or kind. This is the real power of the genitive. If I say, 'a bird of the water,' 'of the water' defines the genus to which a certain bird belongs; it refers it to the genus of water-birds. 'Man of the mountains,' means a mountaineer. In phrases such as 'son of the father,' or 'father of the son,' the genitives have the same effect. They predicate something of the son or of the father; and if we distinguished between the sons of the father, and the sons of the mother, the genitives would mark the class or genus to which the sons respectively belonged. They would answer the same purpose as the adjectives, paternal and maternal. It can be proved etymologically that the termination of the genitive is, in most cases, identical with those derivative suffixes by which substantives are changed into adjectives.*

* In the Tibetan language the rule is, 'Adjectives are formed from substantives by the addition of the genitive sign,' which might be inverted into, 'The genitive is formed from the nominative by the addition of the adjective sign.' For instance, *shing*, wood: *shing-gi*, of wood, or wooden: *ser*, gold; *ser-gyi*, of gold, or golden: *mi*, man; *mi-yi*, of man, or human. The same in Garo, where the sign of the genitive is *ni*, we have: *manû-ni jak*, the hand of man, or the human hand; *ambal-ni kathâli*, a wooden knife, or a knife of wood. In Hindustâni the genitive is so clearly an adjective, that it actually takes the marks of gender according to the words to which it refers. But how is it in Sanskrit and Greek? In Sanskrit we may form adjectives by the addition of *tya*. (*Turanian Languages*, p. 41 seq.; *Essay on Bengâli*, p. 333.) For instance, *dakshiṇâ*, south; *dakshiṇâ-tya*, southern. This *tya* is clearly a demonstrative pronoun, the same as the Sanskrit *syas*, *syâ*, *tyad*, this or that. *Tya* is a pronominal base, and therefore such adjectives as *dakshiṇâ-tya*, southern, or *âp-tya*, aquatic, from *âp*, water, must have been conceived originally as 'water-there,' or 'south-there.' Followed by the terminations of the nominative singular, which was again

It is hardly necessary to trace the history of what I call the empirical study, or the grammatical analysis of language, beyond Rome. With Dionysius Thrax the framework of grammar was finished. Later writers have improved and completed it, but they have added nothing really new and original. We can follow the stream of grammatical science from Dionysius Thrax to our own time in an almost uninterrupted chain of Greek and Roman writers. We find M. Verrius Flaccus, the tutor of the grandsons of Augustus, and Quintilian in the first century; Scaurus, Apollonius Dyscolus, and his son, Herodianus, in the second; Probus and Donatus, the

---

an original pronoun, ὀρίγας would mean ἀρ-τυα-ς, i.e. water-there-be. Now, it makes little difference whether I say an aquatic bird or a bird of the water. In Sanskrit the genitive of water would be, if we take *udaka*, *udaka-sya*. This *sya* is the same pronominal base as the adjective termination *tya*, only that the former does not, like the adjective, take any sign for the gender. The genitive *udakasya* is therefore the same as an adjective without gender. Now let us look to Greek. We there form adjectives by σως, which is the same as the Sanskrit *tya* or *sya*. For instance, from δῆμος, people, the Greeks formed δημόσιος, belonging to the people. Here ος, α, ον, mark the gender. Leave the gender out, and you get δημοσιο. Now, there is a rule in Greek that an ε between two vowels, in grammatical terminations, is elided. Thus the genitive of γένος is not γένεσος, but γένεος, or γένους; hence δημοσιο would necessarily become δήμοιο (Cf. φάος=φῶς). And what is δήμοιο but the regular Homeric genitive of δῆμος, which in later Greek was replaced by δήμου? Thus we see that the same principles which governed the formation of adjectives and genitives in Tibetan, in Garo, and Hindustani, were at work in the primitive stages of Sanskrit and Greek; and we perceive how accurately the real power of the genitive was determined by the ancient Greek grammarians, who called it the general or predicative case, whereas the Romans spoiled the term by wrongly translating it into *genitivus*.

teacher of St. Jerome, in the fourth. After Constantine had moved the seat of government from Rome, grammatical science received a new home in the academy of Constantinople. There were no less than twenty Greek and Latin grammarians who held professorships at Constantinople. Under Justinian, in the sixth century, the name of Priscianus gave a new lustre to grammatical studies, and his work remained an authority during the middle ages to nearly our own times. We ourselves have been taught grammar according to the plan which was followed by Dionysius at Rome, by Priscianus at Constantinople, by Alcuin at York; and whatever may be said of the improvements introduced into our system of education, the Greek and Latin grammars used at our public schools are mainly founded on the first empirical analysis of language, prepared by the philosophers of Athens, applied by the scholars of Alexandria, and transferred to the practical purpose of teaching a foreign tongue by the Greek professors at Rome.

LECTURE IV.

THE CLASSIFICATORY STAGE.

WE traced, in our last lecture, the origin and progress of the empirical study of languages from the time of Plato and Aristotle to our own school-boy days. We saw at what time, and under what circumstances, the first grammatical analysis of language took place; how its component parts, the parts of speech, were named, and how, with the aid of a terminology, half philosophical and half empirical, a system of teaching languages was established, which, whatever we may think of its intrinsic value, has certainly answered that purpose for which it was chiefly intended.

Considering the process by which this system of grammatical science was elaborated, it could not be expected to give us an insight into the nature of language. The division into nouns and verbs, articles and conjunctions, the schemes of declension and conjugation, were a merely artificial network thrown over the living body of language. We must not look in the grammar of Dionysius Thrax for a correct and well-articulated skeleton of human speech. It is curious, however, to observe the striking coincidences between the grammatical terminology of the Greeks and the Hindús, which would seem to prove that there must be some true and natural foundation for the much-abused grammatical system of the schools. The Hindús are the only nation that cultivated the science of grammar without having received any impulse, directly or indirectly, from the Greeks. Yet we find in Sanskrit too the same system of cases, called *vibhakti*, or inflections, the active, passive, and middle voices, the tenses, moods, and persons, divided not exactly, but very nearly, in the same manner as in Greek.* In Sanskrit, grammar is called *vyâkarana*, which means analysis or taking to pieces. As Greek grammar owed its origin to the critical study of Homer, Sanskrit grammar arose from the study of the Vedas, the most ancient poetry of the Brahmans. The differences between the dialect of these sacred hymns and the literary Sanskrit of later ages were noted and preserved with a religious care. We still possess the first essays in the grammatical science of the Brahmans, the so-called *prâtiśâkhyas*. These works, though they merely profess to give rules on the proper pronunciation of the ancient dialect of the Vedas, furnish us at the same time with observations of a grammatical character, and particularly with those valuable lists of words, irregular or in any other way remarkable, the Ganas. These supplied that solid basis on which successive generations of scholars erected the astounding structure that reached its perfection in the grammar of Pânini. There is no form, regular or irregular, in the whole Sanskrit language, which is not provided for in the grammar of Pânini and his commentators. It is the perfection of a merely empirical analysis of language, unsurpassed, nay even unapproached, by anything in the grammatical literature of other nations. Yet

* See M. M.'s *History of Ancient Sanskrit Literature*, p. 158.

of the real nature, and natural growth of language, it teaches us nothing.

What then do we know of language after we have learnt the grammar of Greek or Sanskrit, or after we have transferred the network of classical grammar to our own tongue? We know certain forms of language which correspond to certain forms of thought. We know that the subject must assume the form of the nominative, the object that of the accusative. We know that the more remote object may be put in the dative, and that the predicate, in its most general form, may be rendered by the genitive. We are taught that whereas in English the genitive is marked by a final *s*, or by the preposition *of*, it is in Greek expressed by a final *os*, in Latin by *is*. But what this *os* and *is* represent, why they should have the power of changing a nominative into a genitive, a subject into a predicate, remains a riddle. It is self-evident that each language, in order to be a language, must be able to distinguish the subject from the object, the nominative from the accusative. But how a mere change of termination should suffice to convey so material a distinction would seem almost incomprehensible. If we look for a moment beyond Greek and Latin, we see that there are in reality but few languages which have distinct forms for these two categories of thought. Even in Greek and Latin there is no outward distinction between the nominative and accusative of neuters. The Chinese language, it is commonly said, has no grammar at all, that is to say, it has no inflections, no declension and conjugation, in our sense of these words; it makes no formal distinction of the various parts of speech, noun, verb, adjective, adverb, &c. Yet there is no shade of thought that cannot be rendered in Chinese. The Chinese have no more difficulty in distinguishing between 'James beats John,' and 'John beats James,' than the Greeks and Romans or we ourselves. They have no termination for the accusative, but they attain the same by always placing the subject before, and the object after the verb, or by employing words, before or after the noun, which clearly indicate that it is to be taken as the object of the verb.* There are other

* The following and some other notes were kindly sent to me by the first Chinese scholar in Europe, M. Stanislas Julien, Membre de l'Institut.

The Chinese do not decline their substantives, but they indicate the cases distinctly—

    A. By means of particles.
    B. By means of position.

1. The nominative or the subject of a sentence is always placed at the beginning.

2. The genitive may be marked—

(a) By the particle *tchi* placed between the two nouns, of which the first is in the genitive, the second in the nominative. Example, *jin tchi kiun* (hominum princeps, literally, man, sign of the genitive, prince).

(b) By position, placing the word which is in the genitive first, and the word which is in the nominative second. Ex. *koue* (kingdom) *jin* (man), i.e. a man of the kingdom.

3. The dative may be expressed—

(a) By the preposition *yu*, to. Ex. *eve* (to give) *yen* (money) *yu* (to) *jin* (man).

(b) By position, placing first the verb, then the word which stands in the dative, lastly, the word which stands in the accusative. Ex. *yu* (to give) *jin* (to a man) *pe* (white) *yu* (jade), *hoang* (yellow) *kin* (metal), i.e. gold.

4. The accusative is either left without any mark, for instance, *pao* (to protect) *min* (the people), or it is preceded by certain words which had originally a more tangible meaning, but gradu-

languages which have more terminations even than Greek and Latin. In Finnish there are fifteen cases,

ally dwindled away into mere signs of the accusative. [These were first discovered and correctly explained by M. Stanislas Julien in his *Vindiciæ Philologicæ in Linguam Sinicam*, Paris, 1830.] The particles most frequently used for this purpose by modern writers are *pa* and *tsiang*, to grasp, to take. Ex. *pa* (taking) *tchoung-jin* (crowd of men) *t'eou* (secretly) *k'an* (he looked), i.e. he looked secretly at the crowd of men (hominum turbam furtim aspiciebat). In the more ancient Chinese (*Kou-wen*) the words used for the same purpose are *i* (to employ, etc.), *in*, *iu*, *hou*. Ex. *i* (employing) *jin* (humanity) *t'sun* (he preserves) *sin* (in the heart), i.e. humanitatem conservat corde. *I* (taking) *tchi* (right) *wéi* (to make) *k'iû* (crooked), i.e. rectum facere curvum. *Pao* (to protect) *hou* (sign of accus.) *min* (the people).

5. The ablative is expressed—

(*a*) By means of prepositions, such as *thsong*, *yeou*, *tseu*, *hou*. Ex. *thsong*, (ex) *thien* (cœlo) *lai* (venire); *te* (obtinere) *hou* (ab) *thien* (cœlo).

(*b*) By means of position, so that the word in the ablative is placed before the verb. Ex. *thien* (heaven) *kiang-tchi* (descended, *tchi* being the relative particle or sign of the genitive) *tsai* (calamities), i.e. the calamities which Heaven sends to men.

6. The instrumental is expressed—

(*a*) By the preposition *yu*, with. Ex. *yu* (with) *kien* (the sword) *cha* (to kill) *jin* (a man).

(*b*) By position, the substantive which stands in the instrumental case being placed before the verb, which is followed again by the noun in the accusative. Ex. *i* (by hanging) *cha* (he killed) *tchi* (him).

7. The locative may be expressed by simply placing the noun before the verb. Ex. *ti* (in the East or East) *yeou* (there is) *sou-tou-po* (a sthûpa); or by prepositions as described in the text.

The adjective is always placed before the substantive to which it belongs. Ex. *mei jin*, a beautiful woman.

The adverb is generally followed by a particle which produces the same effect as *e* in bone, or *ter* in coloriter. Ex. *cho-jen*, in silence, silently; *ngeou-jen*, perchance; *kiu-jen*, with fear.

Sometimes an adjective becomes an adverb through position. Ex. *chen*, good; but *chen ko*, to sing well.

expressive of every possible relation between the subject and the object; but there is no accusative, no purely objective case.* In English and French the distinctive terminations of the nominative and accusative have been worn off by phonetic corruption, and these languages are obliged, like Chinese, to mark the subject and object by the collocation of words. What we learn therefore at school in being taught that *rex* in the nominative becomes *regem* in the accusative, is simply a practical rule. We know when to say *rex* and when to say *regem*. But why the king as a subject should be called *rex*, and as an object *regem*, remains entirely unexplained. In the same manner we learn that *amo* means I love, *amavi* I loved; but why that tragical change from *love* to *no love* should be represented by the simple change of *o* to *avi*, or, in English, by the addition of a mere *d*, is neither asked nor answered.

Now if there is a science of language, these are the questions which it will have to answer. If they cannot be answered, if we must be content with paradigms and rules, if the terminations of nouns and verbs must be looked upon either as conventional contrivances or as mysterious excrescences, there is no such thing as a science of language, and we must be satisfied with what has been called the art (τέχνη) of language or grammar.

Before we either accept or decline the solution of any problem, it is right to determine what means

* From a similar cause the North-Indians have innumerable verbs to express every shade of action; they have different words for eating as applied to fish, flesh, animal or human, soup, vegetables, &c. But they cannot say either *I am* or *I have*. Cf. Du Ponceau, pp. 195, 200.

there are for solving it. Beginning with English we should ask, what means have we for finding out why *I love* should mean I am actually loving, whereas *I loved* indicates that that feeling is past and gone? Or, if we look to languages richer in inflections than English, we should try to discover by what process, and under what circumstances, *amo*, I love, was changed in Latin, through the mere addition of an *r*, into *amor*, expressing no longer *I love*, but *I am loved*? Did declensions and conjugations bud forth like the blossoms of a tree? Were they imparted to man ready-made by some mysterious power? Or did some wise people invent them, assigning certain letters to certain phases of thought, as mathematicians express unknown quantities by freely chosen algebraic exponents? We are here brought at once face to face with the highest and most difficult problem of our science, the origin of language. But it will be well for the present to turn our eyes away from theories, and fix our attention at first entirely on facts.

Let us keep to the English perfect, *I loved*, as compared with the present, *I love*. We cannot embrace at once the whole English grammar, but if we can track one form to its true lair, we shall probably have no difficulty in digging out the rest of the brood. Now if we ask how the addition of a final *d* could express the momentous transition from being in love to being indifferent, the first thing we have to do, before attempting any explanation, would be to establish the earliest and most original form of *I loved*. This is a rule which even Plato recognised in his philosophy of language, though, we must confess, he seldom obeyed it. We know what havoc phonetic corruption may make both in the dictionary and the grammar of a language, and it would be a pity to waste our conjectures on formations which a mere reference to the history of language would suffice to explain. Now a very slight acquaintance with the history of the English language teaches us that the grammar of modern English is not the same as the grammar of Wycliffe. Wycliffe's English, again, may be traced back to what, with Sir Frederick Madden, we may call Middle English, from 1500 to 1330; Middle English to Early English, from 1330 to 1230; Early English to Semi-Saxon, from 1230 to 1100; and Semi-Saxon to Anglo-Saxon.* It is evident that if we are to discover the original intention of the syllable which changes *I love* into *I loved*, we must consult the original form of that syllable wherever we can find it. We should never have known that *priest* meant originally *an elder*, unless we had traced it back to its original form *presbyter*, in which a Greek scholar at once recognises the comparative of *presbys*, old. If left to modern English alone, we might attempt to connect *priest* with *praying* or *preaching*, but we should not thus arrive at its true derivation. The modern word *Gospel* conveys no meaning at all. As soon as we trace it back to the original *Goddspell*, we see that it is a literal translation of *Evangelium*, or good news, good tidings.† *Lord* would be nothing but an empty title in English, unless we could discover its original form and meaning in the Anglo-Saxon

---

* See some criticisms on this division in Marsh's *Lectures on the English Language*, p. 48.

† 'Goddspell onu Enuglissh oemnnedd iss God word, annd goṭ tipennde, God errḍa.' &c.—*Ormulum*, pref. 157. ' And beode per godes godd-spel.'—*Layamon*, iii. 182, v. 29, 508.

hláf-ord, meaning the source of bread, from *hláf*, a loaf, and *ord*, place.*

But even after this is done, after we have traced a modern English word back to Anglo-Saxon, it follows by no means that we should there find it in its original form, or that we should succeed in forcing it to disclose its original intention. Anglo-Saxon is not an original or aboriginal language. It points by its very name to the Saxons and Angles of the continent. We have, therefore, to follow our word from Anglo-Saxon through the various Saxon and Low-German dialects, till we arrive at last at the earliest stage of German which is within our reach, the Gothic of the fourth century after Christ. Even here we cannot rest. For, although we cannot trace Gothic back to any earlier Teutonic language, we see at once that Gothic, too, is a modern language, and that it must have passed through numerous phases of growth before it became what it is in the mouth of Bishop Ulfilas.

What then are we to do?—We must try to do what is done when we have to deal with the modern Romance languages. If we could not trace a French word back to Latin, we should look for its corresponding form in Italian, and endeavour to trace the Italian to its Latin source. If, for instance, we were doubtful about the origin of the French word for fire, *feu*, we have but to look to the Italian *fuoco*, in order to see at once that both *fuoco* and *feu* are derived from the Latin *focus*. We can do this because we know that French and Italian are cognate dialects, and because we have ascertained beforehand the exact degree of relationship in which

* Grimm, *Deutsche Grammatik*, l. p. 229. Lady in A.-S. hláf-dige; l. c. ii. p. 405.

they stand to each other. Had we, instead of looking to Italian, looked to German for an explanation of the French *feu*, we should have missed the right track; for the German *fauer*, though more like *feu* than the Italian *fuoco*, could never have assumed in French the form *feu*.

Again, in the case of the preposition *hors*, which in French means *without*, we can more easily determine its origin after we have found that *hors* corresponds with the Italian *fuora*, the Spanish *fuera*. The French *fromage*, cheese, derives no light from Latin. But as soon as we compare the Italian *formaggio*,[*] we see that *formaggio* and *fromage* are derived from *forma*; cheese being made in Italy by keeping the milk in small baskets or forms. Feeble, the French *faible*, is clearly derived from Latin; but it is not till we see the Italian *fievole* that we are reminded of the Latin *flebilis*, tearful. We should never have found the etymology, that is to say the origin, of the French *payer*, the English *to pay*, if we did not consult the dictionary of the cognate dialects, such as Italian and Spanish. Here we find that *to pay* is expressed in Italian by *pagare*, in Spanish by *pagar*, whereas in Provençal we actually find the two forms *pagar* and *payar*. Now *pagar* clearly points back to Latin *pacare*, which means *to pacify, to appease*. To appease a creditor meant to pay him; in the same manner as *une quittance*, a quittance or receipt, was originally *quietantia*, a quieting, from *quietus*, quiet.[†]

---

[*] Diez, *Lexicon Comparativum*. Columella, vii. 8.

[†] In mediæval Latin *fredum* is ' compositio qua fisco exsoluta reus pacem a principe assequitur.' It is the German *frida*, peace, latinised. From it the French *les frais*, expense, and *défrayer*, to pay. Cf. Scheler, *Dictionnaire d'Étymologie française*, s. v.

If, therefore, we wish to follow up our researches—if, not satisfied with having traced an English word back to Gothic, we want to know what it was at a still earlier period of its growth—we must determine whether there are any languages that stand to Gothic in the same relation in which Italian and Spanish stand to French—we must restore, as far as possible, the genealogical tree of the various families of human speech. In doing this we enter on the second or classificatory stage of our science; for genealogy, where it is applicable, is the most perfect form of classification.

Before we proceed to examine the results which have been obtained by the recent labours of Schlegel, Humboldt, Pritchard, Bopp, Burnouf, Grimm, Pott, Benfey, Kuhn, Curtius, Schleicher, and others in this branch of the science of language, it will be well to glance at what had been achieved before their time in the classification of the numberless dialects of mankind.

The Greeks never thought of applying the principle of classification to the varieties of human speech. They only distinguished between Greek on one side, and all other languages on the other, comprehended under the convenient name of 'Barbarous.' They succeeded, indeed, in classifying four of their own dialects with tolerable correctness,* but they applied the term 'barbarous' so promiscuously to the other

---

* Strabo, viii. p. 333. Τὴν μὲν Ἰάδα τῇ παλαιᾷ Ἀτθίδι τὴν αὐτὴν φαμέν, τὴν δὲ Δωρίδα τῇ Αἰολίδι. The same writer, at the commencement of the Christian era, has the following remark on the numerous spoken dialects of Greece: σχεδὸν δ' ἔτι καὶ νῦν κατὰ πόλεις, ἄλλοι ἄλλως διαλέγονται· δοκοῦσι δὲ δωρίζειν ἅπαντες διὰ τὴν συμβᾶσαν ἐπιφάνειαν. See Romaic and Modern Greek, by James Clyde, 1855, p. 25.

more distant relatives of Greek (the dialects of the Pelasgians, Carians, Macedonians, Thracians, and Illyrians), that, for the purposes of scientific classification, it is almost impossible to make any use of the statements of ancient writers about these so-called barbarous idioms.*

* Herodotus (vii. 94, 509) gives Pelasgi as the old name of the Æolians and of the Ionians in the Peloponnesus and the islands. Nevertheless he argues (i. 57) from the dialect spoken in his time by the Pelasgi of the towns of Kreston, Plakia, and Skylake, that the old Pelasgi spoke a barbarous tongue (βάρβαρον τὴν γλῶσσαν ἱέντες). He has, therefore, to admit that the Attic race, being originally Pelasgic, unlearns its language (τὸ Ἀττικὸν ἔθνος ἐὸν Πελασγικόν, ἅμα τῇ μεταβολῇ τῇ ἐς Ἕλληνας, καὶ τὴν γλῶσσαν μετέμαθε). See Diefenbach, *Originies Europæe*, p. 59. Dionysius of Halicarnassus (l. 17) avoids this difficulty by declaring the Pelasgi to have been from the beginning a Hellenic race. This, however, is merely his own theory. The *Karians* are called βαρβαρόφωνοι by Homer (*Il.* v. 867); but Strabo (xiv. 662) takes particular care to show that they are not therefore to be considered as βάρβαροι. He distinguishes between βαρβαροφωνεῖν, i.e. κακῶς ἑλληνίζειν and Καριστὶ λαλεῖν, καρίζειν καὶ βαρβαρίζειν. But the same Strabo says that the Karians were formerly called Λέλεγες (xii. p. 572); and these, together with Pelasgians and Kaukones, are reckoned by him (vii. p. 321) as the earlier *barbarous* inhabitants of Hellas. Again, he (vii. p. 321), as well as Aristotle and Dionysius of Halicarnassus (i. 17), considers the Locrians as descendants of the Leleges, though they would hardly call the Locrians barbarians.

The *Macedonians* are mentioned by Strabo (x. p. 460) together with 'the other Hellenes.' Demosthenes speaks of Alexander as a barbarian; Isokrates as a Heraclide. To judge from a few extant words, Macedonian might have been a Greek dialect. (Diefenbach, *Orig. Europ.* p. 62.) Justine (vii. 1) says of the Macedonians, 'Populus Pelasgi, regio Pæonia dicebatur.' There was a tradition that the country occupied by the Macedonians belonged formerly to Thracians or Pierians (Thuc. II. 99; Strabo, vii. p. 321); part of it to Thessalians (Ibid.).

The *Thracians* are called by Herodotus (v. 3) the greatest people after the Indians. They are distinguished by Strabo

Plato, indeed, in his *Cratylus* (c. 36), throws out a
hint that the Greeks might have received their own
words from the barbarians, the barbarians being
older than the Greeks. But he was not able to
see the full bearing of this remark. He only points
out that some words, such as the names of *fire,
water,* and *dog,* were the same in Phrygian and
Greek; and he supposes that the Greeks borrowed
them from the Phrygians (c. 26). The idea that
the Greek language and that of the barbarians could
have had a common source never entered his mind.
It is strange that even so comprehensive a mind
as that of Aristotle should have failed to perceive

from Illyrians (Diefenbach, p. 65), from Celts (ibid.), and from Scythians (Thuc. ii. 96). What we know of their language rests on a statement of Strabo (vii. 303, 305), that the Thracians spoke the same language as the Getæ, and the Getæ the same as the Dacians. We possess fragments of Dacian speech in the botanical names collected by Dioskorides, and these, as interpreted by Grimm, are clearly Aryan, though not Greek. The Dacians are called barbarians by Strabo, together with Illyrians and Epirotes. (Strabo, vii. p. 321.)

The *Illyrians* were barbarians in the eyes of the Greeks. They are now considered as an independent branch of the Aryan family. Herodotus refers the Veneti to the Illyrians (i. 196); and the Veneti, according to Polybius (ii. 17), who knew them, spoke a language different from that of the Celts. He adds that they were an old race, and in their manner and dress like the Celts. Hence many writers have mistaken them for Celts, neglecting the criterion of language, on which Polybius lays proper stress. The Illyrians were a widely extended race; the Pannonians, the Dalmatians, and the Dardanians (from whom the Dardanelles were called), are all spoken of as Illyrians. (Diefenbach, *Origines Europææ*, pp. 74, 75). It is lost labour to try to extract anything positive from the statements of the Greeks and Romans on the race and the language of their barbarian neighbours.

in languages some of that law and order which he tried to discover in every realm of nature. As Aristotle, however, did not attempt this, we need not wonder that it was not attempted by any one else for the next two thousand years. The Romans, in all scientific matters, were merely the parrots of the Greeks. Having themselves been called barbarians, they soon learnt to apply the same name to all other nations, except, of course, to their masters, the Greeks. Now *barbarian* is one of those lazy expressions which seem to say everything but in reality say nothing. It was applied as recklessly as the word *heretic* during the middle ages. If the Romans had not received this convenient name of barbarian ready-made for them, they would have treated their neighbours, the Celts and Germans, with more respect and sympathy: they would, at all events, have looked at them with a more discriminating eye. And, if they had done so, they would have discovered, in spite of outward differences, that these barbarians were, after all, not very distant cousins. There was as much similarity between the language of Cæsar and the barbarians against whom he fought in Gaul and Germany as there was between his language and that of Homer. A man of Cæsar's sagacity would have seen this, if he had not been blinded by traditional phraseology. I am not exaggerating. For let us look at one instance only. If we take a verb of such constant occurrence as *to have*, we shall find the paradigms almost identical in Latin and Gothic:—

	In Latin.	In Gothic.
I have	habeo	haba
Thou hast	habes	habais
He has	habet	habaiþ

	In Latin.	In Gothic.
We have	habemus	habam
You have	habetis	habaiþ
They have	habent	habant.

It surely required a certain amount of blindness, or rather of deafness, not to perceive such similarity, and that blindness or deafness arose, I believe, entirely from the single word *barbarian*. Not till that word barbarian was struck out of the dictionary of mankind, and replaced by brother, not till the right of all nations of the world to be classed as members of one genus or kind was recognised, can we look even for the first beginnings of our science. This change was effected by Christianity. To the Hindú, every man not twice-born was a Mlechchha; to the Greek, every man not speaking Greek was a barbarian; to the Jew, every person not circumcised was a Gentile; to the Mohammedan, every man not believing in the prophet is a Káfir, an unbeliever, or a Gaur, a fire-worshipping infidel. It was Christianity which first broke down the barriers between Jew and Gentile, between Greek and barbarian, between the white and the black. *Humanity* is a word which you look for in vain in Plato or Aristotle; the idea of mankind as one family, as the children of one God, is an idea of Christian growth; and the science of mankind, and of the languages of mankind, is a science which, without Christianity, would never have sprung into life. When people had been taught to look upon all men as brethren, then, and then only, did the variety of human speech present itself as a problem that called for a solution in the eyes of thoughtful observers; and I, therefore, date the real beginning of the science of language from the first day of Pentecost. After that day of eleven tongues a new light is spreading over the world, and objects rise into view which had been hidden from the eyes of the nations of antiquity. Old words assume a new meaning, old problems a new interest, old sciences a new purpose. The common origin of mankind, the differences of race and language, the susceptibility of all nations of the highest mental culture—these become, in the new world in which we live, problems of scientific, because of more than scientific, interest. It is no valid objection that so many centuries should have elapsed before the spirit which Christianity infused into every branch of scientific inquiry produced visible results. We see in the oaken fleet which rides the ocean the small acorn which was buried in the ground hundreds of years ago, and we recognise in the philosophy of Albertus Magnus,* though nearly 1200 years after the death of Christ, in the aspirations of Kepler,† and in the researches of the

---

* Albert, Count of Bollstädten, or, as he is more generally called, Albertus Magnus, the pioneer of modern physical science, wrote: 'God has given to man His spirit, and with it also intellect, that man might use it for to know God. And God is known through the soul and by faith from the Bible, through the intellect from nature.' And again: 'It is to the praise and glory of God, and for the benefit of our brethren, that we study the nature of created things. In all of them, not only in the harmonious formation of every single creature, but likewise in the variety of different forms, we can and we ought to admire the majesty and wisdom of God.'

† These are the last words in Kepler's *Harmony of the World*, 'Thou who by the light of nature has kindled in us the longing after the light of Thy grace, in order to raise us to the light of Thy glory, thanks to Thee, Creator and Lord, that Thou lettest me rejoice in Thy works. Lo, I have done the work of my life with that power of intellect which Thou hast given. I

greatest philosophers of our own age, the sound of that key-note of thought which had been struck for

have recorded to men the glory of Thy works, as far as my mind could comprehend their infinite majesty. My senses were awake to search as far as I could, with purity and faithfulness. If I, a worm before Thine eyes, and born in the bonds of sin, have brought forth anything that is unworthy of Thy counsels, inspire me with Thy spirit, that I may correct it. If, by the wonderful beauty of Thy works, I have been led into boldness, if I have sought my own honour among men as I advanced in the work which was destined to Thine honour, pardon me in kindness and charity, and by Thy grace grant that my teaching may be to Thy glory, and the welfare of all men. Praise ye the Lord, ye heavenly Harmonies, and ye that understand the new harmonies, praise the Lord. Praise God,' O my soul, so long as I live. From Him, through Him, and in Him is all, the material as well as the spiritual—all that we know and all that we know not yet —for there is much to do that is yet undone.'

These words are all the more remarkable, because written by a man who was persecuted by theologians as a heretic, but who nevertheless was not ashamed to profess himself a Christian.

I end with an extract from one of the most distinguished of living naturalists:—'The antiquarian recognises at once the workings of intelligence in the remains of an ancient civilization. He may fail to ascertain their age correctly, he may remain doubtful as to the order in which they were successively constructed, but the character of the whole tells him they are works of art, and that men like himself originated these relics of bygone ages. So shall the intelligent naturalist read at once in the pictures which nature presents to him, the works of a higher Intelligence: he shall recognise in the minute perforated cells of the coniferæ, which differ so wonderfully from those of other plants, the hieroglyphics of a peculiar age; in their needle-like leaves, the escutcheon of a peculiar dynasty; in their repeated appearance under most diversified circumstances, a thoughtful and thought-eliciting adaptation. He beholds, indeed, the works of a being *thinking* like himself, but he feels, at the same time, that he stands as much below the Supreme Intelligence, in wisdom, power, and goodness, as the works of art are inferior to the wonders of nature. Let naturalists look at the

the first time by the apostle of the Gentiles:* 'For the invisible things of Him from the creation of the world are clearly seen, being understood by the things that are made, even His eternal power and Godhead.'

But we shall see that the science of language owes more than its first impulse to Christianity. The pioneers of our science were those very apostles who were commanded 'to go into all the world, and preach the gospel to every creature;' and their true successors, the missionaries of the whole Christian Church. Translations of the Lord's Prayer or of the Bible into every dialect of the world, form even now the most valuable materials for the comparative philologist. As long as the number of known languages was small, the idea of classification hardly suggested itself. The mind must be bewildered by the multiplicity of facts before it has recourse to division. As long as the only languages studied were Greek, Latin, and Hebrew, the simple division into sacred and profane, or classical and oriental, sufficed. But when theologians extended their studies to Arabic, Chaldee, and Syriac, a step, and a very important step, was made towards the establishment of a class or family of languages.†

---

world under such impressions, and evidence will pour in upon us that all creatures are expressions of the thoughts of Him whom we know, love, and adore unseen.'

* *Rom.* i. 20. Locke, *Essay concerning Human Understanding*, iv. 10, 7.

† Hervas (*Catalogo*, i. 37) mentions the following works, published during the sixteenth century, bearing on the science of language:—*Introductio in Chaldaicam Linguam, Siriacam, atque Armenicam, et decem alias Linguas*, a Theseo Ambrosio, Papiæ. 1639, 4to. *De Ratione communi omnium Linguarum et Littera-*

No one could help seeing that these languages were most intimately related to each other, and that they differed from Greek and Latin on all points on which they agreed among themselves. As early as 1606 we find *Guichard,** in his *Harmonie Etymo-*

rum Commentarius, a Theodoro Bibliandro, Tiguri, 1548, 4to. It contains the Lord's Prayer in fourteen languages. Bibliander derives Welsh and Cornish from Greek, Greek having been carried there from Marseilles, through France. He states that Armenian differs little from Chaldee, and cites Postel, who derived the Turks from the Armenians, because Turkish was spoken in Armenia. He treats the Persians as descendants of Shem, and connects their language with Syriac and Hebrew. Servian and Georgian are, according to him, dialects of Greek.

Other works on language published during the sixteenth century are:—Perion, *Dialogorum de Linguæ Gallicæ Origine ejusque cum Græca Cognatione, libri quatuor,* Parisiis, 1554. He says that as French is not mentioned among the seventy-two languages which sprang from the Tower of Babel, it must be derived from Greek. He quotes Cæsar (*De Bello Gallico,* vi. 14) to prove that the Druids spoke Greek, and then derives from it the modern French language!

The works of Henri Estienne (1528–1598) stand on a much sounder basis. He has been unjustly accused of having derived French from Greek. See his *Traicté de la Conformité du Langage français avec le grec,* about 1566. It contains chiefly syntactical and grammatical remarks, and its object is to show that modes of expression in Greek, which sound anomalous and difficult, can be rendered easy by a comparison of analogous expressions in French.

The Lord's Prayer was published in 1548 in fourteen languages, by Bibliander; in 1591 in twenty-six languages, by Roccha (*Bibliotheca Apostolica Vaticana,* a fratre Angelo Roccha, Romæ, 1591, 4to.); in 1592 in forty languages, by Megiseras (*Specimen XL Linguarum et Dialectorum ab Hieronymo Megisero à diversis auctoribus collectarum quibus Oratio Dominica est expressa,* Francofurti, 1592); in 1593 in fifty languages, by the same author (*Oratio Dominica L. diversis linguis,* cura H. Megiseri, Francofurti, 1593, 8vo.)

* At the beginning of the seventeenth century was published

logique, placing Hebrew, Chaldee, and Syriac as a class of languages by themselves, and distinguishing besides between the Romance and Teutonic dialects.

What prevented, however, for a long time the progress of the science of language was the idea that Hebrew was the primitive language of mankind, and that, therefore, all languages must be derived from Hebrew. The fathers of the Church never expressed any doubt on this point. St. Jerome, in one of his epistles to Damasus,* writes: 'The whole of antiquity (universa antiquitas) affirms that Hebrew, in which the Old Testament is written, was the beginning of all human speech.' Origen, in his eleventh Homily on the book of Numbers, expresses

---

Trésor de l'Histoire des Langues de cet Univers, par Claude Duret, seconde édition, Yverdon, 1619, 4to. Hervas says that Duret repeats the mistakes of Postel, Bibliander, and other writers of the sixteenth century.

Before Duret came Estienne Guichard, *L'Harmonie Etymologique des Langues Hébraïque, Chaldaïque, Syriaque—Grecque—Latine, Françoise, Italienne, Espagnole—Allemande, Flamende, Anglaise,* &c., Paris, 1606.

Hervas only knows the second edition, Paris, 1618, and thinks the first was published in 1606. The title of his book shows that Guichard distinguished between four classes of languages, which we should now call the Semitic, the Hellenic, Italic, and Teutonic: he derives, however, Greek from Hebrew.

J. J. Scaliger, in his *Diatriba de Europæorum Linguis* (*Opuscula varia*, Parisiis, 1610), p. 119. distinguishes eleven classes: Latin, Greek, Teutonic, Slavonic, Epirotic or Albanian, Tartaric, Hungarian, Finnic, Irish, British in Wales and Brittany, and Bask or Cantabrian.

* 'Initium oris et communis eloquii, et hoc omne quod loquimur, Hebræam esse linguam qua vetus Testamentum scriptum est, universa antiquitas tradidit.' In another place (*Isaia*, c. 7) he writes, 'Omnium enim fere linguarum verbis utuntur Hebræi.' See also *Journal Asiatique*, 1850, Juillet, p. 20.

his belief that the Hebrew language, originally given
through Adam, remained in that part of the world
which was the chosen portion of God, not, like the
rest, left to one of His angels.* When, therefore,
the first attempts at a classification of languages were
made, the problem, as it presented itself to scholars
such as Guichard and Thomassin, was this: 'As
Hebrew is undoubtedly the mother of all languages,
how are we to explain the process by which Hebrew
became split into so many dialects, and how can
these numerous dialects, such as Greek and Latin,
Coptic, Persian, Turkish, be traced back to their
common source, the Hebrew?'

It is astonishing what an amount of real learning
and ingenuity was wasted on this question during
the seventeenth and eighteenth centuries. It finds,
perhaps, but one parallel in the laborious calculations
and constructions of early astronomers, who had to
account for the movements of the heavenly bodies,
always taking it for granted that the earth must
be the fixed centre of our planetary system. But,
although we know now that the labours of such
scholars as Thomassin were, and could not be otherwise than fruitless, it would be a most discouraging
view to take of the progress of the human race,
were we to look upon the exertions of eminent men
in former ages, though they may have been in a
wrong direction, as mere vanity and vexation of
spirit. We must not forget that the very fact of
the failure of such men contributed powerfully to a
general conviction that there must be something

* 'Mansit lingua per Adam primitus data, et putamus, He-
brææ, in ea parte hominum, quæ qua pars alicujus angeli, sed quæ
Dei portio permansit.'

wrong in the problem itself, till at last a bolder genius inverted the problem and thereby solved it. When books after books had been written to show how Greek and Latin and all other languages were derived from Hebrew,* and when not one single system proved satisfactory, people asked at last — 'Why then *should* all languages be derived from Hebrew?' — and this very question solved the problem. It might have been natural for theologians in the fourth and fifth centuries, many of whom knew neither Hebrew nor any language except their own, to take it for granted that Hebrew was the source of all languages, but there is neither in the Old nor the New Testament a single word to necessitate this view. Of the language of Adam we know nothing; but if Hebrew, as we know it, was one of the languages that sprang from the confusion of tongues at Babel, it could not well have been the language of Adam or of the whole earth, 'when the whole earth was still of one speech.'†

Although, therefore, a certain advance was made towards a classification of languages by the Semitic

---

* Guichard went so far as to maintain that as Hebrew was written from right to left, and Greek from left to right, Greek words might be traced back to Hebrew by being simply read from right to left.

† Among the different systems of Rabbinical exegesis, there is one according to which every letter in Hebrew is reduced to its numerical value, and the word is explained by another of the same quantity; thus, from the passage, 'And all the inhabitants of the earth were of one language' (*Gen.* xi. 1), is deduced that they all spoke Hebrew, אחת being changed for its synonym קדש, and קדש (5 + 100 + 4 + 300 = 409) is substituted for its equivalent אחת (1 + 8 + 400 = 409). *Coheleth*, ed. Ginsburg, p. 31. Cf. Quatremère, *Mélanges*, p. 138.

scholars of the seventeenth century, yet this partial advance became in other respects an impediment. The purely scientific interest in arranging languages according to their characteristic features was lost sight of, and erroneous ideas were propagated, the influence of which has even now not quite subsided.

The first who really conquered the prejudice that Hebrew was the source of all language was Leibniz, the contemporary and rival of Newton. 'There is as much reason,' he said, 'for supposing Hebrew to have been the primitive language of mankind, as there is for adopting the view of Goropius, who published a work at Antwerp, in 1580, to prove that Dutch was the language spoken in Paradise.'* In a letter to Tenzel, Leibniz writes : 'To call Hebrew the primitive language, is like calling branches

---

* *Hermathena Joannis Goropii Becani:* Antwerpiæ, 1580. *Origines Antverpianæ,* 1569. André Kempe, in his work on the language of Paradise, maintains that God spoke to Adam in Swedish, Adam answered in Danish, and the serpent spoke to Eve in French.

Chardin relates that the Persians believe three languages to have been spoken in Paradise; Arabic by the serpent, Persian by Adam and Eve, and Turkish by Gabriel.

J. B. Erro, in his *El Mundo primitivo,* Madrid, 1814, claims Bask as the language spoken by Adam.

A curious discussion took place about two hundred years ago in the Metropolitan Chapter of Pampeluna. The decision, as entered in the minutes of the chapter, is as follows:—1. Was Bask the primitive language of mankind? The learned members confess that, in spite of their strong conviction on the subject, they dare not give an affirmative answer. 2. Was Bask the only language spoken by Adam and Eve in Paradise? On this point the chapter declares that no doubt can exist in their minds, and that 'it is impossible to bring forward any serious or rational objection.' See Hyanoquin, *Essai sur l'Analogie des Langues,* Bordeaux, 1838, p. 60.

of a tree primitive branches, or like imagining that in some country hewn trunks could grow instead of trees. Such ideas may be conceived, but they do not agree with the laws of nature, and with the harmony of the universe, that is to say, with the Divine Wisdom.'*

But Leibniz did more than remove this one great stumbling-block from the threshold of the science of language. He was the first to apply the principle of sound inductive reasoning to a subject which before him had only been treated at random. He pointed out the necessity of collecting, first of all, as large a number of facts as possible.† He appealed to missionaries, travellers, ambassadors, princes, and emperors, to help him in a work which he had so much at heart. The Jesuits in China had to work for him. Witsen,‡ the traveller, sent him a most precious present, a translation of the Lord's Prayer into the jargon of the Hottentots. 'My friend,'

---

* Guhrauer's *Life of Leibniz*, ii. p. 129.

† Guhrauer, vol. ii. p. 127. In his *Dissertation on the Origin of Nations*, 1710, Leibniz says:—'The study of languages must not be conducted according to any other principles but those of the exact sciences. Why begin with the unknown instead of the known? It stands to reason that we ought to begin with studying the modern languages which are within our reach, in order to compare them with one another, to discover their differences and affinities, and then to proceed to those which have preceded them in former ages, in order to show their filiation and their origin, and then to ascend step by step to the most ancient tongues, the analysis of which must lead us to the only trustworthy conclusions.'

‡ Nicolaes Witsen, Burgomaster of Amsterdam, travelled in Russia, 1666–1672; published his travels in 1677, dedicated to Peter the Great. Second edition, 1705. It contains many collections of words.

writes Leibniz in thanking him, 'remember, I implore you, and remind your Muscovite friends, to make researches in order to procure specimens of the Scythian languages, the Samoyedes, Siberians, Bashkirs, Kalmuks, Tungusians, and others.' Having made the acquaintance of Peter the Great, Leibniz wrote to him the following letter, dated Vienna, October the 26th, 1713:—

'I have suggested that the numerous languages, hitherto almost entirely unknown and unstudied which are current in the empire of your Majesty and on its frontiers, should be reduced to writing; also that dictionaries, or at least small vocabularies, should be collected, and translations be procured in such languages of the Ten Commandments, the Lord's Prayer, the Apostolic Symbolum, and other parts of the Catechism, *ut omnis lingua laudet Dominum*. This would increase the glory of your Majesty, who reigns over so many nations, and is so anxious to improve them; and it would, likewise, by means of a comparison of languages, enable us to discover the origin of those nations who from Scythia, which is subject to your Majesty, advanced into other countries. But principally it would help to plant Christianity among the nations speaking those dialects, and I have, therefore, addressed the Most Rev. Metropolitan on the same subject.'*

Leibniz drew up a list of the most simple and necessary terms which should be selected for com-

---

* *Catherinens der Grossen Verdienste um die vergleichende Sprachkunde*, von F. Adelung, Petersburg, 1915. Another letter of his to the Vice-Chancellor, Baron Schaffiroff, is dated Pirmont, June 22, 1716.

parison in various languages. At home, while engaged in historical researches, he collected whatever could throw light on the origin of the German language, and he encouraged others, such as Eccard, to do the same. He pointed out the importance of dialects, and even of provincial and local terms, for elucidating the etymological structure of languages.* Leibniz never undertook a systematic classification of the whole realm of language, nor was he successful in classing the dialects with which he had become acquainted. He distinguished between a Japhetic and Aramaic class, the former occupying the north, the latter the south, of the continent of Asia and Europe. He believed in a common origin of languages, and in a migration of the human race from east to west. But he failed to distinguish the exact degrees of relationship in which languages stood to each other, and he mixed up some of the Turanian dialects, such as Finnish and Tataric, with the Japhetic family of speech. If Leibniz had found time to work out all the plans which his fertile and comprehensive genius conceived, or if he had been understood and supported by cotemporary scholars, the science of language, as one of the inductive sciences, might have been established a century earlier. But a man like Leibniz, who was equally distinguished as a scholar, a theologian, a lawyer, an historian, and a mathematician, could only throw out hints as to how language ought to be studied. Leibniz was not only the discoverer of the differen-

* *Collectanea Etymologica*, ii. 255. 'Malim sine discrimine Dialectorum corrogari Germanicas voces. Puto quasdam origines ex superioribus Dialectis melius apparituras; ut ex Ulfilæ Pontogothicis, Otfridi Franciscis.'

tial calculus. He was one of the first to watch the geological stratification of the earth. He was engaged in constructing a calculating machine, the idea of which he first conceived as a boy. He drew up an elaborate plan of an expedition to Egypt, which he submitted to Louis XIV. in order to avert his attention from the frontiers of Germany. The same man was engaged in a long correspondence with Bossuet to bring about a reconciliation between Protestants and Romanists, and he endeavoured, in his *Theodicée* and other works, to defend the cause of truth and religion against the inroads of the materialistic philosophy of England and France. It has been said, indeed, that the discoveries of Leibniz produced but little effect, and that most of them had to be made again. This is not the case, however, with regard to the science of language. The new interest in languages, which Leibniz had called into life, did not die again. After it had once been recognised as a desideratum to bring together a complete *Herbarium* of the languages of mankind, missionaries and travellers felt it their duty to collect lists of words and draw up grammars wherever they came in contact with a new race. The two great works in which, at the beginning of our century, the results of these researches were summed up— I mean the *Catalogue of Languages* by Hervas, and the *Mithridates* of Adelung—can both be traced back directly to the influence of Leibniz. As to Hervas, he had read Leibniz carefully, and though he differs from him on some points, he fully acknowledges his merits in promoting a truly philosophical study of languages. Of Adelung's *Mithridates* and his obligations to Leibniz we shall have to speak presently.

Hervas lived from 1735 to 1809. He was a Spaniard by birth, and a Jesuit by profession. While working as a missionary among the polyglottous tribes of America, his attention was drawn to a systematic study of languages. After his return, he lived chiefly at Rome in the midst of the numerous Jesuit missionaries who had at that time been recalled from all parts of the world, and who, by their communications on the dialects of the tribes among whom they had been labouring, assisted him greatly in his researches.

Most of his works were written in Italian, and were afterwards translated into Spanish. We cannot enter into the general scope of his literary labours, which are of the most comprehensive character. They were intended to form a kind of Kosmos, for which he chose the title of *Idea del Universo*. What is of interest to us is that portion which treats of man and language as part of the universe; and here, again, chiefly his *Catalogue of Languages*, in six volumes, published in Spanish in the year 1800.

If we compare the work of Hervas with a similar work which excited much attention towards the end of the last century, and is even now more widely known than Hervas—I mean Court de Gebelin's *Monde Primitif*[*]—we shall see at once how far superior the Spanish Jesuit is to the French philosopher. Gebelin treats Persian, Armenian, Malay, and Coptic as dialects of Hebrew; he speaks of Bask as a dialect of Celtic, and he tries to discover Hebrew, Greek, English, and French words in the idioms of America. Hervas, on the contrary, though en-

[*] *Monde primitif analysé et comparé avec le monde moderne*, Paris, 1773.

bracing in his catalogue five times the number of languages that were known to Gebelin, is most careful not to allow himself to be carried away by theories not warranted by the evidence before him. It is easy now to point out mistakes and inaccuracies in Hervas, but I think that those who have blamed him most are those who ought most to have acknowledged their obligations to him. To have collected specimens and notices of more than three hundred languages is no small matter. But Hervas did more. He himself composed grammars of more than forty languages.* He was the first to point out that the true affinities of languages must be determined chiefly by grammatical evidence, not by mere similarity of words.† He proved, by a comparative list of declensions and conjugations, that Hebrew, Chaldee, Syriac, Arabic, Ethiopic and Amharic are all but dialects of one original language, and constitute one family of speech, the Semitic.‡ He scouted the idea of deriving all the languages of mankind from Hebrew. He had perceived clear traces of affinity in

---

* *Catalogo*, i. 63.

† 'Mas se deben consultar gramaticas para conocer su caracter proprio por medio de su artificio gramatical.'—*Catalogo*, i. 65. The same principle was expressed by Lord Monboddo, about 1795, in his *Ancient Metaphysics*, vol. iv. p. 326. 'My last observation is, that, as the art of a language is less arbitrary and more determined by rule than either the sound or sense of words, it is one of the principal things by which the connection of languages with one another is to be discovered. And, therefore, when we find that two languages practise these great arts of language,—derivation, composition, and flexion,—in the same way, we may conclude, I think, with great certainty, that the one language is the original of the other, or that they are both dialects of the same language.'

‡ *Catalogo*, ii. 468.

Hungarian, Lapponian, and Finnish, three dialects now classed as members of the Turanian family.* He had proved that Bask was not, as was commonly supposed, a Celtic dialect, but an independent language, spoken by the earliest inhabitants of Spain, as proved by the names of the Spanish mountains and rivers.† Nay, one of the most brilliant discoveries in the history of the science of language, the establishment of the Malay and Polynesian family of speech, extending from the island of Madagascar east of Africa, over 208 degrees of longitude, to the Easter Islands west of America,‡ was made by

---

* *Catalogo*, i. 49. Witsen, too, in a letter to Leibniz, dated Mai 22, 1698, alludes to the affinity between the Tataric and Mongolic languages. 'On m'a dit que ces deux langues (la langue Moegala et Tartare) sont différentes à peu près comme l'Allemand l'est du Flamand, et qu'il est de même des Kalmucs et Moegals.'—*Collectanea Etymologica*, ii. p. 363.

† Leibniz held the same opinion (see Hervas, *Catalogo*, i. 50), though he considered the Celts in Spain as descendants of the Iberians.

‡ *Catalogo*, i. 30. 'Verá que la lengua llamada malaya, la qual se habla en la península de Malaca, es matriz de innumerables dialectos de naciones isleñas, que desde dicha península se extienden por mas de doscientos grados de longitud en los mares oriental y pacífico.'

Ibid. ii. 10. 'De esta península de Malaca han salido enjambres de pobladores de las islas del mar Indiano y Pacífico, en las que, aunque parece haber otra nacion, que es de negros, la *malaya* es generalmente la mas dominante y extendida. La lengua malaya se habla en dicha península, continente del Asia, en las islas Maldivas, en la de Madagascar (perteneciente al Africa), en las de Sonda, en las Molucas, en las Filipinas, en las del archipiélago de San Lázaro, y en muchísimas del mar del Sur desde dicho archipiélago hasta islas, que por su poca distancia de América se creian pobladas por americanos. La isla de Madagascar se pone á 60 grados de longitud, y á los 268 se pone la isla de Pasqua ó de Davis, en la que se habla otro dialecto

Hervas long before it was announced to the world by Humboldt.

Hervas was likewise aware of the great grammatical similarity between Sanskrit and Greek, but the imperfect information which he received from his friend, the Carmelite missionary, Fra Paolino de San Bartolomeo, the author of the first Sanskrit grammar, published at Rome in 1790, prevented him from seeing the full meaning of this grammatical similarity. How near Hervas was to the discovery of the truth may be seen from his comparing such words as *Theos*, God, in Greek, with *Deva*, God, in Sanskrit. He identified the Greek auxiliary verb *eimi, eis, esti*, I am, thou art, he is, with the Sanskrit *asmi, asi, asti*. He even pointed out that the terminations of the three genders* in Greek, *os, ê, on*, are the same as the Sanskrit, *as, â, am*. But believing, as he did, that the Greeks derived their philosophy and mythology from India,† he supposed that they had likewise borrowed from the Hindus some of their words, and even the art of distinguishing the gender of words.

The second work which represents the science of language at the beginning of this century, and which is, to a still greater extent, the result of the impulse which Leibniz had given, is the *Mithridates* of Adelung.‡ Adelung's work depends partly on Hervas, partly on the collections of words which

malayo; por lo que la extension de los dialectos malayos es de 208 grados de longitud.'

* *Catalogo*, ii. 134.   † *Ibid.* ii. 135.
‡ The first volume appeared in 1806. He died before the second volume was published, which was brought out by Vater in 1809. The third and fourth volumes followed in 1816 and 1817, edited by Vater and the younger Adelung.

had been made under the auspices of the Russian government. Now these collections are clearly due to Leibniz. Although Peter the Great had no time or taste for philological studies, the government kept the idea of collecting all the languages of the Russian empire steadily in view.* Still greater luck was in store for the science of language. Having been patronised by Cæsar at Rome, it found a still more devoted patroness in the great Cesarina of the North, Catherine the Great (1762-1796). Even as Grand-duchess Catherine was engrossed with the idea of a Universal Dictionary, on the plan suggested by Leibniz. She encouraged the chaplain of the British Factory at St. Petersburg, the Rev. Daniel Dumaresq, to undertake the work, and he is said to have published, at her desire, a *Comparative Vocabulary of Eastern Languages*, in quarto; a work, however, which, if ever published, is now completely lost. The reputed author died in London in 1805, at the advanced age of eighty-four. When Catherine came to the throne, her plans of conquest hardly absorbed more of her time than her philological studies; and she once shut herself up nearly a year, devoting all her time to the compilation of her Comparative Dictionary. A letter of hers to Zimmermann, dated the 9th of May, 1785, may interest some of my hearers:—

'Your letter,' she writes, 'has drawn me from the solitude in which I had shut myself up for nearly

* Evidence of this is to be found in Strahlenberg's work on the *North and East of Europe and Asia*, 1730, with tabula polyglotta, &c.; in Messerschmidt's *Travels in Siberia*, from 1720-1739; in Bachmeister, *Idea et desideria de colligendis linguarum speciminibus*, Petropoli, 1773; in Güldenstädt's *Travels in Caucasus*; &c.

nine months, and from which I found it hard to stir.
You will not guess what I have been about. I will
tell you, for such things do not happen every day.
I have been making a list of from two to three
hundred radical words of the Russian language, and
I have had them translated into as many languages
and jargons as I could find. Their number exceeds
already the second hundred. Every day I took one
of these words and wrote it out in all the languages
which I could collect. This has taught me that the
Celtic is like the Ostiakian: that what means sky in
one language means cloud, fog, vault, in others; that
the word God in certain dialects means Good, the
Highest, in others, sun or fire. [As far as this her
letter is written in French; then follows a line of
German.] I became tired of my hobby, after I had
read your book on Solitude. [Then again in French.]
But as I should have been sorry to throw such a
mass of paper in the fire;—besides, the room, six
fathoms in length, which I use as a boudoir in my
hermitage, was pretty well warmed—I asked Professor Pallas to come to me, and after making an
honest confession of my sin, we agreed to publish
these collections, and thus make them useful to those
who like to occupy themselves with the forsaken toys
of others. We are only waiting for some more dialects of Eastern Siberia. Whether the world at large
will or will not see in this work bright ideas of different kinds, must depend on the disposition of their
minds, and does not concern me in the least.'

If an empress rides a hobby, there are many ready
to help her. Not only were all Russian ambassadors
instructed to collect materials; not only did German

professors* supply grammars and dictionaries, but Washington himself, in order to please the empress, sent her list of words to all governors and generals of the United States, enjoining them to supply the equivalents from the American dialects. The first volume of the Imperial Dictionary† appeared in 1787, containing a list of 285 words translated into fifty-one European and one hundred and forty-nine Asiatic languages. Though full credit should be given to the empress for this remarkable undertaking, it is but fair to remember that it was the philosopher who, nearly a hundred years before, sowed the seed that fell into good ground.

As collections, the works of Hervas, of the Empress Catherine, and of Adelung, are highly important, though such is the progress made in the classification of languages during the last fifty years, that few people would now consult them. Besides, the principle of classification which is followed in these works can hardly claim to be called scientific. Languages are arranged geographically, as the languages of Europe, Asia, Africa, America, and Polynesia, though, at the same time, natural affinities are admitted which would unite

---

* The empress wrote to Nicolai at Berlin to ask him to draw up a catalogue of grammars and dictionaries. The work was sent to her in manuscript from Berlin, in 1785.

† *Glossarium comparativum Linguarum totius Orbis,* Petersburg, 1787. A second edition, in which the words are arranged alphabetically, appeared in 1790-91, in 4 vols., edited by Jankiewitsch de Miriewo. It contains 279 (272) languages, i.e. 171 for Asia, 55 for Europe, 30 for Africa, and 23 for America. According to Pott, *Ungleichheit,* p. 230, it contains 277 languages, 185 for Asia, 22 for Europe, 28 for Africa, 15 for America. This would make 280. It is a very scarce book.

dialects spoken at a distance of 208 degrees. Languages seemed to float about like islands on the ocean of human speech; they did not shoot together to form themselves into larger continents. This is a most critical period in the history of every science, and if it had not been for a happy accident, which, like an electric spark, caused the floating elements to crystallise into regular forms, it is more than doubtful whether the long list of languages and dialects, enumerated and described in the works of Hervas and Adelung, could long have sustained the interest of the student of languages. This electric spark was the discovery of Sanskrit. Sanskrit is the ancient language of the Hindus. It had ceased to be a spoken language at least 300 B.C. At that time the people of India spoke dialects standing to the ancient Vedic Sanskrit in the relation of Italian to Latin. We know some of these dialects, for there were more than one in various parts of India, from the inscriptions which the famous King Asoka had engraved on the rocks of Dhauli, Girnar, and Kapurdigiri, and which have been deciphered by Prinsep, Norris, Wilson, and Burnouf. We can watch the further growth of these local dialects in the *Pâli*, the sacred language of Buddhism in Ceylon, and once the popular dialect of the country where Buddhism took its origin, the modern Behar, the ancient Magadha.* We meet the same local dialects again in what are called the Prâkrit idioms, used in the later plays, in the sacred literature of the Jainas, and in a few poetical compositions; and we see at last how, through a mixture with the languages of

* The Singhalese call Pali, Mungata; the Burmese, Magadabâsâ.

the various conquerors of India, the Arabic, Persian, Mongolic, and Turkish, and through a concomitant corruption of their grammatical system, they were changed into the modern Hindí, Hindustání, Mahratti, and Bengálí. During all this time, however, Sanskrit continued as the literary language of the Brahmans. Like Latin, it did not die in giving birth to its numerous offspring; and even at the present day an educated Brahman would write with greater fluency in Sanskrit than in Bengálí. Sanskrit was what Greek was at Alexandria, what Latin was during the middle ages. It was the classical and at the same time the sacred language of the Brahmans, and in it were written their sacred hymns, the Vedas, and the later works, such as the laws of Manu and the Puránas.

The existence of such a language as the ancient idiom of the country, and the vehicle of a large literature, was known at all times; and if there are still any doubts, like those expressed by Dugald Stewart in his *Conjectures concerning the Origin of the Sanskrit,*[*] as to its age and authenticity, they will be best removed by a glance at the history of India, and at the accounts given by the writers of different nations that became successively acquainted with the language and literature of that country.

The argument that nearly all the names of persons and places in India mentioned by Greek and Roman writers are pure Sanskrit, has been handled so fully and ably by others, that nothing remains to be said on the subject.

The next nation after the Greeks that became ac-

---

[*] *Works,* vol. iii. p. 72.

quainted with the language and literature of India was the Chinese. Though Buddhism was not recognised as a third state-religion before the year 65 A.D., under the Emperor Ming-ti,* Buddhist missionaries had reached China from India as early as the third century B.C. One Buddhist missionary is mentioned in the Chinese annals in the year 217; and about the year 120 B.C., a Chinese general, after defeating the barbarous tribes north of the desert of Gobi, brought back as a trophy a golden statue, the statue of Buddha. The very name of Buddha, changed in Chinese into Fo-t'o and Fo,† is pure Sanskrit, and so is every word and every thought of that religion. The language which the Chinese pilgrims went to India to study, as the key to the sacred literature of Buddhism, was Sanskrit. They call it Fan; but Fan, as M. Stanislas Julien has shown, is an abbreviation of Fan-lan-mo, and this is the only way in which the Sanskrit Brahman could be rendered in Chinese.‡ We read of the Emperor Ming-ti, of the dynasty of Han, sending Tsai-in and other high officials to India, in order to study there the doctrine of Buddha. They engaged the services of two learned Buddhists, Matánga and Tchou-fa-lan, and some of the most important Buddhist works were translated by them into Chinese. The intellectual intercourse between

---

* M. M.'s *Buddhism and Buddhist Pilgrims*, p. 23.

† *Méthode pour déchiffrer et transcrire les noms Sanscrits qui se rencontrent dans les livres chinois, inventée et démontrée* par M. Stanislas Julien: Paris, 1861, p. 103.

‡ 'Fan-chou (brahmâkshara), les caractères de l'écriture indienne, inventée par Fan, c'est-à-dire Fan-lan-mo (brahmâ).'— Stanislas Julien, *Voyages des Pèlerins Bouddhistes*, vol. ii. p. 505.

the Indian peninsula and the northern continent of Asia continued uninterrupted for several centuries. Missions were sent from China to India to report on the religious, political, social, and geographical state of the country; and the chief object of interest, which attracted public embassies and private pilgrims across the Himalayan mountains, was the religion of Buddha. About three hundred years after the public recognition of Buddhism by the Emperor Ming-ti, the great stream of Buddhist pilgrims began to flow from China to India. The first account which we possess of these pilgrimages refers to the travels of Fa-hian, who visited India towards the end of the fourth century. His travels were translated into French by A. Remusat. After Fa-hian, we have the travels of Hœi-seng and Song-yun, who were sent to India, in 518, by command of the empress, with the view of collecting sacred books and relics. Then followed Hiouen-thsang, whose life and travels, from 629–645 have been rendered so popular by the excellent translation of M. Stanislas Julien. After Hiouen-thsang the principal works of Chinese pilgrims are the Itineraries of the Fifty-six Monks, published in 730, and the travels of Khi-nie, who visited India in 964, at the head of 300 pilgrims.

That the language employed for literary purposes in India during all this time was Sanskrit, we learn, not only from the numerous names and religious and philosophical terms mentioned in the travels of the Chinese pilgrims, but from a short paradigm of declension and conjugation in Sanskrit which one of them (Hiouen-thsang) has inserted in his diary.

As soon as the Muhammedans entered India, we hear of translations of Sanskrit works into Persian and Arabic.* As early as the reign of the second Abasside Khalif Almansur,† in the year 773 A.D., an Indian astronomer, well versed in the science which he professed, visited the court of the Khalif, bringing with him tables of the equations of planets according to the mean motions, with observations relative to both solar and lunar eclipses and the ascension of the signs; taken, as he affirmed, from tables computed by an Indian prince, whose name, as the Arabian author writes it, was Phighar. The Khalif, embracing the opportunity thus happily presented to him, commanded the book to be translated into Arabic, to be published for a guide to the Arabians in matters pertaining to the stars. The task devolved on Muhammed ben Ibrahim Alfazári, whose version is known to astronomers by the name of the greater Sind-hind or Hind-sind,‡ for the term occurs written both ways.

* Sir Henry Elliot's *Historians of India*, p. 289.
† Colebrooke, *Miscellaneous Essays*, ii. p. 504, quotes from the preface to the astronomical tables of Ben al Adami, published by his continuator, Al Cásom, in 920 A.D. On Sanskrit figures, Strachey, *As. Res.* xii. 184, Colebrooke, *Algebra*, p. lii.
‡ Sindhind signifies the revolving ages, according to Ben al Adami; Casiri translates it perpetuum æternumque. Colebrooke conjectures Siddhânta, and supposes the original to have been Brahmagupta's work, *Brahmasiddhânta*. M. Reinaud, in his *Mémoire sur l'Inde*, p. 312, quotes the following passage from the *Taryk-al-Hokumá*: 'En l'anée 156 de l'hégire (773 de J. C.), il arriva de l'Inde à Bagdad un homme fort instruit dans les doctrines de son pays. Cet homme possédait la méthode du Sindhind, relative aux mouvements des astres et aux équations calculées au moyen de sinus du quart en quart de degré. Il connaissait aussi diverses manières de déterminer les éclipses, ainsi que le lever des signes du zodiaque. Il avait composé un abrégé d'un ouvrage relatif à ces matières qu'on attribuait à un prince nommé Fygar. Dans cet écrit les Kardagia, (i.e. Kramajyá; see *Súryasiddhânta*, ed. Burgess and Whitney, p. 57 and p. 59) étaient calculés par

About the same time Yacub, the son of Tharee, composed an astronomical work, founded on the Sind-hind.* Harun-al-Rashid (786-809) had two Indians, Manka and Saleh, as physicians at his court. Manka translated the classical work on medicine, Suśruta,† and a treatise on poisons, ascribed to Chânakya, from Sanskrit into Persian.‡ During the Chalifate of Al Mámún, a famous treatise on Algebra was translated by Mohammed ben Musa from Sanskrit into Arabic (edited by F. Rosen, 1831).

About 1000 A.D., Abu Rihan al Birúni (born 970, died 1038) spent forty years in India, and composed his excellent work, the Tarikhu-l-Hind, which gives a complete account of the literature and sciences of the Hindus at that time. Albirúni had been appointed by the Sultan of Khuwarazm to accompany an embassy which he sent to Mahmud of Ghazni and Masud of Lahore. The learned Avicenna had been invited to join the same embassy, but had declined. Albirúni must have acquired a complete knowledge of Sanskrit, for he not only translated one work on

---

minutes. Le Khalife ordonna qu'on traduisît le traité indien en arabe, afin d'aider les musulmans à acquérir une connaissance exacte des étoiles. Le soin de la traduction fut confié à Mohammed, fils d'Ibrahim-al-Fazary, le premier entre les musulmans qui s'était livré à une étude approfondie de l'astronomie: on désigne plus tard cette traduction sous le titre de Grand Sindhind.' Albirúni places the translation in the year 771.

* Reinaud, l.c. p. 314.

† Cf. Steinschneider, Wissenschaftliche Blätter, vol. l. p. 79.

‡ See Professor Flügel, in *Zeitschrift der D.M.G.* xi. s. 148 and 325. A Hebrew treatise on poisons ascribed to the Indian Zaalk, is mentioned by Steinschneider, Wissenschaftliche Blätter, vol. i. p. 65. Albirúni mentions an Indian Kankah as astrologer of Harun-al-Rashid (Reinaud, *Mémoire sur l'Inde*, p. 315). He is likewise mentioned as a physician. Another Indian physician of Harun-al-Rashid is called Mankba (Reinaud, l.c.)

the Sânkhya, and another on the Yoga philosophy from Sanskrit into Arabic, but likewise two works from Arabic into Sanskrit.*

About 1150 we hear of Abu Saleh translating a work on the education of kings from Sanskrit into Arabic.†

Two hundred years later, we are told that Firoz Shah, after the capture of Nagarcote, ordered several Sanskrit words on philosophy to be translated from Sanskrit by Maulâna Izzu-d-din Khâlid Khâni. A work on veterinary medicine ascribed to Sâlotar,‡

---

* Elliot's *Historians of India*, p. 96. Albirúni knew the Harivansa, and fixes the date of the five Siddhántas. The great value of Albirúni's work was first pointed out by M. Reinaud, in his excellent *Mémoire sur l'Inde*, Paris, 1849.

† In the Persian work *Mujmulu-t-Towárikh* there are chapters translated from the Arabic of Abu Saleh ben Shib ben Jawa, who had himself abridged them, a hundred years before, from a Sanskrit work called *Instruction of Kings* (*Rájaníti?*). The Persian translator lived about 1150. See Elliot, *l.c.*

‡ Sâlotar is not known as the author of such a work. Sâlotariya occurs instead of Sâlâturiya, in Rája Rádhakant; but Sâlâturiya is a name of Pâṇini, and the teacher of Suśruta is said to have been Divodâsa. Professor Weber, in his *Catalogue of Sanskrit MSS.* (p. 296) has pointed out Sâlihotra, who is mentioned in the *Panchatantra* as a teacher of veterinary medicine, and who is quoted by Garga in the *Atvdyurveda*. Salotrí is the everyday Urdu and Hindi word for a horse-doctor. Professor Aufrecht has discovered a work on medicine by Sâlihotra in the Library of the E. I. H. A medical work by Sâlinâtha is mentioned in the *Catalogue of Sanskrit MSS. of the College of Fort William*, p. 24. An Arabic translation of a Sanskrit work on veterinary medicine by Chânakya is mentioned by Hâji Chalfa, v. p. 59. A translation of the Charaka from Sanskrit into Persian, and from Persian into Arabic, is mentioned in the Fihrist (finished 987 A.D.). It is likewise mentioned by Albirúni (Reinaud, *Mémoire sur l'Inde*, p. 316); the translation is said to have been made for the Barmekides. The names of the persons by whom the doctrines contained in this work were supposed to have been handed down, should be restored, in Albirúni as

said to have been the tutor of Suśruta, was likewise translated from Sanskrit in the year 1381. A copy of it was preserved in the Royal Library of Lucknow.

Two hundred years more bring us to the reign of Akbar (1556–1605). A more extraordinary man never sat on the throne of India. Brought up as a Muhammedan, he discarded the religion of the Prophet as superstitious,[*] and then devoted himself to a search after the true religion. He called Brahmans and fire-worshippers to his court, and ordered them to discuss in his presence the merits of their religions with the Muhammedan doctors. When he heard of the Jesuits at Goa, he invited them to his capital, and he was for many years looked upon as a secret convert to Christianity. He was, however, a rationalist and deist, and never believed anything, as he declared himself, that he could not understand. The religion which he founded, the so-called Ilahi religion, was pure Deism mixed up with the worship of the sun[†] as the purest and highest emblem of the Deity. Though Akbar himself could neither read nor write,[‡] his court was the home of literary men of all persuasions. Whatever book, in any language, promised to throw light on the problems nearest to the emperor's heart, he ordered to be translated into Persian. The New Testament[§] was thus translated

follows: Brahman, Prajâpati, the Asvinau, Indra, the sons of Atri, Agnivesa, Cf. *Ashtangahridaya*, introd. (MS. Wilson, 296).

[*] See Vans Kennedy, *Notice respecting the Religion introduced by Akbar*, Transactions of the Literary Society of Bombay, 1820, vol. ii. p. 242–270.

[†] Elliot, *Historians of India*, p. 249.

[‡] Müllbauer, *Geschichte der Katholischen Missionem Ostindiens*, p. 134.

[§] Elliot, *Historians of India*, p. 248.

at his command; so were the *Mahábhárata*, the *Rámáyana*, the *Amarakosha*,* and other classical works of Sanskrit literature. But though the emperor set the greatest value on the sacred writings of different nations, he does not seem to have succeeded in extorting from the Brahmans a translation of the *Veda*. A translation of the *Atharva-veda* † was made for him by Haji Ibrahim Sirhindi; but that Veda never enjoyed the same authority as the other three Vedas, and it is doubtful even whether by *Atharva-veda* is meant more than the *Upanishads*, some of which may have been composed for the special benefit of Akbar. There is a story which, though evidently of a legendary character, shows how the study of Sanskrit was kept up by the Brahmans during the reign of the Mogul emperors.

'Neither the authority (it is said) nor promises of Akbar could prevail upon the Brahmans to disclose the tenets of their religion: he was therefore obliged to have recourse to artifice. The stratagem he made use of was to cause a boy, of the name of *Feizi*, to

---

* Elliot, *Historians of India*, p. 259, 260. The *Tarikh-i-Badaoni*, or *Muntakhabu-t-Tawárikh*, written by Mulla Abdu-l-Kádir Maluk, Shah of Badáún, and finished in 1595, is a general history of India from the time of the Ghaznevides to the 40th year of Akbar. The author is a bigoted Muhammadan, and judges Akbar severely, though he was himself under great obligations to him. He was employed by Akbar to translate from Arabic and Sanskrit into Persian: he translated the *Rámáyana*, two out of the eighteen sections of the *Mahábhárata*, and abridged a history of Cashmir. These translations were made under the superintendence of Faizi, the brother of the minister Abu-l-Fazl. 'Abulfacel, ministro de Akbar, se valió del Amarasinha y del Mahabhárata, que traduxo en persiano el año de 1586.'—*Herrera*, II. 136.

† See M. M.'s *History of Ancient Sanskrit Literature*, p. 327.

be committed to the care of these priests, as a poor orphan of the sacerdotal line, who alone could be initiated into the sacred rites of their theology. Feizi, having received the proper instructions for the part he was to act, was conveyed privately to Benares, the seat of knowledge in Hindostan; he was received into the house of a learned Brahman, who educated him with the same care as if he had been his son. After the youth had spent ten years in study, Akbar was desirous of recalling him; but he was struck with the charms of the daughter of his preceptor. The old Brahman laid no restraint on the growing passion of the two lovers. He was fond of Feizi, and offered him his daughter in marriage. The young man, divided between love and gratitude, resolved to conceal the fraud no longer, and falling at the feet of the Brahman, discovered the imposture, and asked pardon for his offences. The priest, without reproaching him, seized a poniard which hung at his girdle, and was going to plunge it in his heart, if Feizi had not prevented him by taking hold of his arm. The young man used every means to pacify him, and declared himself ready to do anything to expiate his treachery. The Brahman, bursting into tears, promised to pardon him on condition that he should swear never to translate the *Vedas*, or sacred volumes, or disclose to any person whatever the symbol of the Brahman creed. Feizi readily promised him: how far he kept his word is not known; but the sacred books of the Indians have never been translated.'*

We have thus traced the existence of Sanskrit,

* *History of the Settlements of the Europeans in the East and West Indies*, translated from the French of the Abbé Bernal by J. Justamond, Dublin, 1776, vol. i. p. 34.

as the language of literature and religion of India, from the time of Alexander to the reign of Akbar. A hundred years after Akbar the eldest son of Shah Jehan, the unfortunate Dárá, manifested the same interest in religious speculations which had distinguished his great grandsire. He became a student of Sanskrit, and translated the *Upanishads*, philosophical treatises appended to the *Vedas*, into Persian. This was in the year 1657, a year before he was put to death by his younger brother, the bigoted Aurengzebe. This prince's translation was translated into French by Anquetil Duperron, in the year 1795, the fourth year of the French Republic; and was for a long time the principal source from which European scholars derived their knowledge of the sacred literature of the Brahmans.

At the time at which we have now arrived, the reign of Aurengzebe (1658–1707), the contemporary and rival of Louis XIV., the existence of Sanskrit and Sanskrit literature was known, if not in Europe generally, at least to Europeans in India, particularly to missionaries. Who was the first European that knew of Sanskrit, or that acquired a knowledge of Sanskrit, is difficult to say. When Vasco du Gama landed at Calicut, on the 9th of May, 1498, Padre Pedro began at once to preach to the natives, and had suffered a martyr's death before the discoverer of India returned to Lisbon. Every new ship that reached India brought new missionaries; but for a long time we look in vain in their letters and reports for any mention of Sanskrit or Sanskrit literature. Francis, now St. Francis, Xavier, was the first to organise the great work of preaching the Gospel in India (1542); and such were his zeal and devotion, such his success in winning the hearts of high and low, that his friends ascribed to him, among other miraculous gifts, the gift of tongues*— a gift never claimed by St. Francis himself. It is not, however, till the year 1559 that we first hear of the missionaries at Goa studying, with the help of a converted Brahman,† the theological and philosophical literature of the country, and challenging the Brahmans to public disputations.

The first certain instance of a European missionary having mastered the difficulties of the Sanskrit language, belongs to a still later period—to what may be called the period of Roberto de Nobili, as distinguished from the first period, which is under the presiding spirit of Francis Xavier. Roberto de Nobili went to India in 1606. He was himself a man of high family, of a refined and cultivated mind, and he perceived the more quickly the difficulties which kept the higher castes, and particularly the Brahmans, from joining the Christian communities formed at Madura and other places. These communities consisted chiefly of men of low rank, of no education, and no refinement. He conceived the bold plan of presenting himself as a Brahman, and thus obtaining access to the high and noble, the wise and learned, in the land. He shut himself up for years, acquiring in secret a knowledge, not only of Tamil and Telugu,

---

* Müllbauer, p. 67.

† Ibid. p. 80. These Brahmans, according to Robert de Nobili, were of a lower class, not initiated in the sacred literature. They were ignorant, he says, 'of the books *Smarta*, *Apastamba*, and *Sutra*.' (*Müllbauer*, p. 189.) Robert himself quotes from the *Apastamba-Sutra*, in his defence, ibid. p. 192. He also quotes *Scanda Purana*, p. 193; *Kadambari*, p. 193.

but of Sanskrit. When, after a patient study of the language and literature of the Brahmans, he felt himself strong enough to grapple with his antagonists, he showed himself in public, dressed in the proper garb of the Brahmans, wearing their cord and their frontal mark, observing their diet, and submitting even to the complicated rules of caste. He was successful, in spite of the persecutions both of the Brahmans, who were afraid of him, and of his own fellow-labourers, who could not understand his policy. His life in India, where he died as an old blind man, is full of interest to the missionary. I can only speak of him here as the first European Sanskrit scholar. A man who could quote from *Manu*, from the *Purânas*, and even from works such as the *Apastamba-Sûtras*, which are known even at present to only those few Sanskrit scholars who can read Sanskrit MSS., must have been far advanced in a knowledge of the sacred language and literature of the Brahmans; and the very idea that he came, as he said, to preach a new or a fourth Veda,* which had been lost, shows how well he knew the strong and weak points of the

---

* The *Ezour-Veda* is not the work of Robert de Nobili. It was probably written by one of his converts. It is in Sanskrit verse, in the style of the Purânas, and contains a wild mixture of Hindu and Christian doctrine. The French translation was sent to Voltaire and printed by him in 1778, '*L'Ezour Vedam traduit du Sanscritam par un Brame.*' Voltaire expressed his belief that the original was four centuries older than Alexander, and that it was the most precious gift for which the West had been ever indebted to the East. Mr. Ellis discovered the Sanskrit original at Pondichery. (*Asiatic Researches*, vol. xiv.) There is no evidence for ascribing the work to Robert, and it is not mentioned in the list of his works. (Bertrand, *La Mission du Maduré*, Paris, 1847-50, t. iii. p. 116; Müllbauer, p. 205, note.)

theological system which he came to conquer. It is surprising that the reports which he sent to Rome, in order to defend himself against the charge of idolatry, and in which he drew a faithful picture of the religion, the customs, and literature of the Brahmans, should not have attracted the attention of scholars. The 'Accommodation Question,' as it was called, occupied cardinals and popes for many years; but not one of them seems to have perceived the extraordinary interest attaching to the existence of an ancient civilisation so perfect and so firmly rooted as to require accommodation even from the missionaries of Rome. At a time when the discovery of one Greek MS. would have been hailed by all the scholars of Europe, the discovery of a complete literature was allowed to pass unnoticed. The day of Sanskrit had not yet come.

The first missionaries who succeeded in rousing the attention of European scholars to the extraordinary discovery that had been made were the French Jesuit missionaries, whom Louis XIV. had sent out to India after the treaty of Ryswick, in 1697.* Father Pons drew up a comprehensive account of the literary treasures of the Brahmans; and his report, dated Karikal, dans le Maduré, November 23, 1740, and addressed to Father Duhalde, was published in the *Lettres édifiantes*.† Father Pons gives in it a most interesting and, in general, a very accurate description of the various branches of Sanskrit literature,—of the four Vedas, the gramma-

---

* In 1677 a Mr. Marshall is said to have been a proficient in Sanskrit. Elliot's *Historians of India*, p. 265.

† See an excellent account of this letter in an article of M. Biot in the *Journal des Savants*, 1861.

tical treatises, the six systems of philosophy, and the astronomy of the Hindus. He anticipated, on several points, the researches of Sir William Jones.

But, although the letter of Father Pons excited a deep interest, that interest remained necessarily barren, as long as there were no grammars, dictionaries, and Sanskrit texts to enable scholars in Europe to study Sanskrit in the same spirit in which they studied Greek and Latin. The first who endeavoured to supply this want was a Carmelite friar, a German of the name of Johann Philip Wesdin, better known as Paulinus a Santo Bartholomeo. He was in India from 1776 to 1789; and he published the first grammar of Sanskrit at Rome, in 1790. Although this grammar has been severely criticised, and is now hardly ever consulted, it is but fair to bear in mind that the first grammar of any language is a work of infinitely greater difficulty than any later grammar.*

We have thus seen how the existence of the Sanskrit language and literature was known ever since India had first been discovered by Alexander and his companions. But what was not known was, that this language, as it was spoken at the time of Alexander, and at the time of Solomon, and for centuries before his time, was intimately related to Greek and Latin, in fact, stood to them in the same relation as French to Italian and Spanish. The

* *Sidharubam seu Grammatica Samscrdamica*, cui accedit dissertatio historico-critica in linguam Samscrdamicam, vulgo Samscret dictam, in qua hujus linguæ existentia, origo, præstantia, antiquitas, extensio, maternitas ostenditur, libri aliqui in ea exarati critice recensentur, et simul aliquæ antiquissimæ gentilium orationes liturgicæ paucis attinguntur et explicantur autore Paulino a S. Bartholomæo. Romæ, 1790.

history of what may be called European Sanskrit philology dates from the foundation of the Asiatic Society at Calcutta, in 1784.* It was through the labours of Sir William Jones, Carey, Wilkins, Forster, Colebrooke, and other members of that illustrious Society, that the language and literature of the Brahmans became first accessible to European scholars; and it would be difficult to say which of the two, the language or the literature, excited the deepest and most lasting interest. It was impossible to look, even in the most cursory manner, at the declensions and conjugations, without being struck by the extraordinary similarity, or, in some cases, by the absolute identity, of the grammatical forms in Sanskrit, Greek, and Latin. As early as 1778, Halhed remarked, in the preface to his Grammar of Bengali,† 'I have been astonished to find this similitude of Sanskrit words with those of Persian and Arabic, and even of Latin and Greek; and these not in technical and metaphorical terms, which the mutation of refined arts and improved manners might have occasionally introduced; but in the main groundwork of language, in monosyllables, in the names of numbers, and the appellations of

* The earliest publications were the *Bhagavadgita*, translated by Wilkins, 1785; the *Hitopadesa*, translated by Wilkins, 1787; and the *Sakuntala*, translated by W. Jones, 1789. Original grammars, without mentioning mere compilations, were published by Colebrooke, 1805; by Carey, 1806; by Wilkins, 1808; by Forster, 1810; by Yates, 1820; by Wilson, 1841. In Germany, Bopp published his grammars in 1827, 1832, 1834; Benfey, in 1852 and 1855.

† Halhed had published in 1776 the *Code of Gentoo Laws*, a digest of the most important Sanskrit law-books made by eleven Brahmans, by the order of Warren Hastings. Halhed translated from a Persian translation of the originals.

such things as could be first discriminated on the immediate dawn of civilisation.' Sir William Jones (died 1794), after the first glance at Sanskrit, declared that, whatever its antiquity, it was a language of most wonderful structure, more perfect than the Greek, more copious than the Latin, and more exquisitely refined than either, yet bearing to both of them a strong affinity. 'No philologer,' he writes, 'could examine the Sanskrit, Greek, and Latin, without believing them to have sprung from some common source, which, perhaps, no longer exists. There is a similar reason, though not quite so forcible, for supposing that both the Gothic and Celtic had the same origin with the Sanskrit. The old Persian may be added to the same family.'

But how was that affinity to be explained? People were completely taken by surprise. Theologians shook their heads; classical scholars looked sceptical; philosophers indulged in the wildest conjectures in order to escape from the only possible conclusion which could be drawn from the facts placed before them, but which threatened to upset their little systems of the history of the world. Lord Monboddo had just finished his great work* in which he derives all mankind from a couple of apes, and all the dialects of the world from a language originally framed by some Egyptian gods,† when the

* *On the Origin and Progress of Language*, second edition, 6 vols. Edinburgh, 1774.

† 'I have supposed that language could not be invented without supernatural assistance, and, accordingly, I have maintained that it was the invention of the Dæmon kings of Egypt, who, being more than men, first taught themselves to articulate, and then taught others. But, even among them, I am persuaded there was a progress in the art, and that such a language as the

discovery of Sanskrit came on him like a thunderbolt. It must be said, however, to his credit, that he at once perceived the immense importance of the discovery. He could not be expected to sacrifice his primæval monkeys or his Egyptian idols; but, with that reservation, the conclusions which he drew from the new evidence placed before him by his friend Wilkins, the author of one of our first Sanskrit grammars, are highly creditable to the acuteness of the Scotch Judge. 'There is a language,' he writes* (in 1792), 'still existing, and preserved among the Bramins of India, which is a richer and in every respect a finer language than even the Greek of Homer. All the other languages of India have a great resemblance to this language, which is called the Shanscrit. But those languages are dialects of it, and formed from it, not the Shanscrit from them. Of this, and other particulars concerning this language, I have got such certain information from India, that if I live to finish my history of man, which I have begun in my third volume of *Antient Metaphysics*, I shall be able clearly to prove that the Greek is derived from the Shanscrit, which was the antient language of Egypt and was carried by the Egyptians into India, with their other arts, and into Greece by the colonies which they settled there.'

A few years later (1795) he had arrived at more definite views on the relation of Sanskrit to Greek; and he writes,† 'Mr. Wilkins has proved to my con-

Shanskrit was not at once invented.'—Monboddo, *Antient Metaphysics*, vol. iv. p. 357.

* *Origin and Progress of Language*, vol. vi. p. 97.
† *Antient Metaphysics*, vol. iv. p. 322.

viction such a resemblance betwixt the Greek and the Shanscrit, that the one must be a dialect of the other, or both of some original language. Now the Greek is certainly not a dialect of the Shanscrit, any more than the Shanscrit is of the Greek. They must, therefore, be both dialects of the same language; and that language could be no other than the language of Egypt, brought into India by Osiris, of which, undoubtedly, the Greek was a dialect, as I think I have proved.'

Into these theories of Lord Monboddo's on Egypt and Osiris, we need not inquire at present. But it may be of interest to give one other extract, in order to show how well, apart from his men with, and his monkeys without, tails, Lord Monboddo could sift and handle the evidence that was placed before him:—

'To apply these observations to the similarities which Mr. Wilkins has discovered betwixt the Shanscrit and the Greek;—I will begin with these words, which must have been original words in all languages, as the things denoted by them must have been known in the first ages of civility, and have got names; so that it is impossible that one language could have borrowed them from another, unless it was a derivative or dialect of that language. Of this kind are the names of numbers, of the members of the human body, and of relations, such as that of father, mother, and brother. And first, as to numbers, the use of which must have been coeval with civil society. The words in the Shanscrit for the numbers, from one to ten are, *ek, dwee, tree, chatoor, panch, shat, sapt, aght, nara, das,* which certainly have an affinity to the Greek or Latin names for those numbers. Then they proceed towards twenty, saying ten and one, ten and two, and so forth, till they come to twenty; for their arithmetic is decimal as well as ours. Twenty they express by the word *veensatee*. Then they go on till they come to thirty, which they express by the word *treensut*, of which the word expressing three is part of the composition, as well as it is of the Greek and Latin names for those numbers. And in like manner they go on expressing forty, fifty, &c., by a like composition with the words expressing simple numerals, namely, four, five, &c., till they come to the number one hundred, which they express by *sat*, a word different from either the Greek or Latin name for that number. But, in this numeration, there is a very remarkable conformity betwixt the word in Shanscrit expressing twenty or twice ten, and the words in Greek and Latin expressing the same number; for in none of the three languages has the word any relation to the number two, which, by multiplying ten, makes twenty; such as the words expressing the numbers thirty, forty, &c., have to the words expressing three or four; for in Greek the word is *eikosi*, which expresses no relation to the number two; nor does the Latin *viginti*, but which appears to have more resemblance to the Shanscrit word *veensatee*. And thus it appears that in the anomalies of the two languages of Greek and Latin, there appears to be some conformity with the Shanscrit.'

Lord Monboddo compares the Sanskrit *pada* with the Greek *pous, podos*; the Sanskrit *nasa* with the

Latin *nasus*; the Sanskrit *deva*, god, with the Greek *Theos* and Latin *deus*; the Sanskrit *ap*, water, with the Latin *aqua*; the Sanskrit *vidhavâ* with the Latin *vidua*, widow. Sanskrit words such as *gonia*, for angle, *kentra*, for centre, *hora*, for hour, he points out as clearly of Greek origin, and imported into Sanskrit. He then proceeds to show the grammatical coincidences between Sanskrit and the classical languages. He dwells on compounds such as *tripada*, from *tri*, three, and *pada*, foot—a tripod; he remarks on the extraordinary fact that Sanskrit, like Greek, changes a positive into a negative adjective by the addition of the *a* privative; and he then produces what he seems to consider as the most valuable present that Mr. Wilkins could have given him, namely, the Sanskrit forms, *asmi*, I am; *asi*, thou art; *asti*, he is; *santi*, they are; forms clearly of the same origin as the corresponding forms, *esmi*, *eis*, *esti*, in Greek, and *sunt* in Latin.

Another Scotch philosopher, Dugald Stewart, was much less inclined to yield such ready submission. No doubt it must have required a considerable effort for a man brought up in the belief that Greek and Latin were either aboriginal languages, or modifications of Hebrew, to bring himself to acquiesce in the revolutionary doctrine that the classical languages were intimately related to a jargon of mere savages; for such all the subjects of the Great Mogul were then supposed to be. However, if the facts about Sanskrit were true, Dugald Stewart was too wise not to see that the conclusions drawn from them were inevitable. He therefore denied the reality of such a language as Sanskrit altogether, and wrote his famous essay to prove that Sanskrit had been put together, after the model of Greek and Latin, by those arch-forgers and liars the Brahmans, and that the whole of Sanskrit literature was an imposition. I mention this fact, because it shows, better than anything else, how violent a shock was given by the discovery of Sanskrit to prejudices most deeply engrained in the mind of every educated man. The most absurd arguments found favour for a time, if they could only furnish a loophole by which to escape from the unpleasant conclusion that Greek and Latin were of the same kith and kin as the language of the black inhabitants of India. The first who dared boldly to face both the facts and the conclusions of Sanskrit scholarship was the German poet, Frederick Schlegel. He had been in England during the peace of Amiens (1801–1802), and had acquired a smattering of Sanskrit from Mr. Alexander Hamilton. After carrying on his studies for some time at Paris, he published, in 1808, his work *On the Language and Wisdom of the Indians*. This work became the foundation of the science of language. Though published only two years after the first volume of Adelung's *Mithridates*, it is separated from that work by the same distance which separates the Copernican from the Ptolemean system. Schlegel was not a great scholar. Many of his statements have proved erroneous; and nothing would be easier than to dissect his essay and hold it up to ridicule. But Schlegel was a man of genius; and when a new science is to be created, the imagination of the poet is wanted, even more than the accuracy of the scholar. It surely required somewhat of poetic vision to embrace with *one* glance the languages of India, Persia, Greece, Italy, and Germany, and to rivet them together by the simple name of Indo-Germanic. This was Schlegel's work; and in the history of the intellect, it has been truly called 'the discovery of a new world.'

We shall see, in our next lecture, how Schlegel's idea was taken up in Germany, and how it led almost immediately to a genealogical classification of the principal languages of mankind.

LECTURE V.

GENEALOGICAL CLASSIFICATION OF LANGUAGES.

WE traced, in our last lecture, the history of the various attempts at a classification of languages to the year 1808, the year in which Frederick Schlegel published his little work on *The Language and Wisdom of the Indians*. This work was like the wand of a magician. It pointed out the place where a mine should be opened; and it was not long before some of the most distinguished scholars of the day began to sink their shafts and raise the ore. For a time, everybody who wished to learn Sanskrit had to come to England. Bopp, Schlegel, Lassen, Rosen, Burnouf, all spent some time in this country, copying manuscripts at the East-India House, and receiving assistance from Wilkins, Colebrooke, Wilson, and other distinguished members of the old Indian Civil Service. The first minute and scholar-like comparison of the grammar of Sanskrit with that of Greek and Latin, Persian, and German, was made by Francis Bopp, in 1816.* Other essays of his followed; and in 1833 appeared the first volume of his *Comparative Grammar of Sanskrit, Zend, Greek, Latin, Lithuanian, Slavonic, Gothic, and German*. This work was not finished till nearly twenty years later, in 1852;† but it will

---

* *Conjugationssystem*, Frankfurt, 1816.
† New edition in 1856, much improved.

form for ever the safe and solid foundation of comparative philology. August Wilhelm von Schlegel, the brother of Frederick Schlegel, used the influence which he had acquired as a German poet, to popularise the study of Sanskrit in Germany. His *Indische Bibliothek* was published from 1819 to 1830, and though chiefly intended for Sanskrit literature, it likewise contained several articles on Comparative Philology. This new science soon found a still more powerful patron in Wilhelm von Humboldt, the worthy brother of Alexander von Humboldt, and at that time one of the leading statesmen in Prussia. His essays, chiefly on the philosophy of language, attracted general attention during his lifetime; and he left a lasting monument of his studies in his great work on the Kawi language, which was published after his death, in 1836. Another scholar who must be reckoned among the founders of Comparative Philology is Professor Pott, whose *Etymological Researches* appeared first in 1833 and 1836.[*] More special in its purpose, but based on the same general principles, was Grimm's *Teutonic Grammar*, a work which has truly been called colossal. Its publication occupied nearly twenty years, from 1819 to 1837. We ought, likewise, to mention here the name of an eminent Dane, Erasmus Rask, who devoted himself to the study of the northern languages of Europe. He started, in 1816, for Persia and India, and was the first to acquire a knowledge of Zend, the language of the Zend-Avesta; but he died before he had time to publish all the results of his learned researches. He had proved, however, that

[*] Second edition, 1859 and 1861. Pott's work on the *Language of the Gipsies*, 1846; his work on *Proper Names*, 1856.

the sacred language of the Parsis was closely connected with the sacred language of the Brahmans, and that, like Sanskrit, it had preserved some of the earliest formations of Indo-European speech. These researches into the ancient Persian language were taken up again by one of the greatest scholars that France ever produced, by Eugène Burnouf. Though the works of Zoroaster had been translated before by Anquetil Duperron, his was only a translation of a modern Persian translation of the original. It was Burnouf who, by means of his knowledge of Sanskrit and Comparative Grammar, deciphered for the first time the very words of the founder of the ancient religion of light. He was, likewise, the first to apply the same key with real success to the cuneiform inscriptions of Darius and Xerxes; and his premature death will long be mourned, not only by those who, like myself, had the privilege of knowing him personally and attending his lectures, but by all who have the interest of oriental literature and of real oriental scholarship at heart.

I cannot give here a list of all the scholars who followed in the track of Bopp, Schlegel, Humboldt, Grimm, and Burnouf. How the science of language has flourished and abounded may best be seen in the library of any comparative philologist. There has been for the last ten years a special journal of Comparative Philology in Germany. The Philological Society in London publishes every year a valuable volume of its transactions; and in almost every continental university there is a professor of Sanskrit who lectures likewise on Comparative Grammar and the science of language.

But why, it may naturally be asked — why should

the discovery of Sanskrit have wrought so complete a change in the classificatory study of languages? If Sanskrit had been the primitive language of mankind, or at least the parent of Greek, Latin, and German, we might understand that it should have led to quite a new classification of these tongues. But Sanskrit does not stand to Greek, Latin, the Teutonic, Celtic, and Slavonic languages, in the relation of Latin to French, Italian, and Spanish. Sanskrit, as we saw before, could not be called their parent, but only their elder sister. It occupies with regard to the classical languages a position analogous to that which Provençal occupies with regard to the modern Romance dialects. This is perfectly true; but it was exactly this necessity of determining distinctly and accurately the mutual relation of Sanskrit and the other members of the same family of speech, which led to such important results, and particularly to the establishment of the laws of phonetic change as the only safe means for measuring the various degrees of relationship of cognate dialects, and thus restoring the genealogical tree of human speech. When Sanskrit had once assumed its right position, when people had once become familiarised with the idea that there must have existed a language more primitive than Greek, Latin, and Sanskrit, and forming the common background of these three, as well as of the Teutonic, Celtic, and Slavonic branches of speech, all languages seemed to fall by themselves into their right position. The key of the puzzle was found, and all the rest was merely a work of patience. The same arguments by which Sanskrit and Greek had been proved to hold co-ordinate rank were perceived to apply with equal strength to Latin and Greek; and after Latin had once been shown to be more primitive on many points than Greek, it was easy to see that the Teutonic, the Celtic, and the Slavonic languages also, contained each a number of formations which it was impossible to derive from Sanskrit, Greek, or Latin. It was perceived that all had to be treated as co-ordinate members of one and the same class.

The first great step in advance, therefore, which was made in the classification of languages, chiefly through the discovery of Sanskrit, was this, that scholars were no longer satisfied with the idea of a general relationship, but began to inquire for the different degrees of relationship in which each member of a class stood to another. Instead of mere *classes*, we hear now for the first time of well-regulated *families* of language.

A second step in advance followed naturally from the first. Whereas, for establishing in a general way the common origin of certain languages, a comparison of numerals, pronouns, prepositions, adverbs, and the most essential nouns and verbs, had been sufficient, it was soon found that a more accurate standard was required for measuring the more minute degrees of relationship. Such a standard was supplied by Comparative Grammar; that is to say, by an intercomparison of the grammatical forms of languages supposed to be related to each other; such intercomparison being carried out according to certain laws which regulate the phonetic changes of letters.

A glance at the modern history of language will make this clearer. There could never be any doubt that the so-called Romance languages, Italian, Wallachian,

Provençal, French, Spanish, and Portuguese, were closely related to each other. Everybody could see that they were all derived from Latin. But one of the most distinguished French scholars, Raynouard, who has done more for the history of the Romance languages and literature than any one else, maintained that Provençal only was the daughter of Latin; whereas French, Italian, Spanish, and Portuguese were the daughters of Provençal. He maintained that Latin passed, from the seventh to the ninth century, through an intermediate stage, which he called Langue Romane, and which he endeavoured to prove was the same as the Provençal of Southern France, the language of the Troubadours. According to him, it was only after Latin had passed through this uniform metamorphosis, represented by the Langue Romane or Provençal, that it became broken up into the various Romance dialects of Italy, France, Spain, and Portugal. This theory, which was vigorously attacked by August Wilhelm von Schlegel, and afterwards minutely criticised by Sir George Cornewall Lewis, can only be refuted by a comparison of the Provençal grammar with that of the other Romance dialects. And here, if you take the auxiliary verb *to be*, and compare its forms in Provençal and French, you will see at once that, on several points, French has preserved the original Latin forms in a more primitive state than Provençal, and that, therefore, it is impossible to classify French as the daughter of Provençal, and as the granddaughter of Latin. We have in Provençal:—

sem, corresponding to the French *nous sommes*
etz   ,,   *vous êtes*
son   ,,   *ils sont*

And it would be a grammatical miracle if crippled forms, such as *sem*, *etz*, and *son*, had been changed back again into the more healthy, more primitive, more Latin, *sommes*, *êtes*, *sont*; *sumus*, *estis*, *sunt*.

Let us apply the same test to Sanskrit, Greek, and Latin; and we shall see how their mutual genealogical position is equally determined by a comparison of their grammatical forms. It is as impossible to derive Latin from Greek, or Greek from Sanskrit, as it is to treat French as a modification of Provençal. Keeping to the auxiliary verb *to be*, we find that *I am* is in

Sanskrit	Greek	Lithuanian
asmi	*esmi*	*esmi*

The root is *as*, the termination *mi*.

Now, the termination of the second person is *si*, which, together with *as*, or *es*, would make

| *as-si* | *es-si* | *es-si* |

But here Sanskrit, as far back as its history can be traced, has reduced *assi* to *asi*; and it would be impossible to suppose that the perfect, or, as they are sometimes called, organic, forms in Greek and Lithuanian, *es-si*, could first have passed through the mutilated state of the Sanskrit *asi*.

The third person is the same in Sanskrit, Greek, and Lithuanian, *as-ti* or *es-ti*; and, with the loss of the final *i*, we recognise the Latin *est*, Gothic *ist*, and Russian *est'*.

The same auxiliary verb can be made to furnish sufficient proof that Latin never could have passed through the Greek, or what used to be called the Pelasgic stage, but that both are independent modifications of the same original language. In the singular, Latin is less primitive than Greek; for *sum* stands for *es-um*, *es* for *es-is*, *est* for *es-ti*. In the first person plural, too, *sumus* stands for *es-umus*, the Greek *es-mes*, the Sanskrit *'smas*. The second person, *es-tis*, is equal to Greek *es-te*, and more primitive than Sanskrit *stha*. But in the third person plural Latin is more primitive than Greek. The regular form would be *as-anti*; this, in Sanskrit, is changed into *santi*. In Greek, the initial *s* is dropped, and the Æolic *enti* is finally reduced to *eisi*. The Latin, on the contrary, has kept the radical *s*, and it would be perfectly impossible to derive the Latin *sunt* from the Greek *eisi*.

I need hardly say that the modern English, *I am, thou art, he is*, are only secondary modifications of the same primitive verb. We find in Gothic

im	for	*ism*
is	„	*iss*
ist		

The Anglo-Saxon changes the *s* into *r*, thus giving

singular:	*eom* for *eorm*	plural:	*sind* for *isind*
	eart „ *ears*	„	*sind*
	is „ *is*	„	*sind*

By applying this test to all languages, the founders of comparative philology soon reduced the principal dialects of Europe and Asia to certain families, and they were able in each family to distinguish different branches, each consisting again of numerous dialects, both ancient and modern.

There are many languages, however, which as yet have not been reduced to families, and though there is no reason to doubt that some of them will hereafter be comprehended in a system of genealogical classification, it is right to guard from the beginning against the common but altogether gratuitous supposition, that the principle of genealogical classification must be applicable to all. Genealogical classification is no doubt the most perfect of all classifications, but there are but few branches of physical science in which it can be carried out, except very partially. In the science of language, genealogical classification must rest chiefly on the formal or grammatical elements, which, after they have been affected by phonetic change, can be kept up only by a continuous tradition. We know that French, Italian, Spanish, and Portuguese must be derived from a common source, because they share grammatical forms in common, which none of these dialects could have supplied from their own resources, and which have no meaning, or, so to say, no life in any one of them. The termination of the imperfect *ba* in Spanish, *va* in Italian, by which *canto*, I sing, is changed into *cantaba* and *cantava*, has no separate existence, and no independent meaning in either of these modern dialects. It could not have been formed with the materials supplied by Spanish and Italian. It must have been handed down from an earlier generation in which this *ba* had a meaning. We trace it back to Latin *bam*, in *cantabam*, and here it can be proved that *bam* was originally an independent auxiliary verb, the same which exists in Sanskrit *bhavâmi*, and in the Anglo-Saxon *beom*, I am. Genealogical classification, therefore, applies properly only to decaying languages, to languages in which grammatical growth has been arrested, through the influence of literary cultivation; in which little new is added, everything old is retained as long as possible, and where what we call growth or history is nothing but the progress of phonetic corruption. But before languages decay, they have passed through a period of growth; and it seems to have been completely overlooked, that dialects which diverged during that early period, would naturally resist every attempt at genealogical classification. If you remember the manner in which, for instance, the plural was formed in Chinese, and other languages examined by us in a former Lecture, you will see that where each dialect may choose its own term expressive of plurality, such as *heap, class, kind, flock, cloud*, &c., it would be unreasonable to expect similarity in grammatical terminations, after these terms have been ground down by phonetic corruption to mere exponents of plurality. But, on the other hand, it would by no means follow that therefore these languages had no common origin. Languages may have a common origin, and yet the words which they originally employed for marking case, number, person, tense, and mood, having been totally different, the grammatical terminations to which these words would gradually dwindle down could not possibly yield any results if submitted to the analysis of comparative grammar. A genealogical classification of such languages is, therefore, from the nature of the case, simply impossible, at least if such classification is chiefly to be based on grammatical or formal evidence.

It might be supposed, however, that such languages, though differing in their grammatical articulation, would yet evince their common origin by the identity of their radicals or roots. No doubt, they will in many instances. They will probably have retained their numerals in common, some of their pronouns, and some of the commonest words of every-day life. But even here we must not expect too much, nor be surprised if we find even less than we expected. You remember how the names for father varied in the numerous Friesian dialects. Instead of *frater*, the Latin word for brother, you find *hermano* in Spanish. Instead of *ignis*, the Latin word for fire, you have in French *feu*, in Italian *fuoco*. Nobody would doubt the common origin of German and English; yet the English numeral 'the first,' though preserved in *Fürst* (princeps, prince), is quite different from the German 'Der Erste;' 'the second' is quite different from 'Der Zweite;' and there is no connection between the possessive pronoun *its* and the German *sein*. This dialectic freedom works on a much larger scale in ancient and illiterate languages; and those who have most carefully watched the natural growth of dialects will be the least surprised that dialects which had the same origin should differ, not only in their grammatical framework, but likewise in many of those test-words which are very properly used for discovering the relationship of literary languages. How it is possible to say anything about the relationship of such dialects we shall see hereafter. For the present, it is sufficient if I have made it clear why the principle of genealogical classification is not of necessity applicable to all languages; and secondly, why languages, though they cannot be classified genealogically, need not therefore be supposed to have been different from the beginning. The assertion so frequently repeated, that the impossibility of classing all languages genealogically proves the impossibility of a common origin of language, is nothing but a kind of scientific dogmatism which, more than anything else, has impeded the free progress of independent research.

But let us see now how far the genealogical classification of languages has advanced, how many families of human speech have been satisfactorily established. Let us remember what suggested to us the necessity of a genealogical classification. We wished to know the original intention of certain words and grammatical forms in English, and we saw that before we could attempt to fathom the origin of such words as 'I love,' and 'I loved,' we should have to trace them back to their most primitive state. We likewise found, by a reference to the history of the Romance dialects, that words existing in one dialect had frequently been preserved in a more primitive form in another, and that therefore it was of the highest importance to bring ancient languages into the same genealogical connection by which French, Italian, Spanish, and Portuguese are held together as the members of one family.

Beginning, therefore, with the living language of England, we traced it, without difficulty, to Anglo-Saxon. This carries us back to the seventh century after Christ, for it is to that date that Kemble and Thorpe refer the ancient English epic, the Beowulf. Beyond this we cannot go on English soil. But we know that the Saxons, the Angles, and Jutes came from the continent, and there their descendants, along the northern coast of Germany, still speak *Low German*,* or Nieder-Deutsch, which in the lar-

---

* ' Het echt engelsch is oud nederduitsch,' 'the genuine Eng-

bours of Antwerp, Bremen, and Hamburg, has been mistaken by many an English sailor for a corrupt English dialect. The Low-German comprehends many dialects in the north or the lowlands of Germany; but in Germany proper they are hardly ever used for literary purposes. The Friesian dialects are Low-German, so are the Dutch and Flemish. The Friesian had a literature of its own as early, at least, as the twelfth century, if not earlier.* The Dutch, which is still a national and literary language, though confined to a small area, can be traced back to literary documents of the sixteenth century. The Flemish, too, was at that time the language of the court of Flanders and Brabant, but has since been considerably encroached upon, though not yet extinguished, by the official languages of the kingdoms of Holland and Belgium. The oldest literary document of Low-German on the Continent is the Christian epic, the *Heljand* (Heljand=Heiland, the Healer or Saviour), which is preserved to us in two MSS. of the ninth century, and was written at that time for the benefit of the newly converted Saxons. We

lish is old Low-Dutch.'—Bilderdyk. See Delfortrie, *Analogie des Langues*, p. 13.

* ' Although the Old Friesian documents rank, according to their dates, with Middle rather than with Old German, the Friesian language appears there in a much more ancient stage, which very nearly approaches the Old High-German. The political isolation of the Friesians, and their noble attachment to their traditional manners and rights, have imparted to their language also a more conservative spirit. After the fourteenth century the old inflections of the Friesian decay most rapidly, whereas in the twelfth and thirteenth centuries they rival the Anglo-Saxon of the ninth and tenth centuries.'—Grimm, *German Grammar* (1st ed.), vol. i. p. lxviii.

have traces of a certain amount of literature in Saxon or Low-German from that time onward through the Middle Ages up to the seventeenth century. But little only of that literature has been preserved; and, after the translation of the Bible by Luther into High-German, the fate of Low-German literature was sealed.

The literary language of Germany is, and has been ever since the days of Charlemagne, the *High-German*. It is spoken in various dialects all over Germany.* Its history may be traced through three periods. The present, or New High-German period dates from Luther: the Middle High-German period extends from Luther backwards to the twelfth century; the Old High-German period extends from thence to the seventh century.

Thus we see that we can follow the High-German as well as the Low-German branch of Teutonic speech, back to about the seventh century after Christ. We must not suppose that before that time there was one common Teutonic language spoken by all German tribes, and that it afterwards diverged into two streams—the High and Low. There never was a common, uniform Teutonic language; nor is there any evidence to show that there existed at any time a uniform High-German or Low-German language, from which all High-German and Low-German dialects are respectively derived. We cannot derive Anglo-Saxon, Friesian, Flemish, Dutch, and Platt-Deutsch from the ancient Low-German, which is preserved in the continental Saxon of the ninth century. All we can say is this, that these

---

* The dialects of Swabia (the Allemanish), of Bavaria and Austria, of Franconia along the Main, and of Saxony, &c.

various Low-German dialects in England, Holland, Friesia, and Lower Germany, passed at different times through the same stages, or, so to say, the same latitudes, of grammatical growth. We may add that, with every century that we go back, the convergence of these dialects becomes more and more decided; but there is no evidence to justify us in admitting the historical reality of *one* primitive and uniform Low-German language from which they were all derived. This is a mere creation of grammarians who cannot understand a multiplicity of dialects without a common type. They would likewise demand the admission of a primitive High-German language, as the source, not only of the literary Old, Middle, and Modern High-German, but likewise of all the local dialects of Austria, Bavaria, Swabia, and Franconia. And they would wish us to believe that, previous to the separation into High and Low German, there existed one complete Teutonic language, as yet neither High nor Low, but containing the germs of both. Such a system may be convenient for the purposes of grammatical analysis, but it becomes mischievous as soon as these grammatical abstractions are invested with an historical reality. As there were families, clans, confederacies, and tribes, before there was a nation, so there were dialects before there was a language. The grammarian who postulates an historical reality for the one primitive type of Teutonic speech, is no better than the historian who believes in a *Francus*, the grandson of Hector, and the supposed ancestor of all the Franks, or in a *Brutus*, the mythical father of all the Britons. When the German races descended, one after the other, from the Danube and from the Baltic, to take possession of Italy and the Roman provinces — when the Goths, the Lombards, the Vandals, the Franks, the Burgundians, each under their own Kings, and with their own laws and customs, settled in Italy, Gaul, and Spain, to act their several parts in the last scene of the Roman tragedy — we have no reason to suppose that they all spoke one and the same dialect. If we possessed any literary documents of those ancient German races, we should find them all dialects again, some with the peculiarities of High, others with those of Low, German. Nor is this mere conjecture: for it so happens that, by some fortunate accident, the dialect of one at least of these ancient German races has been preserved to us in the Gothic translation of the Bible by Bishop Ulfilas.

I must say a few words on this remarkable man. The accounts of ecclesiastical historians with regard to the date and the principal events in the life of Ulfilas are very contradictory. This is partly owing to the fact that Ulfilas was an Arian bishop, and that the accounts which we possess of him come from two opposite sides, from Arian and Athanasian writers. Although in forming an estimate of his character it would be necessary to sift this contradictory evidence, it is but fair to suppose that, when dates and simple facts in the life of the Bishop have to be settled, his own friends had better means of information than the orthodox historians. It is, therefore, from the writings of his own coreligionists that the chronology and the historical outline of the Bishop's life should be determined.

The principal writers to be consulted are Philostorgius, as preserved by Photius, and Auxentius, as preserved by Maximinus in a MS. lately discovered by Professor Waitz* in the Library at Paris. (Supplement. Latin. No. 594.) This MS. contains some writings of Hilarius, the first two books of Ambrosius *De Fide*, and the acts of the Council of Aquileja (381). On the margin of this MS. Maximinus repeated the beginning of the acts of the Council of Aquileja, adding remarks of his own in order to show how unfairly Palladius had been treated in that council by Ambrose. He jotted down his own views on the Arian controversy; and on fol. 282, seq., he copied an account of Ulfilas written by Auxentius, the bishop of Dorostorum (Silistria on the Danube), a pupil of Ulfilas. This is followed again by some dissertations of Maximinus, and on fol. 314—327, a treatise addressed to Ambrose by a Semi-Arian, a follower of Eusebius, possibly by Prudentius himself, was copied and slightly abbreviated for his own purposes by Maximinus.

It is from Auxentius, as copied by Maximinus, that we learn that Ulfilas died at Constantinople, where he had been invited by the emperor to a disputation. This could not have been later than the year 381, because, according to the same Auxentius, Ulfilas had been bishop for forty years, and, according to Philostorgius, he had been consecrated by Eusebius. Now Eusebius of Nicomedia died 341, and as Philostorgius says that Ulfilas was consecrated by 'Eusebius and the bishops who were with him,' the consecration has been referred with great plausibility to the beginning of the year 341, when Eusebius presided at the Synod of Antioch. As Ulfilas was

---

* *Ueber das Leben und die Lehre des Ulfila*, Hannover, 1840; *Ueber das Leben des Ulfila* von Dr. Bessell, Göttingen, 1860.

thirty years old at the time of his consecration, he must have been born in 311, and as he was seventy years of age when he died at Constantinople, his death must have taken place in 381.

Professor Waitz fixed the death of Ulfilas in 388, because it is stated by Auxentius that other Arian bishops had come with Ulfilas on his last journey to Constantinople, and had actually obtained the promise of a new council from the emperor, but that the heretical party, i.e. the Athanasians, succeeded in getting a law published, prohibiting all disputation on the faith, whether in public or private. Maximinus, to whom we owe this notice, has added two laws from the Codex Theodosianus, which he supposed to have reference to this controversy, dated respectively 388 and 386. This shows that Maximinus himself was doubtful as to the exact date. Neither of these laws, however, is applicable to the case, as has been fully shown by Dr. Bessell. They are quotations from the Codex Theodosianus made by Maximinus at his own risk, and made in error. If the death of Ulfilas were fixed in 388, the important notice of Philostorgius, that Ulfilas was consecrated by Eusebius, would have to be surrendered, and we should have to suppose that as late as 388 Theodosius had been in treaty with the Arians, whereas after the year 383, when the last attempt at a reconciliation had been made by Theodosius, and had failed, no mercy was any longer shown to the party of Ulfilas and his friends.

If, on the contrary, Ulfilas died at Constantinople in 381, he might well have been called there by the Emperor Theodosius, not to a council, but to a disputation (ad disputationem), as Dr. Bessell ingeniously maintains, against the Psathyropolistæ,* a new sect of Arians at Constantinople. About the same time, in 380, Sozomen† refers to efforts made by the Arians to gain influence with Theodosius. He mentions, like Auxentius, that these efforts were defeated, and a law published to forbid disputations on the nature of God. This law exists in the Codex Theodosianus, and is dated January 10, 381. But what is most important is, that this law actually revokes a rescript that had been obtained fraudulently by the Arian heretics, thus confirming the statement of Auxentius that the emperor had held out to him and his party a promise of a new council.

We now return to Ulfilas. He was born in 311. His parents, as Philostorgius tells us, were of Cappadocian origin, and had been carried away by the Goths as captives from a place called Sadagolthina, near the town of Parnassus. It was under Valerian and Gallienus (about 267) that the Goths made this raid from Europe to Asia, Galatia, and Cappadocia, and the Christian captives whom they carried back to the Danube were the first to spread the light of the Gospel among the Goths. Philostorgius was himself a Cappadocian, and there is no reason to doubt this statement of his on the parentage of Ulfilas. Ulfilas was born among the Goths; Gothic was his native language, though he was able in after-life to speak and write both in Latin and Greek. Philostorgius, after speaking of the death of Crispus (326), and before proceeding to the last years of Constantine, says that 'about that time' Ulfilas led his Goths from beyond the Danube into the Roman Empire. They

---

* Bossell, l. c. p. 38. † Sozomenus, H. E. vii. 6.

had to leave their country, being persecuted on account of their Christianity. Ulfilas was the leader of the faithful flock, and came to Constantine (not Constantius) as ambassador. This must have been before 337, the year of Constantine's death. It may have been in 328, when Constantine had gained a victory over the Goths; and though Ulfilas was then only seventeen years of age, this would be no reason for rejecting the testimony of Philostorgius, who says that Constantine treated Ulfilas with great respect, and called him the Moses of his time. Having led his faithful flock across the Danube into Mœsia, he might well have been compared by the emperor to Moses leading the Israelites from Egypt through the Red Sea. It is true that Auxentius institutes the same comparison between Ulfilas and Moses, after stating that Ulfilas had been received with great honours by Constantius, not by Constantine. But this refers to what took place after Ulfilas had been for seven years bishop among the Goths, in 348, and does not invalidate the statement of Philostorgius as to the earlier intercourse between Ulfilas and Constantine. Sozomen * clearly distinguishes between the first crossing of the Danube by the Goths, with Ulfilas as their ambassador, and the later attacks of Athanarich on Fridigern or Fritiger, which led to the settlement of the Goths in the Roman Empire. We must suppose that, after having crossed the Danube, Ulfilas remained for some time with his Goths, or at Constantinople. Auxentius says that he officiated as Lector, and it was only when he had reached the requisite age of thirty, that he was made bishop by

* *H. E.* vi. 3, 7.

Eusebius in 341. He passed the first seven years of his episcopate among the Goths, and the remaining thirty-three of his life 'in solo Romaniæ,' where he had migrated together with Fritiger and the Thervingi. There is some confusion as to the exact date of the Gothic Exodus, but it is not at all unlikely that Ulfilas acted as their leader on more than one occasion.

There is little more to be learnt about Ulfilas from other sources. What is said by ecclesiastical historians about the motives of his adopting the doctrines of Arius, and his changing from one side to the other, deserves no credit. Ulfilas, according to his own confession, was always an Arian (semper sic credidi). Socrates says that Ulfilas was present at the Synod of Constantinople in 360, which may be true, though neither Auxentius nor Philostorgius mentions it. The author of the Acts of Nicetas speaks of Ulfilas as present at the Council of Nicæa, in company with Theophilus. Theophilus, it is true, signed his name as a Gothic bishop at that council, but there is nothing to confirm the statement that Ulfilas, then fourteen years of age, was with Theophilus.

Ulfilas translated the whole Bible, except the Books of Kings. For the Old Testament he used the Septuagint; for the New, the Greek text, but not exactly in that form in which we have it. Unfortunately, the greater part of his work has been lost, and we have only considerable portions of the Gospels, all the genuine epistles of St. Paul, though these again not complete; fragments of a Psalm, of Ezra, and Nehemiah.*

---

* Auxentius thus speaks of Ulfilas (*Waitz*): p. 19, 'Et [ita prædic]anto et per Cristum cum dilectione Deo patri gratias

Though Ulfilas belonged to the western Goths, his translation was used by all Gothic tribes, when

agente, haec et his' similia exsequente, quadraginta annis in episcopatu glorioso florens, apostolica gratia Graecam et Latinam et Goticam linguam sine intermissione in una et sola eclesia Cristi predicavit. .... Qui et ipsis tribus linguis plures tractatus et multas interpretationes volentibus ad utilitatem et ad aedificationem, sibi ad aeternam memoriam et mercedem post se dereliquid. Quem condigno laudare non sufficio et penitus tacere non audeo: cui plus omnium ego sum debitor, quantum et amplius in me laboravit, qui me a prima etate mea a parentibus meis discipulum suscepit et sacras litteras docuit et veritatem manifestavit et per misericordiam Dei et gratiam Cristi et carnaliter et spiritaliter ut filium suum in fide educavit.

'Ille Dei providentia et Cristi misericordia propter multorum salutem in gente Gothorum de lectore triginta annorum episkopus est ordinatus, ut non solum esset heres Dei et coheres Cristi, sed et in hoc per gratiam Cristi imitator Cristi et sanctorum ejus, ut quemadmodum sanctus David triginta annorum rex et profeta est constitutus, ut regeret et doceret populum Dei et filios Hisdrael, ita et iste beatus tamquam profeta est manifestatus et sacerdos Cristi ordinatus, ut regeret et corrigeret et doceret et aedificaret gentem Gothorum; quod et Deo volente et Cristo auxiliante per ministerium ipsius admirabiliter est adinpletum, et sicuti Iosef in Aegypto triginta annorum est manifes[tatus et] quemadmodum dominus et Deus noster Ihesus Cristus filius Dei triginta annorum secundum carnem constitutus et baptizatus, coepit evangelium predicare et animas hominum pascere: ita et iste sanctus, ipsius Cristi dispositione et ordinatione, et in famo et penuria predicationis indifferenter agentem ipsam gentem Gothorum secundum evangelicam et apostolicam et profeticam regulam emendavit et vivere [Deo] docuit, et cristianos, vero cristianos esse, manifestavit et multiplicavit.

'Ubi et ex invidia et operatione inimici thune ab inreligioso et sacrilego indice Gothorum tyrannico terrore in varbarico cristianorum persecutio est excitata, ut satanas, qui male facere cupiebat, nolen[s] faceret bene, ut quos desiderabat prevaricatores facere et desertores, Cristo opitulante et propugnante, fierent martyres et confessores, ut persecutor confunderetur, et qui persecutionem patiebantur, coronarentur ut hic, qui temtabat vincere,

they advanced into Spain and Italy. The Gothic language died out in the ninth century, and after the

> victus erubesceret, et qui temtabantur, victores gauderent. Ubi et post multorum servorum et ancillarum Cristi gloriosum martyrium, imminente vehementer ipsa persecutione, conpletis septem annis tantummodo in episkopatum, supradictus sanctissimus vir beatus Ulfila cum grandi populo confessorum de varbarico pulsus, in solo Romaniae a tha[n]c beatae memorie Constantio principe honorifice est susceptus, ut sicuti Deus per Moysem de potentia et violentia Faraonis et Egyptorum po[pulum s]uum l[iberav]it [et rubrum] mare transire fecit et sibi servire providit, ita et per nepo dictum Deus confessores sancti filii sui unigeniti de varbarico liberavit et per Danubium transire fecit, et in montibus secundum sanctorum imitationem sibi servire de[crevit] . . . . . eo populo in solo Romaniae, ubi sine illis septem annis triginta et tribus annis veritatem predicavit, ut et in hoc quorum sanctorum imitator erat [similis esset], quod quadraginta annorum spatium et tempus ut multos . . . . . re et . . . . s[an]orum . . . . . a vita.' . . 'Qu[i] c[um] precepto imperiali, conpletis quadraginta annis, ad Constantinopolitanam urbem ad disputationem . . . . . contra p . , . le . . . [p] . t . etas perrexit, et eundo in . . . . an . . ue . p . . . ocias sibi ax . . . . . to docerent et contestarent[ur] . . . . abat, et inge . e . . . . supradictam [ci]vitatem, recogitato ei im . . . . de statu concilii, ne arguerentur miseris miserabiliores, proprio judicio damnati et perpetuo supplicio plectendi, statim cepit infirmari ; qua in infirmitate susceptus est ad similitudine Eliaei prophete. Considerare modo oportet meritum viri, qui ad hoc duce Domino obit Constantinopolim, immo vero Cristianopolim, ut sanctus et immaculatus sacerdos Cristi a sanctis et consacerdotibus, a dignis dignus digno [per] tantam multitudinem cristianorum pro meritis [suis] mire et gloriose honoraretur.'—(Bessell, p. 37.)
>
> 'Unde et cum sancto Hulfila ceterisque consortibus ad alium comitatum Constantinopolis venissent, illique etiam et imperatore adissent, atque eis promissum fuisset concil[li]um, ut sanctus Aux[en]tius exposuit, [a]gnite promissi[o]ne profati pr[e]positi heretic[i] omnibus viribus[a] institerunt u[t] lex daretur, q[uae] concilium pro[hi]beret, sed nec p[ri]vatim in domo [nec] in publico, vel i[n] quolibet loco di[s]putatio de fide haberetur, sic[ut] textus indicat [lo]gis, etc.'—(Waitz, p. 23 ; Bessell, p. 15.)

extinction of the great Gothic empires, the translation of Ulfilas was lost and forgotten. But a MS. of the fifth century had been preserved in the Abbey of Werden, and towards the end of the sixteenth century, a man of the name of Arnold Mercator, who was in the service of William IV., the Landgrave of Hessia, drew attention to this old parchment containing large fragments of the translation of Ulfilas. The MS., known as the Codex Argenteus, was afterwards transferred to Prague, and when Prague was taken in 1648 by Count Königsmark, he carried this Codex to Upsala in Sweden, where it is still preserved as one of the greatest treasures. The parchment is purple, the letters in silver, and the MS. bound in solid silver.

In 1818, Cardinal Mai and Count Castiglione discovered some more fragments in the monastery of Bobbio, where they had probably been preserved ever since the Gothic empire of Theodoric the Great in Italy had been destroyed.

Ulfilas must have been a man of extraordinary power to conceive, for the first time, the idea of translating the Bible into the vulgar language of his people. At his time, there existed in Europe but two languages which a Christian bishop would have thought himself justified in employing, Greek and Latin. All other languages were still considered as barbarous. It required a prophetic sight, a faith in the destinies of these half-savage tribes, and a conviction also of the utter effeteness of the Roman and Byzantine empires, before a bishop could have brought himself to translate the Bible into the vulgar dialect of his barbarous countrymen. Soon after the death of Ulfilas, the number of Christian

Goths at Constantinople had so much increased as to induce Chrysostom, the bishop of Constantinople (397–405), to establish a church in the capital, where the service was to be read in Gothic.*

The language of Ulfilas, the Gothic, belongs, through its phonetic structure, to the Low-German class, but in its grammar it is, *with few exceptions*, far more primitive than the Anglo-Saxon of the Beowulf, or the Old High-German of Charlemagne. These few exceptions, however, are very important, for they show that it would be grammatically, and therefore historically, impossible to derive either Anglo-Saxon or High-German, or both,† from Gothic. It would be impossible, for instance, to treat the first person plural of the indicative present, the Old High-German *nerjamês*, as a corruption of the Gothic *nasjam*; for we know, from the Sanskrit *masi*, the Greek *mes*, the Latin *mus*, that this was the original termination of the first person plural.

Gothic is but one of the numerous dialects of the German race; other dialects became the feeders of the literary languages of the British Isles, of Holland, Friesia, and of Low and High Germany, others became extinct, and others rolled on from century to century unheeded, and without ever producing any literature at all. It is because Gothic is the only one of these parallel dialects that can be traced back to the fourth century, whereas the others disappear from our sight in the seventh, that it has been mistaken by some for the original source of all

---

* Theodoret, H. E. V. 30.
† For instances where Old High-German is more primitive than Gothic, see Schleicher, *Zeitschrift für V. S.* b. iv. s. 266; Bopp, *ibid.* b. v. s. 69; Pott, *Etym. Forsch.* ii. p. 57, note.

Teutonic speech. The same arguments, however, which we used against Raynouard, to show that Provençal could not be considered as the parent of the six Romance dialects, would tell with equal force against the pretensions of Gothic to be considered as more than the eldest sister of the Teutonic branch of speech.

There is, in fact, a third stream of Teutonic speech, which asserts its independence as much as High-German and Low-German, and which it would be impossible to place in any but a co-ordinate position with regard to Gothic, Low and High-German. This is the *Scandinavian* branch. It consists at present of three literary dialects, those of Sweden, Denmark, and Iceland, and of various local dialects, particularly in the secluded valleys and fiords of Norway,* where, however, the literary language is Danish.

It is commonly supposed † that, as late as the eleventh century, identically the same language was spoken in Sweden, Norway, and Denmark, and that this language was preserved almost intact in Iceland, while in Sweden and Denmark it grew into two new national dialects. Nor is there any doubt that the Icelandic skald recited his poems in Iceland, Norway, Sweden, Denmark, nay, even among his countrymen in England and Gardariki, without fear of not being understood, till, as it is said, William introduced Welsh, i.e. French, into England, and Slavonic tongues grew up in the east.‡ But though one and the same language (then called Danish

---

* See Schleicher, *Deutsche Sprache*, p. 94.
† *Ibid.* s 60.
‡ Weinhold, *Altnordisches Leben*, p. 27; *Gunnlaugssaga*, c. 7.

or Norrœnish) was understood, I doubt whether one and the same language was spoken by all Northmen, and whether the first germs of Swedish and Danish did not exist long before the eleventh century, in the dialects of the numerous clans and tribes of the Scandinavian race. That race is clearly divided into two branches, called by Swedish scholars the East and West Scandinavian. The former would be represented by the old language of Norway and Iceland, the latter by Swedish and Danish. This division of the Scandinavian race had taken place before the Northmen settled in Sweden and Norway. The western division migrated westward from Russia, and crossed over from the continent to the Aland Islands, and from thence to the southern coast of the peninsula. The eastern division travelled along the Bothnian Gulf, passing the country occupied by the Finns and Lapps, and settled in the northern highlands, spreading towards the south and west.

The earliest fragments of Scandinavian speech are preserved in the two *Eddas*, the elder or poetical Edda containing old mythic poems, the younger or Snorri's Edda giving an account of the ancient mythology in prose. Both Eddas were composed, not in Norway, but in Iceland, an island about as large as Ireland, and which became first known through some Irish monks who settled there in the eighth century.* In the ninth century voyages of discovery were made to Iceland by Naddodd, Gardar, and Flokki, 860-870, and soon after the remote island, distant about 750 English miles from Norway, became a kind of America to the Puritans and Republicans of the Scandinavian peninsula. Harald

* See Dasent's *Burnt Njal*, Introduction.

Haarfagr (850-933) had conquered most of the Norwegian kings, and his despotic sway tended to reduce the northern freemen to a state of vassalage. Those who could not resist, and could not bring themselves to yield to the sceptre of Harald, left their country and migrated to France, to England, and to Iceland (874). They were mostly nobles and freemen, and they soon established in Iceland an aristocratic republic, such as they had had in Norway before the days of Harald. This northern republic flourished; it adopted Christianity in the year 1000. Schools were founded, two bishoprics were established, and classical literature was studied with the same zeal with which their own national poems and laws had been collected and interpreted by native scholars and historians. The Icelanders were famous travellers, and the names of Icelandic students are found not only in the chief cities of Europe, but in the holy places of the East. At the beginning of the twelfth century Iceland counted 50,000 inhabitants. Their intellectual and literary activity lasted to the beginning of the thirteenth century, when the island was conquered by Hakon VI., king of Norway. In 1380, Norway, together with Iceland, was united with Denmark; and when, in 1814, Norway was ceded to Sweden, Iceland remained, as it is still, under Danish sway.

The old poetry which flourished in Norway in the eighth century, and which was cultivated by the skalds in the ninth, would have been lost in Norway itself had it not been for the jealous care with which it was preserved by the emigrants of Iceland. The most important branch of their traditional poetry were short songs (hliod or Quida), relating the deeds of their gods and heroes. It is impossible to determine their age, but they existed at least previous to the migration of the Northmen to Iceland, and probably as early as the seventh century, the same century which yields the oldest remnants of Anglo-Saxon, Low-German, and High-German. They were collected in the middle of the twelfth century by *Saemund Sigfusson* (died 1133). In 1643 a similar collection was discovered in MSS. of the thirteenth century, and published under the title of *Edda*, or Great-Grandmother. This collection is called the old or poetic Edda, in order to distinguish it from a later work ascribed to Snorri Sturluson (died 1241). This, the younger or prose Edda, consists of three parts: the mocking of Gylfi, the speeches of Bragi, and the Skalda, or *Ars poetica*. Snorri Sturluson has been called the Herodotus of Iceland; and his chief work is the *Heimskringla*, the world-ring, which contains the northern history from the mythic times to the time of King Magnus Erlingsson (died 1177). It was probably in preparing this history that, like Cassiodorus, Saxo Grammaticus, Paulus Diaconus, and other historians of the same class, Snorri collected the old songs of the people; for his *Edda*, and particularly his *Skalda*, are full of ancient poetic fragments.

The *Skalda*, and the rules which it contains, represent the state of poetry in the thirteenth century; and nothing can be more artificial, nothing more different from the genuine poetry of the old *Edda*, than this *Ars poetica* of Snorri Sturluson. One of the chief features of this artificial or skaldic poetry was that nothing should be called by its proper name. A ship was not to be called a ship, but the beast of the sea; blood, not blood, but the dew of pain, or the water of the sword. A warrior was not spoken of as a warrior, but as an armed tree, the tree of battle. A sword was the flame of wounds. In this poetical language, which every skald was bound to speak, there were no less than 115 names for Odin; an island could be called by 120 synonymous titles. The specimens of ancient poetry which Snorri quotes are taken from the skalds, whose names are well known in history, and who lived from the tenth to the thirteenth century. But he never quotes from any song contained in the old *Edda*,* whether it be that those songs were considered by himself as belonging to a different and much more ancient period of literature, or that they could not be used in illustration of the scholastic rules of skaldic poets, these very rules being put to shame by the simple style of the national poetry, which expressed what it had to express without effort and circumlocution.

We have thus traced the modern Teutonic dialects back to four principal channels—the *High-German*, *Low-German*, *Gothic*, and *Scandinavian*; and we have seen that these four, together with several minor dialects, must be placed in a co-ordinate position from the beginning, as so many varieties of Teutonic speech. This Teutonic speech may, for convenience sake, be spoken of as one—as one branch of that great family of language to which, as we shall see, it belongs; but

---

* The name Edda is not found before the fourteenth century. Snorri Sturlason does not know the word Edda, nor any collection of ancient poems attributed to Saemund; and though Saemund may have made the first collection of national poetry, it is doubtful whether the work which we possess under his name is his.

it should always be borne in mind that this primitive and uniform language never had any real historical existence, and that, like all other languages, that of the Germans began with dialects which gradually formed themselves into several distinct national deposits.

We must now advance more rapidly, and, instead of the minuteness of an Ordnance-map, we must be satisfied with the broad outlines of Wyld's Great Globe in our survey of the languages which, together with the Teutonic, form the Indo-European or Aryan family of speech.

And first the Romance, or modern Latin languages. Leaving mere local dialects out of sight, we have at present six literary modifications of Latin, or, more correctly, of ancient Italian—the languages of Portugal, of Spain, of France, of Italy, of Wallachia,* and

---

* The people whom we call Wallachians, call themselves Románi, and their language Románia.

This Romance language is spoken in Wallachia and Moldavia, and in parts of Hungary, Transylvania, and Bessarabia. On the right bank of the Danube it occupies some parts of the old Thracia, Macedonia, and even Thessaly.

It is divided by the Danube into two branches: the Northern or Daco-romanic, and the Southern or Macedo-romanic. The former is less mixed, and has received a certain literary culture; the latter has borrowed a larger number of Albanian and Greek words, and has not yet been fixed grammatically.

The modern Wallachian is the daughter of the language spoken in the Roman province of Dacia.

The original inhabitants of Dacia were called Thracians, and their language Illyrian. We have hardly any remains of the ancient Illyrian language to enable us to form an opinion as to its relationship with Greek or any other family of speech.

219 B.C. the Romans conquered Illyria; 30 B.C. they took Moesia; and 107 A.D. the Emperor Trajan made Dacia a Roman province. At that time the Thracian population had been displaced by the advance of Sarmatian tribes, particularly the

of the Grisons of Switzerland, called the Roumansch or Romanese.* The Provençal, which, in the poetry of the Troubadours, attained at a very early time to a high literary excellence, has now sunk down to a mere *patois*. The earliest Provençal poem, the Song of Boëthius, is generally referred to the tenth century: Le Bœuf referred it to the eleventh. But in the lately discovered Song of Eulalia, we have now a specimen of the Langue d'Oil, or the ancient Northern French, anterior in date to the earliest poetic specimens of the Langue d'Oc, or the ancient Provençal. Nothing can be a better preparation for the study of the comparative grammar of the ancient Aryan languages than a careful perusal of the *Comparative Grammar of the Six Romance Languages* by Professor Diez.

Though in a general way we trace these six Romance languages back to Latin, yet it has been pointed out before that the classical Latin would fail to supply a complete explanation of their origin. Many of the ingredients of the Neo-Latin dialects must be sought for in the ancient dialects of Italy and her provinces. More than one dialect of Latin was spoken there before the rise of Rome, and some important fragments have been preserved to us, in inscriptions, of the

---

Yazyges. Roman colonists introduced the Latin language; and Dacia was maintained as a colony up to 272, when the Emperor Aurelian had to cede it to the Goths. Part of the Roman inhabitants then emigrated and settled south of the Danube.

In 489 the Slavonic tribes began their advance into Mœsia and Thracia. They were settled in Mœsia by 678, and eighty years later a province was founded in Macedonia, under the name of Slavinia.

* The entire Bible has been published by the Bible Society in Romanese, for the Grisons in Switzerland; and in Lower Romanese, or Enghadine, as spoken on the borders of the Tyrol.

Umbrian spoken in the North, and of the Oscan spoken to the south of Rome. The Oscan language, spoken by the Samnites, now rendered intelligible by the labours of Mommsen, had produced a literature before the time of Livius Andronicus; and the tables of Iguvium, so elaborately treated by Aufrecht and Kirchhoff, bear witness to a priestly literature among the Umbrians at a very early period. Oscan was still spoken under the Roman emperors, and so were minor local dialects in the south and the north. As soon as the literary language of Rome became classical and unchangeable, the first start was made in the future career of those dialects which, even at the time of Dante, are still called *vulgar* or *popular*.* A great deal, no doubt, of the corruption of these modern dialects is due to the fact that, in the form in which we know them after the eighth century, they are really Neo-Latin dialects as adopted by the Teutonic barbarians: full, not only of Teutonic words, but of Teutonic idioms, phrases, and constructions. French is provincial Latin as spoken by the Franks, a Teutonic race; and,to a smaller extent, the same *barbarising* has affected all other Roman dialects. But, from the very beginning, the stock with which the Neo-Latin dialects started was not the classical Latin, but the vulgar, local, provincial dialects of the middle, the lower, and the lowest classes of the Roman empire. Many of the words which give to French and Italian their classical appearance, are really of much later date, and were imported into them by mediæval

* 'E lo primo, che cominciò a dire siccome poeta volgare, si mosse però che volle fare intendere le sue parole a donna, alla quale era malagevole ad intendere versi Latini.'—Dante's *Vita Nuova*; *Opere Minori di Dante Alighieri*, tom. iii. p. 327. Firenze, 1857.

scholars, lawyers, and divines; thus escaping the rough treatment to which the original vulgar dialects were subjected by the Teutonic conquerors.

The next branch of the Indo-European family of speech is the *Hellenic*. Its history is well known from the time of Homer to the present day. The only remark which the comparative philologist has to make is that the idea of making Greek the parent of Latin is more preposterous than deriving English from German; the fact being that there are many forms in Latin more primitive than their corresponding forms in Greek. The idea of Pelasgians as the common ancestors of Greeks and Romans is another of those grammatical myths, but it hardly requires at present any serious refutation.

The fourth branch of our family is the *Celtic*. The Celts seem to have been the first of the Aryans to arrive in Europe; but the pressure of subsequent migrations, particularly of Teutonic tribes, has driven them towards the westernmost parts, and latterly from Ireland across the Atlantic. At present the only remaining dialects are the Kymric and Gaedhelic. The *Kymric* comprises the *Welsh*; the *Cornish*, lately extinct; and the *Armorican*, of Brittany. The *Gaedhelic* comprises the *Irish*; the *Gaelic* of the west coast of Scotland; and the dialect of the *Isle of Man*. Although these Celtic dialects are still spoken, the Celts themselves can no longer be considered an independent nation, like the Germans or Slaves. In former times, however, they not only enjoyed political autonomy, but asserted it successfully against Germans and Romans. Gaul, Belgium, and Britain were Celtic dominions, and the north of Italy was chiefly inhabited by them. In the time of Herodotus we find Celts in Spain;

and Switzerland, the Tyrol, and the country south of the Danube have once been the seats of Celtic tribes. But after repeated inroads into the regions of civilisation, familiarising Latin and Greek writers with the names of their kings, they disappear from the east of Europe. Brennus is supposed to mean king, the Welsh *brennin*. A Brennus conquered Rome (390), another Brennus threatened Delphi (280). And about the same time a Celtic colony settled in Asia, and founded Galatia, where the language spoken at the time of St. Jerome was still that of the Gauls. Celtic words may be found in German, Slavonic, and even in Latin, but only as foreign terms, and their amount is much smaller than commonly supposed. A far larger number of Latin and German words have since found their way into the modern Celtic dialects, and these have frequently been mistaken by Celtic enthusiasts for original words, from which German and Latin might, in their turn, be derived.

The fifth branch, which is commonly called *Slavonic*, I prefer to designate by the name of *Windic*, *Winidæ* being one of the most ancient and comprehensive names by which these tribes were known to the early historians of Europe. We have to divide these tribes into two divisions, the *Lettic* and the *Slavonic*, and we shall have to subdivide the Slavonic again into a *South-East Slavonic* and a *West Slavonic* branch.

The *Lettic* division consists of languages hardly known to the student of literature, but of great importance to the student of language. *Lettish* is the language now spoken in Kurland and Livonia. *Lithuanian* is the name given to a language still spoken by about 200,000 people in Eastern Prussia, and by more than a million of people in the coterminous parts of Russia. The earliest literary document of Lithuanian is a small catechism of 1547.* In this, and even in the language as now spoken by the Lithuanian peasant, there are some grammatical forms more primitive and more like Sanskrit than the corresponding forms in Greek and Latin.

The *Old Prussian*, which is nearly related to Lithuanian, became extinct in the seventeenth century, and the entire literature which it has left behind consists in an old catechism.

Lettish is the language of Kurland and Livonia, more modern in its grammar than Lithuanian, yet not immediately derived from it.

We now come to the *Slavonic* languages, properly so called. The eastern branch comprehends the *Russian* with various local dialects, the *Bulgarian*, and the *Illyrian*. The most ancient document of this eastern branch is the so-called Ecclesiastical Slavonic, i.e. the ancient Bulgarian, into which Cyrillus and Methodius translated the Bible, in the middle of the ninth century. This is still the authorised version † of the Bible for the whole Slavonic race; and to the student of the Slavonic languages, it is what Gothic is to the student of German. The modern Bulgarian, on the contrary, as far as grammatical forms are concerned, is the most reduced among the Slavonic dialects.

Illyrian is a convenient or inconvenient name to

* Schleicher, *Beiträge*, i. 19.
† Oldest dated MS. of 1056, written for Prince Ostromir. Some older MSS. are written with Glagolitic letters. Schleicher, *Beiträge*, b. I. s. 20.

comprehend the *Serrian*, *Croatian*, and *Slovinian* dialects. Literary fragments of *Slovinian* go back as far as the tenth century.*

The western branch comprehends the language of *Poland*, *Bohemia*, and *Lusatia*. The oldest specimen of Polish belongs to the fourteenth century: the Psalter of Margarite. The Bohemian language was, till lately, traced back to the ninth century. But most of the old Bohemian poems are now considered spurious; and it is doubtful, even, whether an ancient interlinear translation of the Gospel of St. John can be ascribed to the tenth century.†

The language of Lusatia is spoken, probably, by no more than 150,000 people, known in Germany by the name of *Wends*.

We have examined all the dialects of our first or Aryan family, which are spoken in Europe, with one exception, the *Albanian*. This language is clearly a member of the same family; and as it is sufficiently distinct from Greek or any other recognised language, it has been traced back to one of the neighbouring races of the Greeks, the Illyrians, and is supposed to be the only surviving representative of the various so-called barbarous tongues which surrounded and interpenetrated the dialects of Greece.

We now pass on from Europe to Asia; and here we begin at once, on the extreme south, with the languages of India. As I sketched the history of Sanskrit in one of my former Lectures, it must suffice, at present, to mark the different periods of that language, beginning about 1500 B.C., with the dialect of the Vedas, which is followed by the modern

* Schleicher, *Beiträge*, b. L s. 22.
† Schleicher, *Deutsche Sprache*, s. 77.

Sanskrit; the popular dialects of the third century B.C.; the Prakrit dialects of the plays; and the spoken dialects, such as Hindi, Hindustáni, Mahratti, Bengali. There are many points of great interest to the student of language, in the long history of the speech of India; and it has been truly said that Sanskrit is to the science of language what mathematics is to astronomy. In an introductory course of lectures, however, like the present, it would be out of place to enter on a minute analysis of the grammatical organism of this language of languages.

There is one point only on which I may be allowed to say a few words. I have frequently been asked, 'But how can you prove that Sanskrit literature is so old as it is supposed to be? How can you fix any Indian dates before the time of Alexander's conquest? What dependence can be placed on Sanskrit manuscripts which may have been forged or interpolated?' It is easier to ask such questions than to answer them, at least to answer them briefly and intelligibly. But, perhaps, the following argument will serve as a partial answer, and show that Sanskrit was the spoken language of India at least some centuries before the time of Solomon. In the hymns of the Veda, which are the oldest literary compositions in Sanskrit, the geographical horizon of the poets is, for the greater part, limited to the north-west of India. There are very few passages in which any allusions to the sea or the sea-coast occur, whereas the Snowy Mountains, and the rivers of the Penjáb, and the scenery of the Upper Ganges valley, are familiar objects to the ancient bards. There is no doubt, in fact, that the

people who spoke Sanskrit came into India from the
north, and gradually extended their sway to the south
and east. Now, at the time of Solomon, it can be
proved that Sanskrit was spoken at least as far south
as the mouth of the Indus.

You remember the fleet of Tharshish[*] which
Solomon had at sea, together with the navy of
Hiram, and which came once in three years, bringing *gold* and *silver*, *ivory*, *apes*, and *peacocks*. The
same navy, which was stationed on the shore of the
Red Sea, is said to have fetched gold from *Ophir*,[†]
and to have brought likewise from thence great plenty
of *algum-[‡]trees* and precious stones.

Well, a great deal has been written to find out
where this Ophir was; but there can be little doubt
that it was in India. The names for *apes*, *peacocks*,
ivory, and *algum-trees* are foreign words in Hebrew,
as much as *gutta-percha* or *tobacco* are in English.
Now, if we wished to know from what part of the
world *gutta-percha* was first imported into England,
we might safely conclude that it came from that
country where the name, *gutta-percha*, formed part
of the spoken language.[§] If, therefore, we can find
a language in which the names for peacock, ape,
ivory, and algum-tree, which are foreign in Hebrew,
are indigenous, we may be certain that the country
in which that language was spoken must have been
the Ophir of the Bible. That language is no other
but Sanskrit.

Apes are called, in Hebrew, *koph*, a word without an

---

[*] 1 Kings viii. 21.   [†] 1 Kings ix. 26.   [‡] 1 Kings x. 11.

[§] *Gutta* in Malay means *gum*, *percha* is the name of the tree
(Isonandra gutta), or of an island from which the tree was first
imported (Pulo-percha).

etymology in the Semitic languages, but nearly identical in sound with the Sanskrit name of ape, *kapi*.

Ivory is called either *karnoth-shen*, horns of tooth; or *shen habbim*. This *habbim* is again without a derivation in Hebrew, but it is most likely a corruption of the Sanskrit name for elephant, *ibha*, preceded by the Semitic article.*

Peacocks are called in Hebrew *tukhi-im*, and this finds its explanation in the old classical name of the pea-fowl in Tamil, *tôkei*, dialectically pronounced *tôgei*. In modern Tamil *tôkei* generally signifies only the peacock's tail, but in the old classical Tamil it signifies the peacock itself.†

All these articles, ivory, gold, apes, peacocks, are indigenous in India, though of course they might have been found in other countries likewise. Not so the *algum-tree*, at least if interpreters are right in taking *algum* or *almug* for sandal-wood. Sandalwood is found indigenous on the coast of Malabar only; and one of its numerous names there, and in

---

* See Lassen, *Indische Alterthumskunde*, b. i. s. 537.

† Cf. Caldwell, *Dravidian Grammar*, p. 66. This excellent scholar points out that *tôkei* cannot be a corruption of Sanskrit *sikhin*, crested, as I had supposed, *sikhin* existing in Tamil under the form of *sigi*, peacock. *Tôgei* does not occur either in Canarese, Telugu, or Malayâlim. Dr. Gundert, who has for many years devoted himself to the study of the Dravidian languages, derives *tôgei* from a root *tô* or *tû*. From this, by the addition of *ngu*, a secondary base, *tongu*, is formed in Tamil, meaning to hang, to be pendant. Hence the Tamil *tongal*, a peacock's tail, ornaments, &c.; in Malayâlim, *tôngal*, plumage, ornaments for the ear, drapery, &c. By adding the suffix *kei* or *gei* we get *togei*, what hangs down, tail, &c. If this etymology be right it would be an important confirmation of the antiquity of the Tamulic languages spoken in India before the advent of the Aryan tribes.

Sanskrit, is *valguka*. This *valgu* (*ka*) is clearly the name which Jewish and Phœnician merchants corrupted into *algum* (2 Chron. ii. 7; 9, 10; 11), and which in Hebrew was still further changed into *almug* (1 Kings x. 11; 12).

Now, the place where the navy of Solomon and Hiram, coming down the Red Sea, would naturally have landed, was the mouth of the Indus. There *gold* and *precious stones* from the north would have been brought down the Indus; and *sandal-wood*, *peacocks*, and *apes* would have been brought from Central and Southern India. In this very locality Ptolemy (vii. 1) gives us the name of *Abiria*, above *Pattalene*. In the same locality Hindu geographers place the people called *Abhīra* or *Abhīra*; and in the same neighbourhood MacMurdo, in his account of the province of Cutch, still knows a race of *Ahirs*,[*] the descendants, in all probability, of the people who sold to Hiram and Solomon their gold and precious stones, their apes, peacocks, and sandal-wood.[†]

If, then, in the Veda the people who spoke Sanskrit were still settled in the north of India, whereas at the time of Solomon their language had extended to Cutch and even the Malabar coast, this will show that at all events Sanskrit is not of yesterday, and

---

[*] See also Sir Henry Elliot's *Supplementary Glossary*, s. v. Aheer.

[†] The arguments brought forward by Quatremère, in his *Mémoire sur le Pays d'Ophir*, against fixing Ophir on the Indian coast, are not conclusive. The arguments derived from the names of the articles exported from Ophir were unknown to him. It is necessary to mention this, because Quatremère's name deservedly carries great weight, and his essay on Ophir has lately been republished in the *Bibliothèque Classique des Célébrités Contemporaines*, 1861.

that it is as old, at least, as the book of Job, in which the gold of Ophir is mentioned.*

* Job xxii. 24. Some of my critics have demurred to this argument because the Books of Kings are not cotemporaneous with Solomon. The articles themselves, however, must have had names at the time of Solomon; and it has never been proved that at his time they had Semitic names, and that these were replaced by Indian names at a later time, when all maritime commercial intercourse between India and Palestine had ceased. As to the name of sandal-wood, my critics ought to have known that both forms, *algum* as well as *almug*, occur in the Bible. The different opinions on the geographical position of Ophir have lately been most carefully examined and impartially summed up by the Hon. E. T. B. Twisleton, in his article on Ophir in Dr. Smith's *Biblical Dictionary*. Mr. Twisleton himself leans strongly towards the opinion of those scholars who, like Michaelis, Niebuhr, Gosselin, and Vincent, place Ophir in Arabia; and he argues very ingeniously that if we consider Ophir simply as an emporium, the principal objection, viz. that gold or any other article brought from Ophir to Palestine, was not a natural product of Arabia, falls to the ground. It is not necessary to discuss here all the controverted points of this question, for the conclusions drawn from the names of sandal-wood, and of other articles of trade brought by the navy of Tharshish, such as ivory, apes, and peacocks, remain, as far as I can judge, unaffected by Mr. Twisleton's arguments. These names, as found in the O. T., are by all competent Hebrew scholars admitted not to be of Semitic growth. They are foreign words in Hebrew, and they do not receive any light either from the dialects of Arabic, including the Himyaritic inscriptions, or from the languages spoken on the Mozambique coast of Africa, where, according to some authorities, Ophir was situated. Several of these names have been traced back to Sanskrit and to the languages spoken on the Malabar coast of the Dekhan; and though it must be admitted that, as foreign words, they have suffered considerable corruptions in the mouths of ignorant sailors, yet, allowing the same latitude of phonetic change, it has been impossible to trace them back to any other family of speech. If, therefore, there existed any evidence that Ophir was a mere *entrepôt*, not in India, but in Arabia or Africa, the spreading of Sanskrit names to Africa or Arabia before they reached Palestine

Most closely allied to Sanskrit, more particularly to the Sanskrit of the Veda, is the ancient language of the Zend-Avesta,* the so-called *Zend*, or sacred

would only serve to increase the antiquity of Sanskrit as spoken in those parts of India from whence alone the natural products of her language and of her soil could have been exported. And if we consider that there is no other language which can claim these names as her own—that there is no country in which *all* the articles brought by the fleet of Tharshish, whether from Ophir or elsewhere, are indigenous—that sandal-wood, fixed upon as the meaning of *algummim* quite independently of any theory as to Ophir being in India, could in ancient times have been exported to Palestine from the Malabar coast only; if to these remarkable coincidences, all pointing to India, is added the fact pointed out by Lassen, that the names of *cotton*, *nard*, and probably *bdellium*, have likewise found their way from Sanskrit into Hebrew, we shall, I think, feel inclined to admit, with Lassen and Ritter and others, a very early commercial intercourse between India and Palestine, and look, until stronger evidence is brought forward, on Abhira at the mouth of the Indus as the place where the fleets of Hiram and Solomon went to fetch the articles indigenous to India, though procurable, it may be, in smaller quantities, in any of the *entrepôts* along the Arabian, Persian, or African coasts.

The statement of Mr. Twisleton that the peacock is too delicate a bird for a long voyage in small vessels, deserves consideration, but would seem to require further proof.

* *Zend-Avesta* is the name used by Chaqâni and other Mohammedan writers. The Parsis use the name '*Avesta* and *Zend*,' taking *Avesta* in the sense of text, and *Zend* as the title of the Pehlevi commentary. I doubt, however, whether this was the original meaning of the word *Zend*. *Zend* was more likely the same word as the Sanskrit *chhandas* (scandere), a name given to the Vedic hymns, and *avesta*, the Sanskrit *avasthâna*, a word which, though it does not occur in Sanskrit, would mean settled text. *Avasthita*, in Sanskrit, means laid down, settled. The Zend-avesta now consists of four books, Yasna, Vispered, Yashts and Vendidad (Vendidad = vidaera dâta; in Pehlevi, Juddivdad). Dr. Haug, in his interesting lecture on the *Origin of the Parsee Religion*, Bombay, 1861, takes *Avesta* in the sense of the most

language of the Zoroastrians or worshippers of Ormuzd. It was, in fact, chiefly through the Sanskrit, and with the help of comparative philology, that the ancient dialect of the Parsis or so-called Fire-worshippers was deciphered. The MSS. had been preserved by the Parsi priests at Bombay, where a colony of Zoroastrians had fled in the tenth century,* and where it has risen since to considerable wealth and influence. Other settlements of Guebres are to be found in Yezd and parts of Kerman. A Frenchman, Anquetil Duperron, was the first to translate the Zend-avesta, but his translation was not from the original, but from a modern Persian translation. The first European who attempted to read the original words of Zoroaster was Rask, the Dane; and after his premature death, Burnouf, in France, achieved one of the greatest triumphs in modern scholarship by deciphering the language of the Zend-avesta, and establishing its close relationship with Sanskrit. The same doubts which were expressed about the age and

ancient texts, Zend as commentary, and Pazend as explanatory notes, all equally written in what we shall continue to call the Zend language.

* 'According to the Kissah-i-Sanján, a tract almost worthless as a record of the early history of the Parsis, the fire-worshippers took refuge in Khorassan forty-nine years before the era of Yezdegerd (632 A.D.), or about 583. Here they stayed a hundred years, to 683, then departed to the city of Hormaz (Ormus, in the Persian Gulf), and after staying fifteen years, proceeded in 698 to Diu, an island on the south-west coast of Katiawar. Here they remained nineteen years, to 717, and then proceeded to Sanján, a town about twenty-four miles south of Damaun. After three hundred years they spread to the neighbouring towns of Guzerat, and established the sacred fire successively at Bacsulah, Nausári, near Surat, and Bombay.'—*Bombay Quarterly Review*, 1856, No. viii. p. 67.

the genuineness of the Veda, were repeated with regard to the Zend-avesta, by men of high authority as oriental scholars, by Sir W. Jones himself, and even by the late Professor Wilson. But Burnouf's arguments, based at first on grammatical evidence only, were irresistible, and have of late been most signally confirmed by the discovery of the cuneiform inscriptions of Darius and Xerxes. That there was a Zoroaster, an ancient sage, was known long before Burnouf. Plato speaks of a teacher of Zoroaster's Magic (Μαγεία), and calls Zoroaster the son of *Oromazes*.*

This name of Oromazes is important; for Oromazes is clearly meant for *Ormuzd*, the god of the Zoroastrians. The name of this god, as read in the inscriptions of Darius and Xerxes, is *Auramazda*, which comes very near to Plato's Oromazes.† Thus Darius says, in one passage: 'Through the grace of Auramazda I am king; Auramazda gave me the kingdom.' But what is the meaning of *Auramazda*? We receive a hint from one passage in the Achæmenian inscriptions, where Auramazda is divided into two words, both being declined. The genitive of Auramazda occurs there as *Aurahya mazdâha*. But even this is unintelligible, and is, in fact, nothing

* Alc. I. p. 122, a. Ὁ μὲν μαγείαν διδάσκει τὴν Ζωροάστρου τοῦ Ὡρομάζου· ἔστι δὲ τοῦτο θεῶν θεραπεία. Aristotle knew not only Oromasdes as the good, but likewise Areimanios as the evil spirit, according to the doctrine of the Magi. See *Diogenes Laertius*, I, 8. Ἀριστοτέλης δ' ἐν πρώτῳ Περὶ φιλοσοφίας καὶ πρεσβυτέρους [τοὺς Μάγους] φησὶν εἶναι τῶν Αἰγυπτίων καὶ δύο κατ' αὐτοὺς εἶναι ἀρχάς, ἀγαθὸν δαίμονα καὶ κακὸν δαίμονα, καὶ τῷ μὲν ὄνομα εἶναι Ζεὺς καὶ Ὡρομάσδης, τῷ δὲ Ἅιδης καὶ Ἀρειμάνιος. Cf. Bernays, *Die Dialoge des Aristoteles*, Berlin, 1863; p. 95.

† In the inscriptions we find—nom. *Auramazdâ*, gen. *Auramazdâha*, acc. *Auramazdam*.

but a phonetic corruption of the name of the supreme Deity as it occurs on every page of the Zend-avesta, namely, *Ahurô mazdâo* (nom). Here, too, both words are declined: and instead of *Ahurô mazdâo*, we also find *Mazdâo ahurô*.* Well, this *Ahurô mazdâo* is represented in the Zend-avesta as the creator and ruler of the world; as good, holy, and true; and as doing battle against all that is evil, dark, and false. 'The wicked perish through the wisdom and holiness of the living wise spirit.' In the oldest hymns, the power of darkness which is opposed to *Ahurô mazdâo* has not yet received its proper name, which is *Angrô mainyus*, the later *Ahriman*; but it is spoken of as a power, as *Drukhs* or deceit; and the principal doctrine which Zoroaster came to preach was that we must choose between these two powers, that we must be good, and not bad. These are his words:—

'In the beginning there was a pair of twins, two spirits, each of a peculiar activity. These are the Good and the Base in thought, word, and deed. Choose one of these two spirits. Be good, not base!'†

Or, again:—

'Ahuramazda is holy, true, to be honoured through veracity, through holy deeds.' 'You cannot serve both.'

Now, if we wanted to prove that Anglo-Saxon was a real language, and more ancient than English a mere comparison of a few words such as *lord* and *hlaford*, *gospel* and *godspel*, would be sufficient.

---

* Gen. *Ahurahe mazdâo*, dat. *mazdâi*, acc. *mazdum*.
† Haug, *Lecture*, p. 11; and in Bunsen's *Egypt*.

Hlaford has a meaning;* *lord* has none; therefore we may safely say that without such a compound as *hlaford*, the word *lord* could never have arisen. The same, if we compare the language of the Zend-avesta with that of the cuneiform inscriptions of Darius. *Auramazdâ* is clearly a corruption of *Ahurô mazdâo*, and if the language of the Mountain-records of Behistun is genuine, then, *à fortiori*, is the language of the Zend-avesta genuine, as deciphered by Burnouf, long before he had deciphered the language of Cyrus and Darius. But what is the meaning of *Ahurô mazdâo*? Here Zend does not give us an answer; but we must look to Sanskrit, as the more primitive language, just as we looked from French to Italian, in order to discover the original form and meaning of *feu*. According to the rules which govern the changes of words, common to Zend and Sanskrit, *Ahurô mazdâo* corresponds to the Sanskrit *Asura medhas*; and this would mean the 'Wise Spirit,'—neither more nor less.

---

* The following remarks on the original meaning of *lord*, or *breadgiver*, the German *Brotherr*, I owe to the kindness of the Rev. Dr. Bosworth, Professor of Anglo-Saxon at Oxford:—

' *Lord* is from the Anglo-Saxon *hláf-ord*, composed of *hláf*, a loaf (the long *á* has the sound of *oa*, as the *á* in *fám*, *bát*, foam, boat), and *órd*, *-es*; m. origin, cause, author. Thus *órd moncynnes*, *origo humani generis*, Cd. 55. Hence, the meaning of *lord*, the Anglo-Saxon *hláf-órd*, loaf or bread origin, the origin, cause, or author of bread or support.

' *Lady* is from A.S. *hláf-dige*, *-dia*. *Hláf*, or *hláf*, *-es*; m. a loaf, bread; and *dige*, *die*, *-an*; f. from dugan, digan, heo dige, to care for, help, serve. Hence, *lady* means one who helps or serves bread to the family. In *Psalm* cxii. 3, we find *hire hlæfdigum*, or *hlæfdian*, *suæ dominæ*. R. Glouc., for *hlæfdie*, writes *lowedie*, *lowedy*: Gower and Spenser *ladie*, at present *lady*.'—J.B.

We have editions, translations, and commentaries of the Zend-avesta by Burnouf, Brockhaus, Spiegel, and Westergaard. Yet there still remains much to be done. Dr. Haug, now settled at Poona, has lately taken up the work which Burnouf left unfinished. He has pointed out that the text of the Zend-avesta, as we have it, comprises fragments of very different antiquity, and that the most ancient only, the so-called Gâthâs, can be ascribed to Zarathustra. 'This portion,' he writes in a lecture just received from India, 'compared with the whole bulk of the Zend fragments is very small; but by the difference of dialect it is easily recognised. The most important pieces written in this peculiar dialect are called Gâthâs or songs, arranged in five small collections; they have different metres, which mostly agree with those of the Veda; their language is very near to the Vedic dialect.' It is to be regretted that in the same lecture, which holds out the promise of so much that will be extremely valuable, Dr. Haug should have lent his authority to the opinion that Zoroaster or Zarathustra is mentioned in the Rig-Veda as Jaradashṭi. The meaning of jaradashṭi in the Rig-Veda may be seen in the Sanskrit Dictionary of the Russian Academy, and no Sanskrit scholar would seriously think of translating the word by Zoroaster.

At what time Zoroaster lived, is a more difficult question, which we cannot discuss at present.* It

---

* Berosus, as preserved in the Armenian translation of Eusebius, mentions a Median dynasty of Babylon, beginning with a king Zoroaster, long before Ninus; his date would be 2234 B.C.

Xanthus, the Lydian (470 B.C.) as quoted by Diogenes Laertius, places Zoroaster, the prophet, 600 before the Trojan war (1800 B.C.).

must suffice if we have proved that he lived, and that his language, the Zend, is a real language, and anterior in time to the language of the cuneiform inscriptions.

We trace the subsequent history of the Persian language from Zend to the inscriptions of the Achæmenian dynasty; from thence to what is called *Pehlevi* or *Huzvaresh* (better Huzûresh), the language of the Sassanian dynasty (226–651), as it is found in the dialect of the translations of the Zend-avesta, and in the official language of the Sassanian coins and inscriptions. This is considerably mixed with Semitic elements, probably imported from Syria. In a still later form, freed also from the Semitic elements which abound in Pehlevi, the language of Persia appears again as *Parsi*, which differs but little from the language of *Firdusi*, the great epic poet of Persia, the author of the Shahnâmeh, about 1000 A.D. The later history of Persian consists entirely in the gradual increase of Arabic words, which have crept into the language since the conquest of Persia and the conversion of the Persians to the religion of Mohammed.

The other languages which evince by their grammar and vocabulary a general relationship with Sanskrit and Persian, but which have received too distinct and national a character to be classed as mere dialects, are the languages of *Afghanistan* or the *Pushtu*, the language of the *Kurds*, the *Ossetian* language in the Caucasus, and the *Armenian*. The

---

Aristotle and Eudoxus, according to Pliny (*Hist. Nat.* xxx. 1), placed Zoroaster 6000 before Plato; Hermippus 5000 before the Trojan war (Diog. Laert. *proœm.*)

Pliny (*Hist. Nat.* xxx. 2) places Zoroaster several thousand years before Moses the Judæan, who founded another kind of Mageia.

language of Bokhára is a mere dialect of Persian, and does not deserve to be classed as an independent member of the Aryan family. Much might be said on every one of these tongues and their claims to be classed as independent members of the Aryan family; but our time is limited, nor has any one of them acquired, as yet, that importance which belongs to the vernaculars of India, Persia, Greece, Italy, and Germany, and to other branches of Aryan speech which have been analysed critically, and may be studied historically in the successive periods of their literary existence. There is only one other Aryan language which we have omitted to mention, and which belongs equally to Asia and Europe, the language of the *Gipsies*. This language, though most degraded in its grammar, and with a dictionary stolen from all the countries through which the Zingari passed, is clearly an exile from Hindustán.

You see, from the diagram before you,* that it is possible to divide the whole Aryan family into two divisions: the *Southern*, including the Indic and Iranic classes, and the *Northern* or *North-western*, comprising all the rest. Sanskrit and Zend share certain words and grammatical forms in common which do not exist in any of the other Aryan languages; and there can be no doubt that the ancestors of the poets of the Veda and of the worshippers of *Ahúró mazdáo* lived together for some time after they had left the original home of the whole Aryan race. For let us see this clearly: the genealogical classification of languages, as drawn in this diagram, has an historical meaning. As sure as the six Romance dialects point to an original home of Italian shepherds on the seven hills at Rome, the Aryan languages together point to an

* Printed at the end of these Lectures.

earlier period of language, when the first ancestors of the Indians, the Persians, the Greeks, the Romans, the Slaves, the Celts, and the Germans were living together within the same enclosures, nay, under the same roof. There was a time when out of many possible names for *father, mother, daughter, son, dog, cow, heaven,* and *earth,* those which we find in all the Aryan languages were framed, and obtained a mastery *in the struggle for life* which is carried on among synonymous words as much as among plants and animals. Look at the comparative table of the auxiliary verb AS, to be, in the different Aryan languages. The selection of the root AS out of many roots, equally applicable to the idea of being, and the joining of this root with one set of personal terminations, all originally personal pronouns, were individual acts, or, if you like, historical events. They took place once, at a certain date and in a certain place; and as we find the same forms preserved by all the members of the Aryan family, it follows that before the ancestors of the Indians and Persians started for the south, and the leaders of the Greek, Roman, Celtic, Teutonic, and Slavonic colonies marched towards the shores of Europe, there was a small clan of Aryans, settled probably on the highest elevation of Central Asia, speaking a language, not yet Sanskrit or Greek or German, but containing the dialectic germs of all; a clan that had advanced to a state of agricultural civilisation; that had recognised the bonds of blood, and sanctioned the bonds of marriage; and that invoked the Giver of Light and Life in heaven by the same name which you may still hear in the temples of Benares, in the basilicas of Rome, and in our own churches and cathedrals.

After this clan broke up, the ancestors of the

Indians and Zoroastrians must have remained together for some time in their migrations or new settlements; and I believe that it was the reform of Zoroaster which produced at last the split between the worshippers of the Vedic gods and the worshippers of Ormuzd. Whether, besides this division into a southern and northern branch, it is possible by the same test (the community of particular words and forms) to discover the successive periods when the Germans separated from the Slaves, the Celts from the Italians, or the Italians from the Greeks, seems more than doubtful. The attempts made by different scholars have led to different and by no means satisfactory results;[*] and it seems best, for the present, to trace each of the northern classes back to its own dialect, and to account for the more special coincidences between such languages as, for instance, the Slavonic and Teutonic, by admitting that the ancestors of these races preserved from the beginning certain dialectical peculiarities which existed before, as well as after, the separation of the Aryan family.

[*] See Schleicher, *Deutsche Sprache*, s. 81.

LECTURE VI.

COMPARATIVE GRAMMAR.

THE genealogical classification of the Aryan languages was founded, as we saw, on a close comparison of the grammatical characteristics of each; and it is the object of such works as Bopp's *Comparative Grammar* to show that the grammatical articulation of Sanskrit, Zend, Greek, Roman, Celtic, Teutonic, and Slavonic, was produced once and for all; and that the apparent differences in the terminations of Sanskrit, Greek, and Latin, must be explained by laws of phonetic decay, peculiar to each dialect, which modified the original common Aryan type, and changed it into so many national languages. It might seem, therefore, as if the object of comparative grammar was attained as soon as the exact genealogical relationship of languages had been settled; and those who only looked to the higher problems of the science of language have not hesitated to declare that 'there is no painsworthy difficulty nor dispute about declension, number, case, and gender of nouns.' But although it is certainly true that comparative grammar is only a means, and that it has wellnigh taught us all that it has to teach—at least in the Aryan family of speech—it is to be hoped that, in the science of language, it will always retain that prominent place which it has obtained through the labours of Bopp, Grimm, Pott, Benfey, Curtius, Kuhn, and others. Besides, comparative grammar has more to do than simply to compare. It would be easy enough to place side by side the paradigms of declension and conjugation in Sanskrit, Greek, Latin, and the other Aryan dialects, and to mark both their coincidences and their differences. But after we have done this, and after we have explained the phonetic laws which cause the primitive Aryan type to assume that national variety which we admire in Sanskrit, Greek, and Latin, new problems arise of a more interesting nature. We know that grammatical terminations, as they are now called, were originally independent words, and had their own purpose and meaning. Is it possible, after comparative grammar has established the original forms of the Aryan terminations, to trace them back to independent words, and to discover their original purpose and meaning? You will remember that this was the point from which we started. We wanted to know why the termination *d* in *I loved* should change a present into a past act. We saw that before answering this question we had to discover the most original form of this termination by tracing it from English to Gothic, and afterwards, if necessary, from Gothic, to Sanskrit. We return now to our original question, namely, What is language that a mere formal change, such as that of *I love* into *I loved*, should produce so very material a difference?

Let us clearly see what we mean if we make a distinction between the radical and formal elements of a language; and by formal elements I mean not only the terminations of declension and conjugation.

but all derivative elements; all, in fact, that is not radical. Our view on the origin of language must chiefly depend on the view which we take of these formal, as opposed to the radical, elements of speech. Those who consider that language is a conventional production, base their arguments principally on these formal elements. The inflections of words, they maintain, are the best proof that language was made by mutual agreement. They look upon them as mere letters or syllables without any meaning by themselves; and if they were asked why the mere addition of a *d* changes *I love* into *I loved*, or why the addition of the syllable *rai* gave to *j'aime*, I love, the power of a future, *j'aimerai*, they would answer, that it was so because, at a very early time in the history of the world, certain persons, or families, or clans, agreed that it should be so.

This view was opposed by another which represents language as an organic and almost a living being, and explains its formal elements as produced by a principle of growth inherent in its very nature. 'Languages,'* it is maintained, 'are formed by a process, not of crystalline accretion, but of germinal development. Every essential part of language existed as completely (although only implicitly) in the primitive germ, as the petals of a flower exist in the bud before the mingled influences of the sun and the air caused it to unfold.' This view was first propounded by Frederick Schlegel,† and it is still held

---

* Farrar, *Origin of Languages*, p. 35.

† 'It has been common among grammarians to regard those terminational changes as evolved by some unknown process from the body of a noun as the branches of a tree spring from the stem—or as elements, unmeaning in themselves, but employed

by many with whom poetical phraseology takes the place of sound and severe reasoning.

The science of language adopts neither of these views. As to imagining a congress for settling the proper exponents of such relations as nominative, genitive, singular, plural, active, and passive, it stands to reason that if such abstruse problems could have been discussed in a language void of inflections, there was no inducement for agreeing on a more perfect means of communication. And as to imagining language, that is to say, nouns and verbs, endowed with an inward principle of growth, all we can say is, that such a conception is really inconceivable. Language may be conceived as a production, but it cannot be conceived as a substance that could itself arbitrarily or conventionally to modify the meanings of words. This latter view is countenanced by Schlegel. "Languages with inflexions," says Schlegel, "are organic languages because they include a living principle of development and increase, and alone possess, if I may so express myself, a fruitful and abundant vegetation. The wonderful mechanism of these languages consists in forming an immense variety of words, and in marking the connection of ideas expressed by these words by the help of an inconsiderable number of syllables, *which, viewed separately, have no signification*, but which determine with precision the sense of the words to which they are attached. By modifying radical letters and by adding derivative syllables to the roots, derivative words of various sorts are formed, and derivatives from those derivatives. Words are compounded from several roots to express complex ideas. Finally, substantives, adjectives, and pronouns are declined, with gender, number, and case; verbs are conjugated throughout voices, moods, tenses, numbers, and persons, by employing, in like manner, terminations and sometimes augments, which by themselves signify nothing. This method is attended with the advantage of enunciating in a single word the principal idea, frequently greatly modified, and extremely complex already, with its whole array of accessory ideas and mutable relations."¹ — *Transactions of the Philological Society*, vol. ii. p. 39.

produce. But the science of language has nothing to do with mere theories, whether conceivable or not. It collects facts, and its only object is to account for these facts, as far as possible. Instead of looking on inflections in general either as conventional signs or natural excrescences, it takes each termination by itself, establishes its most primitive form by means of comparison, and then treats that primitive syllable as it would treat any other part of language—namely, as something which was originally intended to convey a meaning. Whether we are still able to discover the original intention of every part of language is quite a different question, and it should be admitted at once, that many grammatical forms, after they have been restored to their most primitive type, are still without an explanation. But with every year new discoveries are made by means of careful inductive reasoning. We become more familiar every day with the secret ways of language, and there is no reason to doubt that in the end grammatical analysis will be as successful as chemical analysis. Grammar, though sometimes very bewildering to us in its later stages, is originally a much less formidable undertaking than is commonly supposed. What is grammar after all but declension and conjugation? Originally declension could not have been anything but the composition of a noun with some other word expressive of number and case. How the number was expressed, we saw in a former lecture. A very similar process led to the formation of cases.

Thus the locative is formed in various ways in Chinese:[*] one is by adding such words as *tung*, the

---

[*] Endlicher, *Chinesische Grammatik*, s. 172.

middle, or *nĕi*, inside. Thus, *kiŏ-čung*, in the empire, *ĭ sŭi ung*, within a year. The instrumental is formed by the preposition *ў*, which preposition is an old root, meaning *to use*. Thus, *ў ting*, with a stick, where in Latin we should use the ablative, in Greek the dative. Now, however complicated the declensions, regular and irregular, may be in Greek and Latin, we may be certain that originally they were formed by this simple method of composition.

There was originally in all the Aryan languages a case expressive of locality, which grammarians call the *locative*. In Sanskrit every substantive has its locative, as well as its genitive, dative, and accusative. Thus, *heart* in Sanskrit is *hṛid*; in the heart, is *hṛidi*. Here, therefore, the termination of the locative is simply short *i*. This short *i* is a demonstrative root, and in all probability the same root which in Latin produced the preposition *in*. The Sanskrit *hṛidi* represents, therefore, an original compound, as it were, *heart-within*, which gradually became settled as one of the recognised cases of nouns ending in consonants. If we look to Chinese,[*] we find that the locative is expressed there in the same manner, but with a greater freedom in the choice of the words expressive of locality. 'In the empire,' is expressed by *kiŏ-čung*; 'within a year,' is expressed by *ĭ sŭi čung*. Instead of *čung*, however, we might have employed other terms, such, for instance, as *nĕi*, inside. It might be said that the formation of so primitive a case as the locative offers little difficulty, but that this process of composition fails to account for the origin of the more abstract cases, the accusative,

---

[*] Endlicher, *Chinesische Grammatik*, s. 172.

the dative, and the genitive. If we derive our notions of the cases from philosophical grammar, it is true, no doubt, that it would be difficult to realise by a simple composition the abstract relations supposed to be expressed by the terminations of the genitive, dative, and accusative. But remember that these are only general categories under which philosophers and grammarians have endeavoured to arrange the facts of language. The people with whom language grew up knew nothing of datives and accusatives. Everything that is abstract in language was originally concrete. If people wanted to say the King of Rome, they meant really the King at Rome, and they would readily have used what I have just described as the locative; whereas the more abstract idea of the genitive would never enter into their system of thought. But more than this, it can be proved that the locative has actually taken, in some cases, the place of the genitive. In Latin, for instance, the old genitive of nouns in *a* was *as*. This we find still in *pater familiâs*, instead of *pater familiûn* or *pater familiæ*. The Umbrian and Oscan dialects retained the *s* throughout as the sign of the genitive after nouns in *a*. The *æ* of the Latin genitive, however, was originally *ai*, that is to say, the old locative in *i*. 'King of Rome,' if rendered by *Rex Romæ*, meant really 'King at Rome.' And here you will see how grammar, which ought to be the most logical of all sciences, is frequently the most illogical. A boy is taught at school, that if he wants to say 'I am staying at Rome,' he must use the genitive to express the locative. How a logician or grammarian can so twist and turn the meaning of the genitive as to make it express rest in a place, it is not for us to inquire; but, if he succeeded, his pupil would at once use the genitive of Carthage (Carthaginis) or of Athens (Athenarum) for the same purpose, and he would then have to be told that these genitives could not be used in the same manner as the genitive of nouns in *a*. How all this is achieved by what is called philosophical grammar, we know not; but comparative grammar at once removes all difficulty. It is only in the first declension that the locative has supplanted the genitive, whereas *Carthaginis* and *Athenarum*, being real genitives, could never be employed to express a locative. A special case, such as the locative, may be generalised into the more general genitive, but not *vice versâ*.

You see thus by one instance how what grammarians call a genitive was formed by the same process of composition which we can watch in Chinese, and which we can prove to have taken place in the original language of the Aryans. And the same applies to the dative. If a boy is told that the dative expresses a relation of one object to another, less direct than that of the accusative, he may well wonder how such a flying arch could ever have been built up with the scanty materials which language has at her disposal; but he will be still more surprised if, after having realised this grammatical abstraction, he is told that in Greek, in order to convey the very definite idea of being in a place, he has to use after certain nouns the termination of the dative. 'I am staying at Salamis,' must be expressed by the dative *Salamini*. If you ask why? comparative grammar again can alone give an answer. The termination of the Greek dative in *i* was originally the termination of the locative. The locative may well convey the meaning of the dative, but the faded features of the dative can never express the freshness and distinctness of the locative. The dative *Salamini* was first a locative. 'I live at Salamis,' never conveyed the meaning, 'I live to Salamis.' On the contrary, the dative, in such phrases as 'I give it to the father,' was originally a locative; and after expressing at first the palpable relation of 'I give it unto the father,' or 'I place it on or in the father,' it gradually assumed the more general, and less local, less coloured aspect which logicians and grammarians ascribe to their datives.*

If the explanation just given of some of the cases in Greek and Latin should seem too artificial or too forced, we have only to think of French in order to see exactly the same process repeated under our eyes. The most abstract relations of the genitive, as, for instance, 'The immortality of the soul' (*l'immortalité de l'âme*); or of the dative, as, for instance, 'I trust myself to God' (*je me fie à Dieu*), are expressed by prepositions, such as *de* and *ad*, which in Latin had the distinct local meanings of 'down from' and 'towards.' Nay, the English *of* and *to*, which have taken the place of the German terminations *s* and *m*, are likewise prepositions of an originally local character. The only difference between our cases and those of the ancient languages consists in this,—that the determining element is now placed before the word, whereas, in the original language of the Aryans, it was placed at the end.

What applies to the cases of nouns, applies with equal truth to the terminations of verbs. It may

* 'The Algonquins have but one case, which may be called locative.'—*Du Ponceau*, p. 158.

seem difficult to discover in the personal terminations of Greek and Latin the exact pronouns which were added to a verbal base in order to express *I* love, *thou* lovest, *he* loves; but it stands to reason that originally these terminations must have been the same in all languages — namely, personal pronouns. We may be puzzled by the terminations of *thou lovest* and *he loves*, where *st* and *s* can hardly be identified with the modern *thou* and *he*; but we have only to place all the Aryan dialects together, and we shall see at once that they point back to an original set of terminations which can easily be brought to tell their own story.

Let us begin with modern formations, because we have here more daylight for watching the intricate and sometimes wayward movements of language; or better still, let us begin with an imaginary case, or with what may be called the language of the future, in order to see quite clearly how what we should call grammatical forms may arise. Let us suppose that the slaves in America were to rise against their masters, and, after gaining some victories, were to sail back in large numbers to some part of Central Africa, beyond the reach of their white enemies or friends. Let us suppose these men availing themselves of the lessons they had learnt in their captivity, and gradually working out a civilisation of their own. It is quite possible that, some centuries hence, a new Livingstone might find among the descendants of the American slaves, a language, a literature, laws, and manners, bearing a striking similitude to those of his own country. What an interesting problem for any future historian and ethnologist! Yet there are problems in the past history

of the world of equal interest, which have been and
are still to be solved by the student of language.
Now I believe that a careful examination of the
language of the descendants of those escaped slaves
would suffice to determine with perfect certainty
their past history, even though no documents and no
tradition had preserved the story of their captivity
and liberation. At first, no doubt, the threads might
seem hopelessly entangled. A missionary might
surprise the scholars of Europe by an account of
that new African language. He might describe it at
first as very imperfect—as a language, for instance,
so poor that the same word had to be used to express
the most heterogeneous ideas. He might point out
how the same sound, without any change of accent,
meant *true*, a *ceremony*, a *workman*, and was used
also as a verb in the sense of literary composition.
All these, he might say, are expressed in that strange
dialect by the sound *rait* (right, rite, wright, write).
He might likewise observe that this dialect, as poor
almost as Chinese, had hardly any grammatical inflections, and that it had no genders, except in a few
words such as man-of-war and a railway-engine,
which were both conceived as feminine beings, and
spoken of as *she*. He might then mention an even
more extraordinary feature, namely, that although this
language had no terminations for the masculine and
feminine genders of nouns, it employed a masculine
and feminine termination after the affirmative particle,
according as it was addressed to a lady or a gentleman. Their affirmative particle being the same as the
English, *Yes*, they added a final *r* to it if addressed
to a man, and a final *m* if addressed to a lady: that
is to say, instead of simply saying *Yes*, those descen-

dants of the escaped American slaves said *Yes'r* to a man, and *Yes'm* to a lady.

Absurd as this may sound, I can assure you that the descriptions which are given of the dialects of savage tribes, as explained for the first time by travellers or missionaries, are even more extraordinary. But let us consider now what the student of language would have to do, if such forms as *Yes'r* and *Yes'm* were, for the first time, brought under his notice. He would first have to trace them back historically, as far as possible, to their more original types, and if he discovered their connection with *Yes Sir* and *Yes Ma'm*, he would point out how such contractions were most likely to spring up in a vulgar dialect. After having traced back the *Yes'r* and *Yes'm* of the free African negroes to the idiom of their former American masters, the etymologist would next inquire how such phrases as *Yes Sir* and *Yes Madam* came to be used on the American continent.

Finding nothing analogous in the dialects of the aboriginal inhabitants of America, he would be led, by a mere comparison of words, to the languages of Europe, and here again, first to the language of England. Even if no historical documents had been preserved, the documents of language would show that the white masters, whose language the ancestors of the free Africans adopted during their servitude, came originally from England, and, within certain limits, it would even be possible to fix the time when the English language was first transplanted to America. That language must have passed at least the age of Chaucer before it migrated to the New World. For Chaucer has two affirmative particles, *Yes* and *Yes*, and he distinguishes between the two.

He uses *Yes* only in answer to negative questions. For instance, in answer to 'Does he not go?' he would say *Yes*. In all other cases Chaucer uses *Yea*. To a question, 'Does he go?' he would answer *Yea*. He observes the same distinction between *No* and *Nay*, the former being used after negative, the latter after all other questions. This distinction became obsolete soon after Sir Thomas More,* and it must have become obsolete before phrases such as *Yes Sir* and *Yes Madam* could have assumed their stereotyped character.

But there is still more historical information to be gained from these phrases. The word *Yes* is Anglo-Saxon, the same as the German *Ja*, and it therefore reveals the fact that the white masters of the American slaves who crossed the Atlantic after the time of Chaucer, had crossed the Channel at an earlier period after leaving the continental fatherland of the Angles and Saxons. The words *Sir* and *Madam* tell us still more. They are Norman words, and they could only have been imposed on the Anglo-Saxons of Britain by Norman conquerors. They tell us more than this. For these Normans or Northmen spoke originally a Teutonic dialect, closely allied to Anglo-Saxon, and in that dialect words such as *Sir* and *Madam* could never have sprung up. We may conclude, therefore, that, previous to the Norman conquest, the Teutonic Northmen must have made a sufficiently long stay in one of the Roman provinces to forget their own and adopt the language of the Roman provincials.

We may now trace back the Norman *Madam* to

---

* Marsh. p. 579.

the French *Madame*, and we recognise in this a corruption of the Latin *Mea domina*, my mistress. *Domina* was changed into *domna*, *donna*, and *dame*, and the same word *Dame* was also used as a masculine in the sense of lord, as a corruption of *Domino*, *Domno*, and *Donno*. The temporal lord ruling as ecclesiastical seigneur under the bishop, was called a *vidame*, as the Vidame of Chartres, &c. The French interjection *Dame!* has no connection with a similar exclamation in English, but it simply means Lord! *Dame-Dieu* in old French is Lord God.* A derivative of *Domina*, mistress, was *dominicella*, which became *Demoiselle* and *Damsel*. The masculine *Dame* for *Domino*, Lord, was afterwards replaced by the Latin *Senior*, a translation of the German *elder*. This word *elder* was a title of honour, and we have it still both in *alderman*, and in what is originally the same, the English *earl* (the Norse *Jarl*), a comparative analogous to the A.-S. *ealdor*. This title *Senior*, meaning originally *older*, was but rarely † applied to ladies as a title of honour. *Senior* was changed into *Seigneur*, *Seigneur* into *Sieur*, and *Sieur* soon dwindled down to *Sir*.

Thus we see how in two short phrases, such as *Yesr* and *Yesm*, long chapters of history might be

---

* *Dame-Dieu :*—

'Ja dame Dieus non vuelha
Qu'en ma colpa sia'l departimens.'
(Que jamais le Seigneur Dieu ne veuille
Qu'en ma faute soit la séparation.)

(*Anc. Franç.*) 'Grandes miracles fit dames Dex par lui.'(*Romans de Garin*, Du Cange, t. ii. col. 16, 19).—Raynouard, *Lexique*, s. v. *Don*.

† In Old Portuguese, Diez mentions *senhor rainha*, *min sennor formosa*, my beautiful mistress.

read. If a general destruction of books, such as took place in China under the Emperor Thsin-chi-hoang-ti (213 B.C.), should sweep away all historical documents, language, even in its most depraved state, would preserve the secrets of the past, and would tell future generations of the home and migrations of their ancestors from the East to the West Indies.

It may seem startling at first to find the same name, the *East Indies* and the *West Indies*, at the two extremities of the Aryan migrations; but these very names are full of historical meaning. They tell us how the Teutonic race, the most vigorous and enterprising of all the members of the Aryan family, gave the name of *West Indies* to the country which, in their world-compassing migrations, they imagined to be India itself; how they discovered their mistake, and then distinguished between the East Indies and West Indies; how they planted new states in the west, and regenerated the effete kingdoms in the east; how they preached Christianity, and at last practised it by abolishing slavery of body and mind among the slaves of West Indian landholders, and the slaves of Brahmanical soulholders, until they greeted at last the very homes from which the Aryan family had started when setting out on their discovery of the world. All this, and even more, may be read in the vast archives of language. The very name of India has a story to tell, for India is not a native name. We have it from the Romans, the Romans from the Greeks, the Greeks from the Persians. And why from the Persians? Because it is only in Persian that an initial *s* is changed into *h*, which initial *h* was as usual dropped in Greek. It is only in Persian that the country of the *Sindhu* (*sindhu* is the Sanskrit name for *river*), or of the *seven sindhus*, could have been called *Hindia* or *India* instead of *Sindia*. Unless the followers of Zoroaster had pronounced every *s* like *h*, we should never have heard of the West Indies!

We have thus seen by an imaginary instance what we must be prepared for in the growth of language, and we shall now better understand why it must be laid down as a fundamental principle in Comparative Grammar to look upon nothing in language as merely formal, till every attempt has been made to trace the formal elements of language back to their original and substantial prototypes. We are accustomed to the idea of grammatical terminations modifying the meaning of words. But words can be modified by words only; and though in the present state of our science it would be too much to say that all grammatical terminations have been traced back to original independent words, so many of them have, even in cases where only a single letter was left, that we may well lay it down as a rule that all formal elements of language were originally substantial. Suppose English had never been written down before the time of Piers Ploughman. What should we make of such a form as *nadistou*,* instead of *ne hadst thou? Ne rechi*, instead of *I reck not? At ô'm* in Dorsetshire is *all of them. I midden* is *I may not; I cooden, I could not.* Yet the changes which Sanskrit had undergone before it was reduced to writing, must have been more considerable by far than what we see in these dialects.†

* Marsh, p. 387. Barnes, *Poems in Dorsetshire Dialect.*

† In Anglo-Saxon we find *nat* for *ne wat*, I do not know; *niste* for he did not know; *niston* for they did not know; *nolde,*

Let us now look to modern classical languages such as French and Italian. Most of the grammatical terminations are the same as in Latin, only changed by phonetic corruption. Thus *j'aime* is *ego amo*; *tu aimes, tu amas; il aime, ille amat*. There was originally a final *t* in French *il aime*, and it comes out again in such phrases as *aime-t-il?* Thus the French imperfect corresponds to the Latin imperfect, the Parfait défini to the Latin perfect. But what about the French future? There is no similarity between *amabo* and *j'aimerai*. Here then we have a new grammatical form, sprung up, as it were, within the recollection of men; or, at least, in the broad daylight of history. Now did the termination *rai* bud forth like a blossom in spring? or did some wise people meet together to invent this new termination, and pledge themselves to use it instead of the old termination *bo?* Certainly not. We see first of all that in all the Romance languages the terminations of the future are identical with the auxiliary verb *to have.** In French you find—

J'ai	and	je chanter-ai	nous avons	and	nous chanterons
tu as	,,	tu chanter-as	vous avez	,,	vous chanterez
il a	,,	il chanter-a	ils ont	,,	ils chanteront

But besides this, we actually find in Spanish and Provençal the apparent termination of the future used as an independent word and not yet joined to the infinitive. We find in Spanish, instead of '*lo haré*,' I shall do it, the more primitive form *hacer lo he*, i.e.

noldest, for I would not, thou wouldst not; *nyle* for I will not: *naebbe* for I have not; *naefth* for he has not; *naeron* for they were not, &c.

* *Survey of Languages,* p. 21.

facere id habeo. We find in Provençal *dir vos ai* instead of *je vous dirai*; *dir vos em* instead of *nous vous dirons*. There can be no doubt, therefore, that the Romance future was originally a compound of the auxiliary verb *to have* with an infinitive; and *I have to say* easily took the meaning of *I shall say*.

Here, then, we see clearly how grammatical forms arise. A Frenchman looks upon his futures as merely grammatical forms. He has no idea, unless he is a scholar, that the terminations of his futures are identical with the auxiliary verb *avoir*. The Roman had no suspicion that *amabo* was a compound; but it can be proved to contain an auxiliary verb as clearly as the French future. The Latin future was destroyed by means of phonetic corruption. When the final letters lost their distinct pronunciation, it became impossible to keep the imperfect *amabam* separate from the future *amabo*. The future was then replaced by dialectical regeneration, for the use of *habeo* with an infinitive is found in Latin, in such expressions as *habeo dicere*, I have to say, which would imperceptibly glide into I shall say.* In fact, wherever we look, we see that the future is expressed by means of composition. We have in English *I shall* and *thou wilt*, which mean originally *I am bound* and *thou intendest*. In German we use *werden*, the Gothic *vairthan*, which means originally to go, to turn towards. In modern Greek we find *thelō*, I will, in *thelō dōsei*, I shall give. In Roumansch we meet with *vegnir*, to come, forming the future *veng a vegnir*, I shall come; whereas in French *je viens de dire*, I come from saying, is equivalent to 'I have

* Fuchs, *Romanische Sprachen*, s. 344.

just said.' The French *je vais dire* is almost a future, though originally it is *vado dicere*, I go to say. The Dorsetshire, 'I be gwîin to goo a-pickèn stuones,' is another case in point. Nor is there any doubt that in the Latin *bo* of *amabo* we have the old auxiliary *bhû*, to become, and in the Greek future in -σω, the old auxiliary *as*, to be.*

We now go back another step, and ask the question which we asked many times before, How can a mere *d* produce so momentous a change as that from *I love* to *I loved*? As we have learnt in the meantime that English goes back to Anglo-Saxon, and is closely related to continental Saxon and Gothic, we look at once to the Gothic imperfect in order to see whether it has preserved any traces of the original compound; for, after what we have seen in the previous cases, we are no doubt prepared to find here, too, gram-

---

* The Greek term for the future is ὁ μέλλων, and μέλλω is used as an auxiliary verb to form certain futures in Greek. It has various meanings, but they can all be traced back to the Sanskrit *man* (*manyate*), to think. As *anya*, other, is changed to ἄλλος, so *manye*, I think, to μέλλω. *Il.* ii. 39: θήσειν ἐπ' ἐμέλλεν ἐπ' ἄλγεά τε στοναχάς τε Τρωσί τε καὶ Δαναοῖσι, 'he still thought to lay sufferings on Trojans and Greeks.' *Il.* xxiii. 544: μέλλεις ἀφαιρήσεσθαι ἄεθλον, 'thou thinkest thou wouldst have stripped me of the prize.' *Od.* xlii. 293: οὐκ ἄρ' ἐμέλλες λήξειν; 'did you not think of stopping?' i.e. were you not going to stop? Or again in such phrases as *Il.* ii. 36, τά οὐ τελέεσθαι ἔμελλον, 'these things were not meant to be accomplished,' literally, these things did not mean to be accomplished. Thus μέλλω was used of things that were likely to be, as if those things themselves meant or intended to be or not to be; and, the original meaning being forgotten, μέλλω came to be a mere auxiliary expressing probability. Μέλλω and μέλλομαι, in the sense of 'to hesitate,' are equally explained by the Sanskrit *man*, to think or consider. In Old Norse the future is likewise formed by *man*, to mean.

matical terminations mere remnants of independent words.

In Gothic there is a verb *nasjan*, to nourish. Its preterite is as follows:—

Singular	Dual	Plural
nas-i-da	nas-i-dêdu	nas-i-dêdum
nas-i-dôs	nas-i-dêduts	nas-i-dêdup
nas-i-da	——	nas-i-dêdun

The subjunctive of the preterite:

nas-i-dêdjau	nas-i-dêdeiva	nas-i-dêdeima
nas-i-dêdeis	nas-i-dêdeits	nas-i-dêdeip
nas-i-dêdi	——	nas-i-dêdeina

This is reduced in Anglo-Saxon to

Singular	Plural
ner-e-do	ner-e-don
ner-e-dest	ner-e-don
ner-e-do	ner-e-don

Subjunctive:

ner-e-de	ner-e-don
ner-e-de	ner-e-don
ner-e-de	ner-e-don

Let us now look to the auxiliary verb *to do*, in Anglo-Saxon.

Singular	Plural
dide	didon
didest	didon
dide	didon

If we had only the Anglo-Saxon preterite *nerêde* and the Anglo-Saxon *dide*, the identity of the *de* in *nerêde* with *dide* would not be very apparent. But here you will perceive the advantage which Gothic has over all other Teutonic dialects for the purposes of grammatical comparison and analysis. It is in Gothic, and in Gothic in the plural only, that the full auxiliary *dêdum, dêduþ, dêdun,* has been preserved. In the Gothic singular *nasida, nasidês, nasida* stand for *nasidedu, nasidedês, nasidedu.* The same contraction has taken place in Anglo-Saxon, not only in the singular but in the plural also. Yet, such is the similarity between Gothic and Anglo-Saxon that we cannot doubt their preterites having been formed on the same last. If there be any truth in inductive reasoning, there must have been an original Anglo-Saxon preterite*—

Singular	Plural
ner-ĕ-dide	ner-ĕ-didon
ner-ĕ-didest	ner-ĕ-didon
ner-ĕ-dide	ner-ĕ-didon

And as *ner-ĕ-dide* dwindled down to *nerêde,* so *nerĕde* would, in modern English, become *nered.* The *d* of the preterite, therefore, which changes *I love* into *I loved* is originally the auxiliary verb *to do,* and *I loved* is the same as *I love did,* or *I did love.* In English dialects, as, for instance, in the Dorset dialect, every preterite, if it expresses a lasting or repeated action, is formed by *I did,*† and a distinction is thus established between "e died eesterdae," and ' the vo'ke did die by scores ;' though originally *died* is the same as *die did.*

It might be asked, however, very properly, how *did* itself, or the Anglo-Saxon *dide,* was formed, and how it received the meaning of a preterite. In *dide* the final *de* is not a termination, but it is the root, and the first syllable *di* is a reduplication of the root.

---

* Bopp, *Comp. Grammar,* § 620. Grimm, *German Grammar,* ii. 845.

† Barnes, *Dorsetshire Dialect,* p. 39.

The fact being that all preterites of old, or, as they are called, strong verbs, were formed as in Greek and Sanskrit by means of reduplication, reduplication being one of the principal means by which roots were invested with a verbal character.* The root *do* in Anglo-Saxon is the same as the root *thē* in *tithēmi* in Greek, and the Sanskrit root *dhâ* in *dadhâmi*. Anglo-Saxon *dide* would therefore correspond to Sanskrit *dadhau*, I placed.

Now, in this manner, the whole, or nearly the whole, grammatical framework of the Aryan or Indo-European languages has been traced back to original independent words, and even the slightest changes which at first sight seem so mysterious, such as *foot* into *feet*, or *I find* into *I found*, have been fully accounted for. This is what is called comparative grammar, or a scientific analysis of all the formal elements of a language preceded by a comparison of all the varieties which one and the same form has assumed in the numerous dialects of the Aryan family. The most important dialects for this purpose are Sanskrit, Greek, Latin, and Gothic; but in many cases Zend, or Celtic, or Slavonic dialects come in to throw an unexpected light on forms unintelligible in any of the four principal dialects. The result of such a work as Bopp's *Comparative Grammar* of the Aryan languages may be summed up in a few words. The whole framework of grammar—the elements of derivation, declension, and conjugation—had become settled before the separation of the Aryan family. Hence the broad outlines of grammar, in Sanskrit, Greek, Latin, Gothic, and the rest, are in reality the

---

* See M. M.'s *Letter on the Turanian Languages*, pp. 44, 46.

same; and the apparent differences can be explained by phonetic corruption, which is determined by the phonetic peculiarities of each nation. On the whole, the history of all the Aryan languages is nothing but a gradual process of decay. After the grammatical terminations of all these languages have been traced back to their most primitive form, it is possible, in many instances, to determine their original meaning. This, however, can be done by means of induction only; and the period during which, as in the Provençal *dir vos ai*, the component elements of the old Aryan grammar maintained a separate existence in the language and the mind of the Aryans, had closed before Sanskrit was Sanskrit or Greek Greek. That there was such a period we can doubt as little as we can doubt the real existence of fern forests previous to the formation of our coal fields. We can do even more. Suppose we had no remnants of Latin; suppose the very existence of Rome and of Latin were unknown to us; we might still prove, on the evidence of the six Romance dialects, that there must have been a time when these dialects formed the language of a small settlement; nay, by collecting the words which all these dialects share in common, we might to a certain extent reconstruct the original language, and draw a sketch of the state of civilisation, as reflected by these common words. The same can be done if we compare Sanskrit, Greek, Latin, Gothic, Celtic, and Slavonic. The words which have as nearly as possible the same form and meaning in all the languages must have existed before the people, who afterwards formed the prominent nationalities of the Aryan family, separated; and, if carefully interpreted, they, too, will serve as evidence as to the state of

civilisation attained by the Aryans before they left
their common home. It can be proved by the evidence of language, that before their separation the
Aryans led the life of agricultural nomads — a life
such as Tacitus describes that of the ancient Germans.
They knew the arts of ploughing, of making roads, of
building ships, of weaving and sewing, of erecting
houses; they had counted at least as far as one
hundred. They had domesticated the most important
animals, the cow, the horse, the sheep, the dog; they
were acquainted with the most useful metals, and
armed with iron hatchets, whether for peaceful or
warlike purposes. They had recognised the bonds of
blood and the bonds of marriage; they followed
their leaders and kings, and the distinction between
right and wrong was fixed by laws and customs.
They were impressed with the idea of a Divine Being,
and they invoked it by various names. All this, as I
said, can be proved by the evidence of language. For
if you find that languages like Greek, Latin, Gothic,
Celtic, or Slavonic, which, after their first separation, have had but little contact with Sanskrit, have
the same word, for instance, for *iron* which exists in
Sanskrit, this is proof absolute that iron was known
previous to the Aryan separation. Now, *iron* is *ais*
in Gothic, and *ayas* in Sanskrit, a word which, as it
could not have been borrowed by the Indians from
the Germans or by the Germans from the Indians,
must have existed previous to their separation. We
could not find the same name for house in Sanskrit,
Greek, Latin, Slavonic, and Celtic,* unless houses
had been known before the separation of these dialects.
In this manner a history of Aryan civilisation has

---

* Sk. *dama*; Gr. δόμος; L. *domus*; Slav. *domŭ*; Celt. *daimh*.

been written from the archives of language, stretching back to times far beyond the reach of any documentary history.*

The very name of *Arya* belongs to this history, and I shall devote the rest of this lecture to tracing the origin and gradual spreading of this old word. I had intended to include, in to-day's lecture, a short account of *comparative mythology*, a branch of our science which restores the original form and meaning of decayed words by the same means by which comparative grammar recovers the original form and meaning of terminations. But my time is too limited; and, as I have been asked repeatedly why I applied the name of *Aryan* to that family of language which we have just examined, I feel that I am bound to give an answer.

Arya is a Sanskrit word, and in the later Sanskrit it means *noble, of a good family*. It was, however, originally a national name, and we see traces of it as late as the Law-book of the Mânavas, where India is still called *Arya-âvarta*, the abode of the *Aryas*.† In the old Sanskrit, in the hymns of the Veda, *ârya* occurs frequently as a national name and as a name of honour, comprising the worshippers of the gods of the Brahmans, as opposed to their enemies, who are called in the Veda *Dasyus*. Thus one of the gods, *Indra*, who, in some respects, answers to the Greek Zeus, is invoked in the following words (*Rig-veda*, i. 57, 8): 'Know thou the Aryas, O Indra, and they who are Dasyus; punish the lawless, and

---

* See M. M.'s *Essay on Comparative Mythology*, Oxford Essays, 1856.

† Arya-bhûmi, and Arya-desa are used in the same sense.

deliver them unto thy servant! Be thou the mighty helper of the worshippers, and I will praise all these thy deeds at the festivals.'

In the later dogmatic literature of the Vedic age, the name of Ârya is distinctly appropriated to the three first castes—the Brahmans, Kshatriyas, Vaiśyas—as opposed to the fourth, or the Sûdras. In the *Satapatha-Brâhmana* it is laid down distinctly: 'Âryas, are only the Brahmans, the Kshatriyas, and Vaiśyas, for they are admitted to the sacrifices. They shall not speak with everybody, but only with the Brahman, the Kshatriya, and the Vaiśya. If they should fall into a conversation with a Sûdra, let them say to another man, "Tell this Sûdra so." This is the law.'

In the *Atharva-veda* (iv. 20, 4; xix. 62, 1) expressions occur such as, 'seeing all things, whether Sûdra or Ârya,' where Sûdra and Ârya are meant to express the whole of mankind.

This word *ârya* with a long *â* is derived from *arya* with a short *a*, and this name *arya* is applied in the later Sanskrit to a Vaiśya, or a member of the third caste.* What is called the third class must originally have constituted the large majority of the Brahmanic society, for all who were not soldiers or priests were Vaiśyas. We may well understand, therefore, how a name, originally applied to the cultivators of the soil and householders, should in time have become the general name of all Aryans.† Why

---

* *Pân.* iii. 1, 103.

† In one of the Vedas, *arya* with a short *a* is used like *ârya*, as opposed to Sûdra. For we read (*Vâj-San.* xx. 17): 'Whatever sin we have committed in the village, in the forest, in the house, in the open air, against a Sûdra, against an Arya — thou art our deliverance.'

the householders were called *arya* is a question which would carry us too far at present. I can only state that the etymological signification of Arya seems to be, 'one who ploughs or tills,' and that it is connected with the root of *arare*. The Aryans would seem to have chosen this name for themselves as opposed to the nomadic races, *the Turanians*, whose original name *Tura* implies the swiftness of the horseman.

In India, as we saw, the name of Ârya, as a national name, fell into oblivion in later times, and was preserved only in the term Âryâvarta, the abode of the Aryans. But it was more faithfully preserved by the Zoroastrians who migrated from India to the north-west, and whose religion has been preserved to us in the *Zend-avesta*, though in fragments only. Now *Airya* in Zend means venerable, and is at the same time the name of the people.* In the first chapter of the *Vendidâd*, where Ahuramazda explains to Zarathustra the order in which he created the earth, sixteen countries are mentioned, each, when created by Ahuramazda, being pure and perfect; but each being tainted in turn by Angro mainyus or Ahriman. Now the first of these countries is called *Airyanem vaêjô, Arianum semen*, the Aryan seed, and its position is supposed to have been as far east as the western slopes of the Belurtag and Mustag, near the sources of the Oxus and Yaxartes, the highest elevation of Central Asia.† From this country, which is called their seed, the Aryans, according to their own traditions, advanced towards the south and west, and in the *Zend-avesta* the whole extent of country occupied by the Aryans is likewise called *Airyâ*. A line

* Lassen, *Ind. Alt.* b. i. s. 6.   † *Ibid.* b. i. s. 528.

drawn from India along the Paropamisus and Caucasus Indicus in the east, following in the north the direction between the Oxus and Yaxartes,* then running along the Caspian Sea, so as to include Hyrcania and Rágha, then turning south-east on the borders of Nisaea, Aria (i.e. Haria), and the countries washed by the Etymandrus and Arachotus, would indicate the general horizon of the Zoroastrian world. It would be what is called in the fourth cardé of the Yasht of Mithra, 'the whole space of Aria,' *vîspem airyâ-śayanem* (totum Ariæ situm).† Opposed to the Aryan we find in the Zendavesta the non-Aryan countries (anairyâo dainhâvô)‡, and traces of this name are found in the 'Αναριάκαι, a people and town on the frontiers of Hyrcania.§ Greek geographers use the name of Ariana in a wider sense even than the *Zend-avesta*. All the country between the Indian Ocean in the south and the Indus in the east, the Hindu-kush and Paropamisus in the north, the Caspian gates, Karmania, and the mouth of the Persian gulf in the west, is included by Strabo (xv. 2) under the name of Ariana; and Bactria is thus called‖ by him 'the

* Ptolemy knows 'Αριάκαι, near the mouth of the Yaxartes. Ptol. vi. 14; Lassen, *loc. cit.* L 6.

† Burnouf, *Yaçna*, Notes, 61. In the same sense the *Zend-avesta* uses the expression. Aryan provinces, 'airyanâm daṅyunâm' gen. plur., or 'airyâo dainhâvô,' provinciæ Arianæ. Burnouf, *Yaçna*, 442; and *Notes*, p. 70.

‡ Burnouf, *Notes*, p. 62.

§ Strabo, xi. 7, 11; Plin. *Hist. Nat.* vi. 19; Ptol. vi. 2; De Sacy, *Mémoires sur diverses Antiquités de la Perse*, p. 48; Lassen, *Indische Alterthumskunde*, L 6.

‖ Strabo, xi. 11; Burnouf, *Notes*, p. 110. 'In another place Eratosthenes is cited as describing the western boundary to be a line separating Parthiens from Media, and Karmania from Para-

ornament of the whole of Ariana.' As the Zoroastrian religion spread westward, Persia, Elymais, and Media all claimed for themselves the Aryan title. Hellanicus, who wrote before Herodotus, knows of Aria as a name of Persia.* Herodotus (vii. 62) attests that the Medians called themselves Arii; and even for Atropatene, the northernmost part of Media, the name of Ariania (not Aria) has been preserved by Stephanus Byzantinus. As to Elymais its name has been derived from *Ailama*, a supposed corruption of *Airyama*.† The Persians, Medians, Bactrians, and Sogdians all spoke, as late as the time of Strabo,‡ nearly the same language, and we may well understand, therefore, that they should have claimed for themselves one common name, in opposition to the hostile tribes of Turan.

That *Aryan* was used as a title of honour in the Persian empire is clearly shown by the cuneiform inscriptions of Darius. He calls himself *Ariya* and *Ariya-chitra*, an Aryan and of Aryan descent; and Ahuramazda, or, as he is called by Darius, Auramazda, is rendered in the Turanian translation of

---

takene and Persia, thus taking in Yezd and Kerman, but excluding Fars.'—Wilson, *Ariana antiqua*, p. 120.

* Hellanicus, fragm. 166, ed. Müller. Ἀρία Περσική χώρα.

† Joseph Müller, *Journal Asiatique*, 1839, p. 298. Lassen, loc. cit. L 6. From this the Elam of *Genesis*. *Mélanges Asiatiques*, i. p. 623. In the cuneiform inscriptions which represent the pronunciation of Persian under the Achaemenian dynasty, the letter *l* is wanting altogether. In the names of Babylon and Arbela it is replaced by *r*. The *l* appears, however, in the Sassanian inscriptions, where both Allán and Airán, Anillán and Aniran occur.

‡ Heeren, *Ideen*, L p. 337: ὁμόγλωττοι παρὰ μικρόν. Strabo, p. 1054.

the inscription of Behistun, 'the god of the Aryans.' Many historical names of the Persians contain the same element. The great-grandfather of Darius is called in the inscriptions Ariyârâmna, the Greek *Ariaramnês* (Herod. vii. 90). Ariobarzanés (i. e. Euergetés), Ariomanes (i. e. Eumenés), Ariomardos, all show the same origin.*

About the same time as these inscriptions, Eudemos, a pupil of Aristotle, as quoted by Damascius, speaks of 'the Magi and the whole Aryan race,'† evidently using Aryan in the same sense in which the *Zend-avesta* spoke of 'the whole country of Aria.'

And when after years of foreign invasion and occupation, Persia rose again under the sceptre of the Sassanians to be a national kingdom, we find the new national kings, the worshippers of Masdanes, calling themselves, in the inscriptions deciphered by De Sacy,‡ 'Kings of the Aryan and un-Aryan races;' in Pehlevi, *Irân va Anirân*; in Greek, Ἀριάνων καὶ Ἀναριάνων.

The modern name of Irân for Persia still keeps up the memory of this ancient title.

In the name of *Armenia* the same element of *Arya* has been supposed to exist.§ The name of Armenia,

---

* One of the Median classes is called Ἀριζαντοί, which may be *âryajantu*. Herod. i. 101.

† Μάγοι δὲ καὶ πᾶν τὸ Ἄρειον γένος, ὡς καὶ τοῦτο γράφει ὁ Εὔδημος, οἱ μὲν τόπον, οἱ δὲ χρόνον καλοῦσι τὸ νοητὸν ἅπαν καὶ τὸ ἡνωμένον· ἐξ οὗ διακριθῆναι ἢ θεὸν ἀγαθὸν καὶ δαίμονα κακὸν ἢ φῶς καὶ σκότος πρὸ τούτων, ὡς ἐνίους λέγειν. Οὕτω δὲ οὖν καὶ αὐτοὶ μετὰ τὴν ἀδιάκριτον φύσιν διακρινομένην ποιοῦσι τὴν διττὴν συστοιχίαν τῶν κρειττόνων, τῆς μὲν ἡγεῖσθαι τὸν Ὡρομάσδην, τῆς δὲ τὸν Ἀρειμάνιον. Damascius, *Quæstiones de primis Principiis*, ed. Kopp, 1826, cap. 125, p. 384.

‡ De Sacy, *Mémoire*, p. 47; Lassen, *Ind. Alt.* i. 8.

§ Burnouf, *Notes*, 107. Spiegel, *Beiträge zur vergl. Sprachf.*

however, does not occur in Zend, and the name *Armina*, which is used for Armenia in the cuneiform inscriptions, is of doubtful etymology.* In the language of Armenia, *ari* is used in the widest sense for Aryan or Iranian; it means also brave, and is applied more especially to the Medians.† The word *arya*, therefore, though not contained in the name of Armenia, can be proved to have existed in the Armenian language as a national and honourable name.

West of Armenia, on the borders of the Caspian Sea, we find the ancient name of *Albania*. The Armenians call the Albanians *Aghovan*, and as *gh* in Armenian stands for *r* or *l*, it has been conjectured by Boré, that in *Aghovan* also the name of Aria is contained. This seems doubtful. But in the valleys of the Caucasus we meet with an Aryan race speaking an Aryan language, the *Os* of *Ossethi*, and they call themselves *Iron*.‡

Along the Caspian, and in the country washed by

i. 31. Anquetil had no authority for taking the Zend *airyanam* for Armenia.

* Bochart shows (*Phaleg*, l. 1, c. 3, col. 20) that the Chaldee paraphrast renders the Mini of Jeremiah by Har Mini, and as the same country is called Minyas by Nicolaus Damascenus, he infers that the first syllable is the Semitic Har, a mountain (see Rawlinson's *Glossary*, s. v.).

† Lassen, *Ind. Alt.* I. 8, note. *Arikh* also is used in Armenian as the name of the Medians, and has been referred by Jos. Müller to Aryaka as a name of Media. *Journ. As.* 1839, p. 299. If, as Quatremère says, *ari* and *asuri* are used in Armenian for Medians and Persians, this can only be ascribed to a misunderstanding, and must be a phrase of later date.

‡ Sjögren, *Ossetic Grammar*, p. 396. Scylax and Apollodorus mention Ἄριοι and Ἀμάρια, south of the Caucasus. Pictet, *Origines*, 67; Scylax, *Perip.* p. 213, ed. Klausen; *Apollodori Biblioth.* p. 433, ed Heyne.

the Oxus and Yaxartes, Aryan and non-Aryan tribes were mingled together for centuries. Though the relation between Aryans and Turanians was hostile, and though there were continual wars between them, as we learn from the great Persian epic, the Shahnámeh, it does not follow that all the nomad races who infested the settlements of the Aryans were of Tatar blood and speech. Turvaśa and his descendants, who represent the Turanians, are described in the later epic poems of India as cursed and deprived of their inheritance in India; but in the Vedas Turvaśa is represented as worshipping Aryan gods. Even in the Shahnámeh, Persian heroes go over to the Turanians and lead them against Iran, very much as Coriolanus led the Samnites against Rome. We may thus understand why so many Turanian or Scythian names, mentioned by Greek writers, should show evident traces of Aryan origin. *Aspa* was the Persian name for *horse*, and in the Scythian names *Aspabotu*, *Aspakara*, and *Asparatha*,* we can hardly fail to recognise the same element. Even the name of the Aspasian mountains, placed by Ptolemy in Scythia, indicates a similar origin. Nor is the word Arya unknown beyond the Oxus. There is a people called *Ariaca*,† another called *Antariani*.‡ A king of the Scythians, at the time of Darius, was called *Ariantes*. A contemporary of Xerxes is known by the name of *Aripithes* (i. e. Sanskrit *aryapati*; Zend *airyapaiti*): and *Sparapithes* seems to have some connection with the Sanskrit *svargapati*, lord of heaven.

* Burnouf, *Notes*, p. 105.
† Ptol. vi. 2, and vi. 14. There are 'Αραρίκαι on the frontiers of Hyrcania. Strabo, xi. 7; Pliny, *Hist. Nat.* vi. 19.
‡ On Arimaspi and Aramati, see Burnouf, *Notes*, p. 105; Plin. vi. 9.

We have thus traced the name of Árya from India to the west, from Áryâvarta to Ariana, Persia, Media, more doubtfully to Armenia and Albania, to the Iron in the Caucasus, and to some of the nomad tribes in Transoxiana. As we approach Europe the traces of this name grow fainter, yet they are not altogether lost.

Two roads were opened to the Aryans of Asia in their westward migrations. One through Chorasan * to the north, through what is now called Russia, and thence to the shores of the Black Sea and Thrace. Another from Armenia, across the Caucasus or across the Black Sea to Northern Greece, and along the Danube to Germany. Now on the former road the Aryans left a trace of their migrations in the old name of Thrace, which was *Aria* ;† on the latter we meet in the eastern part of Germany, near the Vistula, with a German tribe called *Arii*. And as in Persia we found many proper names in which *Arya* formed an important ingredient, so we find again in German history names such as *Ariovistus*.‡

Though we look in vain for any traces of this old national name among the Greeks and Romans, some scholars believe that it may have been preserved in the extreme west of the Aryan migrations, in the very name of *Ireland*. The common etymology of *Erin* is that it means 'island of the west,' *iar-innis*, or land of

---

* Qairizem in the Zend-avesta, *Uvârazmis* in the inscriptions of Darius.

† Stephanus Byzantinus.

‡ Grimm, *Rechtsalterthümer*, p. 292, traces Arii and Ariovistus back to the Gothic *harji*, army. If this etymology be right, this part of our argument must be given up.

the west, *iar-in*. But this is clearly wrong.* The old name is *Eriu* in the nominative, more recently *Eire*. It is only in the oblique cases that the final *n* appears, as in Latin words such as *regio, regionis*. *Erin* therefore has been explained as a derivative of *Er* or *Eri*, said to be the ancient name of the Irish Celts as preserved in the Anglo-Saxon name of their country, *Ireland*.† It is maintained by O'Reilly, though denied by others, that *er* is used in Irish in the sense of noble, like the Sanskit *árya*.‡

* Pictet, *Les Origines Indo-Européennes*, p. 31. ' *Iar*, l'ouest, ne s'écrit jamais *er* ou *air*, et la forme *Iariu* ne se rencontre nulle part pour Erin.' Zeuss gives *iar-rend*, insula occidentalis. But *rend* (recte *rind*) makes *rendo* in the gen. sing.

† Old Norse *irar*, Irishmen, Anglo-Saxon *ira*, Irishman.

‡ Though I state these views on the authority of M. Pictet, I think it right to add the following note which an eminent Irish scholar has had the kindness to send me :—

The ordinary name of Ireland, in the oldest Irish MSS, is (*h*)*Eriu*, gen. (*h*)*Erenn*, dat. (*h*)*Erinn*. The initial *h* is often omitted. Before etymologising on the word, we must try to fix its Old Celtic form. Of the ancient names of Ireland which are found in Greek and Latin writers, the only one which *hériu* can formally represent is *Hiberio*. The abl. sing. of this form — *Hiberione* — is found in the Book of Armagh, a Latin MS of the early part of the ninth century. From the same MS we also learn that a name of the Irish people was *Hyberionaces*, which is obviously a derivative from the stem of *Hiberio*. Now if we remember that the Old Irish scribes often prefixed *h* to words beginning with a vowel (e.g. *h-abunde, h-arundo, h-erimus, h-ostium*), and that they also often wrote *b* for the *v* consonant (e. g. *babes, fribulus, corbus, sabonius*); if, moreover, we observe that the Welsh and Breton names for Ireland — *Iwerddon, Iwerdon*, point to an Old Celtic name beginning with IVER—, we shall have little difficulty in giving *Hiberio* a correctly Latinised form, viz. *Iverio*. This in Old Celtic would be *Iveriu*, gen. *Iveriones*. So the Old Celtic form of *Fronto* was *Frontiu*, as we see from the

Some of the evidence here collected in tracing the ancient name of the Aryan family, may seem doubtful, and I have pointed out myself some links of the chain uniting the earliest name of India with the modern name of Ireland, as weaker than the rest. But the principal links are safe. Names of countries, peoples, rivers, and mountains, have an extraordinary vitality, and they will remain while cities, kingdoms, and nations pass away. *Rome* has the same name

Gaulish inscription at Vieux Poitiers. As *v* when flanked by vowels is always lost in Irish, *Iveriu* would become *ieriu*, and then, the first two vowels running together, *ériu*. As regards the double *n* in the oblique cases of *ériu*, the genitive *Érenn* (e.g.) is to *Iverionos* as the Old Irish *anmann* 'names' is to the Skr. *námáni*, Lat. *nomina*. The doubling of the *n* may perhaps be due to the Old Celtic accent. What then is the etymology of *Ieeriú*? I venture to think that it may (like the Lat. *Aver-nus*, Gr. Ἄφερ-νος) be connected with the Skr. *avara*, 'posterior,' 'western.' So the Irish *des*, Welsh *deheu*, 'right,' 'south,' is the Skr. *dakshina*, 'dexter,' and the Irish *áir*, (in *an-áir*), if it stand for *páir*, 'east,' is the Skr. *púrva*, 'anterior.'

M. Pictet regards Ptolemy's Ἰουερνία (Ivernia) as coming nearest to the Old Celtic form of the name in question. He further sees in the first syllable what he calls the Irish *ibh*, 'land,' 'tribe of people,' and he thinks that this *ibh* may be connected not only with the Vedic *ibha*, 'family,' but with the Old High German *eiba*, 'a district.' But, first, according to the Irish phonetic laws, *ibha* would have appeared as *eb* in Old, *eabh* in Modern-Irish. Secondly, the *ei* in *eiba* is a diphthong = Gothic *ái*, Irish *óí*, *óe*, Skr. *é*. Consequently *ibh* and *ibha* cannot be identified with *eiba*. Thirdly, there is no such word as *ibh* in the nom. sing., although it *is* to be found in O'Reilly's dictionary, along with his explanation of the intensive prefix *er*—, as 'noble,' and many other blunders and forgeries. The form *ibh* is, no doubt, producible, but it is a very modern dative plural of *úa*, 'a descendant.' Irish districts were often called by the names of the occupying clans. These clans were often called 'descendants (*húi, hí, í*) of such an one.' Hence the blunder of the Irish lexicographer.—W. S.

to-day, and will probably have it for ever, which was given to it by the earliest Latin and Sabine settlers; and wherever we find the name of Rome, whether in Wallachia, which by the inhabitants is called Rumunia, or in the dialects of the Grisons, the Romansch, in the title of the Romance languages, or in the name of Rouma, given by the Arabs to the Greeks, and in that of Roumelia, we know that some threads would lead us back to the Rome of Romulus and Remus, the stronghold of the earliest warriors of Latium. The ruined city near the mouth of the Upper Zab, now usually known by the name of Nimrud, is called *Athur* by the Arabic geographers, and in Athur we recognise the old name of Assyria, which Dio Cassius writes Atyria, remarking that the barbarians changed the Sigma into Tau. Assyria is called Athurâ in the inscriptions of Darius.[*] We hear of battles fought on the *Sutledge*, and we hardly think that the battlefield of the Sikhs was nearly the same where Alexander fought the kings of the Penjâb. But the name of the *Sutledge* is the name of the same river as the *Hesudrus* of Alexander, the *Śatadru* of the Indians, and among the oldest hymns of the Veda, about 1500 B.C., we find a war-song referring to a battle fought on the two banks of the same stream.

No doubt there is danger in trusting to mere similarity of names. Grimm may be right that the Arii of Tacitus were originally Harii, and that their name is not connected with Arya. But the evidence on either side being merely conjectural, this must remain an open question. In most cases, however, a strict observation of the phonetic laws peculiar to each language will remove all uncertainty. Grimm,

[*] See Rawlinson's *Glossary*, s. v.

in his *History of the German Language* (p. 228), imagined that *Hariva*, the name of *Herat* in the cuneiform inscriptions, is connected with Arii, the name which, as we saw, Herodotus gives to the Medes. This cannot be, for the initial aspiration in *Hariva* points to a word which in Sanskrit begins with *s*, and not with a vowel, like *Arya*. The following remarks will make this clearer.

Herat is called *Herat* and *Heri*,[*] and the river on which it stands is called *Heri-rud*. This river *Heri* is called by Ptolemy 'Αρείας,[†] by other writers *Arius*; and *Aria* is the name given to the country between Parthia (Parthuwa) in the west, Margiana (Murghush) in the north, Bactria (Bakhtrish) and Arachosia (Harauwatish) in the east, and Drangiana (Zaraka) in the south. This, however, though without the initial *h*, is not Ariana, as described by Strabo, but an independent country, forming part of it. It is supposed to be the same as the *Haraiva* (Hariva) of the cuneiform inscriptions, though this is doubtful. But it is mentioned in the *Zend-avesta* under the name of *Haróyu*,[‡] as the sixth country created by Ormuzd. We can trace this name with the initial *h* even be-

---

[*] W. Ouseley, *Orient. Geog. of Ebn Haukal*. Burnouf, *Yaçna*, Notes, p. 102.

[†] Ptol. vi. c. 17.

[‡] It has been supposed that *haróyúm* in the *Zend-avesta* stands for *haraivem*, and that the nominative was not *Haróyu*, but *Haraivó*. (Oppert, *Journal Asiatique*, 1851, p. 280.) Without denying the possibility of the correctness of this view, which is partially supported by the accusative *vidóyúm*, from *vidaivo*, enemy of the Divs, there is no reason why *Haróyúm* should not be taken for a regular accusative of *Haróyu*, the long *ú* in the accusative being due to the final nasal. (Burnouf, *Yaçna*, Notes, p. 103.) This *Haróyu* would be in the nominative as regular a form as *Suruyu* in Sanskrit, nay even more regular, as *haróyu* would presuppose a Sanskrit *sarasyu* or *sarayu*, from *saras*.

yond the time of Zoroaster. The Zoroastrians were a colony from northern India. They had been together for a time with the people whose sacred songs have been preserved to us in the Veda. A schism took place, and the Zoroastrians migrated westward to Arachosia and Persia. In their migrations they did what the Greeks did when they founded new colonies, what the Americans did in founding new cities. They gave to the new cities and to the rivers along which they settled, the names of cities and rivers familiar to them, and reminding them of the localities which they had left. Now, as a Persian *h* points to a Sanskrit *s*, *Haroyu* would be in Sanskrit *Saroyu*. One of the sacred rivers of India, a river mentioned in the Veda, and famous in the epic poems as the river of Ayodhyâ, one of the earliest capitals of India, the modern Awadh or Hanumân-garhi, has the name of *Sarayu*, the modern *Sarju*.*

As Comparative Philology has thus traced the ancient name of Ârya from India to Europe, as the original title assumed by the Aryans before they left their common home, it is but natural that it should have been chosen as the technical term for the family of languages which was formerly designated as Indo-Germanic, Indo-European, Caucasian, or Japhetic.

Sarayû occurs also with a long *û*; see Wilson, s. v. M. Oppert rightly identifies the people of *Harôiva* with the 'Αρειοι, not, like Grimm, with the Άριοι.

* It is derived from a root *sar* or *sṛi* to go, to run, from which *saras*, water, *sarit*, river, and *Sarayu*, the proper name of the river near the capital of Oude; and we may conclude with great probability that this Sarayu or Sarasyu gave the name to the river Arius or Heri, and to the country of ῎Αρια or Herat. Anyhow ῎Αρια as the name of Herat has no connection with ῎Αρια the wide country of the Aryas.

LECTURE VII.

THE CONSTITUENT ELEMENTS OF LANGUAGE.

OUR analysis of some of the nominal and verbal formations in the Aryan or Indo-European family of speech has taught us that, however mysterious and complicated these grammatical forms appear at first sight, they are in reality the result of a very simple process. It seems at first almost hopeless to ask such questions as why the addition of a mere *d* should change love present into love past, or why the termination *ai* in French, if added to *aimer*, should convey the idea of love to come. But, once placed under the microscope of comparative grammar, these and all other grammatical forms assume a very different and much more intelligible aspect. We saw how what we now call terminations were originally independent words. After coalescing with the words which they were intended to modify, they were gradually reduced to mere syllables and letters, unmeaning in themselves, yet manifesting their former power and independence by the modification which they continue to produce in the meaning of the words to which they are appended. The true nature of grammatical terminations was first pointed out by a philosopher, who, however wild some of his speculations may be, had certainly caught many a glimpse of the real life and growth of language; I mean Horne Tooke. This is what he writes of terminations :*—

'For though I think I have good reasons to believe that all terminations may likewise be traced to their respective origin; and that, however artificial they may now appear to us, they were not originally the effect of premeditated and deliberate art, but separate words by length of time corrupted and coalescing with the words of which they are now considered as the terminations; yet this was less likely to be suspected by others. And if it had been suspected, they would have had much further to travel to their journey's end, and through a road much more embarrassed; as the corruption in those languages is of much longer standing than in ours, and more complex.'

Horne Tooke, however, though he saw rightly what road should be followed to track the origin of grammatical terminations, was himself without the means to reach his journey's end. Most of his explanations are quite untenable, and it is curious to observe in reading his book, the *Diversions of Purley*, how a man of a clear, sharp, and powerful mind, and reasoning according to sound and correct principles, may yet, owing to his defective knowledge of facts, arrive at conclusions directly opposed to truth.

When we have once seen how grammatical terminations are to be traced back in the beginning to independent words, we have learnt at the same time that the component elements of language, which remain in our crucible at the end of a complete

* *Diversions of Purley*, p. 190.

grammatical analysis, are of two kinds, namely, *Roots predicative* and *Roots demonstrative*.

We call *root* or *radical* whatever, in the words of any language or family of languages, cannot be reduced to a simpler or more original form. It may be well to illustrate this by a few examples. But, instead of taking a number of words in Sanskrit, Greek, and Latin, and tracing them back to their common centre, it will be more instructive if we begin with a root which has been discovered, and follow it through its wanderings from language to language. I take the root AR, to which I alluded in our last Lecture as the source of the word *Arya*, and we shall thus, while examining its ramification, learn at the same time why that name was chosen by the agricultural nomads, the ancestors of the Aryan race.

This root AR* means *to plough*, to open the soil. From it we have the Latin *ar-are*, the Greek *ar-oun*, the Irish *ar*, the Lithuanian *ar-ti*, the Russian *ora-ti*, the Gothic *ar-jan*, the Anglo-Saxon *er-jan*, the modern English *to ear*. Shakespeare says (Richard II. iii. 2), 'to ear the land that has some hope to grow.' We read in Deut. xxi. 4, 'a rough valley which is neither eared nor sown.'

From this we have the name of the plough, or the instrument of earing: in Latin, *ara-trum*; in Greek, *aro-tron*; in Bohemian, *oradlo*; in Lithuanian, *arkla-s*; in Cornish, *aradar*; in Welsh, *arad*;† in

---

* AR might be traced back to the Sanskrit root, *ri*, to go (Pott, *Etymologische Forschungen*, i. 218); but for our present purposes the root AR is sufficient.

† If, as has been supposed, the Cornish and Welsh words were corruptions of the Latin *aratrum*, they would have appeared as *areader*, *arad*, respectively.

Old Norse, *ardhr*. In Old Norse, however, *ardhr*, meaning originally the plough, came to mean earnings or wealth; the plough being, in early times, the most essential possession and means of livelihood. In the same manner the Latin name for money, *pecunia*, was derived from *pecus*, cattle; the word *fee*, which is now restricted to the payment made to a doctor or lawyer, was in Old English *feh*, and in Anglo-Saxon *feoh*, meaning cattle and wealth; for *feoh*, and Gothic *faihu*, are really the same word as the Latin *pecus*, the modern German *vieh*.

The act of ploughing is called *aratio* in Latin; *arosis* in Greek: and I believe that *aroma*, too, in the sense of perfume, had the same origin; for what is sweeter or more aromatic than the smell of a ploughed field? In Genesis xxviii. 27, Jacob says 'the smell of my son is as the smell of a field which the Lord has blessed.'

A more primitive formation of the root *ar* seems to be the Greek *era*, earth, the Sanskrit *ira*, the Old High-German *ero*, the Gaelic *ire*, *irionn*. It meant originally the ploughed land, afterwards earth in general. Even the word *earth*, the Gothic *airtha*,[*] the Anglo-Saxon *eorthe*, must have been taken originally in the sense of ploughed or cultivated land. The derivative *ar-mentum*, formed like *ju-mentum*, would

---

[*] Grimm remarks justly that *airtha* could not be derived from *arjan*, on account of the difference in the vowels. But *airtha* is a much more ancient formation, and comes from the root *ar*, which root, again, was originally *pi* or *ir* (Benfey, *Kurze Gr.* p. 27). From this primitive root *pi* or *ir*, we must derive both the Sanskrit *irâ* or *idâ*, and the Gothic *airtha*. The latter would correspond to the Sanskrit *rita*. The true meaning of the Sanskrit *idâ* has never been discovered. The Brahmans explain it as prayer, but this is not its original meaning.

naturally have been applied to any animal fit for ploughing and other labour in the field, whether ox or horse.

As agriculture was the principal labour in that early state of society when we must suppose most of our Aryan words to have been formed and applied to their definite meanings, we may well understand how a word which originally meant this special kind of labour was afterwards used to signify labour in general. The most natural tendency in the growth of words and of their meanings is from the special to the general: thus *regere* and *gubernare*, which originally meant to steer a ship, took the general sense of governing. To *equip*, which originally was to furnish a ship (French *équiper* and *esquif*, from *schifo*, ship), came to mean furnishing in general. Now in modern German, *arbeit* means simply *labour*; *arbeitsam* means industrious. In Gothic, too, *arbaips* is only used to express labour and trouble in general. But in Old Norse, *erfidhi* means chiefly *ploughing*, and afterwards labour in general; and the same word in Anglo-Saxon, *earfodh* or *earfedhe*, is labour. Of course we might equally suppose that, as labourer, from meaning one who labours in general, came to take the special sense of an agricultural labourer, so *arbeit*, from meaning work in general, came to be applied, in Old Norse, to the work of ploughing. But as the root of *erfidhi* seems to be *ar*, our first explanation is the more plausible. Besides, the simple *ar* in Old Norse means ploughing and labour, and the Old High-German *art* has likewise the sense of ploughing.*

* Grimm derives *arbeit*, Gothic *arbaiths*, Old High-German *arapeit*, Modern High-German *arbeit*, directly from the Gothic *arbja*, heir; but admits a relationship between *arbja* and the

The Greek Aroura and the Latin *arvum*, a field, have to be referred to the root *ar*, to plough. And as ploughing was not only one of the earliest kinds of labour, but also one of the most primitive arts, I have no doubt that the Latin *ars*, *artis*, and our own word *art*, meant originally the art of all arts, first taught to mortals by the goddess of all wisdom, the art of cultivating the land. In Old High-German *aranti*, in Anglo-Saxon *arend*, means simply work; but they too must originally have meant the special work of agriculture; and in the English *errand*, and *errand-boy*, the same word is still in existence.

But *ar* did not only mean to plough, or to cut open the land; it was transferred at a very early time to the ploughing of the sea, or rowing. Thus Shakspeare says:—

> Make the sea serve them; which they *ear* and wound
> With keels.

In a similar manner, we find that Sanskrit derives from *ar* the substantive *aritra*, not in the sense of a plough, but in the sense of a rudder. In Anglo-Saxon we find the simple form *ár*, the English *oar*, as it were the plough-share of the water. The Greek also had used the root *ar* in the sense of rowing; for eretēs* in Greek is a rower, and, their word tri-ēr-ēs,

---

root *arjam*, to plough. He identifies *arôja* with the Slavonic *rab*, servant, slave, and *arbeit* with *rabota*, corvée, supposing that sons and heirs were the first natural slaves. He supposes even a relationship between *rabota* and the Latin *labor* (German Dictionary, s. v. Arbeit).

* Latin *remus* (O. Irish *rám*) for *resmus*, connected with ἐρετ- μός. From ἐρέτης, ἐρέσσω; and ὑπηρέτης, servant, helper. *Rostrum* from *rodere*.

meant originally a ship with three oars, or with three rows of oars,* a trireme.

This comparison of ploughing and rowing is of frequent occurrence in ancient languages. The English word *plough*, the Slavonic *ploug*, has been identified with the Sanskrit *plava*,† a ship, and with the Greek *ploion*, ship. As the Aryans spoke of a ship ploughing the sea, they also spoke of a plough sailing across the field; and thus it was that the same names were applied to both.‡ In English dialects, *plough* or *plow* is still used in the general sense of wagon or conveyance.§

We might follow the offshoots of this root *ar* still further, but the number of words which we have examined in various languages will suffice to show what is meant by a predicative root. In all these words *ar* is the radical element, all the rest is merely formative. The root *ar* is called a predicative root, because in whatever composition it enters, it predicates one and the same conception, whether of the plough, or the rudder, or the ox, or the field. Even

---

* Cf. Eur. *Her.* 455, κώπη ἀλώπηξ. Ἀμφήρης means having oars on both sides.

† From Sanskrit *plu*, πλέω: cf. *fleet* and *float*.

‡ Other similes: ὕρις, and ὕρριξ, ploughshare, derived by Plutarch from ὗς, boar. A plough is said to be called a pig's-nose. The Latin *porca*, a ploughed field, is derived from *porcus*, hog; and the German *fwricka*, furrow, is connected with *farah*, boar. The Sanskrit *vṛika*, wolf, from *vraich*, to tear, is used for plough (*Rv.* i. 117, 21). *Godaraṇa*, earth-tearer, is another word for plough in Sanskrit. Gothic *hoha*, plough = Sk. *kaka*, wolf. See Grimm, *Deutsche Sprache*, and Kuhn, *Indische Studien*, vol. i. p. 321.

§ In the Vale of Blackmore, a wagon is called *plough*, or *plow*, and *sull* (A.-S. *syl*) is used for *aratrum* (Barnes, *Dorset Dialect*, p. 369).

in such a word as *artistic*, the predicative power of the root *ar* may still be perceived, though, of course, as it were by means of a powerful telescope only. The Brahmans, who call themselves *ârya* in India, were no more aware of the real origin of this name and its connection with agricultural labour, than the artist who now speaks of *his art* as a divine inspiration suspects - that the word which he uses was originally applicable only to so primitive an art as that of ploughing.

We shall now examine another family of words, in order to see by what process the radical elements of words were first discovered.

Let us take the word *respectable*. It is a word of Latin, not of Saxon origin. In *respectabilis* we easily distinguish the verb *respectare* and the termination *bilis*. We then separate the prefix *re*, which leaves *spectare*, and we trace *spectare* as a participial formation back to the Latin verb *spicere* or *specere*, meaning to see, to look. In *specere*, again, we distinguish between the changeable termination *ere* and the unchangeable remnant *spec*, which we call the root. This root we expect to find in Sanskrit and the other Aryan languages; and so we do. In Sanskrit the more usual form is *paś*, to see, without the *s*; but *spaś* also is found in *spaśa*, a spy. in *spashṭa* and *vi-spashṭa*, clear, manifest, and in the Vedic *spaś*, a guardian. In the Teutonic family we find *spëhôn* in Old High-German meaning to look, to spy, to contemplate; and *spëha*, the English spy.* In Greek, the root *spek* has been changed into *skep*, which exists

---

* Pott, *Etymologische Forschungen*, p. 267; Benfey, *Griechisches Wurzelwörterbuch*, p. 236.

in *skeptomai*, I look, I examine; from whence *akeptikos*, an examiner or inquirer, in theological language, a sceptic; and *episkopos*, an overseer, a bishop. Let us now examine the various ramifications of this root. Beginning with *respectable*, we found that it originally meant a person who deserves *respect*, *respect* meaning *looking back*. We pass by common objects or persons without noticing them, whereas we turn back to look again at those which deserve our admiration, our regard, our respect. This was the original meaning of *respect* and *respectable*, nor need we be surprised at this if we consider that *noble*, *nobilis* in Latin, conveyed originally no more than the idea of a person that deserves to be known; for *nobilis* stands for *gnobilis*, just as *nomen* stands for *gnomen*, or *natus* for *gnatus*.

'With respect to' has now become almost a mere preposition. For if we say, 'With respect to this point I have no more to say,' this is the same as 'I have no more to say on this point.'

Again, as in looking back we single out a person, the adjective *respective*, and the adverb *respectively*, are used almost in the same sense as special, or singly.

The English *respite* is the Norman modification of *respectus*, the French *répit*. *Répit* meant originally looking back, reviewing the whole evidence. A criminal received so many days *ad respectum*, to re-examine the case. Afterwards it was said that the prisoner had received a respit, that is to say, had obtained a re-examination; and at last a verb was formed, and it was said that a person had been respited.

As *specere*, to see, with the preposition *re*, came

to mean respect, so with the preposition *de*, down, it forms the Latin *despicere*, meaning to look down, the English *despise*. The French *dépit* (Old French *despit*) means no longer contempt, though it is the Latin *despectus*, but rather *anger*, *vexatim*. *Se dépiter* is, to be vexed, to fret. '*En dépit de lui*' is originally 'angry with him,' then 'in spite of him;' and the English *spite*, *in spite of*, *spiteful*, are mere abbreviations of *despite*, *in despite of*, *despiteful*, and having nothing whatever to do with the spitting of cats.

As *de* means down from above, so *sub* means up from below, and this added to *specere*, to look, gives us *suspicere*, *suspicari*, to look up, in the sense of to suspect.* From it *suspicion*, *suspicious*; and likewise the French *soupçon*, even in such phrases as 'There is a soupçon of chicory in this coffee,' meaning just a touch, just the smallest atom of chicory.

As *circum* means round about, so *circumspect* means, of course, cautious, careful.

With *in*, meaning into, *specere* forms *inspicere*, to inspect; hence *inspector*, *inspection*.

With *ad* towards, *specere* becomes *adspicere*, to look at a thing. Hence *adspectus*, the aspect, the look or appearance of things.

So with *pro*, forward, *specere* became *prospicere*; and gave rise to such words as *prospectus*, as it were a look out, *prospective*, &c. With *con*, with, *specere* forms *conspicere*, to see together, *conspectus*, con-

---

* The Greek ὀπώπα, askance, is derived from ἀπό, and ὄπα, which is connected with δέρκομαι, I see: the Sanskrit *driś*. In Sanskrit, however, the more primitive root *dṛi*, or *dar*, has likewise been preserved, and is of frequent occurrence, particularly if joined with the preposition *â*; *tad âdṛitya*, with respect to this.

spicuous. We saw before in *respectable*, that a new word, *spectare*, is formed from the participle of *spicere*. This, with the preposition *ex*, out, gives us the Latin *exspectare*, the English *to expect*, to look out; with its derivatives.

Auspicium is another word which contains our root as the second of its component elements. The Latin *auspicium* stands for *avispicium*, and meant the looking out for certain birds which were considered to be of good or bad omen to the success of any public or private act. Hence *auspicious* is the sense of lucky. *Haru-spex* was the name given to a person who foretold the future from the inspection of the entrails of animals.

Again, from *specere*, *speculum* was formed, in the sense of looking-glass, or any other means of looking at oneself; and from it *speculari*, the English *to speculate*, *speculative*, &c.

But there are many more offshoots of this one root. Thus, the Latin *speculum*, looking-glass, became *specchio* in Italian; and the same word, though in a roundabout way, came into French, as the adjective *espiègle*, waggish. The origin of this French word is curious. There exists in German a famous cycle of stories, mostly tricks played by a half-historical, half-mythical character of the name of *Eulenspiegel*, or *Owl-glass*. These stories were translated into French, and the hero was known at first by the name of *Ulespiègle*, which name, contracted afterwards into *Espiègle*, became a general name for every wag.

As the French borrowed not only from Latin, but likewise from the Teutonic languages, we meet there, side by side with the derivatives of the Latin *specere*, the Old High-German *spëhôn*, slightly disguised as *épier*, to spy, the Italian *spiare*. The German word for a spy was *spëha*, and this appears in old French as *espie*, in modern French as *espion*.

One of the most prolific branches of the same root is the Latin *species*. Whether we take *species* in the sense of a perennial succession of similar individuals in continual generations (Jussieu), or look upon it as existing only as a category of thought (Agassiz), *species* was intended originally as the literal translation of the Greek *eidos* as opposed to *genos*, or *genus*. The Greeks classified things originally according to *kind* and *form*, and though these terms were afterwards technically defined by Aristotle, their etymological meaning is in reality the most appropriate. Things may be classified either because they are of the same *genus* or *kind*, that is to say, because they had the same origin; this gives us a genealogical classification: or they can be classified because they have the same appearance, *eidos*, or *form*, without claiming for them a common origin; and this gives us a morphological classification. It was, however, in the Aristotelian, and not in its etymological sense, that the Greek *eidos* was rendered in Latin by *species*, meaning the subdivision of a genus, the class of a family. Hence the French *espèce*, a kind; the English *special*, in the sense of particular as opposed to general. There is little of the root *spas*, to see, left in a *special train*, or a *special messenger*; yet the connection, though not apparent, can be restored with perfect certainty. We frequently hear the expression *to specify*. A man specifies his grievances. What does it mean? The mediæval Latin *specificus* is a literal translation of the Greek *eidopoios*. This means what makes or constitutes an *eidos* or species. Now, in classification, what constitutes a species is that particular quality which, superadded to other qualities, shared in common by all the members of a genus, distinguishes one class from all other classes. Thus the specific character which distinguishes man from all other animals is reason or language. Specific, therefore, assumed the sense of *distinguishing* or *distinct*, and the verb *to specify* conveyed the meaning of enumerating distinctly, or one by one. I finish with the French *épicier*, a respectable grocer, but originally a man who sold drugs. The different kinds of drugs which the apothecary had to sell were spoken of, with a certain learned air, as *species*, not as drugs in general, but as peculiar drugs and special medicines. Hence the chymist or apothecary is still called *speziale* in Italian, his shop *spezieria*.* In French *species*, which regularly became *espèce*, assumed a new form to express drugs, namely, *épices*; the English *spices*, the German *Specereien*. Hence the famous *pain d'épices*, gingerbread nuts, and *épicier*, a grocer. If you try for a moment to trace *spicy*, or a *well-spiced* article, back to the simple root *specere*, to look, you will understand that marvellous power of language which, out of a few simple elements, has created a variety of names hardly surpassed by the unbounded variety of nature herself.†

I say 'out of a few simple elements,' for the

---

* *Generi coloniali*, colonial goods. *Marsh*, p. 253. In Spanish, *generos*, merchandise.

† Many derivatives might have been added, such as *specimen*, *spectator*, *le spectacle*, *spéciallité*, *spectrum*, *spectacles*, *specious*, *specula*, &c.

number of what we call full predicative roots, such as *ar*, to plough, or *spas*, to look, is indeed small.

A root is necessarily monosyllabic.* Roots consisting of more than one syllable can always be proved to be derivative roots, and even among monosyllabic roots it is necessary to distinguish between primitive, secondary, and tertiary roots.

A. Primitive roots are those which consist
   (1) of one vowel; for instance, *i*, to go.
   (2) of one vowel and one consonant; for instance, *ad*, to eat.
   (3) of one consonant and one vowel; for instance, *dâ*, to give.

B. Secondary roots are those which consist
   (1) of one consonant, vowel, and consonant; for instance, *tud*, to strike.

In these roots either the first or the last consonant is modificatory.

C. Tertiary roots are those which consist
   (1) of consonant, consonant, and vowel; for instance, *plu*, to flow.
   (2) of vowel, consonant, and consonant; for instance, *ard*, to hurt.
   (3) of consonant, consonant, vowel, and consonant; for instance, *spas*, to see.
   (4) of consonant, consonant, vowel, consonant, and consonant; for instance, *spand*, to tremble.

The primary roots are the most important in the

---

* Cf. W. von Humboldt, *Verschiedenheit*, p. 376; Pott, *Etym. Forsch.* ii. pp. 216, 311.

early history of language; but their predicative power being generally of too indefinite a character to answer the purposes of advancing thought, they were soon encroached upon and almost supplanted by secondary and tertiary radicals.

In the secondary roots we can frequently observe that one of the consonants, in the Aryan languages generally the final, is liable to modification. The root retains its general meaning, which is slightly modified and determined by the changes of the final consonants. Thus, besides *tud* (*tudati*), we have in Sanskrit *tup* (*topati, tupati,* and *tumpati*), meaning to strike; Greek *typ-tō*. We meet likewise with *tubh* (*tubhnāti, tubhyati, tobhate*), to strike; and, according to Sanskrit grammarians, with *tuph* (*tophati, tuphati, tumphati*). Then there is a root *tuj* (*tunjati, tojati*), to strike, to excite; another root, *tur* (*tutorti*), to which the same meaning is ascribed; another, *tūr* (*tūryate*), to hurt. Then there is the further derivative *turv* (*tūrvati*), to strike, to conquer; there is *tuh* (*tohati*), to pain, to vex; and there is *tus* (*tosate*), to which Sanskrit grammarians attribute the sense of striking.

Although we may call all these verbal bases roots, they stand to the first class in about the same relation as the triliteral Semitic roots to the more primitive biliteral.[*]

In the third class we shall find that one of the two consonants is always a semivowel, nasal, or sibilant, these being more variable than the other consonants; and we can almost always point to one consonant as of later origin, and added to a biconsonantal root in

---

[*] Benloew, *Aperçu général*, p. 28 seq.

order to render its meaning more special. Thus we have, besides *spaś*, the root *paś*, and even this root has been traced back by Pott to a more primitive *ak*. Thus *vand*, again, is a mere strengthening of the root *rad*, like *mand* of *mad*, like *yu-na-j* and *yu-n-j* of *yuj*. The root *yuj*, to join, and *yudh*, to fight, both point back to a root *yu*, to mingle, and this simple root has been preserved in Sanskrit. We may well understand that a root, having the general meaning of mingling or being together, should be employed to express both the friendly joining of hands and the engaging in hostile combat; but we may equally understand that language, in its progress to clearness and definiteness, should have desired a distinction between these two meanings, and should gladly have availed herself of the two derivatives, *yuj* and *yudh*, to mark this distinction.

Sanskrit grammarians have reduced the whole growth of their language to 1,706 roots,* that is to say, they have admitted so many radicals in order to derive from them, according to their system of grammatical derivation, all nouns, verbs, adjectives, pronouns, prepositions, adverbs, and conjunctions, which occur in Sanskrit. According to our explanation of a root, however, this number of 1,706 would have to be reduced considerably, and though a few new roots would likewise have to be added which Sanskrit grammarians failed to discover, yet the number of

---

* Benfey, *Grammatik*, § 151:—

    Roots of the 2, 3, 5, 7, 8, 9 classes . . 226
    Roots of the 1, 4, 6, 10 classes . . . 1,480
                                          1,706

            including 143 of the 10th class.

primitive sounds, expressive of definite meanings, requisite for the etymological analysis of the whole Sanskrit dictionary would not amount to even one-third of that number. Hebrew has been reduced to about 500 roots,* and I doubt whether we want a larger number for Sanskrit. This shows a wise spirit of economy on the part of primitive language, for the possibility of forming new roots for every new impression was almost unlimited. Even if we put the number of letters only at twenty-four, the possible number of biliteral and triliteral roots would amount together to 14,400 ;† whereas Chinese, though abstaining from composition and derivation, and therefore requiring a larger number of radicals than any other language, was satisfied with about 450. With these 450 sounds, raised to 1,263 by various accents and intonations, the Chinese have produced a dictionary of from 40,000 to 50,000 words.‡

* Renan, *Histoire des Langues sémitiques*, p. 138. Lousden counted 5,642 Hebrew and Chaldee words in the O. T. Benloew estimates the necessary radicals of Gothic at 600, of modern German at 250 (p. 22). Pott thinks that each language has about 1,000 roots. *Etym. Forsch.* ii. p. 73. Grimm has compiled a list of 462 strong verbs in the Teutonic family. Cf. *Grammatik*, i. 1030. Pott, *Etym. Forsch.* ii. p. 76. Dobrowsky, *Instit. linguæ Slavicæ*, p. 236, gives 1,605 radicals of the Slavic languages.

† Leibniz (*De Arte combinatoria*, Opp. t.ii. p.387-388, ed. Dutens). Quoties sitns literarum in alphabeto sit variabilis; 23 literarum linguæ Latinæ variationes sunt 25,852,016,738,884,976,640,000; 24 literarum Germanicæ linguæ, 620,448,701,733,239,739,360,000. Cf. Pott, *Etym. Forsch.* ii. p. 9. Jean Paul, *Lebens Fibels*, p. 180.

‡ The exact number in the Imperial Dictionary of Khang-hi amounts to 42,718. About one fourth part has become obsolete; and one half of the rest may be considered of rare occurrence, thus leaving only about 15,000 words in actual use. 'The exact

It is clear, however, that in addition to these predicative roots, we want another class of radical elements to enable us to account for the full growth of language. With the 400 or 500 predicative roots at her disposal, language would not have been at a loss to coin names for all things that come under our cognisance. Language is a thrifty housewife. Consider the variety of ideas that were expressed by the one root *spac*, and you will see that with 500 such roots she might form a dictionary sufficient to satisfy the wants, however extravagant, of her husband— the human mind. If each root yielded fifty derivatives, we should have 25,000 words. Now, we are told on good authority, by a country clergyman, that some of the labourers in his parish had not 300 words in their vocabulary.* The cuneiform inscriptions of Persia contain no more than 379 words, 131 of these being proper names. The vocabulary of the ancient sages of Egypt, at least as far as it is known to us from the hieroglyphic inscriptions, amounts to about 658 words.† The *libretto* of an Italian opera

number of the classical characters is 42,718. Many of them are no longer in use in the modern language, but they occur in the canonical and the classical books. They may be found sometimes in official documents, when an attempt is made at imitating the old style. A considerable portion of these are names of persons, places, mountains, rivers, &c. In order to compete for the place of imperial historian, it was necessary to know 9,000, which were collected in a separate manual."—Stanislas Julien.

* The study of the English language by A. D'Orsey, p. 15.

† This is the number of words in the Vocabulary given by Bunsen, in the first volume of his Egypt, pp. 463–491. Several of these words, however, though identical in sound, must be separated etymologically, and later researches have still further increased the number. The number of hieroglyphic groups in Sharpe's *Egyptian Hieroglyphics*, 1861, amounts to 2,030.

seldom displays a greater variety.* A well-educated person in England, who has been at a public school and at the university, who reads his Bible, his Shakspeare, the *Times*, and all the books of Mudie's Library, seldom uses more than about 3,000 or 4,000 words in actual conversation. Accurate thinkers and close reasoners, who avoid vague and general expressions, and wait till they find the word that exactly fits their meaning, employ a larger stock; and eloquent speakers may rise to a command of 10,000. Shakspeare, who displayed a greater variety of expression than probably any writer in any language, produced all his plays with about 15,000 words. Milton's works are built up with 8,000; and the Hebrew Testament says all that it has to say with 5,642 words.†

* Marsh, *Lectures*, p. 182. M. Thommerel stated the number of words in the Dictionaries of Robertson and Webster as 43,566. Todd's edition of Johnson, however, is said to contain 58,000 words, and the later editions of Webster have reached the number of 70,000, counting the participles of the present and perfect as independent vocables. Flügel estimated the number of words in his own dictionary at 94,464, of which 65,085 are simple, 29,379 compound. This was in 1843; and he then expressed a hope that in his next edition the number of words would far exceed 100,000. This is the number fixed upon by Mr. Marsh as the minimum of the *copia vocabulorum* in English. See the *Saturday Review*, Nov. 2, 1861. 'Adamantinos Korais invenit in veteri Academiæ Parisiensis dictionario 29,712 contineri; in Johnsoniano 56,784; in linguæ Armeniacæ vocabulario 50,000; sed in thesauri Stephaniani editione Londinensi, 150,000.' Cf. Pott, *Etym. Forsch.* ii. 79.

Varro, L.L. vi. § 35. Horum verborum si primigenia sunt ad mille, ut Cosconius scribit, ex eorum declinationibus verborum discrimina quingenta millia esse possunt. Ideo quis singulis verbis primigeniis circiter quingentæ species declinationibus fiant. Primigenia dicuntur verba, ut lego, scribo, sto, sedeo et cætera quæ non sunt ab aliquo verbo, sed suas habent radices.

† Renan, *Histoire*, p. 138.

Five hundred roots, therefore, considering their fertility and pliancy, was more than was wanted for the dictionary of our primitive ancestors. And yet they wanted something more. If they had a root expressive of light and splendour, that root might have formed the predicate in the names of sun, and moon, and stars, and heaven, day, morning, dawn, spring, gladness, joy, beauty, majesty, love, friend, gold, riches, &c. But if they wanted to express *here* and *there, who, what, this, that, thou, he*, they would have found it impossible to discover any predicative root that could be applied to this purpose. Attempts have indeed been made to trace these words back to predicative roots; but if we are told that the demonstrative root *ta*, this or there, may be derived from a predicative root *tan*, to extend, we find that even in our modern languages, the demonstrative pronouns and particles are of too primitive and independent a nature to allow of so artificial an interpretation. The sound *ta* or *sa*, for this or there, is as involuntary, as natural, as independent an expression as any of the predicative roots, and although some of these demonstrative, or pronominal, or local roots, for all these names have been applied to them, may be traced back to a predicative source, we must admit a small class of independent radicals, not predicative in the usual sense of the word, but simply pointing, simply expressive of existence under certain more or less definite, local or temporal prescriptions.

It will be best to give one illustration at least of a pronominal root and its influence in the formation of words.

In some languages, and particularly in Chinese, a predicative root may by itself be used as a noun, or a verb, or an adjective or adverb. Thus the Chinese sound *ta* means, without any change of form, great, greatness, and to be great.* If *ta* stands before a substantive, it has the meaning of an adjective. Thus *ta jin* means a great man. If *ta* stands after a substantive, it is a predicate, or, as we should say, a verb. Thus, *jin ta* (or *jin ta ye*) would mean the man is great.† Or again, *jin ngô, li pû ngô,* would mean man bad, law not bad. Here we see that there is no outward distinction whatever between a root and a word, and that a noun is distinguished from a verb merely by its collocation in a sentence.

In other languages, however, and particularly in the Aryan languages, no predicative root can by itself form a word. Thus in Latin there is a root *luc,* to shine. In order to have a substantive, such as light, it was necessary to add a pronominal or demonstrative root, this forming the general subject of which the meaning contained in the root is to be predicated. Thus by the addition of the pronominal element *s* we have the Latin noun, *luc-s,* the light, or literally, shining-there. Let us add a personal pronoun, and we have the verb *luc-e-s,* shining-thou, thou shinest. Let us add other pronominal derivatives, and we get the adjectives, *lucidus, luculentus, lucerna,* &c.

It would be a totally mistaken view, however, were

* Endlicher, *Chinesische Grammatik,* § 128.

† If two words are placed like *jin ta,* the first may form the predicate of the second, the second being used as a substantive. Thus *jin ta* might mean the greatness of man, but in this case it is more usual to say *jin tci ta.*

'Another instance—*chen,* virtue; ex. *jin tchi chen,* the virtue of man: *chen,* virtuous; ex. *chen jin,* the virtuous man: *chen,* to approve; ex. *chen tchi,* to find it good: *chen,* well; ex. *chen ko,* to sing well.'—Stanislas Julien.

we to suppose that all derivative elements, all that remains of a word after the predicative root has been removed, must be traced back to pronominal roots. We have only to look at some of our own modern derivatives in order to be convinced that many of them were originally predicative, that they entered into composition with the principal predicative root, and then dwindled down to mere suffixes. Thus *scape* in *landscape*, and the more modern *ship* in *hardship*, are both derived from the same root which we have in Gothic,* *skapa, skôp, skôpum*, to create; in Anglo-Saxon, *scape, scôp, scôpon*. It is the same as the German derivative *schaft*, in *Gesellschaft* &c. So again *dom* in *wisdom* or *christendom* is derived from the same root which we have in *to do*. It is the same as the German *thum* in *Christenthum*, the Anglo-Saxon *dôm* in *cyning-dom, Königthum*.† Sometimes it may seem doubtful whether a derivative element was originally merely demonstrative or predicative. Thus the termination of the comparative in Sanskrit is *tara*, the Greek *teros*. This might, at first sight, be taken for a demonstrative element, but it is in reality the root *tar*, which means *to go beyond*, which we have likewise in the Latin *trans*. This *trans* in its French form *très* is prefixed to adjectives in order to express a higher or transcendent degree, and the same root was well adapted to form the comparative in the ancient Aryan tongues. This root must like-

* Grimm, *Deutsche Grammatik*, b. ii. s. 531.
† Spenser, *Shepheard's Calender*, Februarie 85 (ed. Collier, i. p. 25):—

'Cuddie, I wote thou kenst little good
So vainly t'advaunce thy headlesse hood:'

(for thy headlessness; *hood* is a termination denoting estate, as manhood.—T. Warton).

wise be admitted in one of the terminations of the locative which is *tra* in Sanskrit; for instance, from *ta*, a demonstrative root, we form *ta-tra*, there, originally this way; we form *anyatra*, in another way: the same as in Latin we say *ali-ter*, from *aliud*; compounds no more surprising than the French *autrement* (see p. 47) and the English *otherwise*.

Most of the terminations of declension and conjugation are demonstrative roots, and the *s*, for instance, of the third person singular, he loves, can be proved to have been originally the demonstrative pronoun of the third person. It was originally not *s* but *t*. This will require some explanation. The termination of the third person singular of the present is *ti* in Sanskrit. Thus *dâ*, to give, becomes *dadâti*, he gives; *dhâ*, to place; *dadhâti*, he places.

In Greek this *ti* is changed into *si*; just as the Sanskrit *twam*, the Latin *tu*, thou, appears in Greek as *sy*. Thus Greek *didôsi* corresponds to Sanskrit *dadâti*; *tithêsi* to *dadhâti*. In the course of time, however, every Greek *s* between two vowels, in a termination, was elided. Thus *genous* does not form the genitive *genesos*, like the Latin *genus, genesis* or *generis*, but *geneos = genous*. The dative is not *generi* (the Latin *generi*), but *genei = genei*. In the same manner all the regular verbs have *ei* for the termination of the third person singular. But this *ei* stands for *esi*. Thus *typtei* stands for *typtesi*, and this for *typteti*.

The Latin drops the final *i*, and instead of *ti* has *t*. Thus we get *amat, dicit*.

Now there is a law to which I alluded before, which is called Grimm's Law. According to it every tennis in Latin is in Gothic represented by its corresponding aspirate. Hence, instead of *t*, we should expect in Gothic *th*; and so we find indeed in Gothic *habaiþ*, instead of Latin *habet*. This aspirate likewise appears in Anglo-Saxon, where *he loves* is *lufath*. It is preserved in the Biblical *he loveth*, and it is only in modern English that it gradually sank to *s*. In the *s* of *he loves*, therefore, we have a demonstrative root, added to the predicative root *love*, and this *s* is originally the same as the Sanskrit *ti*. This *ti* again must be traced back to the demonstrative root *ta*, this or there; which exists in the Sanskrit demonstrative pronoun *tad*, the Greek *to*, the Gothic *thata*, the English *that*; and which in Latin we can trace in *talis, tantus, tunc, tam*, and even in *tamen*, an old locative in *men*. We have thus seen that what we call the third person singular of the present is in reality a simple compound of a predicative root with a demonstrative root. It is a compound like any other, only that the second part is not predicative, but simply demonstrative. As in paymaster we predicate pay of master, meaning a person whose office it is to pay, so in *dadâ-ti*, *give-he*, the ancient framers of language simply predicated giving of some third person, and this synthetic proposition, *give-he*, is the same as what we now call the third person singular in the indicative mood, of the present tense, in the active voice.*

We have necessarily confined ourselves in our analysis of language to that family of languages to which our own tongue, and those with which we are best acquainted, belong; but what applies to Sanskrit and the Aryan family applies to the whole realm of

---

* Each verb in Greek, if conjugated through all its voices, tenses, moods, and persons, yields, together with its participles, about 1,300 forms.

human speech. Every language, without a single
exception, that has as yet been cast into the crucible
of comparative grammar, has been found to contain
these two substantial elements, predicative and demonstrative roots. In the Semitic family these two
constituent elements are even more palpable than in
Sanskrit and Greek. Even before the discovery of
Sanskrit, and the rise of comparative philology,
Semitic scholars had successfully traced back the
whole dictionary of Hebrew and Arabic to a small
number of roots, and as every root in these languages
consists of three consonants, the Semitic languages
have sometimes been called by the name of triliteral.

To a still higher degree the constituent elements
are, as it were, on the very surface in the Turanian
family of speech. It is one of the characteristic features of that family, that, whatever the number of
prefixes and suffixes, the root must always stand out
in full relief, and must never be allowed to suffer by
its contact with derivative elements.

There is one language, the Chinese, in which no
analysis of any kind is required for the discovery of
its component parts. It is a language in which no
coalescence of roots has taken place; every word is a
root, and every root is a word. It is, in fact, the
most primitive stage in which we can imagine human
language to have existed. It is language *comme il
faut*; it is what we should naturally have expected
all languages to be.

There are, no doubt, numerous dialects in Asia,
Africa, America, and Polynesia, which have not yet
been dissected by the knife of the grammarian; but
we may be satisfied at least with this negative evidence, that, as yet, no language which has passed

through the ordeal of grammatical analysis has ever disclosed any but these two constituent elements.

The problem, therefore, of the origin of language, which seemed so perplexing and mysterious to the ancient philosophers, assumes a much simpler aspect with us. We have learnt what language is made of; we have found that everything in language, except the roots, is intelligible, and can be accounted for. There is nothing to surprise us in the combination of the predicative and demonstrative roots which led to the building up of all the languages with which we are acquainted, from Chinese to English. It is not only conceivable, as Professor Pott remarks, 'that the formation of the Sanskrit language, as it is handed down to us, may have been preceded by a state of the greatest simplicity and entire absence of inflections, such as is exhibited to the present day by the Chinese and other monosyllabic languages.' It is absolutely impossible that it should have been otherwise. After we have seen that all languages must have started from this Chinese or monosyllabic stage, the only portion of the problem of the origin of language that remains to be solved is this: How can we account for the origin of those predicative and demonstrative roots which form the constituent elements of all human speech, and which have hitherto resisted all attempts at further analysis? This problem will form the subject of our two next Lectures.

LECTURE VIII.

MORPHOLOGICAL CLASSIFICATION.

WE finished in our last Lecture our analysis of language, and we arrived at the result that *predicative* and *demonstrative* roots are the sole constituent elements of human speech.

We now turn back in order to discover how many possible forms of language may be produced by the free combination of these constituent elements; and we shall then endeavour to find out whether each of these possible forms has its real counterpart in some or other of the dialects of mankind. We are attempting in fact to carry out a *morphological classification* of speech, which is based entirely on the form or manner in which roots are put together, and therefore quite independent of the genealogical classification which, according to its very nature, is based on the formations of language handed down ready made from generation to generation.

Before, however, we enter on this, the principal subject of our present Lecture, we have still to examine, as briefly as possible, a second family of speech, which, like the Aryan, is established on the strictest principles of genealogical classification, namely, the *Semitic*.

The Semitic family is divided into three branches, the *Aramaic*, the *Hebraic*, and the *Arabic*.*

The *Aramaic* occupies the north, including Syria, Mesopotamia, and part of the ancient kingdoms of Babylonia and Assyria. It is known to us chiefly in two dialects, the *Syriac* and *Chaldee*. The former name is given to the language which has been preserved to us in a translation of the Bible (the Peshito†) ascribed to the second century, and in the rich Christian literature dating from the fourth. It is still spoken, though in a very corrupt form, by the Nestorians of Kurdistan, near the lakes of Van and Urmia, and by some Christian tribes in Mesopotamia; and an attempt has been made by the American missionaries,‡ stationed at Urmia, to restore this dialect to some grammatical correctness by publishing translations and a grammar of what they call the Neo-Syriac language.§

---

* *Histoire générale et Système comparé des Langues sémitiques*, par Ernest Renan. Seconde édition. Paris, 1858.

† *Peshito* means simple. The Old Testament was translated from Hebrew, the New Testament from Greek, about 200, if not earlier. Ephraem Syrus lived in the middle of the fourth century. During the eighth and ninth centuries the Nestorians of Syria acted as the instructors of the Arabs. Their literary and intellectual supremacy began to fail in the tenth century. It was revived for a time by Gregorius Barhebraeus (Abulfaraj) in the thirteenth century. See Renan, p. 257.

‡ Messrs. Perkins and Stoddard, the latter the author of a grammar, published in the *Journal of the American Oriental Society*, vol. v. 1.

§ The following extract from Allen's *Memoir of Sherman*, will show how easily even intelligent persons deceive themselves or are deceived by others, with regard to languages and their relationship. 'I shall never forget Mr. Sherman's delight when he found that Dr. Nolan, speaking in native Irish, and Asaad y' Kijatt from Beyroot, speaking in Syro-phoenician, could under-

The name of *Chaldee* has been given to the language adopted by the Jews during the Babylonian captivity. Though the Jews always retained a knowledge of their sacred language, they soon began to adopt the dialect of their conquerors, not for conversation only, but also for literary composition.* The book of Ezra contains fragments in Chaldee, contemporaneous with the cuneiform inscription of Darius and Xerxes, and several of the apocryphal books, though preserved to us in Greek only, were most likely composed originally in Chaldee, and not in Hebrew. The so-called *Targums* † again, or translations and paraphrases of the Old Testament, written during the centuries immediately preceding and following the Christian era,‡ give us another specimen of the Aramaic, or the language of Babylonia, as transplanted to Palestine. This Aramaic was the dialect spoken by Christ and his disciples. The few authentic words preserved in the New Testament as spoken by our Lord in His own language, such as *Talitha kumi*, *Ephphatha*, *Abba*, are not in Hebrew, but in the Chaldee, or Aramaic, as then spoken by the Jews.§

After the destruction of Jerusalem the literature of the Jews continued to be written in the same dialect.

---

stand each other, so as to hold conversation. It seemed to settle the long-disputed point as to Ireland having been first peopled by dispersed Phœnician mariners.' p. 215.

* Renan, p. 214 seq., ' Le chaldéen biblique serait un dialecte araméen légèrement hébraïsé.'

† Arabic, *tarjam*, to explain; *Dragoman*, Arabic, *tarjamân*.

‡ The most ancient are those of Onkelos and Jonathan, in the second century after Christ. Others are much later, later even than the Talmud. Renan, p. 220.

§ Renan, pp. 220-222.

The Talmud* of Jerusalem of the fourth, and that of Babylon of the fifth, century exhibit the Aramæan, as spoken by the educated Jews settled in these two localities, though greatly depraved and spoiled by an admixture of strange elements. This language remained the literary idiom of the Jews to the tenth century. The Masora,† and the traditional commentary of the Old Testament, was written in it about that time. Soon after the Jews adopted Arabic as their literary language, and retained it to the thirteenth century. They then returned to a kind of modernised Hebrew, which they still continue to employ for learned discussions.

It is curious that the Aramaic branch of the Semitic family, though originally the language of the great kingdoms of Babylon and Nineveh, should have been preserved to us only in the literature of the Jews, and of the Christians of Syria. There must have been a Babylonian literature, for the wisdom of the Chaldeans had acquired a reputation which could hardly have been sustained without a literature. Abraham must have spoken Aramaic before he emigrated to Canaan. Laban spoke the same dialect, and the name which he gave to the heap of stones that was to be a witness between him and Jacob (Jegar-sahadutha), is Syriac, whereas Galeed, the name by which Jacob called it, is Hebrew.‡ If

* *Talmud* (instruction) consists of *Mishna* and *Gemara*. *Mishna* means repetition, viz. of the Law. It was collected and written down about 218, by Jehudá. *Gemara* is a continuation and commentary of the Mishna: that of Jerusalem was finished towards the end of the fourth, that of Babylon towards the end of the fifth century.

† First printed in the Rabbinic Bible, Venice, 1525.

‡ Quatremère, *Mémoire sur les Nabathéens*, p. 139.

U

we are ever to recover a knowledge of that ancient Babylonian literature, it must be from the cuneiform inscriptions lately brought home from Babylon and Nineveh. They are clearly written in a Semitic language. About this there can be no longer any doubt. And though the progress in deciphering them has been slow, and slower than was at one time expected, yet there is no reason to despair. In a letter, dated April 1853, Sir Henry Rawlinson wrote:—

'On the clay tablets which we have found at Nineveh, and which now are to be counted by thousands, there are explanatory treatises on almost every subject under the sun; the art of writing, grammars, and dictionaries, notation, weights and measures, divisions of time, chronology, astronomy, geography, history, mythology, geology, botany, &c. In fact we have now at our disposal a perfect cyclopædia of Assyrian science.'

Considering what has been achieved in deciphering one class of cuneiform inscriptions, the Persian, there is no reason to doubt that the whole of that cyclopædia will some day be read with the same ease with which we read the mountain records of Darius.

There is, however, another miserable remnant of what was once the literature of the Chaldeans or Babylonians, namely, the *Book of Adam*, and similar works preserved by the *Mendaïtes* or *Nasoreans*, a curious sect settled near Bassora. Though the composition of these works is as late as the tenth century after Christ, it has been supposed that under a modern crust of wild and senseless hallucinations, they contain some grains of genuine ancient Babylonian thought. These *Mendaïtes* have in fact been identified with the *Nabateans*, who are mentioned as late as the tenth century* of our era, as a race purely pagan, and distinct from Jews, Christians, and Mohammedans. In Arabic the name Nabatean† is used for Babylonians—nay, all the people of Aramaic origin, settled in the earliest times between the Euphrates and Tigris, are referred to by that name.‡ It is supposed that the Nabateans, who are mentioned about the beginning of the Christian era as a race distinguished for their astronomical and general scientific knowledge, were the ancestors of the mediæval Nabateans, and the descendants of the ancient Babylonians and Chaldeans. You may have lately seen in some literary journals an account of a work called *The Nabatean Agriculture*. It exists only in an Arabic translation by Ibn-Wahshiyyah, the Chaldean,§ who lived about 900 years after Christ, but the original, which was written by Kuthami in Aramean, has lately been referred to the beginning of the thirteenth century B.C. The evidence is not yet fully before us, but from what is known it seems more likely that this work was the compilation of a Nabatean who lived about the

---

* Renan, p. 241. † Ibid. p. 237.
‡ Quatremère, *Mémoire sur les Nabatéens*, p. 116.
§ Ibn-Wahshiyyah was a Mussulman, but his family had been converted for three generations only. He translated a collection of Nabatean books. Three have been preserved: 1, the Nabatean Agriculture; 2, the book on poisons; 3, the book of Tenkelusha (Teucros) the Babylonian; besides fragments of the book of the secrets of the Sun and Moon. The Nabatean Agriculture was referred by Quatremère (*Journal Asiatique*, 1835) to the period between Belesis who delivered the Babylonians from their Median masters and the taking of Babylon by Cyrus. Prof. Chwolson of St. Petersburg, who has examined all the MSS., places Kuthami at the beginning of the thirteenth century B.C.

fourth century after Christ;* and though it contains ancient traditions, which may go back to the days of the great Babylonian monarchs, these traditions can hardly be taken as a fair representation of the ancient civilisation of the Aramean race.

The second branch of the Semitic family is the *Hebraic*, chiefly represented by the ancient language of Palestine, where Hebrew was spoken and written from the days of Moses to the times of Nehemiah and the Maccabees, though of course with considerable modifications, and with a strong admixture of Aramean forms, particularly since the Babylonian captivity, and the rise of a powerful civilisation in the neighbouring country of Syria. The ancient language of Phœnicia, to judge from inscriptions, was most closely allied to Hebrew, and the language of the Carthaginians too must be referred to the same branch.

Hebrew was first encroached upon by Aramaic dialects, through the political ascendency of Babylon, and still more of Syria; it had to yield to Greek, for a time the language of civilisation in the East; and was at last swept away by Arabic, which, since the conquest of Palestine and Syria in the year 636, has monopolised nearly the whole area formerly occupied by the two older branches of the Semitic stock, the Aramaic and Hebrew.

This third, or Arabic, branch sprang from the Arabian peninsula, where it is still spoken by a compact mass of aboriginal inhabitants. Its most ancient documents are the *Himyaritic* inscriptions. In very early times this Arabic branch was transplanted to

* Renan, *Mémoire sur l'âge du livre intitulé Agriculture Nabatéenne*, p. 38, Paris, 1860; *Times*, January 31, 1862.

Africa, where, south of Egypt and Nubia, on the coast opposite Yemen, an ancient Semitic dialect has maintained itself to the present day. This is the *Ethiopic* or *Abyssinian*, or, as it is called by the people themselves, the *Geez* language. Though no longer spoken in its purity by the people of Habesh, it is still preserved in their sacred writings, translations of the Bible, and similar works, which date from the third and fourth centuries. The modern language of Abyssinia is called *Amharic*.

The earliest literary documents of Arabic go back beyond Mohammed. They are called *Moallakat*, literally, suspended poems, because they are said to have been thus publicly exhibited at Mecca. They are old popular poems, descriptive of desert life. With Mohammed Arabic became the language of a victorious religion, and established its sway over Asia, Africa, and Europe.

These three branches, the Aramaic, the Hebraic, and Arabic, are so closely related to each other, that it was impossible not to recognise their common origin. Every root in these languages, as far back as we know them, must consist of three consonants, and numerous words are derived from these roots by a simple change of vowels, leaving the consonantal skeleton as much as possible intact. It is impossible to mistake a Semitic language; and what is most important—it is impossible to imagine an Aryan language derived from a Semitic, or a Semitic from an Aryan language. The grammatical framework is totally distinct in these two families of speech. This does not exclude, however, the possibility that both are diverging streams of the same source; and the comparisons that have been instituted between the

Semitic roots, reduced to their simplest form, and the roots of the Aryan languages, have made it more than probable that the material elements with which they both started were originally the same.

Other languages which are supposed to belong to the Semitic family are the *Berber* dialects of Northern Africa, spoken on the coast from Egypt to the Atlantic Ocean before the invasion of the Arabs, and now pushed back towards the interior. Some other African languages, too, such as the *Haussa* and *Galla*, have been classed as Semitic; and the language of Egypt, from the earliest hieroglyphic inscriptions to the Coptic, which ceased to be spoken after the seventeenth century, has equally been referred to this class. The Semitic character of these dialects, however, is much less clearly defined, and the exact degree of relationship in which they stand to the Semitic languages, properly so called, has still to be determined.*

Strictly speaking, the Aryan and Semitic are the only *families* of speech which fully deserve that title. They both presuppose the existence of a finished system of grammar, previous to the first divergence of their dialects. Their history is from the beginning a history of decay rather than of growth, and hence the unmistakeable family-likeness which pervades every one even of their latest descendants. The

---

* Some excellent articles on these outlying members of the Semitic family were published by Dr. Lottner in the *Transactions of the Philological Society*, 1861, p. 20, 'On the Sister Families of Languages, especially those connected with the Semitic Family.' The relationship, however, of these languages with Arabic, Hebrew, and Syriac, is hardly so close and definite as might seem to be implied by the term Sister families.

language of the Sepoy and that of the English soldier are, strictly speaking, one and the same language. They are both built up of materials which were definitely shaped before the Teutonic and Indic branches separated. No new root has been added to either since their first separation; and the grammatical forms which are of more modern growth in English or Hindustáni, are, if closely examined, new combinations only of elements which existed from the beginning in all the Aryan dialects. In the termination of the English *he is*, and in the inaudible termination of the French *il est*, we recognise the result of an act performed before the first separation of the Aryan family, the combination of the predicative root *as* with the demonstrative root *ti*; an act performed once for all, and continuing to be felt to the present day.

It was the custom of Nebuchadnezzar to have his name stamped on every brick that was used during his reign in erecting his colossal palaces. Those palaces fell to ruins, but from the ruins the ancient materials were carried away for building new cities; and, on examining the bricks in the walls of the modern city of Bagdad on the borders of the Tigris, Sir Henry Rawlinson discovered on each the clear traces of that royal signature. It is the same if we examine the structure of modern languages. They too were built up with the materials taken from the ruins of the ancient languages, and every word, if properly examined, displays the visible stamp impressed upon it from the first by the founders of the Aryan and the Semitic empires of speech.

The relationship of languages, however, is not always so close. Languages may diverge before their grammatical system has become fixed and hardened;

and in that case they cannot be expected to show the same marked features of a common descent as, for instance, the Neo-Latin dialects, French, Italian, and Spanish. They may have much in common, but they will likewise display an after-growth in words and grammatical forms peculiar to each dialect. With regard to words we see that even languages so intimately related to each other as the six Romance dialects, diverged in some of the commonest expressions. Instead of the Latin *frater*, the French *frère*, we find in Spanish *hermano*. There was a very good reason for this change. The Latin word *frater*, changed into *fray* and *frayle*, had been applied to express a brother or a friar. It was felt inconvenient that the same word should express two ideas which it was sometimes necessary to distinguish, and therefore, by a kind of natural elimination, *frater* was given up as the name of brother in Spanish, and replaced from the dialectical stores of Latin by *germanus*. In the same manner the Latin word for shepherd, *pastor*, was so constantly applied to the shepherd of the people, or the clergyman, *le pasteur*, that a new word was wanted for the real shepherd. Thus *berbicarius*, from *berbex* or *cervex*, a wether, was used instead of *pastor*, and changed into the French *berger*. Instead of the Spanish *enfermo*, ill, we find in French *malade*, in Italian *malato*. Languages so intimately related as Greek and Latin have fixed on different expressions for son, daughter, brother, woman, man, sky, earth, moon, hand, mouth, tree, bird, &c.* That is to say, out of a large number of synonymes which were supplied by the numerous dialects of the Aryan family,

---

* See *Letter on Turanian Languages*, p. 62.

the Greeks perpetuated one, the Romans another. It is clear that when the working of this principle of natural selection is allowed to extend more widely, languages, though proceeding from the same source, may in time acquire a totally different nomenclature for the commonest objects. The number of real synonymes is frequently exaggerated, and if we are told that in Icelandic there are 120 names for island, or in Arabic 500 names for lion,* and 1,000 names for sword,† many of these are no doubt purely poetical. But even where there are in a language only four or five names for the same objects, it is clear that four languages might be derived from it, each in appearance quite distinct from the rest.

The same applies to grammar. When the Romance languages, for instance, formed their new future by placing the auxiliary verb *habere*, to have, after the infinitive, it was quite open to any one of them to fix upon some other expedient for expressing the future. The French might have chosen *je vais dire* or *je dirais* (I wade to say) instead of *je dirai*, and in this case the future in French would have been totally distinct from the future in Italian. If such changes are possible in literary languages of such long standing as French and Italian, we must be prepared for a great deal more in languages which, as I said, diverged before any definite settlement had taken place, either in their grammar or their dictionary. If we were to expect in them the definite criteria of a genealogical relationship which unites the members of the Aryan and Semitic familes of speech, we should necessarily be disappointed. Such criteria could not possibly

---

* Renan, *Histoire des Langues sémitiques*, p. 137.
† Pococke, *Notes to Abulfaragius*, p. 153; *Glossology*, p. 352.

exist in these languages. But there are criteria for determining even these more distant degrees of relationship in the vast realm of speech; and they are sufficient at least to arrest the hasty conclusions of those who would deny the possibility of a common origin of any languages more removed from each other than French and Italian, Sanskrit and Greek, Hebrew and Arabic. You will see this more clearly after we have examined the principles of what I call the *morphological classification* of human speech.

As all languages, so far as we can judge at present, can be reduced in the end to roots, predicative and demonstrative, it is clear that, according to the manner in which roots are put together, we may expect to find three kinds of languages, or three stages in the gradual formation of speech.

1. Roots may be used as words, each root preserving its full independence.

2. Two roots may be joined together to form words, and in these compounds one root may lose its independence.

3. Two roots may be joined together to form words, and in these compounds both roots may lose their independence.

What applies to two roots, applies to three or four or more. The principle is the same, though it would lead to a more varied subdivision.

The first stage, in which each root preserves its independence, and in which there is no formal distinction between a root and a word, I call the *Radical Stage*. This stage is best represented by ancient Chinese. Languages belonging to this first or Radical Stage have sometimes been called *Monosyllabic* or

Isolating. The second stage, in which two or more roots coalesce to form a word, the one retaining its radical independence, the other sinking down to a mere termination, I call the *Terminational Stage.* This stage is best represented by the Turanian family of speech, and the languages belonging to it have generally been called *agglutinative,* from *gluten,* glue. The third stage, in which roots coalesce so that neither the one nor the other retains its substantive independence, I call the *Inflectional Stage.* This stage is best represented by the Aryan and Semitic families, and the languages belonging to it have sometimes been distinguished by the name of *amalgamating* or *organic.*

The first stage excludes phonetic corruption altogether.

The second stage excludes phonetic corruption in the principal root, but allows it in the secondary or determinative elements.

The third stage allows phonetic corruption both in the principal root and in the terminations.

A few instances will make this classification clearer.

In the first stage, which is represented by Chinese, every word is a root, and has its own substantial meaning. Thus, where we say in Latin *baculo,* with a stick, we say in Chinese *y čáng.** Here *y* might be taken for a mere preposition, like the English *with.* But in Chinese this *y* is a root; it is the same word which, if used as a verb, would mean 'to employ.' Therefore in Chinese *y čáng* means literally 'employ stick.' Or again, where we say in English *at home,*

---

* Endlicher, *Chinesische Grammatik,* p. 123.

or in Latin *domi*, the Chinese say *tŏ-li*, *tŏ* meaning *house*, and *li* originally *inside*.* The name for *day* in modern Chinese is *gi-tse*, which means originally *son of the sun*.†

There is in Chinese, as we saw before, no formal distinction between a noun, a verb, an adjective, an adverb, a preposition. The same root, according to its position in a sentence, may be employed to convey the meaning of great, greatness, greatly, and to be great. Everything, in fact, depends in Chinese on the proper collocation of words in a sentence. Thus *ngŏ tă ni* means 'I beat thee;' but *ni tă ngŏ* would mean 'thou beatest me.' Thus *ngŏ gin* means 'a bad man;' *gin ngŏ* would mean 'the man is bad.'

As long as every word, or part of a word, is felt to express its own radical meaning, a language belongs to the first or radical stage. As soon as such words as *tse* in *gi-tse*, day, *li* in *tŏ-li*, at home, or *y* in *y-čäng*, with the stick, lose their etymological meaning and become mere signs of derivation or of case, language enters into the second or *Terminational* stage.

By far the largest number of languages belong to this stage. The whole of what is called the *Turanian* class consists of Terminational or Agglutinative languages, and this Turanian class comprises in reality all languages spoken in Asia and Europe, and not included under the Aryan and Semitic families, with the exception of Chinese and its cognate dialects. In

---

* Endlicher, *Chinesische Grammatik*, s. 329.

† In this word *tse* (tseu) does not signify son; it is an addition of frequent occurrence after nouns, adjectives, and verba. Thus, *lao*, old,+*tseu* is father; *nei*, the interior,+*tseu* is wife; *hiang*, scent,+*tseu* is clove; *hoa*, to beg,+*tseu*, a mendicant; *hi*, to act,+*tseu*, an actor.'—*Stanislas Julien*.

the great continent of the Old World the Semitic and
Aryan languages occupy only what may be called the
four western peninsulas, namely, India with Persia,
Arabia, Asia Minor, and Europe; and we have reason
to suppose that even these countries were held by
Turanian tribes previous to the arrival of the Aryan
and Semitic nations.

This Turanian class is of great importance in the
science of languages. Some scholars would deny it
the name of a family; and if family is only applicable
to dialects so closely connected among themselves as
the Aryan or Semitic, it would no doubt be preferable
to speak of the Turanians as a class or group, and not
as a family of languages. But this concession must
not be understood as an admission that the members
of this class start from different sources, and that they
are held together, not by genealogical affinity, but by
morphological similarity only.

These languages share elements in common which
they must have borrowed from the same source, and
their formal coincidences, though of a different character from those of the Aryan and Semitic families,
are such that it would be impossible to ascribe them
to mere accident.

The name Turanian is used in opposition to Aryan,
and is applied to the nomadic races of Asia as opposed
to the agricultural or Aryan races.

The Turanian family or class consists of two great
divisions, the *Northern* and the *Southern*.

The Northern is sometimes called the *Ural-Altaic*
or *Ugro-Tataric*, and it is divided into five sections, the *Tungusic, Mongolic, Turkic, Finnic,* and
Samoyedic.

The Southern, which occupies the South of Asia,

is divided into four classes, the *Tamulic*, or the languages of the Dekhan ; the *Bhotiya*, or the dialects of Tibet and Bhotan ; the *Taïc*, or the dialects of Siam ; and the *Malaic*, or the Malay and Polynesian dialects.

No doubt, if we expected to find in this immense number of languages the same family likeness which holds the Semitic or Aryan languages together, we should be disappointed. But the very absence of that family likeness constitutes one of the distinguishing features of the Turanian dialects. They are *Nomad* languages, as contrasted with the Aryan and Semitic languages.* In the latter most words and grammatical forms were thrown out but once by the creative power of one generation, and they were not lightly parted with, even though their original distinctness had been blurred by phonetic corruption. To hand down a language in this manner is possible only among people whose history runs on in one main stream, and where religion, law, and poetry supply well-defined borders which hem in on every side the current of language. Among the Turanian nomads no such nucleus of a political, social, or literary character has ever been formed. Empires were no sooner founded than they were scattered again like the sand-clouds of the desert ; no laws, no songs, no stories outlived the age of their authors. How quickly language can change, if thus left to itself without any literary standard, we saw in a former Lecture, when treating of the growth of dialects. The most necessary substantives, such as father, mother, daughter, son, have frequently been

* *Letter on the Turanian Languages*, p. 24.

lost, and replaced by synonymes in the different dialects of Turanian speech, and the grammatical terminations have been treated with the same freedom. Nevertheless some of the Turanian numerals and pronouns, and many Turanian roots, point to a single original source; and the common words and common roots which have been discovered in the most distant branches of the Turanian stock, warrant the admission of a real, though very distant, genealogical relationship of all Turanian speech.

The most characteristic feature of the Turanian languages is what has been called *Agglutination*, or 'gluing together.'* This means not only that, in their grammar, pronouns are *glued* to the verbs in order to form the conjugation, or prepositions to substantives in order to form declension. *That* would not be a distinguishing characteristic of the Turanian or nomad languages; for in Hebrew as well as in Sanskrit, conjugation and declension were originally formed on the same principle. What distinguishes the Turanian languages is, that in them the conjugation and declension can still be taken to pieces; and although the terminations have by no means always retained their significative power as independent words, they are felt as modificatory syllables, and as distinct from the roots to which they are appended.

In the Aryan languages the modifications of words, comprised under declension and conjugation, were likewise originally expressed by agglutination. But the component parts began soon to coalesce, so as to form one integral word, liable in its turn to phonetic

* *Survey of Languages,* p. 90.

corruption to such an extent that it became impossible after a time to decide which was the root and which the modificatory element. The difference between an Aryan and a Turanian language is somewhat the same as between good and bad mosaic. The Aryan words seem made of one piece, the Turanian words clearly show the sutures and fissures where the small stones are cemented together.

There was a very good reason why the Turanian languages should have remained in this second or agglutinative stage. It was felt essential that the radical portion of each word should stand out in distinct relief, and never be obscured or absorbed, as happens in the third or inflectional stage.

The French *âge*, for instance, has lost its whole material body, and is nothing but termination. *Age* in old French was *eage* and *edage*. *Edage* is a corruption of the Latin *ætaticum*; *ætaticum* is a derivative of *ætas*; *ætas* an abbreviation of *ævitas*; *ævitas* is derived from *ævum*, and in *ævum*, *æ* only is the radical or predicative element, the Sanskrit *âj* in *âj-us*, life, which contains the germ from which these various words derive their life and meaning. From *ævum* the Romans derived *æviternus*, contracted into *æternus*, so that *age* and *eternity* flow from the same source. What trace of *æ* or *ævum*, or even *ævitas* and *ætas*, remains in *âge*? Turanian languages cannot afford such words as *âge* in their dictionaries. It is an indispensable requirement in a nomadic language that it should be intelligible to many, though their intercourse be but scanty. It requires tradition, society, and literature to maintain words and forms which can no longer be analysed at once. Such words would seldom spring up in nomadic languages, or if they did they would die away with each generation.

The Aryan verb contains many forms in which the personal pronoun is no longer felt distinctly. And yet tradition, custom, and law preserve the life of these veterans, and make us feel unwilling to part with them. But in the ever-shifting state of a nomadic society no debased coin can be tolerated in language, no obscure legend accepted on trust. The metal must be pure, and the legend distinct; that the one may be weighed, and the other, if not deciphered, at least recognised as a well-known guarantee. Hence the small proportion of irregular forms in all agglutinative languages.*

A Turanian might tolerate the Sanskrit

as-mi,	a-si,	as-ti,	's-mas,	's-tha,	's-anti,
I am,	thou art,	he is,	we are,	you are,	they are;

or even the Latin

| 's-um, | e-s, | es-t, | 'su-mus, | es-tis, | 'sunt. |

In these instances, with a few exceptions, root and affix are as distinguishable as, for instance, in Turkish:

bakar-im,	bakar-sin,	bakar,
I regard,	thou regardest,	he regards.
bakar-iz,	bakar-siniz,	bakar-lar,
we regard,	you regard,	they regard.

But a conjugation like the Hindustáni, which is a modern Aryan dialect,

hún, hai, hai, hain, ho, hain,

would not be compatible with the genius of the

---

* The Abbé Molina states that the language of Chili is entirely free from irregular forms (Du Ponceau, *Mémoire*, p. 90).

Turanian languages, because it would not answer the requirements of a nomadic life. Turanian dialects exhibit either no terminational distinctions at all, as in Mandshu, which is a Tungusic dialect; or a complete and intelligible system of affixes, as in the spoken dialect of Nyertchinsk, equally of Tungusic descent. But a state of conjugation in which, through phonetic corruption, the suffix of the first person singular and plural and of the third person plural are the same, where there is no distinction between the second and third persons singular, and between the first and third persons plural, would necessarily lead, in a Turanian dialect, to the adoption of new and more expressive forms. New pronouns would have to be used to mark the persons, or some other expedient be resorted to for the same purpose.

And this will make it still more clear why the Turanian languages, or in fact all languages in this second or agglutinative stage, though protected against phonetic corruption more than the Aryan and Semitic languages, are so much exposed to the changes produced by dialectical regeneration. A Turanian retains, as it were, the consciousness of his language and grammar. The idea, for instance, which he connects with a plural is that of a noun followed by a syllable indicative of plurality; a passive with him is a verb followed by a syllable expressive of suffering, or eating, or going.* Now these determinative ideas may be expressed in various ways, and though in one and the same clan, and during one period of time, a certain number of terminations would become stationary, and be assigned to

---

* *Letter on the Turanian Languages,* p. 206.

the expression of certain grammatical categories, such as the plural, the passive, the genitive, different hordes, as they separated, would still feel themselves at liberty to repeat the process of grammatical composition, and defy the comparative grammarian to prove the identity of the terminations, even in dialects so closely allied as Finnish and Hungarian, or Tamil and Telugu.

It must not be supposed, however, that Turanian or agglutinative languages are for ever passing through this process of grammatical regeneration. Where nomadic tribes approach to a political organisation, their language, though Turanian, may approach to the system of political or traditional languages, such as Sanskrit or Hebrew. This is indeed the case with the most advanced members of the Turanian family, the Hungarian, the Finnish, the Tamil, Telugu, &c. Many of their grammatical terminations have suffered by phonetic corruption, but they have not been replaced by new and more expressive words. The termination of the plural is *lu* in Telugu, and this is probably a mere corruption of *ynl*, the termination of the plural in Tamil. The only characteristic Turanian feature which always remains is this: the root is never obscured. Besides this, the determining or modifying syllables are generally placed at the end, and the vowels do not become so absolutely fixed for each syllable as in Sanskrit or Hebrew. On the contrary, there is what is called the Law of Harmony, according to which the vowels of each word may be changed and modulated so as to harmonise with the key-note struck by its chief vowel. The vowels in Turkish, for instance, are divided into two classes, *sharp* and *flat*. If a verb contains a sharp vowel in its radical portion, the vowels of the terminations are all sharp, while the same terminations, if following a root with a flat vowel, modulate their own vowels into the flat key. Thus we have *sev-mek*, to love, but *bak-mak*, to regard, *mek* or *mak* being the termination of the infinitive. Thus we say, *ev-ler*, the houses, but *at-lar*, the horses, *ler* or *lar* being the termination of the plural.

No Aryan or Semitic language has preserved a similar freedom in the harmonic arrangement of its vowels, while traces of it have been found among the most distant members of the Turanian family, as in Hungarian, Mongolian, Turkish, the Yakut, spoken in the north of Siberia, in the Tulu,* and in dialects spoken on the eastern frontiers of India.

For completeness' sake I add a short account of the Turanian family, chiefly taken from my *Survey of Languages*, published 1855:—

Tungusic Class.

The *Tungusic* branch extends from China northward to Siberia and westward to 118°, where the river Tunguska partly marks its frontier. The Tungusic tribes in Siberia are under Russian sway. Other Tungusic tribes belong to the Chinese empire, and are known by the name of Mandshu, a name taken after they had conquered China in 1644, and founded the present imperial dynasty.

* 'In Tulu final short *u* is left unchanged only after words containing labial vowels (*buḍuḍu*, having left); it is changed into *ü* after all other vowels (*peẓḍaḍü*, having said).'—*Dr. Gundert.*

Mongolic Class.

The original seats of the people who speak Mongolic dialects lie near the Lake Baikal and in the eastern parts of Siberia, where we find them as early as the ninth century after Christ. They were divided into three classes, the *Mongols* proper, the *Buriäts*, and the *Ölöts* or *Kalmüks*. Chingis-khân (1227) united them into a nation and founded the Mongolian empire, which included, however, not only Mongolic, but Tungusic and Turkic, commonly called Tataric, tribes.

The name of Tatar soon became the terror of Asia and Europe, and it was applied promiscuously to all the nomadic warriors whom Asia then poured forth over Europe. Originally Tatar was a name of the Mongolic races, but through their political ascendency in Asia after Chingis-khân, it became usual to call all the tribes which were under Mongolian sway by the name of Tatar. In linguistic works Tataric is now used in two several senses. Following the example of writers of the middle ages, Tataric, like Scythian in Greek, has been fixed upon as the general term comprising *all* languages spoken by the nomadic tribes of Asia. Hence it is used sometimes in the same sense in which I use Turanian. Secondly, Tataric has become the name of that class of Turanian languages of which the Turkish is the most prominent member. While the Mongolic class—that which in fact has the greatest claims to the name of Tataric—is never so called, it has become an almost universal custom to apply this name to the third or Turkic branch of the Ural-Altaic division; and the races belonging to this branch have in many instances themselves adopted the name. These Turkish, or, as they are more commonly called, Tataric races, were settled on the northern side of the Caspian Sea, and on the Black Sea, and were known as Komanes, Pechenegs, and Bulgars, when conquered by the Mongolic army of the son of Chingis-khán, who founded the Kapchakian empire, extending from the Dniestr to the Yemba and the Kirgisian steppes. Russia for two centuries was under the sway of these Kháns, known as the Kháns of the Golden Horde. This empire was dissolved towards the end of the fifteenth century, and several smaller kingdoms rose out of its ruins. Among these Krim, Kasan, and Astrachan were the most important. The princes of these kingdoms still gloried in their descent from Chingis-khán, and had hence a right to the name of Mongols or Tatars. But their armies and subjects also, who were of Turkish blood, received the name of their princes; and their languages continued to be called Tataric, even after the Turkish tribes by whom they were spoken had been brought under the Russian sceptre, and were no longer governed by kháns of Mongolic or Tataric origin. It would therefore be desirable to use Turkic instead of Tataric, when speaking of the third branch of the northern division of the Turanian family, did not a change of terminology generally produce as much confusion as it remedies. The recollection of their non-Tataric, i.e. non-Mongolic origin, remains, it appears, among the so-called Tatars of Kasan and Astrachan. If asked whether they are Tatars, they reply no; and they call their language Turki or Turuk, but not Tatari. Nay, they consider Tatar as a term of reproach, synony-

mons with robber, evidently from a recollection that
their ancestors had once been conquered and enslaved
by Mongolic, that is, Tataric, tribes. All this rests
on the authority of Klaproth, who during his stay in
Russia had great opportunities of studying the languages spoken on the frontiers of this half-Asiatic
empire.

The conquests of the Mongols or the descendants
of Chingis-khán were not confined, however, to these
Turkish tribes. They conquered China in the east,
where they founded the Mongolic dynasty of Yuan,
and in the west, after subduing the khalifs of Bagdad
and the sultans of Iconium, they conquered Moscow,
and devastated the greater part of Russia. In 1240
they invaded Poland, in 1241 Silesia. Here they
recoiled before the united armies of Germany, Poland, and Silesia. They retired into Moravia, and,
having exhausted that country, occupied Hungary.

At that time they had to choose a new khán, which
could only be done at Karakorum, the old capital of
their empire. Thither they withdrew to elect an
emperor to govern an empire which then extended
from China to Poland, from India to Siberia. But a
realm of such vast proportions could not be long
held together, and towards the end of the thirteenth
century it broke up into several independent states,
all under Mongolian princes, but no longer under one
khán of kháns. Thus new independent Mongolic
empires arose in China, Turkestan, Siberia, Southern
Russia, and Persia. In 1360 the Mongolian dynasty
was driven out of China; in the fifteenth century
they lost their hold on Russia. In Central Asia they
rallied once more under Timur (1369), whose sway
was again acknowledged from Karakorum to Persia

and Anatolia. But in 1468, this empire also fell by its own weight, and for want of powerful rulers like Chingis-khán or Timur. In Jagatai alone—the country extending from the Aral Lake to the Hindu-kush between the rivers Oxus and Yaxartes (Jihon and Sihon), and once governed by Jagatai, the son of Chingis-khán— the Mongolian dynasty maintained itself, and thence it was that Baber, a descendant of Timur, conquered India, and founded there, a Mongolian dynasty, surviving up to our own times in the Great Moguls of Delhi. Most Mongolic tribes are now under the sway of the nations whom they once had conquered, the Tungusic sovereigns of China, the Russian czars, and the Turkish sultans.

The Mongolic language, although spoken (but not continuously) from China as far as the Volga, has given rise to but few dialects. Next to Tungusic the Mongolic is the poorest language of the Turanian family, and the scantiness of grammatical terminations accounts for the fact that, as a language, it has remained very much unchanged. There is, however, a distinction between the language as spoken by the Eastern, Western, and Northern tribes, and incipient traces of grammatical life have lately been discovered by Castrén, the great Swedish traveller and Turanian philologist, in the spoken dialect of the Buriäts. In it the persons of the verb are distinguished by affixes, while, according to the rules of Mongolic grammar, no other dialect distinguishes in the verb between *amu, amas, amat*.

The Mongols who live in Europe have fixed their tents on each side of the Volga and along the coast of the Caspian Sea near Astrachan. Another colony is found south-east of Semkirsk. They belong to the

Western branch, and are Ölöts or Kalmüks, who left their seats on the Koko-nur, and entered Europe in 1662. They proceeded from the clans Dürbet and Torgod, but most of the Torgods returned again in 1770, and their descendants are now scattered over the Kirgisian steppes.

Turkic Class.

Much more important are the languages belonging to the third branch of the Turanian family, most prominent among which is the Turkish or Osmanli of Constantinople. The number of the Turkish inhabitants of European Turkey is indeed small. It is generally stated at 2,000,000; but Shafarik estimates the number of genuine Turks at not more than 700,000, who rule over fifteen millions of people. The different Turkic dialects of which the Osmanli is one, occupy one of the largest linguistic areas, extending from the Lena and the Polar Sea down to the Adriatic.

The most ancient name by which the Turkic tribes of Central Asia were known to the Chinese was Hiung-nu. These Hiung-nu founded an empire (206 B.C.) comprising a large portion of Asia west of China. Engaged in frequent wars with the Chinese, they were defeated at last in the middle of the first century after Christ. Thereupon they divided into a northern and southern empire; and, after the southern Hiung-nu had become subjects of China, they attacked the northern Hiung-nu, together with the Chinese, and, driving them out of their seats between the rivers Amur and Selenga, and the Altai mountains, westward, they are supposed to have given the first impulse to the inroads of the barbarians into Europe. In the beginning of the third century, the Mongolic and Tungusic tribes, who had filled the seats of the northern Hiung-nu, had grown so powerful as to attack the southern Hiung-nu and drive them from their territories. This occasioned a second migration of Asiatic tribes towards the west.

Another name by which the Chinese designate these Hiung-nu or Turkish tribes is Tu-kiu. This Tu-kiu is supposed to be identical with Turk. Although the tribe to which this name was given was originally but small, it began to spread in the sixth century from the Altai to the Caspian, and it was probably to them that in 569 the Emperor Justinian sent an ambassador in the person of Semarchos. The empire of the Tu-kiu was destroyed in the eighth century, by the 'Hui-'he (Chinese Kao-che). This tribe, equally of Turkish origin, maintained itself for about a century, and was then conquered by the Chinese and driven back from the northern borders of China. Part of the 'Hui-'he occupied Tangut, and, after a second defeat by the Mongolians in 1257, the remnant proceeded still further west, and joined the Uigurs, whose tents were pitched near the towns of Turfan, 'Kashgar, 'Hamil, and Aksu.

These facts, gleaned chiefly from Chinese historians, show from the very earliest times the westward tendency of the Turkish nations. In 568 Turkish tribes occupied the country between the Volga and the sea of Azov, and numerous reinforcements have since strengthened their position in those parts.

The northern part of Persia, west of the Caspian Sea, Armenia, the south of Georgia, Shirwan, and

Dagestan, harbour a Turkic population, known by the general name of Turkman or Kisil-bash (Qazal-báshi, i.e. Red-caps). They are nomadic robbers, and their arrival in these countries dates from the eleventh and twelfth centuries.

East of the Caspian Sea the Turkman tribes are under command of the Usbek-Kháns of Khiva, Fergana, and Bukhára. They call themselves, however, not subjects but guests of these Khans. Still more to the east the Turkmans are under Chinese sovereignty, and in the south-west they reach as far as Khorasan and other provinces of Persia.

The Usbeks, descendants of the 'Hui-'he and Uigurs, and originally settled in the neighbourhood of the towns of 'Hoten, Kashgar, Turfan, and 'Hamil, crossed the Yaxartes in the sixteenth century, and, after several successful campaigns, gained possession of Balkh, Kharism (Khiva), Bukhára, and Fergana. In the latter country and in Balkh they have become agricultural; but generally their life is nomadic, and too warlike to be called pastoral.

Another Turkish tribe are the Nogái, west of the Caspian, and also north of the Black Sea. To the beginning of the seventeenth century they lived north-east of the Caspian, and the steppes on the left of the Irtish bore their name. Pressed by the Kalmüks, a Mongolic tribe, the Nogáis advanced westward as far as Astrachan. Peter I. transferred them thence to the north of the Caucasian mountains, where they still graze their flocks on the shores of the Kuban and the Kuma. One horde, that of Kundur, remained on the Volga, subject to the Kalmüks.

Another tribe of Turkish origin in the Caucasus are the Bazianes. They now live near the sources of the Kuban, but before the fifteenth century within the town Majari, on the Kuma.

A third Turkish tribe in the Caucasus are the Kumüks on the rivers Sunja, Aksai, and Koisu: now subjects of Russia, though under native princes.

The southern portion of the Altaic mountains has long been inhabited by the Bashkirs, a race considerably mixed with Mongolic blood, savage and ignorant, subjects of Russia and Mohammedans by faith. Their land is divided into four Roads, called the Roads of Siberia, of Kasan, of Nogai, and of Osa, a place on the Kama. Among the Bashkirs, and in villages near Ufa, is now settled a Turkish tribe, the Mescheräks, who formerly lived near the Volga.

The tribes near the Lake of Aral are called Kara-Kalpak. They are subject partly to Russia, partly to the Kháns of Khiva.

The Turks of Siberia, commonly called Tatars, are partly original settlers, who crossed the Ural, and founded the Khanat of Sibir, partly later colonists. Their chief towns are Tobolsk, Yeniseisk, and Tomsk. Separate tribes are the Uran'hat on the Chulym, and the Barabas in the steppes between the Irtish and the Ob.

The dialects of these Siberian Turks are considerably intermingled with foreign words, taken from Mongolic, Samoyedic, or Russian sources. Still they resemble one another closely in all that belongs to the original stock of the language.

In the north-east of Asia, on both sides of the river Lena, the *Yakuts* form the most remote link in the Turkic chain of languages. Their male population has lately risen to 100,000, while in 1795 it amounted only to 50,066. The Russians became first acquainted with them in 1620. They call themselves Sakha, and are mostly heathen, though Christianity is gaining ground among them. According to their traditions, their ancestors lived for a long time in company with Mongolic tribes, and traces of this can still be discovered in their language. Attacked by their neighbours, they built rafts and floated down the river Lena, where they settled in the neighbourhood of what is now Yakutzk. Their original seats seem to have been north-west of Lake Baikal. Their language has preserved the Turkic type more completely than any other Turco-Tataric dialect. Separated from the common stock at an early time, and removed from the disturbing influences to which the other dialects were exposed, whether in war or in peace, the Yakutian has preserved so many primitive features of Tataric grammar, that even now it may be used as a key to the grammatical forms of the Osmanli and other more cultivated Turkic dialects.

Southern Siberia is the mother country of the Kirgis, one of the most numerous tribes of Turco-Tataric origin. The Kirgis lived originally between the Ob and Yenisei, where Mongolic tribes settled among them. At the beginning of the seventeenth century the Russians became acquainted with the Eastern Kirgis, then living along the Yenisei. In 1606 they had become tributary to Russia, and after several wars with two neighbouring tribes, they were driven more and more south-westward, till they left Siberia altogether at the beginning of the eighteenth century. They now live at Burut, in Chinese Turkestan, together with the Kirgis of the 'Great

Horde,' near the town of Kashgar, north as far as the Irtish.

Another tribe is that of the Western Kirgis, or Kirgis-Kazak, who are partly independent, partly tributary to Russia and China.

Of what are called the three Kirgis Hordes, from the Caspian Sea east as far as Lake Tenghiz, the Small Horde is fixed in the west, between the rivers Yemba and Ural; the Great Horde in the east; while the most powerful occupies the centre between the Sarasu and Yemba, and is called the Middle Horde. Since 1819, the Great Horde has been subject to Russia. Other Kirgis tribes, though nominally subject to Russia, are really her most dangerous enemies.

The Turks of Asia Minor and Syria came from Khorasan and Eastern Persia, and are Turkmans, or remnants of the Seljuks, the rulers of Persia during the Middle Ages. It was here that Turkish received that strong admixture of Persian words and idioms. The Osmanli, whom we are accustomed to call Turks *par excellence*, and who form the ruling portion of the Turkish empire, must be traced to the same source. They are now scattered over the whole Turkish Empire in Europe, Asia, and Africa, and their number amounts to between 11,000,000 and 12,000,000. They form the landed gentry, the aristocracy, and the bureaucracy of Turkey; and their language, the Osmanli, is spoken by persons of rank and education, and by all government authorities in Syria, in Egypt, at Tunis, and at Tripoli. In the southern provinces of Asiatic Russia, along the borders of the Caspian, and through the whole of Turkestan, it is the language of the people. It is heard even at the court of Teheran, and is understood by official personages in Persia.

The rise of this powerful tribe of Osman, and the spreading of that Turkish dialect which is now emphatically called the Turkish, are matters of historical notoriety. We need not search for evidence in Chinese annals, or try to discover analogies between names that a Greek or an Arabic writer may by chance have heard and handed down to us, and which some of those tribes have preserved to the present day. The ancestors of the Osman Turks are men as well known to European historians as Charlemagne or Alfred. It was in the year 1224 that Soliman-shah and his tribe, pressed by Mongolians, left Khorasan and pushed westward into Syria, Armenia, and Asia Minor. Soliman's son, Ertoghrul, took service under Aladdin, the Seljuk Sultan of Iconium (Nicæa), and, after several successful campaigns against Greeks and Mongolians, received part of Phrygia as his own. There he founded what was afterwards to become the basis of the Osman empire. During the last years of the thirteenth century the Sultans of Iconium lost their power, and their former vassals became independent sovereigns. Osman, after taking his share of the spoil in Asia, advanced through the Olympic passes into Bithynia, and was successful against the armies of the Emperors of Byzantium. Osman became henceforth the national name of his people. His son, Orkhan, whose capital was Prusa (Bursa), after conquering Nicomedia (1327) and Nicæa (1330), threatened the Hellespont. He took the title of Padishah, and his court was called the 'High Porte.' His son, Soliman, crossed the Hellespont (1357), and took possession of Gallipoli and

Sestos. He thus became master of the Dardanelles. Murad I. took Adrianople (1362), made it his capital, conquered Macedonia, and, after a severe struggle, overthrew the united forces of the Slavonic races south of the Danube, the Bulgarians, Servians, and Kroatians, in the battle of Kossova-polye (1389). He fell himself, but his successor Bayazeth followed his course, took Thessaly, passed Thermopylæ, and devastated the Peloponnesus. The Emperor of Germany, Sigismund, who advanced at the head of an army composed of French, German, and Slavonic soldiers, was defeated by Bayazeth on the Danube in the battle of Nicopolis, 1399. Bayazeth took Bosnia, and would have taken Constantinople, had not the same Mongolians, who in 1244 drove the first Turkish tribes westward into Persia, threatened again their newly-acquired possessions. Timur had grasped the reins fallen from the hands of Chingis-khán: Bayazeth was compelled to meet him, and suffered defeat (1402) in the battle of Angora (Ankyra) in Galatia.

Europe now had respite, but not long; Timur died, and with him his empire fell to pieces, while the Osman army rallied again under Mahomet I. (1413), and re-attained its former power under Murad II. (1421). Successful in Asia, Murad sent his armies back to the Danube, and after long-continued campaigns, and powerful resistance from the Hungarians and Slaves under Hunyad, he at last gained two decisive victories; Varna in 1444, and Kossova in 1448. Constantinople could no longer be held, and the Pope endeavoured in vain to rouse the chivalry of Western Europe to a crusade against the Turks. Mahomet II. succeeded in 1451, and on the 26th of May, 1453, Constantinople, after a valiant resistance, fell, and became the capital of the Turkish empire.

It is a real pleasure to read a Turkish grammar, even though one may have no wish to acquire it practically. The ingenious manner in which the numerous grammatical forms are brought out, the regularity which pervades the system of declension and conjugation, the transparency and intelligibility of the whole structure, must strike all who have a sense of that wonderful power of the human mind which has displayed itself in language. Given so small a number of graphic and demonstrative roots as would hardly suffice to express the commonest wants of human beings, to produce an instrument that shall render the faintest shades of feeling and thought; given a vague infinitive or a stern imperative, to derive from it such moods as an optative or subjunctive, and tenses as an aorist or paulo-post future; given incoherent utterances, to arrange them into a system where all is uniform and regular, all combined and harmonious; such is the work of the human mind which we see realised in 'language.' But in most languages nothing of this early process remains visible. They stand before us like solid rocks, and the microscope of the philologist alone can reveal the remains of organic life with which they are built up.

In the grammar of the Turkic languages, on the contrary, we have before us a language of perfectly transparent structure, and a grammar the inner workings of which we can study, as if watching the building of cells in a crystal beehive. An eminent orientalist remarked, 'We might imagine Turkish to be the result of the deliberations of some eminent society of learned men;' but no such society could have devised what the mind of man produced, left to itself in the steppes of Tartary, and guided only by its innate laws, or by an instinctive power as wonderful as any within the realm of nature.

Let us examine a few forms. 'To love,' in the most general sense of the word, or love, as a root, is in Turkish *sev*. This does not yet mean 'to love,' which is *sevmek*, or 'love' as a substantive, which is *sevgu* or *sevi*; but it only expresses the general idea of loving in the abstract. This root, as we remarked before, can never be touched. Whatever syllables may be added for the modification of its meaning, the root itself must stand out in full prominence like a pearl set in diamonds. It must never be changed or broken, assimilated, or modified, as in the English I fall, I fell, I take, I took, I think, I thought, and similar forms. With this one restriction, however, we are free to treat it at pleasure.

Let us suppose we possessed nothing like our conjugation, but had to express such ideas as I love, thou lovest, and the rest, for the first time. Nothing would seem more natural now than to form an adjective or a participle, meaning 'loving,' and then add the different pronouns, as I loving, thou loving, &c. Exactly this the Turks have done. We need not inquire at present how they produced what we call a participle. It was a task, however, by no means so facile as we now conceive it. In Turkish, one participle is formed by *er*. *Sev+er* would, therefore, mean lov+er or lov+ing. Thou, in Turkish is *sen*, and as all modificatory syllables are placed at the end of the root, we get *sev-er-sen*, thou lovest. You in Turkish is *siz*; hence *sev-er-siz*, you love. In these cases the pronouns and the terminations of the verb coincide exactly. In other persons the coincidences are less complete, because the pronominal terminations have sometimes been modified, or, as in the third person singular, *sever*, dropped altogether as unnecessary. A reference to other cognate languages, however, where either the terminations or the pronouns themselves have maintained a more primitive form, enables us to say that in the original Turkish verb, all persons of the present were formed by means of pronouns appended to this participle *sever*. Instead of 'I love, thou lovest, he loves,' the Turkish grammarian says, 'lover-I, lover-thou, lover.'

But these personal terminations are not the same in the imperfect as in the present.

PRESENT	IMPERFECT
Sever-im, I love	sever-di-m, I loved
Sever-sen	sever-di-ñ
Sever	sever-di
Sever-iz	sever-di-k (miz)
Sever-siz	sever-di-ñiz
Sever-ler	sever-di-ler.

We need not inquire as yet into the origin of the *di*, added to form the imperfect; but it should be stated that in the first person plural of the imperfect a various reading occurs in other Tataric dialects, and that *miz* is used there instead of *k*. Now, looking at these terminations, *m, ñ, i, miz, ñiz*, and *ler*, we find that they are exactly the same as the possessive pronouns used after nouns. As the Italian says *fratel-mo*, my brother, and as in Hebrew we say *El-i*, God (of) I, *i.e.* my God, the Tataric languages form the phrases 'my house, thy house, his house,' by possessive pronouns appended to substantives. A Turk says

Bâbâ	father	bâbâ-m	my father
Aghâ	lord	aghâ-n	thy lord
El	hand	el-i	his hand
Oghlu	son	oghlu-muz	our son
Anâ	mother	anâ-ñiz	your mother
Kitâb	book	kitâb-leri	their book.

We may hence infer that in the imperfect these pronominal terminations were originally taken in a possessive sense, and that, therefore, what remains after the personal terminations are removed, *sever-di*, was never an adjective or a participle, but must have been originally a substantive capable of receiving terminal possessive pronouns; that is, the idea originally expressed by the imperfect could not have been 'loving-I,' but 'love of me.'

How, then, could this convey the idea of a past tense as contrasted with the present? Let us look to our own language. If desirous to express the perfect, we say, I have loved, *j'ai aimé*. This 'I have' meant originally, I possess, and in Latin 'amicus quem amatum habeo' signified in fact a friend whom I hold dear—not, as yet, whom I *have* loved. In the course of time, however, these phrases 'I have said, I have loved,' took the sense of the perfect, and of time past—and not unnaturally, inasmuch as what I *hold*, or *have* done, *is* done—done, as we say, and past. In place of an auxiliary possessive verb, the Turkish language uses an auxiliary possessive pronoun to the same effect. 'Paying belonging to me,' equals 'I have paid;' in either case a phrase originally possessive, took a temporal signification, and became a past or perfect tense. This, however, is the very anatomy of grammar, and when a Turk says 'severdim,' he is, of course, as unconscious of its literal force, 'loving belonging to me,' as of the circulation of his blood.

The most ingenious part of Turkish is undoubtedly the verb. Like Greek and Sanskrit, it exhibits a variety of moods and tenses, sufficient to express the nicest shades of doubt, of surmise, of hope, and supposition. In all these forms the root remains intact, and sounds like a key-note through all the various modulations produced by the changes of person, number, mood, and time. But there is one feature so peculiar to the Turkish verb, that no analogy can be found in any of the Aryan languages—the power of producing new verbal bases by the mere addition of certain letters, which give to every verb a negative, or causative, or reflexive, or reciprocal meaning.

Sev-mek, for instance, as a simple root, means to love. By adding *in*, we obtain a reflexive verb, *sev-in-mek*, which means to love oneself, or rather, to rejoice, to be happy. This may now be conjugated through all moods and tenses, *sevin* being in every respect equal to a new root. By adding *ish* we form a reciprocal verb, *sev-ish-mek*, to love one another.

To each of these three forms a causative sense may be imparted by the addition of the syllable *dir*. Thus

 I. *sev-mek*, to love, becomes IV. *sev-dir-mek*, to cause to love.
 II. *sev-in-mek*, to rejoice, becomes V. *sev-in-dir-mek*, to cause to rejoice.
 III. *sev-ish-mek*, to love one another, becomes VI. *sev-ish-dir-mek*, to cause one to love one another.

Each of these six forms may again be turned into a passive by the addition of *il*. Thus

I. *sev-mek*, to love, becomes VII. *sev-il-mek*, to be loved.
II. *sev-in-mek*, to rejoice, becomes VIII. *sev-in-il-mek*, to be rejoiced at.
III. *sev-ish-mek*, to love one another, becomes IX. *sev-ish-il-mek*, not translatable.
IV. *sev-dir-mek*, to cause one to love, becomes IX. *sev-dir-il-mek*, to be brought to love.
V. *sev-in-dir-mek*, to cause to rejoice, becomes XI. *sev-in-dir-il-mek*, to be made to rejoice.
VI. *sev-ish-dir-mek*, to cause them to love one another, becomes XII. *sev-ish-dir-il-mek*, to be brought to love one another.

This, however, is by no means the whole verbal contingent at the command of a Turkish grammarian. Every one of these twelve secondary or tertiary roots may again be turned into a negative by the mere addition of *me*. Thus, *sev-mek*, to love, becomes *sev-me-mek*, not to love. And if it is necessary to express the impossibility of loving, the Turk has a new root at hand to convey even that idea. Thus while *sev-me-mek* denies only the fact of loving, *sev-eme-mek*, denies its possibility, and means not to be able to love. By the addition of these two modificatory syllables, the number of derivative roots is at once raised to thirty-six. Thus

I. *sev-mek*, to love, becomes XIII. *sev-me-mek*, not to love.
II. *sev-in-mek*, to rejoice, becomes XIV. *sev-in-me-mek*, not to rejoice.
III. *sev-ish-mek*, to love one another, becomes XV. *sev-ish-me-mek*, not to love one another.
IV. *sev-dir-mek*, to cause to love, becomes XVI. *sev-dir-me-mek*, not to cause one to love.
V. *sev-in-dir-mek*, to cause to rejoice, becomes XVII. *sev-in-dir-me-mek*, not to cause one to rejoice.
VI. *sev-ish-dir-mek*, to cause them to love one another, becomes

XVIII. *sev-ish-dir-me-mek*, not to cause them to love one another.
VII. *sev-il-mek*, to be loved, becomes XIX. *sev-il-me-mek*, not to be loved.
VIII. *sev-in-il-mek*, to be rejoiced at, becomes XX. *sev-in-il-me-mek*, not to be the object of rejoicing.
IX. *sev-ish-il-mek*, if it was used, would become XXI. *sev-ish-il-me-mek*, neither form being translatable.
X. *sev-dir-il-mek*, to be brought to love, becomes XXII. *sev-dir-me-ek*, not to be brought to love.
XI. *sev-in-dir-il-mek*, to be made to rejoice, becomes XXIII. *sev-in-dir-il-me-mek*, not to be made to rejoice.
XII. *sev-ish-dir-il-mek*, to be brought to love one another, becomes XXIV. *sev-ish-dir-il-me-mek*, not to be brought to love one another.*

Some of these forms are of course of rare occurrence, and with many verbs these derivative roots, though possible grammatically, would be logically impossible. Even a verb like 'to love,' perhaps the most pliant of all, resists some of the modifications to which a Turkish grammarian is fain to subject it. It is clear, however, that wherever a negation can be formed, the idea of impossibility also can be superadded, so that by substituting *eme* for *me*, we should raise the number of derivative roots to thirty-six. The very last of these, XXXVI., *sev-ish-dir-il-eme-mek*, would be perfectly intelligible, and might be used, for instance, if, in speaking of the Sultan and the Czar, we wished to say, that it was impossible that they should be brought to love one another.

* Prof. Pott, in the second edition of his *Etymologische Forschungen*, ii. 118, refers to similar verbal formations in Arabic, in the language of the Gallas, &c. Analogous forms, according to Dr. Gundert, exist also in Tulu, but they have not yet been analysed so successfully as in Turkish. Thus, *malpuwe* is I do; *malpuwe*, I do habitually; *maltarace*, I do all at once; *malpawe*, I cause to do; *malpurdye*, I cause not to do.

Finnic Class.

It is generally supposed that the original seat of the Finnic tribes was in the Ural mountains, and their languages have been therefore called *Uralic*. From this centre they spread east and west; and southward in ancient times, even to the Black Sea, where Finnic tribes, together with Mongolic and Turkic, were probably known to the Greeks under the comprehensive and convenient name of Scythians. As we possess no literary documents of any of these nomadic nations, it is impossible to say, even where Greek writers have preserved their barbarous names, to what branch of the vast Turanian family they belonged. Their habits were probably identical before the Christian era, during the Middle Ages, and at the present day. One tribe takes possession of a tract and retains it perhaps for several generations, and gives its name to the meadows where it tends its flocks, and to the rivers where the horses are watered. If the country be fertile, it will attract the eye of other tribes; wars begin, and if resistance be hopeless, hundreds of families fly from their paternal pastures, to migrate perhaps for generations—for migration they find a more natural life than permanent habitation—and after a time we may rediscover their names a thousand miles distant. Or two tribes will carry on their warfare for ages, till with reduced numbers both have perhaps to make common cause against some new enemy.

During these continued struggles their languages lose as many words as men are killed on the field of battle. Some words (we might say) go over, others are made prisoners, and exchanged again during times of peace. Besides, there are parleys and challenges, and at last a dialect is produced which may very properly be called a language of the camp (Urdu-zabán, camp-language, is the proper name of Hindustání, formed in the armies of the Mogul emperors), but where it is difficult for the philologist to arrange the living and to number the slain, unless some salient points of grammar have been preserved throughout the medley. We saw how a number of tribes may be at times suddenly gathered by the command of a Chingis-khán or Timur, like billows heaving and swelling at the call of a thunder-storm. One such wave rolling on from Karakorum to Liegnitz may sweep away all the sheepfolds and landmarks of centuries, and when the storm is over, a thin crust will, as after a flood, remain, concealing the underlying stratum of people and languages.

On the evidence of language, the Finnic stock is divided into four branches,

        The Chudic,
        The Bulgaric,
        The Permic,
        The Ugric.

The Chudic branch comprises the Finnic of the Baltic coasts. The name is derived from Chud (Tchud), originally applied by the Russians to the Finnic nations in the north-west of Russia. Afterwards it took a more general sense, and was used almost synonymously with Scythian for all the tribes of Central and Northern Asia. The Finns, properly so called, or as they call themselves Suomalainen, i.e. inhabitants of fens, are settled in the provinces of

Finland (formerly belonging to Sweden, but since 1809 annexed to Russia), and in parts of the governments of Archangel and Olonetz. Their number is stated at 1,521,515. The Finns are the most advanced of their whole family, and are, the Magyars excepted, the only Finnic race that can claim a station among the civilised and civilising nations of the world. Their literature and, above all, their popular poetry bear witness to a high intellectual development in times which we may call mythical, and in places more favourable to the glow of poetical feelings than their present abode, the last refuge Europe could afford them. The epic songs still live among the poorest, recorded by oral tradition alone, and preserving all the features of a perfect metre and of a more ancient language. A national feeling has lately arisen amongst the Finns, despite of Russian supremacy; and the labours of Sjögern, Lönnrot, Castrén, and Kellgren, receiving hence a powerful impulse, have produced results truly surprising. From the mouths of the aged an epic poem has been collected equalling the *Iliad* in length and completeness—nay, if we can forget for a moment all that we in our youth learned to call beautiful, not less beautiful. A Finn is not a Greek, and Wainamoinen was not a Homer. But if the poet may take his colours from that nature by which he is surrounded, if he may depict the men with whom he lives, *Kalewala* possesses merits not dissimilar from those of the *Iliad*, and will claim its place as the fifth national epic of the world, side by side with the Ionian songs, with the *Mahábhárata*, the *Shahnámah*, and the *Nibelunge*. This early literary cultivation has not been without a powerful influence on the language. It has imparted permanency to its forms and a traditional character to its words, so that at first sight we might almost doubt whether the grammar of this language had not left the agglutinative stage, and entered into the current of inflection with Greek or Sanskrit. The agglutinative type, however, yet remains, and its grammar shows a luxuriance of grammatical combination second only to Turkish and Hungarian. Like Turkish it observes the 'harmony of vowels,' a feature peculiar to Turanian languages, as explained before.

Karelian and Tavastian are dialectical varieties of Finnish.

The Esths or Esthonians, neighbours to the Finns, speak a language closely allied to the Finnish. It is divided into the dialects of Dorpat (in Livonia) and Reval. Except some popular songs, it is almost without literature. Esthonia, together with Livonia and Kurland, forms the three Baltic provinces of Russia. The population on the islands of the Gulf of Finland is mostly Esthonian. In the higher ranks of society Esthonian is hardly understood, and never spoken.

Besides the Finns and Esthonians, the Livonians and the Lapps must be reckoned also amongst the same family. Their number, however, is small. The population of Livonia consists chiefly of Esths, Letts, Russians, and Germans. The number of Livonians speaking their own dialect is not more than 5,000.

The Lapps, or Laplanders, inhabit the most northern part of Europe. They belong to Sweden and Russia. Their number is estimated at 28,000. Their language has lately attracted much attention, and Castrén's travels give a description of their manners most interesting from its simplicity and faithfulness.

The Bulgaric branch comprises the Tcheremissians and Mordvinians, scattered in disconnected colonies along the Volga, and surrounded by Russian and Tataric dialects. Both languages are extremely artificial in their grammar, and allow an accumulation of pronominal affixes at the end of verbs, surpassed only by the Bask, the Caucasian, and those American dialects that have been called Polysynthetic.

The general name given to these tribes, Bulgaric, is not borrowed from Bulgaria, on the Danube; Bulgaria, on the contrary, received its name (replacing Moesia) from the Finnic armies by whom it was conquered in the seventh century. Bulgarian tribes advanced from the Volga to the Don, and after remaining for a time under the sovereignty of the Avars on the Don and Dnieper, they advanced to the Danube in 635, and founded the Bulgarian kingdom. This has retained its name to the present day, though the Finnic Bulgarians have long been absorbed by Slavonic inhabitants, and both brought under Turkish sway since 1392.

The third, or Permic branch, comprises the idioms of the Votiakes, the Sirianes, and the Permians, three dialects of one language. *Perm* was the ancient name for the country between 61°—76° E. long. and 55°—65° N. lat. The Permic tribes were driven westward by their eastern neighbours, the Voguls, and thus pressed upon their western neighbours, the Bulgars of the Volga. The Votiakes are found between the rivers Vyatka and Káma. Northwards follow the Sirianes, inhabiting the country on the

Upper Káma, while the eastern portion is held by the Permians. These are surrounded on the south by the Tatars of Orenburg and the Bashkirs; on the north by the Samoyedes, and on the east by Voguls, who pressed on them from the Ural.

These Voguls, together with Hungarians and Ostiakes, form the fourth and last branch of the Finnic family, the Ugric. It was in 462, after the dismemberment of Attila's Hunnic empire, that these Ugric tribes approached Europe. They were then called Onogurs, Saragurs, and Urogs; and in later times they occur in Russian chronicles as Ugry. They are the ancestors of the Hungarians, and should not be confounded with the Uigurs, an ancient Turkic tribe mentioned before.

The similarity between the Hungarian language and dialects of Finnic origin, spoken east of the Volga, is not a new discovery. In 1253, Wilhelm Ruysbroeck, a priest who travelled beyond the Volga, remarked that a race called Pascatir, who lived on the Yaik, spoke the same language as the Hungarians. They were then settled east of the old Bulgarian kingdom, the capital of which, the ancient Bolgari, on the left of the Volga, may still be traced in the ruins of Spask. If these Pascatir—the portion of the Ugric tribes that remained east of the Volga—are identical with the Bashkir, as Klaproth supposes, it would follow that, in later times, they gave up their language, for the present Bashkir no longer speak a Hungarian, but a Turkic, dialect. The affinity of the Hungarian and the Ugro-Finnic dialects was first proved philologically by Gyáramthi in 1799.

A few instances may suffice to show this connection:—

FINNIC CLASS.

Hungarian	Tcheremissian	English
Atya-m	atya-m	my father
Atya-d	atya-t	thy father
Atya	atya-ze	his father
Atya-nk	atya-na	our father
Atya-tok	atya-da	your father
Aty-ok	atya-st	their father

DECLENSION.

	Hungarian	Esthonian	English
Nom.	vér	werri	blood
Gen.	véré	werre	of blood
Dat.	vérnek	werrele	to blood
Acc.	vért	werd	blood
Abl.	véreztöl	werriat	from blood

CONJUGATION.

Hungarian	Esthonian	English
Lelem	leian	I find
Leled	leiad	thou findest
Leli	leiab	he finds
Leljük	loiame	we find
Lelitek	leiate	you find
Lelik	leiawad	they find

A COMPARATIVE TABLE

OF THE

Numerals of each of the Four Branches of the FINNIC CLASS, showing the degree of their relationship.

	1	2	3	4	5	6	7	8	9	10
Churlic, Finnish	yksi	kaksi	kolme	neljä	viisi	kuusi	seitsemän	kahdeksan	yhdeksän	kymmenen
„ Esthonian	üts	kats	kolm	neli	wiis	kuus	seitse	katteus	ütessa	kümme
Bulgaric, Tchermissian	ik	kok	kum	nil	vis	kut	sim	kändizy	enduxe	lu
„ Mordvinian	vaike	kavto	kolmo	nile	vëtä	köto	sisem	kavsko	vikke	kämen
Permic, Sirianian	ötik	kyk	kujim	njolj	vit	kvais	disim	kökjamys	ökmys	das
Ugric, Ostiakian	it	kat	chudam	njeda	vet	chat	tabet	nida	nrjong	jong
„ Hungarian	egy	két	három	negy	öt	hat	hét	njolcs	kilencz	tiz

We have thus examined the four chief classes of the Turanian family, the Tungusic, Mongolic, Turkic, and Finnic. The Tungusic branch stands lowest; its grammar is not much richer than Chinese, and in its structure there is an absence of that architectonic order which in Chinese makes the Cyclopean stones of language hold together without cement. This applies, however, principally to the Mandshu; other Tungusic dialects spoken, not in China, but in the original seats of the Mandshus, are even now beginning to develope grammatical forms.

The Mongolic dialects excel the Tungusic, but in their grammar can hardly distinguish between the different parts of speech. The spoken idioms of the Mongolians, as of the Tungusians, are evidently struggling towards a more organic life, and Castrén has brought home evidence of incipient verbal growth in the language of the Buriäts and a Tungusic dialect spoken near Nyertchinsk.

This is, however, only a small beginning, if compared with the profusion of grammatical resources displayed by the Turkic languages. In their system of conjugation, the Turkic dialects can hardly be surpassed. Their verbs are like branches which break down under the heavy burden of fruits and blossoms. The excellence of the Finnic languages consists rather in a diminution than increase of verbal forms; but in declension Finnish is even richer than Turkish.

These four classes, together with the Samoyedic, constitute the northern or Ural-Altaic division of the Turanian family.

The southern division consists of the Tamulic, the Gangetic (Trans-Himalayan and Sub-Himalayan), the Lohitic, the Taic, and the Malaic classes.* These two divisions comprehend very nearly all the languages of Asia, with the exception of Chinese, which, together with its neighbouring dialects, forms the only representative of radical or monosyllabic speech. A few, such as Japanese,† the language of Korea, of the Koriaks, the Kamchadales, and the numerous dialects of the Caucasus, &c., remain unclassed; but in them also some traces of a common origin with the Turanian languages have, it is probable, survived, and await the discovery of philological research.

Of the third or inflectional stage I need not say much, as we have examined its structure when analysing, in our former Lectures, a number of words in Sanskrit, Greek, Latin, or any other of the Aryan languages. The chief distinction between an inflectional and an agglutinative language consists in the fact that agglutinative languages preserve the consciousness of their roots, and therefore do not allow them to be affected by phonetic corruption; and, though they have lost the consciousness of the original meaning of their terminations, they feel distinctly the difference between the significative root and the modifying elements. Not so in the inflectional languages. There the various elements which enter into the composition of words, may become so welded together, and suffer so much from phonetic corrup-

---

* Of these I can only give a tabular survey at the end of these Lectures, referring for further particulars to my *Letter on the Turanian Languages*. The Gangetic and Lohitic dialects are those comprehended under the name of Bhotiya.

† Professor Boller of Vienna, who has given a most accurate analysis of the Turanian languages in the *Transactions of the Vienna Academy*, has lately endeavoured to establish the Turanian character of Japanese.

tion, that none but the educated would be aware of an original distinction between root and termination, and none but the comparative grammarian able to discover the seams that separate the component parts.

If you consider the character of our morphological classification, you will see that this classification, differing thereby from the genealogical, must be applicable to all languages. Our classification exhausts all possibilities. If the component elements of language are roots, predicative and demonstrative, we cannot have more than three combinations. Roots may either remain roots without any modification; or, secondly, they may be joined so that one determines the other and loses its independent existence; or, thirdly, they may be joined and be allowed to coalesce, so that both lose their independent character. The number of roots which enter into the composition of a word makes no difference, and it is unnecessary, therefore, to admit a fourth class, sometimes called *polysynthetic*, or *incorporating*, including most of the American languages. As long as in these sesquipedalian compounds the significative root remains distinct, they belong to the agglutinative stage; as soon as it is absorbed by the terminations, they belong to the inflectional stage. Nor is it necessary to distinguish between *synthetic* and *analytical* languages, including under the former name the ancient, and under the latter the modern, languages of the inflectional class. The formation of such phrases as the French *j'aimerai*, for *j'ai à aimer*, or the English *I shall do*, *thou wilt do*, may be called *analytical* or *metaphrastic*. But in their morphological nature these phrases are still inflectional. If we analyse such a phrase as *je vivrai*, we find it was originally *ego* (Sanskrit *aham*) *vivere*

(Sanskrit *jiv-ai-r*, dat. neutr.) *habeo* (Sanskrit *bhá-vayá-mi*); that is to say, we have a number of words in which grammatical articulation has been almost entirely destroyed, but has not been cast off; whereas in Turanian languages grammatical forms are produced by the combination of integral roots, and the old and useless terminations are first discarded before any new combination takes place.*

At the end of our morphological classification a problem presents itself, which we might have declined to enter upon if we had confined ourselves to a genealogical classification. At the end of our genealogical classification we had to confess that only a certain number of languages had as yet been arranged genealogically, and that therefore the time for approaching the problem of the common origin of all languages had not yet come. Now, however, although we have not specified all languages which belong to the radical, the terminational, and inflectional classes, we have clearly laid it down as a principle, that all languages must fall under one or the other of these three categories of human speech. It would not be consistent, therefore, to shrink from the consideration of a problem which, though beset with many difficulties, cannot be excluded from the science of language.

Let us first see our problem clearly and distinctly. The problem of the common origin of languages has no necessary connection with the problem of the common origin of mankind. If it could be proved that languages had had different beginnings, this would in nowise necessitate the admission of different beginnings of the human race. For if we look upon

* *Letter on the Turanian Languages*, p. 75.

language as natural to man, it might have broken out at different times and in different countries among the scattered descendants of one original pair; if, on the contrary, language is to be treated as an artificial invention, there is still less reason why each succeeding generation should not have invented its own idiom.

Nor would it follow, if it could be proved that all the dialects of mankind point to one common source, that therefore the human race must descend from one pair. For language might have been the property of one favoured race, and have been communicated to the other races in the progress of history.

The science of language and the science of ethnology have both suffered most seriously from being mixed up together. The classification of races and languages should be quite independent of each other. Races may change their languages, and history supplies us with several instances where one race adopted the language of another. Different languages, therefore, may be spoken by one race, or the same language may be spoken by different races; so that any attempt at squaring the classification of races and tongues must necessarily fail.*

Secondly, the problem of the common origin of languages has no connection with the statements contained in the Old Testament regarding the creation of man and the genealogies of the patriarchs. If our researches led us to the admission of different beginnings for the languages of mankind, there is nothing

* The opposite view, namely, that a genealogical arrangement of the races of man would afford the best classification of the various languages now spoken throughout the world, is maintained by Darwin, *Origin of Species*, p. 422.

in the Old Testament opposed to this view. For although the Jews believed that for a time the whole earth was of one language and of one speech, it has long been pointed out by eminent divines, with particular reference to the dialects of America, that new languages might have arisen at later times. If, on the contrary, we arrive at the conviction that all languages can be traced back to one common source, we could never think of transferring the genealogies of the Old Testament to the genealogical classification of language. The genealogies of the Old Testament refer to blood, not to language, and as we know that people, without changing their name, did frequently change their language, it is clearly impossible that the genealogies of the Old Testament should coincide with the genealogical classification of languages. In order to avoid a confusion of ideas, it would be preferable to abstain altogether from using the same names to express relationship of language which in the Bible are used to express relationship of blood. It was usual formerly to speak of *Japhetic*, *Hamitic*, and *Semitic* languages. The first name has now been replaced by *Aryan*, the second by *African*; and though the third is still retained, it has received a scientific definition quite different from the meaning which it would have in the Bible. It is well to bear this in mind, in order to prevent not only those who are for ever attacking the Bible with arrows that cannot reach it, but likewise those who defend it with weapons they know not how to wield, from disturbing in any way the quiet progress of the science of language.

Let us now look dispassionately at our problem. The problem of the possibility of a common origin of all languages naturally divides itself into two parts, the *formal* and the *material*. We are to-day concerned with the formal part only. We have examined all possible forms which language can assume, and we have now to ask, Can we reconcile with these three distinct forms, the radical, the terminational, and the inflectional, the admission of one common origin of human speech?—I answer decidedly, Yes.

The chief argument that has been brought forward against the common origin of language is this, that no monosyllabic or radical language has ever entered into an agglutinative or terminational stage, and that no agglutinative or terminational language has ever risen to the inflectional stage. Chinese, it is said, is still what it has been from the beginning; it has never produced agglutinative or inflectional forms; nor has any Turanian language ever given up the distinctive feature of the terminational stage, namely, the integrity of its roots.

In answer to this, it should be pointed out that though each language, as soon as it once becomes settled, retains that morphological character which it had when it first assumed its individual or national existence, it does not lose altogether the power of producing grammatical forms that belong to a higher stage. In Chinese, and particularly in Chinese dialects, we find rudimentary traces of agglutination. The *li* which I mentioned before as the sign of the locative, has dwindled down to a mere postposition, and a modern Chinese is no more aware that *li* originally meant interior, than the Turanian is of the origin of his case terminations.* In the spoken dialects of

* M. Stanislas Julien remarks that the numerous compounds which occur in Chinese prove the wide-spread influence of the

Chinese, agglutinative forms are of more frequent occurrence. Thus, in the Shanghai dialect, *wo* is to speak as a verb; *woda*, a word. Of *woda* a genitive is formed, *woda-ka*, a dative *pela woda*, an accusative *lang woda*.* In agglutinative languages, again, we meet with rudimentary traces of inflection. Thus in Tamil the verb *tûngu*, to sleep, has not retained its full integrity in the derivative *tûkkam*, sleep; and *tûngu* itself might probably be traced back to a simpler root, such as *tu*, to recline, to be suspended, to sleep.

I mention these instances, which might be greatly multiplied, in order to show that there is nothing mysterious in the tenacity with which each language clings in general to that stage of grammar which it had attained at the time of its first settlement. If a family, or a tribe, or a nation, has once accustomed itself to express its ideas according to one system of grammar, that first mould remains and becomes

principle of agglutination in that language. The fact is, that in Chinese every sound has numerous meanings; and in order to avoid ambiguity, one word is frequently followed by another which agrees with it in the particular meaning which is intended by the speaker. Thus

chi-youen	(beginning-origin)	signifies	beginning
hen-youen	(root-origin)	,,	beginning
youen-chi	(origin-beginning)	,,	beginning
mei-miai	(beautiful-remarkable)	,,	beautiful
mei-li	(beautiful-elegant)	,,	beautiful
chen-youen	(charming-lovely)	,,	beautiful
yong-i	(easy-facile)	,,	easily
tsong-yong	(to obey, easy)	,,	easily

In order to express 'to boast,' the Chinese say *king-koua*, *king-fa*, &c., both words having one and the same meaning.

This peculiar system of *juxtaposition*, however, cannot be considered as agglutination in the strict sense of the word.

* *Turanian Languages*, p. 24.

stronger with each generation. But, while Chinese was arrested and became traditional in this very early stage, the radical, other dialects passed on through that stage, retaining their pliancy. They were not arrested, and did not become traditional or national, before those who spoke them had learnt to appreciate the advantage of agglutination. That advantage being once perceived, a few single forms in which agglutination first showed itself, would soon, by that sense of analogy which is inherent in language, extend their influence irresistibly. Languages arrested in that stage would cling with equal tenacity to the system of agglutination. A Chinese can hardly understand how language is possible unless every syllable is significative; a Turanian despises every idiom in which each word does not display distinctly its radical and significative element; whereas we, who are accustomed to the use of inflectional languages, are proud of the very grammar which a Chinese and Turanian would treat with contempt.

The fact, therefore, that languages, if once settled, do not change their grammatical constitution, is no argument against our theory, that every inflectional language was once agglutinative, and every agglutinative language was once monosyllabic. I call it a theory, but it is more than a theory, for it is the only possible way in which the realities of Sanskrit or any other inflectional language can be explained. As far as the formal part of language is concerned, we cannot resist the conclusion that what is now *inflectional* was formerly *agglutinative*, and what is now *agglutinative* was at first *radical*. The great stream of language rolled on in numberless dialects, and changed its grammatical colouring as it passed from time to time through new deposits of thought. The different channels which left the main current and became stationary and stagnant, or, if you like, literary and traditional, retained for ever that colouring which the main current displayed at the stage of their separation. If we call the radical stage *white*, the agglutinative *red*, and the inflectional *blue*, then we may well understand why the white channels should show hardly a drop of red or blue, or why the red channels should hardly betray a shadow of blue; and we shall be prepared to find what we do find, namely, white tints in the red, and white and red tints in the blue channels of speech.

You will have perceived that in what I have said I only argue for the possibility, not for the necessity, of a common origin of language.

I look upon the problem of the common origin of language, which I have shown to be quite independent of the problem of the common origin of mankind, as a question which ought to be kept open as long as possible. It is not, I believe, a problem quite as hopeless as that of the plurality of worlds, on which so much has been written of late, but it should be treated very much in the same manner. As it is impossible to demonstrate by the evidence of the senses that the planets are inhabited, the only way to prove that they are, is to prove that it is impossible that they should not be. Thus, on the other hand, in order to prove that the planets are not inhabited, you must prove that it is impossible that they should be. As soon as the one or the other has been proved, the question will be set at rest; till then it must remain an open question, whatever our own predilections on the subject may be.

I do not take quite as desponding a view of the problem of the common origin of language, but I insist on this, that we ought not to allow this problem to be in any way prejudged. Now it has been the tendency of the most distinguished writers on comparative philology to take it almost for granted, that after the discovery of the two families of language, the Aryan and Semitic, and after the establishment of the close ties of relationship which unite the members of each, it would be impossible to admit any longer a common origin of language. After the criteria by which the unity of the Aryan as well as the Semitic dialects can be proved had been so successfully defined, it was but natural that the absence of similar coincidences between any Semitic and Aryan language, or between these and any other branch of speech, should have led to a belief that no connection was admissible between them. A Linnæan botanist, who has his definite marks by which to recognise an Anemone, would reject with equal confidence any connection between the species Anemone, and other flowers which have since been classed under the same head, though deficient in the Linnæan marks of the Anemone.

But there are surely different degrees of affinity in languages as well as in all other productions of nature, and the different families of speech, though they cannot show the same signs of relationship by which their members are held together, need not of necessity have been perfect strangers to each other from the beginning.

Now I confess that when I found the argument used over and over again, that it is impossible any longer to speak of a common origin of language, because comparative philology had proved that there existed various families of speech, I felt that this was not true, that at all events it was an exaggeration.

The problem, if properly viewed, bears the following aspect:—'*If you wish to assert that language had various beginnings, you must prove it impossible that language could have had a common origin.*'

No such impossibility has ever been established with regard to a common origin of the Aryan and Semitic dialects; while, on the contrary, the analysis of the grammatical forms in either family has removed many difficulties, and made it at least intelligible how, with materials identical or very similar, two individuals, or two families, or two nations, could in the course of time have produced languages so different in form as Hebrew and Sanskrit.

But still greater light was thrown on the formative and metamorphic process of language by the study of other dialects unconnected with Sanskrit or Hebrew, and exhibiting before our eyes the growth of those grammatical forms (grammatical in the widest sense of the word) which in the Aryan and Semitic families we know only as formed, not as forming; as decaying, not as living; as traditional, not as understood and intentional: I mean the Turanian languages. The traces by which these languages attest their original relationship are much fainter than in the Semitic and Aryan families, but they are so of necessity. In the Aryan and Semitic families the agglutinative process by which alone grammatical forms can be obtained, has been arrested at some time, and this could only have been through religious or political influences. By the same power through which an advancing civilisation absorbs the manifold dialects in which every spoken idiom naturally represents itself, the first political or religious centralisation must necessarily have put a check on the exuberance of an agglutinative speech. Out of many possible forms one became popular, fixed, and technical for each word, for each grammatical category; and by means of poetry, law, and religion, a literary or political language was produced to which thenceforth nothing had to be added; which in a short time, after becoming unintelligible in its formal elements, was liable to phonetic corruption only, but incapable of internal resuscitation. It is necessary to admit a primitive concentration of this kind for the Aryan and Semitic families, for it is thus only that we can account for coincidences between Sanskrit and Greek terminations, which were formed neither from Greek nor from Sanskrit materials, but which are still identically the same in both. It is in this sense that I call these languages political or state languages, and it has been truly said that languages belonging to these families must be able to prove their relationship by sharing in common not only what is regular and intelligible, but what is anomalous, unintelligible, and dead.

If no such concentration takes place, languages, though formed of the same materials and originally identical, must necessarily diverge in what we may call dialects, but in a very different sense from the dialects such as we find in the later periods of political languages. The process of agglutination will continue in each clan, and forms becoming unintelligible will be easily replaced by new and more intelligible compounds. If the cases are formed by postpositions, new postpositions can be used as soon as the old ones become obsolete. If the conjugation is formed by pronouns, new pronouns can be used if the old ones are no longer sufficiently distinct.

Let us ask, then, what coincidences we are likely to find in agglutinative dialects which have become separated, and which gradually approach to a more settled state? It seems to me that we can only expect to find in them such coincidences as Castrén and Schott have succeeded in discovering in the Finnic, Turkic, Mongolic, Tungusic, and Samoyedic languages; and such as Hodgson, Caldwell, Logan, and myself have pointed out in the Tamulic, Gangetic, Lohitic, Taic, and Malaic languages. They must refer chiefly to the radical materials of language, or to those parts of speech which it is most difficult to reproduce—I mean pronouns, numerals, and prepositions. These languages will hardly ever agree in what is anomalous or inorganic, because their organism repels continually what begins to be formal and unintelligible. It is astonishing rather that any words of a conventional meaning should have been discovered as the common property of the Turanian languages, than that most of their words and forms should be peculiar to each. These coincidences must, however, be accounted for by those who deny the common origin of the Turanian languages; they must be accounted for, either as the result of accident, or of an imitative instinct which led the human mind everywhere to the same onomatopoëtic formations. This has never been done, and it will require great efforts to achieve it.

To myself the study of the Turanian family was interesting particularly because it offered an opportunity of learning how far languages, supposed to be of a common origin, might diverge and become dissimilar by the unrestrained operation of dialectic regeneration.

In a letter which I addressed to my friend, the late Baron Bunsen, and which was published by him in his *Outlines of the Philosophy of Universal History** (vol. i. pp. 263–521), it had been my object to trace, as far as I was able, the principles which guided the formation of agglutinative languages, and to show how far languages may become dissimilar in their grammar and dictionary, and yet allow us to treat them as cognate dialects. In answer to the assertion that it was impossible, I tried, in the fourth, fifth, and sixth sections of that Essay, to show how it was possible that, starting from a common ground, languages as different as Mandshu and Finnish, Malay and Siamese, should have arrived at their present state, and might still be treated as cognate tongues. And as I look upon this process of agglutination as the only intelligible means by which language can acquire a grammatical organisation, and clear the barrier which has arrested the growth of the Chinese idiom, I felt justified in applying the principles derived from the formation of the Turanian languages to the Aryan and Semitic families. They also must have passed through an agglutinative stage, and it is during that period alone that we can account for the gradual divergence and individualisation of what we afterwards call the Aryan and Semitic forms of speech. If we can account for the different appearance of Mandshu and Finnish, we can also

---

* These *Outlines* form vols. iii. and iv. of Bunsen's work, *Christianity and Mankind*, in 7 vols. (London, 1854: Longman), and are sold separately.

account for the distance between Hebrew and Sanskrit. It is true that we do not know the Aryan speech during its agglutinative period, but we can infer what it was when we see languages like Finnish and Turkish approaching more and more to an Aryan type. Such has been the advance which Turkish has made towards inflectional forms, that Professor Ewald claims for it the title of a synthetic language, a title which he gives to the Aryan and Semitic dialects after they have left the agglutinative stage, and entered into a process of phonetic corruption and dissolution. 'Many of its component parts,' he says, 'though they were no doubt originally, as in every language, independent words, have been reduced to mere vowels, or have been lost altogether, so that we must infer their former presence by the changes which they have wrought in the body of the word. *Göz* means eye, and *gör*, to see; *ish*, deed, and *ir*, to do; *ich*, the interior, *gir*, to enter.'* Nay, he goes so far as to admit some formal elements which Turkish shares in common with the Aryan family, and which therefore could only date from a period when both were still in their agglutinative infancy. For instance, *di*, as exponent of a past action; *ta*, as the sign of the past participle of the passive; *lu*, as a suffix to form adjectives, &c.† This is more than I should venture to assert.

Taking this view of the gradual formation of language by agglutination, as opposed to internal development, it is hardly necessary to say that, if I speak of a Turanian family of speech, I use the word family in a

---

* *Göttingische gelehrte Anzeigen*, 1855, p. 298.
† *Ibid.* p. 302, note.

different sense from that which it has with regard to the Aryan and Semitic languages. In my Letter on the Turanian languages, which has been the subject of such fierce and wild attacks from those who believe in different beginnings of language and mankind, I had explained this repeatedly, and I had preferred the term of *group* for the Turanian languages, in order to express as clearly as possible that the relation between Turkish and Mandshu, between Tamil and Finnish, was a different one, not in degree only, but in kind, from that between Sanskrit and Greek. 'These Turanian languages,' I said (p. 216), 'cannot be considered as standing to each other in the same relation as Hebrew and Arabic, Sanskrit and Greek.' 'They are radii diverging from a common centre, not children of a common parent.' And still they are not so widely distant as Hebrew and Sanskrit, because none of them has entered into that new phase of growth or decay (p. 218) through which the Semitic and Aryan languages passed after they had been settled, individualised, and nationalised.

The real object of my Essay was therefore a defensive one. It was to show how rash it was to speak of different independent beginnings in the history of human speech, before a single argument had been brought forward to establish the necessity of such an admission. The impossibility of a common origin of language has never been proved, but, in order to remove what were considered difficulties affecting the theory of a common origin, I felt it my duty to show practically, and by the very history of the Turanian languages, how such a theory was possible, or, as I say in one instance only, probable. I endeavoured to show how even the most distant members of the Turanian family, the one spoken in the north, the other in the south of Asia, the *Finnic* and the *Tamulic*, have preserved in their grammatical organisation traces of a former unity; and, if my opponents admit that I have proved the ante-Brahmanic or Tamulic inhabitants of India to belong to the Turanian family, they can hardly have been aware that if this, the most extreme point of my argument, be conceded, everything else is involved, and must follow by necessity.

Yet I did not call the last chapter of my Essay, 'On the Necessity of a Common Origin of Language,' but 'On the Possibility;' and, in answer to the opinions advanced by the opposite party, I summed up my defence in these two paragraphs:—

I.

'Nothing necessitates the admission of different independent beginnings for the *material* elements of the Turanian, Semitic, and Aryan branches of speech: nay, it is possible even now to point out radicals which, under various changes and disguises, have been current in these three branches ever since their first separation.'

II.

'Nothing necessitates the admission of different beginnings for the formal elements of the Turanian, Semitic, and Aryan branches of speech; and though it is impossible to derive the Aryan system of grammar from the Semitic, or the Semitic from the Aryan, we can perfectly understand how, either through individual influences, or by the wear and tear of speech in its own continuous working, the different systems of grammar of Asia and Europe may have been produced.'

It will be seen, from the very wording of these two paragraphs, that my object was to deny the necessity of independent beginnings, and to assert the possibility of a common origin of language. I have been accused of having been biassed in my researches by an implicit belief in the common origin of mankind. I do not deny that I hold this belief, and, if it wanted confirmation, that confirmation has been supplied by Darwin's book, *On the Origin of Species*.* But I defy my adversaries to point out one single passage where I have mixed up scientific with theological arguments. Only, if I am told that no 'quiet observer would ever have conceived the idea of deriving all mankind from one pair, unless the Mosaic records had taught it,' I must be allowed to say in reply, that this idea, on the contrary, is so natural, so consistent with all human laws of reasoning, that, as far

---

* ' Here the lines converge as they recede into the geological ages, and point to conclusions which, upon Darwin's theory, are inevitable, but hardly welcome. The very first step backward makes the negro and the Hottentot our blood-relations ; not that reason or Scripture objects to that, though pride may.'—Asa Grey, *Natural Selection not inconsistent with Natural Theology*, 1861. p. 5.

' One good effect is already manifest, its enabling the advocates of the hypothesis of a multiplicity of human species to perceive the double insecurity of their ground. When the races of men are admitted to be of one species, the corollary, that they are of one origin, may be expected to follow. Those who allow them to be of one species must admit an actual diversification into strongly marked and persistent varieties ; while those, on the other hand, who recognise several or numerous human species, will hardly be able to maintain that such species were primordial and supernatural in the ordinary sense of the word.'—*Ibid.* p. 54.

as I know, there has been no nation on earth which, if it possessed any traditions on the origin of mankind, did not derive the human race from one pair, if not from one person. The author of the Mosaic records, therefore, though stripped, before the tribunal of Physical Science, of his claims as an inspired writer, may at least claim the modest title of a quiet observer; and if his conception of the physical unity of the human race can be proved to be an error, it is an error which he shares in common with other quiet observers, such as Humboldt, Bunsen, Prichard, and Owen.[*]

The only question which remains to be answered is this, Was it one and the same volume of water which supplied all the lateral channels of speech? or, to drop all metaphor, are the roots which were joined together according to the radical, the terminational, and inflectional systems, identically the same? The only way to answer, or at least to dispose of, this question is to consider the nature and origin of roots; and we shall then have reached the extreme limits to which inductive reasoning can carry us in our researches into the mysteries of human speech.

[*] Professor Pott, the most distinguished advocate of the polygenetic dogma, has pleaded the necessity of admitting more than one beginning for the human race and for language in an article in the *Journal of the German Oriental Society*, ix. 405, *Max Müller und die Kennzeichen der Sprachverwandtschaft*, 1855; in a treatise *Die Ungleichheit menschlicher Rassen*, 1856; and in the new edition of his *Etymologische Forschungen*, 1861.

LECTURE IX.

THE THEORETICAL STAGE, AND THE ORIGIN OF LANGUAGE.

'IN examining the history of mankind, as well as in examining the phenomena of the material world, when we cannot trace the process by which an event *has been* produced, it is often of importance to be able to show how it *may have been* produced by natural causes. Thus, although it is impossible to determine with certainty what the steps were by which any particular language was formed, yet, if we can show, from the known principles of human nature, how all its various parts *might* gradually have arisen, the mind is not only to a certain degree satisfied, but a check is given to that indolent philosophy which refers to a miracle whatever appearances, both in the natural and moral worlds, it is unable to explain.'[*]

This quotation from an eminent Scotch philosopher contains the best advice that could be given to the student of the science of language, when he approaches the problem which we have to examine to-day, namely, the origin of language. Though we have stripped that problem of the perplexing and mysterious aspect which it presented to the philosophers of old, yet, even in its simplest form, it seems to be almost beyond the reach of the human understanding.

[*] Dugald Stewart, vol. iii. p. 25.

If we were asked the riddle how images of the eye and all the sensations of our senses could be represented by sounds, nay, could be so embodied in sounds as to express thought and excite thought, we should probably give it up, as the question of a madman, who, mixing up the most heterogeneous subjects, attempted to change colour into sound and sound into thought.* Yet this is the riddle which we have now to solve.

It is quite clear that we have no means of solving the problem of the origin of language *historically*, or of explaining it as a matter of fact which happened once in a certain locality and at a certain time. History does not begin till long after mankind had acquired the power of language, and even the most ancient traditions are silent as to the manner in which man came in possession of his earliest thoughts and words. Nothing, no doubt, would be more interesting than to know from historical documents the exact process by which the first man began to lisp his first words, and thus to be rid for ever of all the theories on the origin of speech. But this knowledge is denied us; and, if it had been otherwise, we should probably be quite unable to understand those primitive events in the history of the human mind.† We are told that

* Herder, as quoted by Steinthal, *Ursprung der Sprache*, s. 39.

† 'In all these paths of research, when we travel far backwards, the aspect of the earlier portions becomes very different from that of the advanced part on which we now stand; but in all cases the path is lost in obscurity as it is traced backwards towards its starting-point:—it becomes not only invisible, but unimaginable; it is not only an interruption, but an abyss, which interposes itself between us and any intelligible beginning of things.'— Whewell, *Indications*, p. 166.

the first man was the son of God, that God created him in His own image, formed him of the dust of the ground, and breathed into his nostrils the breath of life. These are simple facts, and to be accepted as such; if we begin to reason on them, the edge of the human understanding glances off. Our mind is so constituted that it cannot apprehend the absolute beginning or the absolute end of anything. If we tried to conceive the first man created as a child, and gradually unfolding his physical and mental powers, we could not understand his living for *one* day without supernatural aid. If, on the contrary, we tried to conceive the first man created full-grown in body and mind, the conception of an effect without a cause would equally transcend our reasoning powers. It is the same with the first beginnings of language. Theologians who claim for language a divine origin drift into the most dangerous anthropomorphism, when they enter into any details as to the manner in which they suppose the Deity to have compiled a dictionary and grammar in order to teach them to the first man as a schoolmaster teaches the deaf and dumb. And they do not see that, even if all their premises were granted, they would have explained no more than how the first man might have learnt a language, if there was a language ready-made for him. How that language was made would remain as great a mystery as ever. Philosophers, on the contrary, who imagine that the first man, though left to himself, would gradually have emerged from a state of mutism and have invented words for every new conception that arose in his mind, forget that man could not by his own power have acquired *the faculty* of speech which is the distinctive character of mankind,* unattained and unattainable by the mute creation. It shows a want of appreciation as to the real bearings of our problem, if philosophers appeal to the fact that children are born without language, and gradually emerge from mutism to the full command of articulate speech. We want no explanation how birds learn to fly, created as they are with organs adapted to that purpose. Nor do we wish to enquire how children learn to use the various faculties with which the human body and soul are endowed. We want to gain, if possible, an insight into the original faculty of speech; and for that purpose I fear it is as useless to watch the first stammerings of children, as it would be to repeat the experiment of the Egyptian king who intrusted two new-born infants to a shepherd, with the injunction to let them suck a goat's milk, and to speak no word in their presence, but to observe what word they would first utter.† The same experiment is said to have been repeated by the Swabian emperor, Frederic II., by James IV. of Scotland, and by one of the

---

* 'Der Mensch ist nur Mensch durch Sprache; um aber die Sprache zu erfinden, müsste er schon Mensch sein.'—W. von Humboldt, *Sämmtliche Werke*, b. iii. s. 252. The same argument is ridden to death by Süssmilch, *Versuch eines Beweises dass die erste Sprache ihren Ursprung nicht vom Menschen, sondern allein vom Schöpfer erhalten habe*, Berlin, 1766.

† Farrar, *Origin of Language*, p. 10; Grimm, *Ursprung der Sprache*, s. 32. The word βεκός, which these children are reported to have uttered, and which, in the Phrygian language, meant bread—thus proving, it was supposed, that the Phrygian was the primitive language of mankind—is derived from the same root which exists in the English, to bake. How these unfortunate children came by the idea of baked bread, involving the ideas of corn, mill, oven, fire, &c., seems never to have struck the ancient sages of Egypt.

Mogul emperors of India. But, whether for the purpose of finding out which was the primitive language of mankind, or of discovering how far language was natural to man, the experiments failed to throw any light on the problem before us. Children, in learning to speak, do not invent language. Language is there ready-made for them. It has been there for thousands of years. They acquire the use of a language, and, as they grow up, they may acquire the use of a second and a third. It is useless to inquire whether infants, left to themselves, would invent a language. It would be impossible, unnatural, and illegal to try the experiment, and, without repeated experiments, the assertions of those who believe and those who disbelieve the possibility of children inventing a language of their own are equally valueless. All we know for certain is, that an English child, if left to itself, would never begin to speak English, and that history supplies no instance of any language having thus been invented.

If we want to gain an insight into the faculty of flying, which is a characteristic feature of birds, all we can do is, first, to compare the structure of birds with that of other animals which are devoid of that faculty, and secondly, to examine the conditions under which the act of flying becomes possible. It is the same with speech. Speech is a specific faculty of man. It distinguishes man from all other creatures; and if we wish to acquire more definite ideas as to the real nature of human speech, all we can do is to compare man with those animals that seem to come nearest to him, and thus to try to discover what he shares in common with these animals, and what is peculiar to him, and to him alone. After we have discovered this, we may proceed to inquire into the conditions under which speech becomes possible, and we shall then have done all that we can do, considering that the instruments of our knowledge, wonderful as they are, are yet far too weak to carry us through all the regions to which we may soar on the wings of our imagination!

In comparing man with the other animals, we need not enter here into the physiological question whether the difference between the body of an ape and the body of a man is one of degree or of kind. However that question is settled by physiologists, we need not be afraid. If the structure of a mere worm is such as to fill the human mind with awe, if a single glimpse which we catch of the infinite wisdom displayed in the organs of the lowest creature gives us an intimation of the wisdom of its Divine Creator far transcending the powers of our conception, how are we to criticise and disparage the most highly organised creatures of His creation, creatures as wonderfully made as we ourselves? Are there not many creatures in many points more perfect even than man? Do we not envy the lion's strength, the eagle's eye, the wings of every bird? If there existed animals altogether as perfect as man in their physical structure, nay, even more perfect, no thoughtful man would ever be uneasy. His true superiority rests on different grounds. 'I confess,' Sydney Smith writes, 'I feel myself so much at ease about the superiority of mankind—I have such a marked and decided contempt for the understanding of every baboon I have ever seen—I feel so sure that the blue ape without a tail will never rival us in poetry, painting, and music, that I see no reason whatever that justice may not be done to the few fragments of soul and tatters of understanding which they may really possess.' The playfulness of Sydney Smith in handling serious and sacred subjects has of late been found fault with by many; but humour is often a safer sign of strong convictions and perfect safety than guarded solemnity.

With regard to our own problem, no one can doubt that certain animals possess all the physical requirements for articulate speech. There is no letter of the alphabet which a parrot will not learn to pronounce.* The fact, therefore, that the parrot is without a language of his own, must be explained by a difference between the *mental*, not between the *physical*, faculties of the animal and man; and it is by a comparison of the mental faculties alone, such as we find them in man and brutes, that we may hope to discover what constitutes the indispensable qualification for language, a qualification to be found in man alone, and in no other creature on earth.

I say *mental faculties*, and I mean to claim a large share of what we call our mental faculties for the higher

---

* 'L'usage de la main, la marche à deux pieds, la ressemblance, quoique grossière, de la face, tous les actes qui peuvent résulter de cette conformité d'organisation, ont fait donner au singe le nom d'*homme sauvage* par des hommes à la vérité qui l'étaient à demi, et qui ne savaient comparer que les rapports extérieurs. Que serait-ce, si, par une combinaison de causes aussi possible que toute autre, le singe eût eu la voix du perroquet, et, comme lui, la faculté de la parole ? Le singe parlant eût rendu muette d'étonnement l'espèce humaine entière, et l'aurait séduite au point que le philosophe aurait eu grand' peine à démontrer qu'avec tous ces beaux attributs humains le singe n'en était pas moins une bête. Il est donc heureux, pour notre intelligence, que la Nature ait séparé et placé, dans deux espèces très-différentes, l'imitation de la parole et celle de nos gestes.'—Buffon, as quoted by Flourens, p. 77.

animals. These animals have *sensation, perception, memory, will,* and *intellect*; only we must restrict intellect to the comparing or interlacing of single perceptions. All these points can be proved by irrefragable evidence, and that evidence has never, I believe, been summed up with greater lucidity and power than in one of the last publications of M. P. Flourens, *De la Raison, du Génie, et de la Folie,* Paris, 1861. There are no doubt many people who are as much frightened at the idea that brutes have souls and are able to think, as by 'the blue ape without a tail.' But their fright is entirely of their own making. If people will use such words as soul or thought without making it clear to themselves and others what they mean by them, these words will slip away under their feet, and the result must be painful. If we once ask the question, Have brutes a soul? we shall never arrive at any conclusion; for *soul* has been so many times defined by philosophers, from Aristotle down to Hegel, that it means everything and nothing. Such has been the confusion caused by the promiscuous employment of the ill-defined terms of mental philosophy that we find Descartes representing brutes as living machines, whereas Leibniz claims for them not only souls, but immortal souls. 'Next to the error of those who deny the existence of God,' says Descartes, 'there is none so apt to lead weak minds from the right path of virtue, as to think that the soul of brutes is of the same nature as our own, and, consequently, that we have nothing to fear or to hope after this life, any more than flies or ants; whereas, if we know how much they differ, we understand much better that *our* soul is quite independent of the body, and consequently not subject to die with the body.'

The spirit of these remarks is excellent, but the argument is extremely weak. It does not follow that brutes have no souls because they have no human souls. It does not follow that the souls of men are not immortal, because the souls of brutes are not immortal; nor has the *major premiss* ever been proved by any philosopher, namely, that the souls of brutes must necessarily be destroyed and annihilated by death. Leibniz, who has defended the immortality of the human soul with stronger arguments than even Descartes, writes—'I found at last how the souls of brutes and their sensations do not at all interfere with the immortality of human souls; on the contrary, nothing serves better to establish our natural immortality than to believe that all souls are imperishable.'

Instead of entering into these perplexities, which are chiefly due to the loose employment of ill-defined terms, let us simply look at the facts. Every unprejudiced observer will admit that—

1. Brutes see, hear, taste, smell, and feel; that is to say, they have five senses, just like ourselves, neither more nor less. They have both sensation and perception—a point which has been illustrated by M. Flourens by the most interesting experiments. If the roots of the optic nerve are removed, the retina in the eye of a bird ceases to be excitable, the iris is no longer movable; the animal is blind, because it has lost the organ of *sensation*. If, on the contrary, the cerebral lobes are removed, the eye remains pure and sound, the retina excitable, the iris movable. The eye is preserved, yet the animal cannot see, because it has lost the organs of perception.

2. Brutes have sensations of pleasure and pain. A dog that is beaten behaves exactly like a child that is chastised, and a dog that is fed and fondled exhibits the same signs of satisfaction as a boy under the same circumstances. We can judge from signs only, and if they are to be trusted in the case of children, they must be trusted likewise in the case of brutes.

3. Brutes do not forget, or, as philosophers would say, brutes have memory. They know their masters, they know their home; they evince joy on recognising those who have been kind to them, and they bear malice for years to those by whom they have been insulted or ill-treated. Who does not recollect the dog Argos in the *Odyssey*, who, after so many years' absence, was the first to recognise Ulysses?*

4. Brutes are able to compare and to distinguish. A parrot will take up a nut, and throw it down again without attempting to crack it. He has found that it is light;—this he could discover only by comparing the weight of the good nuts with that of the bad; and he has found that it has no kernel;—this he could discover only by what philosophers would dignify with the grand title of syllogism, namely, 'All light nuts are hollow; this is a light nut, therefore this nut is hollow.'

5. Brutes have a will of their own. I appeal to any one who has ever ridden a restive horse.

6. Brutes show signs of shame and pride. Here again any one who has to deal with dogs, who has watched a retriever with sparkling eyes placing a partridge at his master's feet, or a hound slinking

---

* *Odyssey*, xvii. 300.

away with his tail between his legs from the huntsman's call, will agree that these signs admit of but one interpretation. The difficulty begins when we use philosophical language, when we claim for brutes a moral sense, a conscience, a power of distinguishing good and evil; and, as we gain nothing by these scholastic terms, it is better to avoid them altogether.

7. Brutes show signs of love and hatred. There are well-authenticated stories of dogs following their masters to the grave, and refusing food from any one. Nor is there any doubt that brutes will watch their opportunity till they revenge themselves on those whom they dislike.

If, with all these facts before us, we deny that brutes have sensation, perception, memory, will, and intellect, we ought to bring forward powerful arguments for interpreting the signs which we observe in brutes so differently from those which we observe in men.

Some philosophers imagine they have explained everything if they ascribe to brutes instinct instead of intellect. But, if we take these two words in their usual acceptations, they surely do not exclude each other.* There are instincts in man as well as in brutes. A child takes his mother's breast by instinct; the spider weaves its net by instinct; the bee builds her cell by instinct. No one would ascribe to the child a knowledge of physiology because it employs the exact muscles which are required for sucking; nor shall we claim for the spider a knowledge of mechanics, or for the bee an acquaintance with

* 'The evident marks of reasoning in the other animals—of reasoning which I cannot but think as unquestionable as the instincts that mingle with it.'—Brown, *Works*, vol. i. p. 446.

geometry, because we could not do what they do without a study of these sciences. But what if we tear a spider's web, and see the spider examining the mischief that is done, and either giving up his work in despair, or endeavouring to mend it as well as may be?* Surely here we have the instinct of weaving controlled by observation, by comparison, by reflection, by judgment. Instinct, whether mechanical or moral, is more prominent in brutes than in man; but it exists in both, as much as intellect is shared by both.

Where, then, is the difference between brute and man?† What is it that man can do, and of which we find no signs, no rudiments, in the whole brute world? I answer without hesitation: the one great barrier between the brute and man is *Language*. Man speaks, and no brute has ever uttered a word. Language is our Rubicon, and no brute will dare to cross it. This is our matter-of-fact answer to those who speak of development, who think they discover the rudiments at least of all human faculties in apes, and who would fain keep open the

* Flourens, *De la Raison*, p. 51.
† To allow that 'brutes have certain mental endowments in common with men,' .... 'desires, affections, memory, simple imagination, or the power of reproducing the sensible past in mental pictures, and even judgment of the simple or intuitive kind;'—that 'they compare and judge' (*Mem. Amer. Acad.* 8, p. 118), is to concede that the intellect of brutes really acts, so far as we know, like human intellect, as far as it goes; for the philosophical logicians tell us that all reasoning is reducible to a series of simple judgments. And Aristotle declares that even reminiscence—which is, we suppose, 'reproducing the sensible past in mental pictures'—is a sort of reasoning (τὶ ἀναμιμνήσκεσθαί ἐστι οἷον συλλογισμός τις). Asa Gray, *Natural Selection &c.*, p. 58, note.

possibility that man is only a more favoured beast, the triumphant conqueror in the primeval struggle for life. Language is something more palpable than a fold of the brain or an angle of the skull. It admits of no cavilling, and no process of natural selection will ever distil significant words out of the notes of birds or the cries of beasts.

Language, however, is only the outward sign. We may point to it in our arguments, we may challenge our opponent to produce anything approaching to it from the whole brute world. But if this were all, if the art of employing articulate sounds for the purpose of communicating our impressions were the only thing by which we could assert our superiority over the brute creation, we might not unreasonably feel somewhat uneasy at having the gorilla so close on our heels.

It cannot be denied that brutes, though they do not use articulate sounds for that purpose, have nevertheless means of their own for communicating with each other. When a whale is struck, the whole shoal, though widely dispersed, are instantly made aware of the presence of an enemy; and when the grave-digger beetle finds the carcase of a mole, he hastens to communicate the discovery to his fellows, and soon returns with his *four* confederates.* It is evident, too, that dogs, though they do not speak, possess the power of understanding much that is said to them, their names and the calls of their master; and other animals, such as the parrot, can pronounce every articulate sound. Hence, although, for the purpose of philosophical warfare, articulate

* Conscience, *Boek der Natuur*, vi., quoted by Marsh, p. 32.

language would still form an impregnable position, yet it is but natural that for our own satisfaction we should try to find out in what the strength of our position really consists; or, in other words, that we should try to discover that inward power of which language is the outward sign and manifestation.

For this purpose it will be best to examine the opinions of those who approached our problem from another point; who, instead of looking for outward and palpable signs of difference between brute and man, inquired into the inward mental faculties, and tried to determine the point where man transcends the barriers of the brute intellect. That point, if truly determined, ought to coincide with the starting-point of language; and, if so, that coincidence ought to explain the problem which occupies us at present.

I shall read an extract from Locke's Essay concerning Human Understanding.

After having explained how universal ideas are produced, how the mind, having observed the same colour in chalk, and snow, and milk, comprehends these single perceptions under the general conception of whiteness, Locke continues: * 'If it may be doubted, whether beasts compound and enlarge their ideas that way to any degree: this, I think, I may be positive in, that the power of abstracting is not at all in them; and that the having of general ideas is that which puts a perfect distinction betwixt men and brutes, and is an excellency which the faculties of brutes do by no means attain to.'

If Locke is right in considering the having general

* Book ii. chapter xi. § 10.

ideas as the distinguishing feature between man and brutes, and if we ourselves are right in pointing to language as the one palpable distinction between the two, it would seem to follow that language is the outward sign and realisation of that inward faculty which is called the faculty of abstraction, but which is better known to us by the homely name of Reason.

Let us now look back to the result of our former Lectures. It was this. After we had explained everything in the growth of language that can be explained, there remained in the end, as the only inexplicable residuum, what we called *roots*. These roots formed the constituent elements of all languages. This discovery has simplified the problem of the origin of language immensely. It has taken away all excuse for those rapturous descriptions of language which invariably precede the argument that language must have a divine origin. We shall hear no more of that wonderful instrument which can express all we see, and hear, and taste, and touch, and smell; which is the breathing image of the whole world; which gives form to the airy feelings of our souls, and body to the loftiest dreams of our imagination; which can arrange in accurate perspective the past, the present, and the future, and throw over everything the varying hues of certainty, of doubt, of contingency. All this is perfectly true, but it is no longer wonderful, at least not in the Arabian Nights sense of that word. 'The speculative mind,' as Dr. Ferguson says, 'in comparing the first and last steps of the progress of language, feels the same sort of amazement with a traveller, who, after rising insensibly on the slope of a hill, comes to look from a precipice of an almost unfathomable depth, to the summit of which he scarcely believes himself to have ascended without supernatural aid.' To certain minds it is a disappointment to be led down again by the hand of history from that high summit. They prefer the unintelligible which they can admire, to the intelligible which they can only understand. But to a mature mind reality is more attractive than fiction, and simplicity more wonderful than complication. Roots may seem dry things as compared with the poetry of Goethe; yet there is something more truly wonderful in a root than in all the lyrics of the world.

What, then, are these roots? In our modern languages roots can only be discovered by scientific analysis, and, even as far back as Sanskrit, we may say that no root was ever used as a noun or as a verb. But originally roots were thus used, and in Chinese we have fortunately preserved to us a representative of that primitive radical stage which, like the granite, underlies all other strata of human speech. The Aryan root *DA*, to give, appears in Sanskrit *dâ-nam*, Latin *do-num*, gift, as a substantive; in Latin *do*, Sanskrit *da-dâ-mi*, Greek *di-dō-mi*, I give, as a verb; but the root DA can never be used by itself. In Chinese, on the contrary, the root TA, as such, is used in the sense of a noun, greatness; of a verb, to be great; of an adverb, greatly or much. Roots therefore are not, as is commonly maintained, merely scientific abstractions, but they were used originally as real words. What we want to find out is this, What inward mental phase is it that corresponds to these roots, as the germs of human speech?

Two theories have been started to solve this

problem, which, for shortness' sake, I shall call the *Bow-wow* theory and the *Pooh-pooh* theory.*

According to the first, roots are imitations of sounds; according to the second, they are involuntary interjections. The first theory was very popular among the philosophers of the eighteenth century, and, as it is still held by many distinguished scholars and philosophers, we must examine it more carefully. It is supposed, then, that man, being as yet mute, heard the voices of birds and dogs and cows, the thunder of the clouds, the roaring of the sea, the rustling of the forest, the murmurs of the brook, and the whisper of the breeze. He tried to imitate these sounds, and finding his mimicking cries useful as signs of the objects from which they proceeded, he followed up the idea and elaborated language. This view was most ably defended by Herder.† 'Man,' he says, 'shows conscious reflection when his soul acts so freely that it may separate, in the ocean of sensations which rush into it through the senses, one single wave, arrest it, regard it, being conscious all the time of regarding this one single wave. Man proves his conscious reflection when, out of the dream of images that float past his senses, he can gather himself up and wake for a moment, dwelling intently

---

* I regret to find that the expressions here used have given offence to several of my reviewers. They were used because the names Onomatopoetic and Interjectional are awkward and not very clear. They were not intended to be disrespectful to those who hold the one or the other theory—some of them scholars for whose achievements in comparative philology I entertain the most sincere respect.

† A fuller account of the views of Herder and other philosophers on the origin of language may be found in Steinthal's useful little work, *Der Ursprung der Sprache*, Berlin, 1858.

on one image, fixing it with a bright and tranquil glance, and discovering for himself those signs by which he knows that *this* is *this* image and no other. Man proves his conscious reflection when he not only perceives vividly and distinctly all the features of an object, but is able to separate and recognise one or more of them as its distinguishing features.' For instance, ' Man sees a lamb. He does not see it like the ravenous wolf. He is not disturbed by any uncontrollable instinct. He wants to know it, but he is neither drawn towards it nor repelled from it by his senses. The lamb stands before him, as represented by his senses, white, soft, woolly. The conscious and reflecting soul of man looks for a distinguishing mark;—the lamb bleats!—the mark is found. The bleating, which made the strongest impression, which stood apart from all other impressions of sight or touch, remains in the soul. The lamb returns— white, soft, woolly. The soul sees, touches, reflects, looks for a mark. The lamb bleats, and now the soul has recognised it. "Ah, thou art the bleating animal," the soul says within herself; and the sound of bleating, perceived as the distinguishing mark of the lamb, becomes the name of the lamb. It was the comprehended mark, the word. And what is the whole of our language but a collection of such words?'

Our answer is, that though there are names in every language formed by mere imitation of sound, yet these constitute a very small proportion of our dictionary. They are the playthings, not the tools, of language, and any attempt to reduce the most common and necessary words to imitative roots ends in complete failure. Herder himself, after having most strenuously defended this theory of Onomatopoieia, as it is called, and having gained a prize which the Berlin Academy had offered for the best essay on the origin of language, renounced it openly towards the latter years of his life, and threw himself in despair into the arms of those who looked upon languages as miraculously revealed. We cannot deny the possibility that a language might have been formed on the principle of imitation: all we say is, that as yet no language has been discovered that was so formed. An Englishman in China,[*] seeing a dish placed before him about which he felt suspicious, and wishing to know whether it was a duck, said, with an interrogative accent,

Quack-Quack?

He received the clear and straightforward answer,

Bow-wow!

This, no doubt, was as good as the most eloquent conversation on the same subject between an Englishman and a French waiter. But I doubt whether it deserves the name of language. We do not speak of a *bow-wow*, but of a dog. We speak of a cow, not of a *moo*; of a lamb, not of a *baa*. It is the same in more ancient languages, such as Greek, Latin, and Sanskrit. If this principle of Onomatopoieia is applicable anywhere, it would be in the formation of the names of animals. Yet we listen in vain for any similarity between goose and cackling, hen and clucking, duck and quacking, sparrow and chirping, dove and cooing, hog and grunting, cat and mewing, between dog and barking, yelping, snarling, or growling.

There are of course some names, such as cuckoo,

[*] Farrar, p. 74.

or the American *whip-poor-will*, which are clearly formed by an imitation of sound. But words of this kind are, like artificial flowers, without a root. They are sterile, and unfit to express anything beyond the one object which they imitate. If you remember the variety of derivatives that could be formed from the root *spak*, to see, you will at once perceive the difference between the fabrication of such a word as *cuckoo*, and the true natural growth of predicative words.

Let us compare two words such as *cuckoo* and *raven*. *Cuckoo* in English is clearly a mere imitation of the cry of that bird, even more so than the corresponding terms in Greek, Sanskrit, and Latin. In these languages the imitative element has received the support of a derivative suffix; we have *kokila* in Sanskrit, and *kokkyx* in Greek, *cuculus* in Latin.[*] *Cuckoo* is, in fact, a modern word, which has taken the place of the Anglo-Saxon *geac*, the German *Gauch*, and being purely onomatopoetic, it is of course not liable to the changes of Grimm's Law. As the word *cuckoo* predicates nothing but the sound of a particular bird, it could never be applied for expressing any general quality in which other animals might share; and the only derivatives to which it might give rise are words expressive of a metaphorical likeness to the bird. The same applies to *cock*, the Sanskrit *kukkuṭa*. Here, too, Grimm's Law does not apply, for both words were intended to convey merely the cackling sound of the bird; and, as this intention continued to be felt, phonetic change was less likely to set in. The Sanskrit *kukkuṭa* is not derived from any root: it simply repeats the cry of the bird,

---

[*] Pott, *Etymologische Forschungen*, I. 87; *Zeitschrift*, iii. 43.

and the only derivatives to which it gives rise are metaphorical expressions, such as the French *coquet*, originally strutting about like a cock; *coquetterie*; *cocart*, conceited; *cocarde*, a cockade; *coquelicot*, originally a cock's comb, then the wild red poppy, likewise so called from its similarity to a cock's comb.

Let us now examine the word *raven*. It might seem at first as if this also was merely onomatopoetic. Some people imagine they perceive a kind of similarity between the word *raven* and the cry of that bird. This seems still more so if we compare the Anglo-Saxon *hræfn*, the German *Rabe*, Old High-German *hraban*. The Sanskrit *kârava* also, the Latin *corvus*, the English *crow*, and the Greek *korōnē*, all are supposed to show some similarity to the unmelodious sound of *Maître Corbeau*. But if we look more closely we find that these words, though so similar in sound, spring from different sources. The English *crow* can claim no relationship whatever with *corvus*, for the simple reason that, according to Grimm's Law, an English c cannot correspond to a Latin c. *Raven*, on the contrary, which in outward appearance differs from *corvus* much more than *crow*, offers much less real difficulty in being traced back to the same source from which sprang the Latin *corvus*. For *raven* is the Anglo-Saxon *hræfen* or *hræfn*, and its first syllable *hræ* would be a legitimate substitute for the Latin *cor*. Opinions differ widely as to the root or roots from which the various names of the crow, the raven, and the rook in the Aryan dialects are derived. Those who look on Sanskrit as the most primitive form of Aryan speech, are disposed to admit the Sanskrit *kârava* as the original type; and as *kârava* is by native etymologists derived from *kâ + rava*, making a harsh noise,* *ru*, to make a noise, the root of *rava*, noise, was readily fixed upon as the etymon for the corresponding words in Latin, Greek, and German. I cannot enter here into the question whether such compounds as *kâ + rava*, in which the initial interrogative or exclamatory element *kâ* or *ku* is supposed to fill the office of the Greek *dys* or the English *mis*, are so numerous as they are supposed to be in Sanskrit. The question has been discussed again and again, and though it is impossible to deny the existence of such compounds in Sanskrit, particularly in the later Sanskrit, I know of no well-established instance where such formations have found their way into Greek, Latin, or German. If, therefore, *kârava*, *corvus*, *korônê*, and *hrafen* are cognate words, it would be more advisable to look upon the *k* as part of the radical, and thus to derive all these words from a root *kru*, a secondary form, it may be, of the root *ru*. This root *kru*, or, in its more primitive form, *ru* (*rauti* and *raviti*), is not a mere imitation of the cry of the raven; it embraces many cries, from the harshest to the softest, and it might have been applied to the nightingale as well as to the raven. In Sanskrit the root *ru* is applied in its verbal and nominal derivatives to the murmuring sound of birds, bees, and trees, to the barking of dogs, the lowing of cows, and the whispering of man.† In Latin we have from it both *raucus*, hoarse, and *rumor*, a whisper; in German *rûnen*, to speak low, and *runa*, mystery. The Latin *lamentum* stands for a more original *lavimentum* or *ravimentum*, for

* See Boehtlingk and Roth, *Sanskrit Dictionary*, s. v.

† Cf. *Hitopadeśa*, I. 76, where *rauti* is used both of the humming of the gnat and the flatteries whispered into the ear by an enemy.

there is no necessity for deriving this noun from the secondary root *kru*, *krav*, *krâv*, and for admitting the loss of the initial guttural in *cravimentum*, particularly as in *clamare* the same guttural is preserved. It is true, however, that this root *ru* appears under many secondary forms. By the addition of an initial *k* it is raised to *kru* and *klu*, well known by its numerous offshoots, such as the Greek *klyo*, *klytos*, the Latin *cluo*, *inclitus*, *cliens*, the English *loud*, the Slavonic *slava*, glory. By the addition of final letters *ru* appears as the Sanskrit *rud*, to cry, and as the Latin *rug* in *rugire*, to howl. By the addition both of initial and final letters we get the Sanskrit *kruś*, to shout; the Gothic *hrukjan*, to crow, and *hropjan*, to cry, the German *rufen*. In the Sanskrit *śru* and the Greek *klyo* the same root has been used to convey the sense of hearing; naturally, because, when a noise was to be heard from a far distance, the man who first perceived it might well have said 'I ring,' for his ears were sounding or ringing; and the same verb, if once used as a transitive, would well come in in such forms as the Homeric *klythí mey*, hear me, or the Sanskrit *śrudhí*, hear!

But although, as far as the meaning of *kârava*, *cornix*, *koróné*, and *hrafen* is concerned, there would seem to be no difficulty in deriving them from a root *kru*, to sound, I have nowhere found a satisfactory explanation of the exact etymological process by which the Sanskrit *kârava* could be formed from *kru*. *Kru*, no doubt, might yield *krava*, but to admit a dialectic corruption of *krava* into *karva*, and of *karva* into *kârava*, is tantamount to giving up any etymological derivation at all. Are we therefore forced to be satisfied with the assertion that *kârava* is no grammatical derivative at all, but a mere imitation of the sound *cor cor*, uttered by the raven? I believe not; but, as I hinted at before, we may treat *kârava* as a regular derivative of the Sanskrit *kâru*. This *kâru* is a Vedic word, and means one who sings praises to the gods, literally one that shouts. It comes from a root *kar*, to shout, to praise, to record, from which the Vedic word *kiri*, a poet, and the well-known *kîrti*, glory, *kîrtayati*, he praises.* *Kâru* from *kar* meant originally a shouter (like the Greek *kēryx*, a herald †), and its derivative *kârava* was therefore applied to the raven in the general sense of the shouter. All the other names of the raven can easily be traced back to the same root *kar*:—*cor-vus* from *kar*, like *tor-vus* from *tar*; ‡ *kor-ōnē* from *kar*, like *chelōnē* from *har*; § *kor-ax* from *kar*, like *phylax* &c. The Anglo-Saxon *hræfen*, as well as the Old High-German *hraban*, might be represented in Sanskrit by such forms as *kar-van* or *kar-van-a*.

The English *crow*, the A.-S. *crâwe*, cannot, as was pointed out before, be derived from the same root *kar*. Beginning with a guttural tenuis in Anglo-Saxon, its corresponding forms in Sanskrit would there begin with the guttural media. There exists in Sanskrit a root *gar* meaning to sound, to praise, from which the Sanskrit *gir*, voice, the Greek *gêrys*, voice, the Latin *garrulus*. From it was framed the name of the crane, *geranos* in Greek, *cran* in Anglo-Saxon,

---

* See Boehtlingk and Roth, *Sanskrit Dictionary*, s. v. *Kar*, 2: Lassen, *Anthol.* 203.

† Cf. Bopp, *Vergleichende Grammatik*, § 949.

‡ Ibid. § 943.

§ Bopp, *l.c.* § 837; Curtius, *Grundzüge*, i. p. 167; Hugo Weber, in Kuhn's *Zeitschrift*, x. p. 257.

and likewise the Latin name for cock, *gallus* instead of *garrus*. The name of the nightingale, O.H.G. *nahti-gal*, has been referred to the same root, but in violation of Grimm's Law.* From this root *gur* or *gal*, *crow* might have been derived, but not from the root *kar* which yielded *corvus*, *korax*, or *kārava*, still less from *cor cor*, the supposed cry of the bird.

It will be clear from these remarks that the process which led to the formation of the word *raven* is quite distinct from that which produced *cuckoo*. *Raven* means a shouter, a caller, a crier. It might have been applied to many birds; but it became the traditional and recognised name of one, and of one only. Cuckoo could never mean anything but the cuckoo, and while a word like *raven* has ever so many relations, cuckoo stands by itself like a stick in a living hedge.†

It is curious to observe how apt we are to deceive ourselves when we once adopt this system of Onomatopoieia. Who does not imagine that he hears in the word 'thunder' an imitation of the rolling and rumbling noise which the old Germans ascribed to their god Thor playing at nine-pins? Yet *thunder*,

---

* Curtius, *Grundzüge*, i. pp. 145, 147.

† The following remarks on the interjectional theory, from Yāska's Nirukta (iii. 18), a work anterior to Pāṇini, and therefore belonging at least to the fourth century B.C., may be of interest.

After mentioning that words like lion and tiger, or dog and crow, may be applied to men to express either admiration or contempt, Yāska continues: '*kāka*, crow, is an imitation of the sound (*kāka kāka*, according to Durga), and this is very common with regard to birds. Aupamanyava, however, maintains that imitation of sound does never take place. He therefore derives *kāka*, crow, from *apakūlayitavya*, i.e. a bird that is to be driven away; *tittiri*, partridge, from *tar*, to jump, or from *tilamiśra-chitra*, with small spots, &c.'

A.S. *thunor*, has clearly the same origin as the Latin *tonitru*. The root is *tan*, to stretch. From this root *tan* we have in Greek *tonos*, our tone, *tone* being produced by the stretching and vibrating of cords; Latin *tonare*. In Sanskrit the sound thunder is expressed by the same root *tan*, but in the derivatives *tanyu*, *tanyatu*, and *tanayitnu*, thundering, we perceive no trace of the rumbling noise which we imagined we perceived in the Latin *tonitru* and the English *thunder*.* The very same root, *tan*, to stretch, yields some derivatives which are anything but rough and noisy. The English *tender*, the French *tendre*, the Latin *tener*, are derived from it. Like *tenuis*, the Sanskrit *tanu*, the English *thin*, *tener* meant originally what was extended over a larger surface, then *thin*, then *delicate*. The relationship betwixt *tender*, *thin*, and *thunder* would be hard to establish if the original conception of thunder had really been its rumbling noise.

Who does not imagine that he hears something sweet in the French *sucre*, *sucré*? Yet sugar came from India, and it is there called *'sarkhara*, which is anything but sweet-sounding. This *'sarkhara* is the same word as *sugar*; it was called in Latin *saccharum*, and we still speak of *saccharine* juice, which is sugar juice.†

---

* A secondary root is *stan*, to sound, from which *stanitnu*, the rattling of thunder; *stanayitnu*, thunder, lightning, cloud (see Wilson's *Dict.*); Greek στένω, I groan, and its numerous derivatives. Professor Bopp (*Vergleichende Grammatik*, § 3) and Professor Kuhn (*Zeitschrift*, iv. 7) consider *stan* as the primitive form; Prof. Pott (*Etym. Forsch.* ii. 293) treats *stan* as formed from *tan*.

† 'Lo nome d'Amore è sì dolce a udire, che impossibile mi pare, che la sua operazione sia nelle più cose altro che dolce, conziossiacosachè i nomi seguitino le nominate cose, siccome è

In *squirrel*, again, some people imagine they hear something of the rustling and whirling of the little animal. But we have only to trace the name back to Greek, and there we find that *skiouros* is composed of two distinct words, the one meaning shade, the other tail; the animal being called shade-tail by the Greeks.

Thus the word *cat*, the German *katze*, is supposed to be an imitation of the sound made by a cat spitting. But if the spitting were expressed by the sibilant, that sibilant does not exist in the Latin *catus*, nor in *cat* or *kitten*, nor in the German *kater*.* The Sanskrit *mârjâra*, cat, might seem to imitate the purring of the cat; but it is derived from the root *mrj*, to clean, *mârjâra* meaning the animal that always cleans itself.

Many more instances might be given to show how easily we are deceived by the constant connection of certain sounds and certain meanings in the words of our own language, and how readily we imagine that there is something in the sound to tell us the meaning of the words. 'The sound must seem an echo to the sense.'

Most of these Onomatopoieias vanish as soon as we trace our own names back to Anglo-Saxon and Gothic, or compare them with their cognates in Greek, Latin, or Sanskrit. The number of names which are really formed by an imitation of sound dwindle down to a very small quotum if cross-examined by the comparative philologist; and we are left in the end with the conviction that though a language might have been made out of the roaring,

---

scritto: Nomina sunt consequentia rerum.'—Dante, *Vita Nuova*, *Opere Minori*. Firenze, 1857, tom. iii. p. 289.

* See Pictet, *Aryas Primitifs*, p. 331.

fizzing, hissing, gobbling, twittering, cracking, banging, slamming, and rattling sounds of nature, the tongues with which *we* are acquainted point to a different origin.*

And so we find many philosophers, and among them Condillac, protesting against a theory which would place man even below the animal. Why should man be supposed, they say, to have taken a lesson from birds and beasts? Does he not utter cries, and sobs, and shouts himself, according as he is affected by fear, pain, or joy? These cries or interjections were represented as the natural and real beginnings of human speech. Everything else was supposed to have been elaborated after their model. This is what I call the Interjectional, or Pooh-pooh, Theory.

Our answer to this theory is the same as to the former. There are no doubt in every language interjections, and some of them may become traditional, and enter into the composition of words. But these interjections are only the outskirts of real language. Language begins where interjections end. There is as much difference between a real word, such as ' to

---

* In Chinese the number of imitative sounds is very considerable. They are mostly written phonetically, and followed by the determinative sign 'mouth.' We give a few, together with the corresponding sounds in Mandshu. The difference between the two will show how differently the same sounds strike different ears, and how differently they are rendered into articulate language:—

The cock crows	kiao kiao	In Chinese	dchor dchor	In Mandshu
The wild goose cries	kao kao	"	kor kor	"
The wind and rain sound	siao siao	"	chor chor	"
Waggon sound	lin lin	"	koongour koongour	"
Dogs coupled together	ling-ling	"	kalang kalang	"
Chains	tsiang-tsiang	"	killing killing	"
Bells	tsiang-tsiang	"	tang tang	"
Drums	kun kun	"	tung tung	"

laugh,' and the interjection ha, ha! between 'I suffer,' and oh! as there is between the involuntary act and noise of sneezing, and the verb 'to sneeze.' We sneeze, and cough, and scream, and laugh in the same manner as animals, but if Epicurus tells us that we speak in the same manner as dogs bark, moved by nature,* our own experience will tell us that this is not the case.

An excellent answer to the interjectional theory has been given by Horne Tooke.

'The dominion of speech,' he says,† 'is erected upon the downfal of interjections. Without the artful contrivances of language, mankind would have had nothing but interjections with which to communicate, orally, any of their feelings. The neighing of a horse, the lowing of a cow, the barking of a dog, the purring of a cat, sneezing, coughing, groaning, shrieking, and every other involuntary convulsion with oral sound, have almost as good a title to be called parts of speech, as interjections have. Voluntary interjections are only employed where the suddenness and vehemence of some affection or passion returns men to their natural state, and makes them for a moment forget the use of speech; or when, from some circumstance, the shortness of time will not permit them to exercise it.'

As in the case of Onomatopoeia, it cannot be denied that with interjections, too, some kind of lan-

* Ὁ γὰρ Ἐπίκουρος ἔλεγεν, ὅτι οὐχὶ ἐπιστημόνως οὗτοι ἔθεντο τὰ ὀνόματα, ἀλλὰ φυσικῶς κινούμενοι, ὡς οἱ βήσσοντες καὶ πταίροντες καὶ μυκώμενοι καὶ ὑλακτοῦντες καὶ στενάζοντες.—Lersch, *Sprachphilosophie der Alten*, i. 40. Cf. Diog. Laert. x. § 75. The statement is taken from Proclus, and I doubt whether he represented Epicurus fairly.

† *Diversions of Purley*, p. 32.

guage might have been formed; but not a language like that which we find in numerous varieties among all the races of men. One short interjection may be more powerful, more to the point, more eloquent than a long speech. In fact, interjections, together with gestures, the movements of the muscles of the mouth, and the eye, would be quite sufficient for all purposes which language answers with the majority of mankind. Lucian, in his treatise on dancing, mentions a king whose dominions bordered on the Euxine. He happened to be at Rome in the reign of Nero, and, having seen a pantomime perform, begged him of the emperor as a present, in order that he might employ him as an interpreter among the nations in his neighbourhood with whom he could hold no intercourse on account of the diversity of language. A pantomime meant a person who could mimic everything, and there is hardly anything which cannot be thus expressed. We, having language at our command, have neglected the art of speaking without words; but in the south of Europe that art is still preserved. If it be true that one look may speak volumes, it is clear that we might save ourselves much of the trouble entailed by the use of discursive speech. Yet we must not forget that *hum! ugh! tut! pooh!* are as little to be called words as the expressive gestures which usually accompany these exclamations.

As to the attempts at deriving some of our words etymologically from mere interjections, they are apt to fail from the same kind of misconception which leads us to imagine that there is something expressive in the sounds of words. Thus it is said 'that the idea of disgust takes its rise in the senses of smell and taste, in the first instance probably in smell alone;

that in defending ourselves from a bad smell we are instinctively impelled to screw up the nose, and to expire strongly through the compressed and protruded lips, giving rise to a sound represented by the interjections faugh! foh! fie! From this interjection it is proposed to derive not only such words as *foul* and *filth*, but, by transferring it from natural to moral aversion, the English *fiend*, the German *Feind*.' If this were true, we should suppose that the expression of contempt was chiefly conveyed by the aspirate *f*, by the strong emission of the breathing with half-opened lips. But *fiend* is a participle from a root *fian*, to hate; in Gothic *fijan*; and as a Gothic aspirate always corresponds to a tenuis in Sanskrit, the same root in Sanskrit would at once lose its expressive power. It exists in fact in Sanskrit as *pîy*, to hate, to destroy; just as *friend* is derived from a root which in Sanskrit is *prî*, to delight.*

There is one more remark which I have to make about the Interjectional and the Onomatopoeïc

---

* The following list of Chinese interjections may be of interest :—

    hu, to express surprise
    fu, the same
    tsai, to express admiration and approbation
    i, to express distress
    tsie, vocative particle
    tsie tsie, exhortative particle
    a'i, to express contempt
    û-hu, to express pain
    shin-i, ah, indeed
    pû sin, alas !
    ngu, stop !

In many cases interjections were originally words, just as the French *hélas* is derived from *lassus*, tired, miserable. Diez, *Lexicon Etymologicum*, s. v. lasso.

theories, namely, this: If the constituent elements of human speech were either mere cries, or the mimicking of the sounds of nature, it would be difficult to understand why brutes should be without language. There is not only the parrot, but the mockingbird and others, which can imitate most successfully both articulate and inarticulate sounds; and there is hardly an animal without the faculty of uttering interjections, such as huff, hiss, baa, &c. It is clear also that if what puts a perfect distinction betwixt man and brutes is the having of general ideas, language which arises from interjections and from the imitation of the cries of animals could not claim to be the outward sign of that distinctive faculty of man. All words, in the beginning at least (and this is the only point which interests us), would have been the signs of individual impressions and individual perceptions, and would only gradually have been adapted to the expression of general ideas.*

The theory which is suggested to us by an analysis of language carried out according to the principles of comparative philology is the very opposite. We arrive in the end at roots, and every one of these expresses a general, not an individual, idea. Every name, if we analyse it, contains a predicate by which the object to which the name applied was known.

There is an old controversy among philosophers, whether language originated in general-appellatives, or in proper names.† It is the question of the *primum cognitum*, and its consideration will help us perhaps in discovering the true nature of the root, or the *primum appellatum*.

* Pott, *Etym. Forsch.* ii. 172.
† Sir W. Hamilton's *Lectures*, ii. p. 319.

Some philosophers, among whom I may mention Locke, Condillac, Adam Smith, Dr. Brown, and with some qualification Dugald Stewart, maintain that all terms, as at first employed, are expressive of individual objects. I quote from Adam Smith. 'The assignation,' he says, ' of particular names to denote particular objects, that is, the institution of nouns substantive, would probably be one of the first steps towards the formation of language. Two savages who had never been taught to speak, but had been bred up remote from the societies of men, would naturally begin to form that language by which they would endeavour to make their mutual wants intelligible to each other by uttering certain sounds whenever they meant to denote certain objects. Those objects only which were most familiar to them, and which they had most frequent occasion to mention, would have particular names assigned to them. The particular cave whose covering sheltered them from the weather, the particular tree whose fruit relieved their hunger, the particular fountain whose water allayed their thirst, would first be denominated by the words *cave, tree, fountain,* or by whatever other appellations they might think proper, in that primitive jargon, to mark them. Afterwards, when the more enlarged experience of these savages had led them to observe, and their necessary occasions obliged them to make mention of, other caves, and other trees, and other fountains, they would naturally bestow upon each of those new objects the same name by which they had been accustomed to express the similar object they were first acquainted with. The new objects had none of them any name of its own, but each of them exactly resembled another object which had such an appellation. It was impossible that those savages could behold the new objects without recollecting the old ones, and the name of the old ones, to which the new bore so close a resemblance. When they had occasion, therefore, to mention, or to point out to each other many of the new objects, they would naturally utter the name of the correspondent old one, of which the idea could not fail, at that instant, to present itself to their memory in the strongest and liveliest manner. And thus those words, which were originally the proper names of individuals, became the common name of a multitude. A child that is just learning to speak calls every person who comes to the house its papa or its mamma; and thus bestows upon the whole species those names which it had been taught to apply to two individuals. I have known a clown who did not know the proper name of the river which ran by his own door. It was *the river*, he said, and he never heard any other name for it. His experience, it seems, had not led him to observe any other river. The general word *river*, therefore, was, it is evident, in his acceptance of it, a proper name signifying an individual object. If this person had been carried to another river, would he not readily have called it *a river*? Could we suppose any person living on the banks of the Thames so ignorant as not to know the general word *river*, but to be acquainted only with the particular word *Thames*, if he were brought to any other river, would he not readily call it a *Thames*? This, in reality, is no more than what they who are well acquainted with the general word are very apt to do. An Englishman, describing any great river which he may have seen in some foreign country, naturally says that it is another Thames.

". . . . It is this application of the name of an individual to a great multitude of objects, whose resemblance naturally recalls the idea of that individual, and of the name which expresses it, that seems originally to have given occasion to the formation of those classes and assortments which, in the schools, are called *genera* and *species*.'

This extract from Adam Smith will give a clear idea of one view of the formation of thought and language. I shall now read another extract, representing the diametrically opposite view. It is taken from Leibniz,* who maintains that general terms are necessary for the essential constitution of languages. He likewise appeals to children. 'Children,' he says, 'and those who know but little of the language which they attempt to speak, or little of the subject on which they would employ it, make use of general terms, as *thing, plant, animal,* instead of using proper names, of which they are destitute. And it is certain that all proper or individual names have been originally appellative or general.' And again: 'Thus, I would make bold to affirm that almost all words have been originally general terms, because it would happen very rarely that man would invent a name, expressly and without a reason, to denote this or that individual. We may, therefore, assert that the names of individual things were names of species, which were given *par excellence*, or otherwise, to some individual; as the name *Great Head* to him of the whole town who had the largest, or who was the man of the most consideration of the great heads known.'

It might seem presumptuous to attempt to arbi-

---

* *Nouveaux Essais*, lib. iii. c. i. p. 297 (Erdmann); Sir W. Hamilton, *Lectures*, ii. 324.

trate between such men as Leibniz and Adam Smith, particularly when both speak so positively as they do on this subject. But there are two ways of judging of former philosophers. One is to put aside their opinions as simply erroneous where they differ from our own. This is the least satisfactory way of studying ancient philosophy. Another way is to try to enter fully into the opinions of those from whom we differ, to make them, for a time at least, our own, till at last we discover the point of view from which each philosopher looked at the facts before him, and catch the light in which he regarded them. We shall then find that there is much less of downright error in the history of philosophy than is commonly supposed; nay, we shall find nothing so conducive to a right appreciation of truth as a right appreciation of the error by which it is surrounded.

Now, in the case before us, Adam Smith is no doubt right, when he says that the first individual cave which is called cave gave the name to all other caves. In the same manner the first *town*, though a mere enclosure, gave the name to all other towns; the first imperial residence on the Palatine hill gave the name to all palaces. Slight differences between caves, towns, or palaces are readily passed by, and the first name becomes more and more general with every new individual to which it is applied. So far Adam Smith is right, and the history of almost every substantive might be cited in support of his view. But Leibniz is equally right when, in looking beyond the first emergence of such names as cave or town or palace, he asks how such names could have arisen. Let us take the Latin names of cave. A cave in Latin is called *antrum, cavea, spelunca*. Now *antrum* means really the same as *internum*. *Antar* in Sanskrit means *between* and *within*.* *Antrum*, therefore, meant originally what is within or inside the earth or anything else. It is clear, therefore, that such a name could not have been given to any individual cave, unless the general idea of being within, or inwardness, had been present in the mind. This general idea once formed, and once expressed by the pronominal root *an* or *antar*, the process of naming is clear and intelligible. The place where the savage could live safe from rain and from the sudden attacks of wild beasts, a natural hollow in the rock, he would call his *within*, his *antrum*; and afterwards similar places, whether dug in the earth or cut in a tree, would be designated by the same name. The same general idea, however, would likewise supply other names, and thus we find that the *entrails* were called *antra* (neuter) in Sanskrit, *enteron* in Greek, originally things within.

Let us take another word for cave which is *cava* or *caverna*. Here again Adam Smith would be perfectly right in maintaining that this name, when first given, was applied to one particular cave, and was afterwards extended to other caves. But Leibniz would be equally right in maintaining that in order to call even the first hollow *cava*, it was necessary that the general idea of *hollow* should have been formed in the mind, and should have received its vocal expression *cav*. Nay, we may go a step beyond, for *cavus*, or hollow, is a secondary, not a primary, idea. Before a cave was called *cava*, a hollow thing, many things hollow had passed before the eyes of men.

* Pott, *Etymologische Forschungen*, p. 324, seq.

Why then was a hollow thing, or a hole, called by the root *car*? Because what had been hollowed out was intended at first as a place of safety and protection, as a cover; and it was called therefore by the root *ku* or *sku*, which conveyed the idea of to cover.* Hence the general idea of covering existed in the mind before it was applied to hiding-places in rocks or trees, and it was not till an expression had thus been framed for things hollow or safe in general, that caves in particular could be designated by the name of *cavea* or hollows.

Another form for *carus* was *koilos*, hollow. The conception was originally the same; a hole was called *koilon* because it served as a cover. But once so used *koilon* came to mean a cave, a vaulted cave, a vault, and thus the heaven was called *cœlum*, the modern *ciel*, because it was looked upon as a vault or cover for the earth.

It is the same with all nouns. They all express originally one out of the many attributes of a thing, and that attribute, whether it be a quality or an action, is necessarily a general idea. The word thus formed was in the first instance intended for one object only, though of course it was almost immediately extended to the whole class to which this object seemed to belong. When a word such as *rivus*, river, was first formed, no doubt it was intended for a certain river, and that river was called *rivus*, from a root *ru* or *sru*, to run, because of its running water. In many instances a word meaning river or runner remained the proper name of one river, without ever rising to the dignity of an appellative. Thus *Rhenus*, the

---

* Benfey, *Griech. Wurzel-Lex.* p. 611. From *sku* or *ku*, σκύτος, skin; *cutis*, hide.

Rhine, means river or runner, but it clung to one river, and could not well be used as an appellative for others.* The Ganges is the Sanskrit *Gangá*, literally the Go-go; a name applied to the sacred river, and to several minor rivers in India. The Indus again is the Sanskrit *Sindhu*, and means the irrigator, from *syand*, to sprinkle. In this case, however, the proper name was not checked in its growth, but was used likewise as an appellative for any great stream.

We have thus seen how the controversy about the *primum cognitum* assumes a new and perfectly clear aspect. The first thing really known is the general. It is through it that we know and name afterwards individual objects of which any general idea can be predicated, and it is only in the third stage that these individual objects, thus known and named, become again the representatives of whole classes, and their names or proper names are raised into appellatives.†

There is a petrified philosophy in language, and if we examine the most ancient word for name we find it is *náman* in Sanskrit, *nomen* in Latin, *namo* in Gothic. This *náman* stands for *gnáman*, which is preserved in the Latin *co-gnomen*. The *g* is dropped

* In Somersetshire the large drains which carry off the abundant water from the Sedgemoor district are locally termed *rhines*, the German *Rinne*.

† Sir William Hamilton (*Lectures on Metaphysics*, ii. p. 327) holds a view intermediate between those of Adam Smith and Leibniz. 'As our knowledge,' he says, 'proceeds from the confused to the distinct, from the vague to the determinate, so, in the mouths of children, language at first expresses neither the precisely general nor the determinately individual, but the vague and confused, and out of this the universal is elaborated by generification, the particular and singular by specification and individualisation.' Some further remarks on this point in the *Literary Gazette*, 1861, p. 173.

as in *natus*, son, for *gnatus*. *Nâman*, therefore, and name are derived from the root *gnâ*, to know, and meant originally that by which we know a thing.

And how do we know things? We perceive things by our senses, but our senses convey to us information about single things only. But to *know* is more than to feel, than to perceive, more than to remember, more than to compare. No doubt words are much abused. We speak of a dog *knowing* his master, of an infant *knowing* his mother. In such expressions, to know means to recognise. But to know a thing means more than to recognise it. We know a thing if we are able to bring it, and any part of it, under more general ideas. We then say not that we have a perception, but a conception, or that we have a general idea of a thing. The facts of nature are perceived by our senses: the thoughts of nature, to borrow an expression of Oersted's, can be conceived by our reason only.[*] Now the first step towards this real knowledge, a step which, however small in appearance, separates man for ever from all other animals, is *the naming of a*

---

[*] 'We receive the impression of the falling of a large mass of water, descending always from the same height and with the same difficulty. The scattering of the drops of water, the formation of froth, the sound of the fall by the roaring and by the froth, are constantly produced by the same causes, and, consequently, are always the same. The impression which all this produces on us is no doubt at first felt as multiform, but it soon forms a whole, or, in other terms, we feel all the diversity of the isolated impressions as the work of a great physical activity which results from the particular nature of the spot. We may, perhaps, till we are better informed, call all that is fixed in the phenomenon, *the thoughts of nature*.'—Oersted, *Esprit dans la Nature*, p. 152.

thing, or the making a thing knowable. All naming is classification, bringing the individual under the general; and whatever we know, whether empirically or scientifically, we know it only by means of our general ideas. Other animals have sensation, perception, memory, and, in a certain sense, intellect; but all these, in the animal, are conversant with single objects only. Man has sensation, perception, memory, intellect, and reason, and it is his reason only that is conversant with general ideas.*

Through reason we not only stand a step above the brute creation; we belong to a different world. We look down on our merely animal experience, on our sensations, perceptions, our memory, and our intellect, as something belonging to us, but not as constituting our most inward and eternal self. Our senses, our memory, our intellect, are like the lenses of a telescope. But there is an eye that looks through them at the realities of the outer world, our own rational and self-conscious soul; a power as distinct from our perceptive faculties as the sun is from the earth which it fills with light, and warmth, and life.

At the very point where man parts company with the brute world, at the first flash of reason as the manifestation of the light within us, there we see the true genesis of language. Analyse any word you like, and you will find that it expresses a general idea peculiar to the individual to which the name belongs. What is the meaning of moon?—

---

* 'Ce qui trompe l'homme, c'est qu'il voit faire aux bêtes plusieurs des choses qu'il fait, et qu'il ne voit pas que, dans ces choses-là même, les bêtes ne mettent qu'une intelligence grossière, bornée, et qu'il met, lui, une intelligence *doublée d'esprit*.'— Flourens, *De la Raison*, p. 73.

the measurer. What is the meaning of sun?—the begetter. What is the meaning of earth?—the ploughed. The old name given to animals, such as cows and sheep, was *paśu*, the Latin *pecus*, which means *feeders*. *Animal* itself is a later name, and derived from *anima*, soul. This *anima* again meant originally blowing or breathing, like spirit from *spirare*, and was derived from a root, *an*, to blow, which gives us *anila*, wind, in Sanskrit, and *anemos*, wind, in Greek. *Ghost*, the German *Geist*, is based on the same conception. It is connected with *gust*, with *yeast*, with *gas*, and even with the hissing and boiling *geysers* of Iceland. *Soul* is the Gothic *saivala*, and this is clearly related to another Gothic word, *saivs*,* which means the sea. The sea was called *saivs*, from a root *si* or *siv*, the Greek *seio*, to shake; it meant the tossed-about water, in contradistinction to stagnant or running water. The soul being called *saivala*, we see that it was originally conceived by the Teutonic nations as a sea within, heaving up and down with every breath, and reflecting heaven and earth on the mirror of the deep.

The Sanskrit name for love is *smara*; it is derived from *smar*, to recollect; and the same root may have supplied the German *schmerz*, pain, and the English *smart*.†

If the serpent is called in Sanskrit *sarpa*, it is because it was conceived under the general idea of creeping, an idea expressed by the word *srip*. But the serpent was also called *ahi* in Sanskrit, in Greek *echis* or *echidna*, in Latin *anguis*. This name is derived

---

* See Heyse, *System der Sprachwissenschaft*, s. 97.
† Cf. Pott, *Etym. Forsch.* ii. 290.

from quite a different root and idea. The root is *ah* in Sanskrit, or *anh*, which means to press together, to choke, to throttle. Here the distinguishing mark from which the serpent was named was his throttling, and *ahi* meant serpent, as expressing the general idea of throttler. It is a curious root this *anh*, and it still lives in several modern words. In Latin it appears as *ango, anxi, anctum*, to strangle, in *angina*, quinsy,[*] in *angor*, suffocation. But *angor* meant not only quinsy or compression of the neck: it assumed a moral import and signifies anguish or anxiety. The two adjectives *angustus*, narrow, and *anxius*, uneasy, both come from the same source. In Greek the root retained its natural and material meaning; in ἐγγύς, near, and *echis*, serpent, throttler. But in Sanskrit it was chosen with great truth as the proper name of sin. Evil no doubt presented itself under various aspects to the human mind, and its names are many ; but none so expressive as those derived from our root *anh*, to throttle. *Anhas* in Sanskrit means sin, but it does so only because it meant originally throttling —the consciousness of sin being like the grasp of the assassin on the throat of his victim. All who have seen and contemplated the statue of Laokoon and his sons, with the serpent coiled round them from head to foot, may realise what those ancients felt and saw when they called sin *anhas*, or the throttler. This *anhas* is the same word as the Greek *agos*, sin. In Gothic the same root has produced *agis*, in the sense of *fear*,

---

[*] The word *quinsy*, as was pointed out to me, offers a striking illustration of the ravages produced by phonetic decay. The root *anh* has here completely vanished. But it was there originally, for *quinsy* is the Greek κυνάγχη, dog-throttling. See Richardson's *Dictionary*, s. v. Quinancy.

and from the same source we have *awe*, in awful. i. e. fearful, and *ug*, in *ugly*. The English *anguish* is from the French *angoisse*, the Italian *angoscia*, a corruption of the Latin *angustiæ*, a strait.*

And how did those early thinkers and framers of language distinguish between man and the other animals? What general idea did they connect with the first conception of themselves? The Latin word *homo*, the French *l'homme*, which has been reduced to *on* in *on dit*, is derived from the same root which we have in *humus*, the soil, *humilis*, humble. *Homo*, therefore, would express the idea of a being made of the dust of the earth.†

Another ancient word for man was the Sanskrit *marta*,‡ the Greek *brotos*, the Latin *mortalis* (a secondary derivative), our own *mortal*. *Marta* means 'he who dies,' and it is remarkable that, where everything else was changing, fading, and dying, this should have been chosen as the distinguishing name for man. Those early poets would hardly have called themselves mortals unless they had believed in other beings as immortal.

There is a third name for man which means simply the thinker, and this, the true title of our race, still lives in the name of *man*. *Mâ* in Sanskrit means to measure, from which, you remember, we had the name of moon. *Man*, a derivative root, means to think. From this we have the Sanskrit *manu*, originally thinker, then man. In the later Sanskrit we find derivatives, such as *mânava*, *mânusha*, *manushya*,

---

* Kuhn, *Zeitschrift*, i. 152, 365.

† Greek χαμαί, Zend *zem*, Lithuanian *zeme*, and *žmones*, *komines*. See Bopp, *Glossarium Sanscritum*, s. v.

‡ See Windischmann, *Fortschritt der Sprachenkunde*, p. 23.

all expressing man or son of man. In Gothic we find both *man* and *mannisks*, the modern German *mann* and *mensch*.

There were many more names for man, as there were many names for all things in ancient languages. Any feature that struck the observing mind as peculiarly characteristic could be made to furnish a new name. In common Sanskrit dictionaries we find 5 words for hand, 11 for light, 15 for cloud, 20 for moon, 26 for snake, 33 for slaughter, 35 for fire, 37 for sun.* The sun might be called the bright, the warm, the golden, the preserver, the destroyer, the wolf, the lion, the heavenly eye, the father of light and life. Hence that superabundance of synonymes in ancient dialects, and hence that *struggle for life* carried on among these words, which led to the destruction of the less strong, the less happy, the less fertile words, and ended in the triumph of *one*, as the recognised and proper name for every object in every language. On a very small scale this process of *natural selection*, or, as it would better be called, *elimination*, may still be watched even in modern languages, that is to say, even in languages so old and stricken in years as English and French. What it was at the first burst of dialects we can only gather from such isolated cases as when Von Hammer counts 5,744 words all relating to the camel.†

* Cf. Yates, *Sanskrit Grammar*, p. xviii.

† Farrar, *Origin of Language*, p. 85. 'Das Kamel,' *Extrait des Mém. de l'Acad. de Vienne*, classe de phil. et d'hist. t. vii. In Arabic a work is mentioned on the 500 names of the lion; another on the 200 names of the serpent. Firuzabadi, the author of the *Kamus*, says he wrote a work on the names of honey, and that he counted 80 without exhausting the subject. The same author maintains that in Arabic there are at least 1,000 words for

The fact that every word is originally a predicate—that names, though signs of individual conceptions, are all, without exception, derived from general ideas—is one of the most important discoveries in the science of language. It was known before that language is the distinguishing characteristic of man; it was known also that the having of general ideas is that which puts a perfect distinction betwixt man and brutes; but that these two were only different expressions of the same fact was not known till the theory of roots had been established as preferable to the theories both of Onomatopoeia and of Interjections. But, though our modern philosophy did not know it, the ancient poets and framers of language must have known it. For in Greek language is *logos*, but *logos* means also reason, and *alogon* was chosen as the name, and the most proper name, for brute. No animal thinks, and no animal speaks, except man. Language and thought are inseparable. Words without thought are dead sounds; thoughts without words are nothing. To think is to speak low; to speak is to think aloud. The word is the thought incarnate.

And now I am afraid I have but a few minutes left to explain the last question of all in our science, namely—How can sound express thought? How did roots become the signs of general ideas? How was the abstract idea of measuring expressed by *má*, the idea of thinking by *man*? How did *gá* come to mean going, *sthá* standing, *sad* sitting, *dá* giving, *mar* dying, *char* walking, *kar* doing?

I shall try to answer as briefly as possible. The 400

---

sword; others maintain that there are 400 to signify misfortune. There is, however, much exaggeration in these statements. See Renan, *Histoire des Langues Sémitiques*, p. 577.

or 500 roots which remain as the constituent elements in different families of language are not interjections, nor are they imitations. They are *phonetic types*, produced by a power inherent in human nature. They exist, as Plato would say, by nature; though with Plato we should add that, when we say by nature, we mean by the hand of God.* There is a law which runs through nearly the whole of nature, that everything which is struck rings. Each substance has its peculiar ring. We can tell the more or less perfect structure of metals by their vibrations, by the answer which they give. Gold rings differently from tin, wood rings differently from stone; and different sounds are produced according to the nature of each percussion. It was the same with man, the most highly organised of nature's works.† Man rings. Man, in his primitive and perfect state, was not only endowed, like the brute, with the power of expressing his sensations by interjections, and his perceptions by onomatopoieia. He possessed likewise the faculty of giving more articulate expression to the rational conceptions of his mind. That faculty was not of his own making. It was an

---

* Θέσω τὰ μὲν φύσει λεγόμενα καλεῖσθαι Θεία τύχη.

† This view was propounded many years ago by Professor Heyse in the lectures which he gave at Berlin, and which have been very carefully published since his death by one of his pupils, Dr. Steinthal. The fact that wood, metals, cords, &c., if struck, vibrate and ring, can, of course, be used as an illustration only, and not as an explanation. The faculty peculiar to man, in his primitive state, by which every impression from without received its vocal expression from within, must be accepted as an ultimate fact. That faculty must have existed in man, because its effects continue to exist. Analogies from the inanimate world, however, are useful, and deserve further examination.

instinct, an instinct of the mind as irresistible as any other instinct. So far as language is the production of that instinct, it belongs to the realm of nature. Man loses his instincts as he ceases to want them. His senses become fainter when, as in the case of scent, they become useless. Thus the creative faculty which gave to each conception, as it thrilled for the first time through the brain, a phonetic expression, became extinct when its object was fulfilled. The number of these *phonetic types* must have been almost infinite in the beginning, and it was only through the same process of *natural elimination* which we observed in the early history of words, that clusters of roots, more or less synonymous, were gradually reduced to one definite type. Instead of deriving language from nine roots, like Dr. Murray,[*] or from *one* root, a feat actually accomplished by a Dr. Schmidt,[†] we must suppose that the first settlement of the radical elements of language was preceded by a period of unrestrained growth—the spring of speech—to be followed by many an autumn.

With the process of elimination, or natural selection, the historical element enters into the science of language. However primitive the Chinese may be as compared with terminational and inflectional languages, its roots or words have clearly passed through a long process of mutual attrition. There are many things of a merely traditional character even in Chinese. The rule that in a simple sentence the first

---

[*] Dr. Murray's primitive roots were ag, bag, dwag, cwag, lag, mag, nag, rag, swag.

[†] Curtius, *Griechische Etymologie*, p. 13. Dr. Schmidt derives all Greek words from the root *e*, and all Latin words from the arch-radical *hi*.

word is the subject, the second the verb, the third the object, is a traditional rule. It is by tradition only that *ngŏ jin*, in Chinese, means a bad man, whereas *jin ngŏ* signifies man is bad. The Chinese themselves distinguish between *full* and *empty* roots,[*] the former being predicative, the latter corresponding to our particles which modify the meaning of full roots and determine their relation to each other. It is only by tradition that roots become empty. All roots were originally full, whether predicative or demonstrative, and the fact that empty roots in Chinese cannot always be traced back to their full prototypes shows that even the most ancient Chinese had passed through successive periods of growth. Chinese commentators admit that all empty words were originally full words, just as Sanskrit grammarians maintain that all that is formal in grammar was originally substantial. But we must be satisfied with but partial proofs of this general principle, and must be prepared to find as many fanciful derivations in Chinese as in Sanskrit. The fact again that all roots in Chinese are no longer capable of being employed at pleasure, either as substantives, or verbs, or adjectives, is another proof that, even in this most primitive stage, language points back to a previous growth. *Fu* is father, *mu* is mother, *fu mu* parents; but neither *fu* nor *mu* is used as a root in its original predicative sense. The simplest proof however, of the various stages through which even so simple a language as Chinese must have passed, is to be found in the comparatively small number of roots, and in the definite meanings attached to each—a

---

[*] Endlicher, *Chinesische Grammatik*, p. 168.

result which could only have been obtained by that constant struggle which has been so well described in natural history as the struggle for life.

But although this sifting of roots, and still more the subsequent combination of roots, cannot be ascribed to the mere working of nature or natural instincts, it is still less, as we saw in a former Lecture, the effect of deliberate or premeditated art, in the sense in which, for instance, a picture of Raphael or a symphony of Beethoven is. Given a root to express flying, or bird, and another to express heap, then the joining together of the two to express many birds, or birds in the plural, is the natural effect of the synthetic power of the human mind, or, to use more homely language, of the power of putting two and two together. Some philosophers maintain indeed that this explains nothing, and that the real mystery to be solved is how the mind can form a synthesis, or conceive many things as one. Into those depths we cannot follow. Other philosophers imagine that the combination of roots to form agglutinative and inflectional language is, like the first formation of roots, the result of a natural instinct. Thus Professor Heyse* maintained that ' the various forms of development in language must be explained by the philosophers as *necessary evolutions*, founded in the very essence of human speech.' This is not the case. We can watch the growth of language, and we can understand and explain all that is the result of that growth. But we cannot undertake to prove that all that is in language is so by necessity, and could not have been otherwise. When we have,

* *System der Sprachwissenschaft*, p. 61.

as in Chinese, two such words as *kiai* and *tu*, both expressing a heap, an assembly, a quantity, then we may perfectly understand why either the one or the other should have been used to form the plural. But if one of the two becomes fixed and traditional while the other becomes obsolete, then we can register the fact as historical, but no philosophy on earth will explain its absolute necessity. We can perfectly understand how, with two such roots as *kŭŏ*, empire, and *čung*, middle, the Chinese should have formed what we call a locative, *kŭŏ čung*, in the empire. But to say that this was the only way to express this conception is an assertion contradicted both by fact and reason. We saw the various ways in which the future can be formed. They are all equally intelligible and equally possible, but not one of them is inevitable. In Chinese *yaó* means to will, *ngŏ* is I; hence *ngò yaó*, I will. The same root *yao*, added to *kiú*, to go, gives us *ngò yaó kiú*, I will go, the first germ of our futures. To say that *ngò yaó kiú* was the necessary form of the future in Chinese would introduce a fatalism into language which rests on no authority whatever. The building up of language is not like the building of the cells in a beehive, nor is it like the building of St. Peter's by Michael Angelo. It is the result of innumerable agencies, working each according to certain laws, and leaving, in the end, the result of their combined efforts freed from all that proved superfluous or useless. From the first combination of two such words as *jin*, man, *kiai*, many, to form the plural *jin kiai*, to the perfect grammar of Sanskrit and Greek, everything is intelligible as the result of the two principles of growth which we considered in our second Lecture.

What is antecedent to the production of roots is the work of nature; what follows after is the work of man, not in his individual and free, but in his collective and moderating, capacity.

I do not say that every form in Greek or Sanskrit has as yet been analysed and explained. There are formations in Greek and Latin and English which have hitherto baffled all tests; and there are certain contrivances, such as the augment in Greek, the change of vowels in Hebrew, the Umlaut and Ablaut in the Teutonic dialects, where we might feel inclined to suppose that language admitted distinctions purely musical or phonetic, corresponding to very palpable and material distinctions of thought. Such a supposition, however, is not founded on any safe induction. It may seem inexplicable to us why *bruder* in German should form its plural as *brüder*; or *brother*, *brethren*. But what is inexplicable and apparently artificial in our modern languages becomes intelligible in their more ancient phases. The change of *u* into *ü*, as in *bruder*, *brüder*, was not intentional; least of all was it introduced to express plurality. The change is phonetic, and due to the influence of an *i* or *j*,[*] which existed originally in the last syllable, and which reacted regularly on the vowel of the preceding syllable—nay, which leaves its effect behind, even after it has itself disappeared. By a false analogy such a change, perfectly justifiable in a certain class of words, may be applied to other words where no such change was called for; and it may then appear as if an arbitrary change of vowels was intended to convey a grammatical change.

[*] See Schleicher, *Deutsche Sprache*, p. 144.

But even into these recesses the comparative philologist can follow language, thus discovering a reason even for what in reality was irrational and wrong. It seems difficult to believe that the augment in Greek should originally have had an independent substantial existence, yet all analogy is in favour of such a view. Suppose English had never been written down before Wycliffe's time, we should then find that in some instances the perfect was formed by the mere addition of a short *a*. Wycliffe spoke and wrote,* *I knowleeh to a felid and seid þus*; i.e. I acknowledge to have felt and said thus. In a similar way we read *it should a fallen*, instead of 'it should have fallen;' and in some parts of England common people still say very much the same: *I should a done it*. Now in some old English books this *a* actually coalesces with the verb—at least they are printed together—so that a grammar founded on them would give us ' to fall ' as the infinitive of the present, *to afallen* as the infinitive of the past. I do not wish for a moment to be understood as if there was any connection between this *a*, a contraction of *have* in English, and the Greek augment which is placed before past tenses. All I mean is, that, if the origin of the augment has not yet been satisfactorily explained, we are not therefore to despair, or to admit an arbitrary addition of a consonant or vowel, used as it were algebraically or by mutual agreement, to distinguish a past from a present tense.

If inductive reasoning is worth anything, we are justified in believing that what has been proved to be true on so large a scale, and in cases where it was

* Marsh, p. 588.

least expected, is true with regard to language in general. We require no supernatural interference, nor any conclave of ancient sages, to explain the realities of human speech. All that is formal in language is the result of rational combination; all that is material, the result of a mental instinct. The first natural and instinctive utterances, if sifted differently by different clans, would fully account both for the first origin and for the first divergence of human speech. We can understand not only the origin of language, but likewise the necessary breaking up of one language into many; and we perceive that no amount of variety in the material or the formal elements of speech is incompatible with the admission of one common source.

The Science of Language thus leads us up to that highest summit from whence we see into the very dawn of man's life on earth, and where the words which we have heard so often from the days of our childhood—'And the whole earth was of one language and of one speech'—assume a meaning more natural, more intelligible, more convincing, than they ever had before.

And now, in concluding this course of Lectures, I have only to express my regret that the sketch of the Science of Language which I endeavoured to place before you was necessarily so very slight and imperfect. There are many points which I could not touch at all, many which I could only allude to: there is hardly one to which I could do full justice. Still I feel grateful to the President and the Council of this Institution for having given me an opportunity of claiming some share of public sympathy for a science which I believe has a great future in store; and I shall be pleased if, among those who have done me the honour of attending these Lectures, I have excited, though I could not have satisfied, some curiosity as to the strata which underlie the language on which we stand and walk, and as to the elements which enter into the composition of the very granite of our thoughts.

APPENDIX.

No. I.—Genealogical Table of the Aryan Family of Languages.

No. II.

GENEALOGICAL TABLE OF THE SEMITIC FAMILY OF LANGUAGES.

LIVING LANGUAGES	DEAD LANGUAGES	CLASSES	
Dialects of Arabic		Arabic	
Amharic	Ethiopic	or	
	Himyaritic Inscriptions	Southern	
The Jews	Biblical Hebrew	Hebraic	SEMITIC FAMILY
	Samaritan (Pentateuch, 3rd cent. A.D.)	or	
	Carthaginian, Phœnician Inscriptions	Middle	
	Chaldee (Masora, Talmud, Targum, Biblical Chaldee)	Aramaic	
Neo-Syrians	Syriac (Peshito, 2nd cent. A.D.)	or	
	Cuneiform Inscriptions of Babylon and Nineveh	Northern	

TURANIAN FAMILY OF LANGUAGES. 413

No. III.

GENEALOGICAL TABLE OF THE TURANIAN FAMILY OF LANGUAGES. NORTHERN DIVISION.

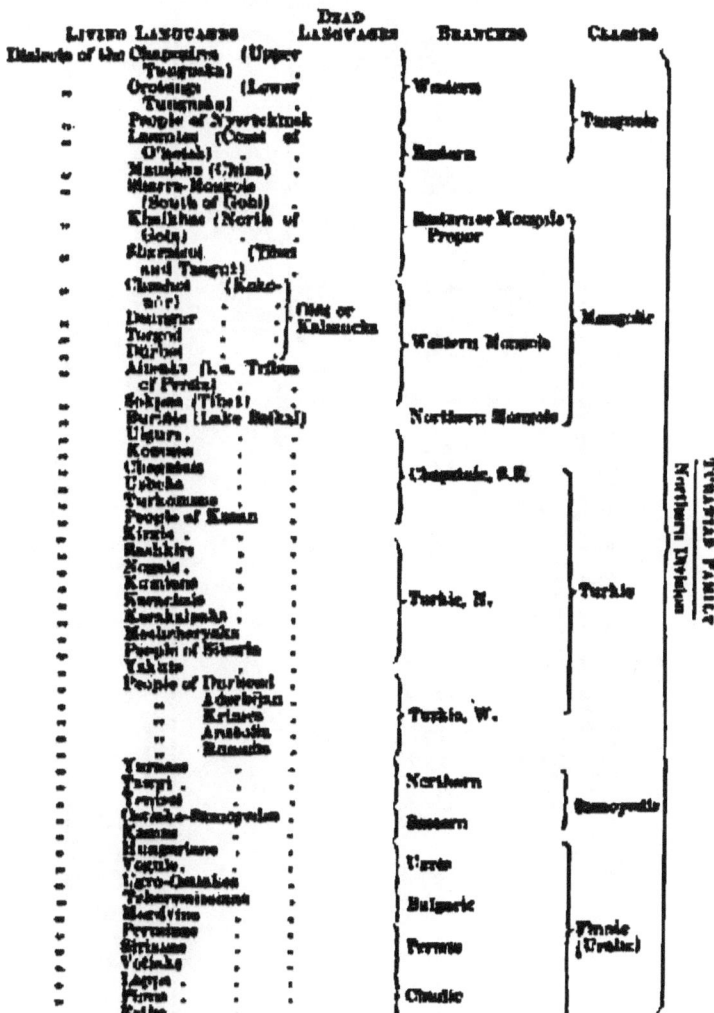

No. IV.

GENEALOGICAL TABLE OF THE TURANIAN FAMILY OF LANGUAGES.
SOUTHERN DIVISION.

LIVING LANGUAGES	DEAD LANGUAGES	BRANCHES	CLASSES
Dialects of Siamese			
Ahom			
Laos			Thai
Khamti			
Shan (Tenasserim)			
Malay and Polynesian Islands. (See Humboldt, Kavi Sprache)			Malaic
Tibetan			
Horpa (N.W. Tibet, Bachards)			
Thochu-Sifan (N.E. Tibet, China)		Trans-Himalayan	
Gyarung-Sifan (N.E. Tibet, China)			
Manyak-Sifan (N.E. Tibet, China)			
Takpa (West of Kwombo)			
Kunawar (Sutlej basin)			
Sérpa (West of Gandakdun basin)			
Sunwar (Gandakdun basin)			
Gurung (Gandakdun basin)			Gangetic
Magar (Gandakdun basin)			
Newar (between Gandakdun and Kansai basins)		Sub-Himalayan	
Murmi (between Gandakdun and Kansai basins)			
Limbu (Kansai basin)			
Kiranti (Kansai basin)			
Lepcha (Teishta basin)			
Bhutanese (Manas-hu basin)			
Gurjara (Nepal-Tarai)			
Garrows (Burrampu and Aracan)			
Haiuzol (between Kondi and Dowria)			
Kassiari-Beta (Migrat. 26°—28°, and 92°—94°)			
Garos (91°—93° E. long.; 25°—26° N. lat.)			
Chemealia (91°—93° E. long.)			
Mishmi (Novempuri)			
Dophla (91° 30′—93° N. lat.)			
Miri (93°—95° E. long. ?)			
Abor-Miri			
Abor (91°—93° E. long.)			
Shampo-Miri			
Sibsagar (91°—93° E. lat.)			
Naga tribes (98°—97° E. long.; 25° N. lat.) (Mishmi N. of Silamper)			Lohitic
Naga tribes (Karnowng)			
Naga tribes (Nowgong)			
Naga tribes (Tengsa)			
Naga tribes (Dalhusa N. of Silampor)			
Naga tribes (Khari Jorhat)			
Naga tribes (Angamili, Sanith)			
Kuki (N.E. of Chittagong)			
Khyeng (Boyu) (19°—22° N. lat. Aracan)			
Kami (Koladan N. Aracan)			
Kumi (Koladan S. Aracan)			
Chotodun (22°—23° and 93°—94°)			
Muru (Aracan, Chittagong)			
Sak (Naaf River, Rose)			
Tulingha (Tenasserim)			
Hu (Kolarian)			
Sonthalese Kol (Cuyahuma)			
Sontal (Copeleuson)			
Khervi (Tributana)			Mundic
Musjokia (Chota Nagpur)			(For Tura-vian Lan-guages, p. 176)
Canarese			
Tamil			
Telugu			
Malayalam			
Gondi			Tamulic
Kookvi			
Pahaïra			
Tudhtin			
Uracen-kat			

Turanian Family, Southern Division

INDEX.

INDEX.

ABD

ABDUL-KADIR Maluk, Mulla, Shekh of Badāūn, his general history of India, and other works, 153 note

Abhīra, or Âbhīra, at the mouth of the Indus, 210

Abiria, the, of Ptolemy, 210

Ablative in Latin, Caesar the inventor of the term, 107

— the, in Chinese, 117 note

Abraham, the language of, 280

Abul Walîd, or Rabbi Junā, author of the first Hebrew grammar, 83 note

Abu Saluh, his translation from Sanskrit into Arabic, 153

Abu Zacariyya Hayyudj, on Hebrew roots, 83 note

Abyssinian language, ancient and modern, 293

Academy, New, doctrines of the, embraced in Rome, 104

Achæmenian dynasty, inscriptions of the, 218

Accusative, formation of the, in Chinese, 117 note

Adelung, his Mithridates, 143

Adjective, formation of, in Tibetan, 110 note

— in Chinese, 117 note

Ælius Stilo, Lucius, his lectures at Rome, on Latin grammar, 106

Affinity, indications of true, in the animal and vegetable world, 16, 17

Afghanistan, the language of, 219

Africa, South, dialects of, 57

African language, an imaginary, 332

Age, history of the French word, 304

Agglutination in the Turanian family of languages, 343

Agrœool, the, of the Greeks, 27

Agriculture of the Chaldæans, work on the, 291

AVA

Agriculture, Punic work of Mago on, 90 note

Ahirs, the, of Catch, 210

Akbar, the Emperor, his search after the true religion, 154

— his foundation of the so-called Ilahi religion, 154

— works translated into Persian for him, 154

— not able to obtain a translation of the Veda, 155

Albania, origin of the name, 252

Albanian language, origin of the, 306

Albertus Magnus, on the humanising influence of Christianity, quoted, 149 note

Albiruni, or Abu Rihan al Birūni, his Tarikhu-l-Hind, 152

Alchemy, causes of the extinction of the science, 9

Alexander the Great, influence of his expedition in giving the Greeks a knowledge of other nations and languages, 48

— his difficulty in conversing with the Brahmans, 89

Alexandria, influence of, on the study of foreign languages, 91

— critical study of ancient Greek at, 93

Algebra, translation of the famous Indian work on, into Arabic, 152

Algonquian, the use case of the, 330, note

America, Central, rapid changes which take place in the language of the savage tribes of, 34

— great number of languages spoken by the natives of, 54

— Hervas's reduction of them to eleven families, 55, 56

Amharic, or modern Abyssinian, 293

Anatomy, comparative, science of, 17

ANG

Anglo-Saxon, the most ancient epic in, 181
Angora, in Galatia, battle of, 320
Anquetil Duperron, his translation of the Persian translation of the Upanishads into French, 157
— his translation of the works of Zoroaster, 173, 243
Apollo, temple of, at Rome, 96
AR, the root, various ramifications of, 262
Arabic, influencing the Persian and influenced by it, 74, 77
— ascendency of, in Palestine and Syria, 292
— original seat of Arabic, 293
— ancient Himyaritic inscriptions, 292
— earliest literary documents in Arabic, 292
— relation of Arabic to Hebrew, 81, 293
Aramaic division of Semitic languages, 287
— two dialects of, 287
Arghi-taari, the Buck name for the moon, 8
Ariana, the, of Greek geographers, 243
Ariaramnes, father of Darius, origin of the name, 251
Aristotle on grammatical categories, 93, 125
Armenia, origin of the name, 251
Armorican, 203
Arpinum, provincial Latin of, 60
Arure, the, original meaning of the word, 91
— the Greek, restored by Zenodotus, 93
Arya. See Aryan
Arya-Avarta, India so called, 246
Aryan, an Indo-European family of languages, 34, 74, 161
— mode of tracing back the grammatical fragments of the Aryan languages to original independent works, 243, 244
— Aryan grammar, 243
— northern and southern divisions of the, 219
— the original Aryan clan of Central Asia, 230
— period when this clan breaks up, 215
— formation of the locative in all the Aryan languages, 227
— Aryan civilization proved by the evidence of language, 243
— origin and gradual spreading of the word Arya, 244
— original seat of the Aryans, 249

AUX

Aryan, the Aryan and Semitic the only families of speech deserving that title, 294
— genealogical table, 411
AŚ, the root, 220
Asia Minor, origin of the Turks of, 318
Asiatic Society, foundation of the, at Calcutta, 162
Asoka, King, his rock inscriptions, 147
Assyria, various forms of the name, 256
Astrology, causes of the extinction of the science, 9
Astronomy, the Ptolemaean system, although wrong, important toscience, 17
Auramazda, of the cuneiform inscriptions, 214. See Ormuzd
Auxentius on Ulfilas, 185, 190 note
Awadh, 259
Ayodhya, 259

BABER, foundation of his Indian empire, 312
Babylonia, literature of, 289
— probability of the recovery of, from the cuneiform inscriptions, 290
Barabas tribe, in the steppes between the Irtish and the Ob, 315
Barbarians, the, of the Greeks, 86
— seem to have possessed greater facility for acquiring languages than either Greeks or Romans, 90
— the term Barbarian as used by the Greeks and Romans, 126
— unfortunate influence of the term, 126
Bashkirs, race of the, in the Altaic mountains, 316
Basil, St., his denial that God had created the names of all things, 81 note
Bezzane tribe, in the Caucasus, 314
Beaver, the, sagacity of, 14
Behar, Pâli once the popular dialect of, 147
Beowulf, the ancient English epic of, 181
Berber, dialects of Northern Africa, origin of the, 284
Bernays, Jakoba, on the expressions proper for certain things, 65
Berosus, his study and cultivation of the Greek language, 90
— his history of Babylon, 90
— his knowledge of the cuneiform inscriptions, 91
Bible, number of obsolete words and names in the English translation of 1611, 36

INDEX.   419

Bible, first complete Hebrew Grammar and Dictionary of the, 83 *note*
Bibliander, his work on language, 131 *note*
Birûni, Abu Rihan al, 152
— his 'Tarikhu-l-Hind,' 152
Bishop and skeptic derived from the same root, 265
Boëthius, Song of, age of the, 201
Bohemian, oldest specimens of, 204
Bonaparte, Prince L., his collection of English dialects, 65
Booker's 'Scripture and Prayer-Book Glossary' referred to, 36
Books, general destruction of, in China in 213 B.C., 336
Bopp, Francis, his great work, 170
— treatise of his 'Comparative Grammar,' 243
Botany, origin of the word, 5
— the Linnæan system, although imperfect, important to science, 16
Brahman, the highest being, known through speech, 83
Brahmans, their deification of language, 82
— their early achievements in grammatical analysis, 83
— difficulties of Alexander in conversing with them, 89
Brâhmanas, the, on language, 82
Brennus, the word, 304
Brown, Rev. Mr., on the dialects of the Burmese, 64
Brutes, faculties of, 264
— instinct and intellect, 266
— language, the difference between man and brute, 267
— the old name given to brutes, 267
Buddhism, date of its introduction into China, 142
Bulgarian Kingdom on the Danube, 332
— language and literature, 205
Bulgaric branch of the Finnic class of languages, 322
— Bulgarian tribes and dialects, 323
Burmese, dialects of the, new phase of grammatical life of the, 57
Between language and literature, 56
— dialects, 56
Burnouf, Eugène, his studies of Zend, 172, 313
— and of cuneiform inscriptions, 172

C

CÆSAR, Julius, publication of his work 'De Analogia,' 107
— invented the term ablative, 107

Carneades forbidden by Cato to lecture at Rome, 105
Carthaginian language, closely allied to Hebrew, 290
Case, history of the word, 106
Cases, formation of, in the Aryan languages, 226
Cassius, Dionysius, of Utica, his translation of the agricultural work of Mago, 90 *note*
Castor and Pollux, worship of, in Italy, 99
Castrén on the Mongolian dialects, 87
Cat, origin of the word, 382
Catherine the Great of Russia, her 'Comparative Dictionary,' 144
Cato, his history of Rome in Latin, 100
— his acquisition of the Greek language in his old age, 102
— reasons for his opposition to everything Greek, 102
Caucasian Isthmus, called 'The Mountain of Languages,' 88
— tribes of the, 315
Celtic language, substantive existence of, 73
— a branch of the Indo-European family of languages, 203
Celts, their former political ascendancy, 203
Chaldee, in what it consisted, 287, 288
— fragments in Ezra, 288
— language of the Targums, 288
— literature of Babylon and Nineveh, 289
— the Modern Mandates or Nazoreans, 290
Changes, historical, affecting every variety of language, 33
— rapid changes in the languages of savage tribes, 35
— words or senses obsolete in English since 1611, 36
— smaller changes, 37
— grammatical changes, 37
— laws of, in language, 40
Children, probable influence of the language of, on the gradual disappearance of irregular conjugations and declensions, 59
Chili, language of, 305 *note*
China, date of the introduction of Buddhism into, 140
— Chinese Buddhist pilgrims to India, 142
— conquered by the Mongols, 311
Chinese language, ancient, no trace of grammar in, 60, 115
— notes by M. Stanislas Julien on

420 INDEX.

C.

Chinese substantives and adjectives, 116 note

Chinese language, formation of the locative in, 117 note, 226, 227
— and of the instrumental, 117 note, 227
— number of roots in Chinese, 274
— number of words in the Chinese dictionary, obsolete, rare, and in use, 275
— no analysis required to discover its component parts, 284
— mode of using a predicative root in, 279, 280
— roots in Chinese, 293
— the parts of speech determined in Chinese by the position of the word in a sentence, 300
— rudimentary traces of agglutination in Chinese, 342
— imitative sounds in, 358 note
— list of Chinese interjections, 366 a.
— natural selection of roots in, 404
Chingis-khán, founds the Mongolian empire, 309
Christianity, humanising influence of, 127
Chudic branch of the Finnic languages, 322
— the national epic of the Finns, 323
Cicero, his provincial Latin, 60, 61
— quoted as an authority on grammatical questions, 107
— Cæsar's 'De Analogia' dedicated to Cicero, 107
Class dialects, 59
Classical, or literary languages, origin of, 59
— stagnation and inevitable decay of, 61
Classification, in the physical sciences, 15
— object of classification, 17
Colchic, dialects of, according to Pliny, 35
Conjugation, most of the terminations of, demonstrative roots, 262
Constantinople, taking of, 320
Copernicus, causes which led to the discovery of his system, 18
Cornish, last person who spoke, 73
— a branch of the Celtic, 70?
Cosmopolitan Club, 104
Crates of Pergamus, his visit to Rome, 106
— his public lectures there on grammar, 105
Crum, the word, 376
Crumbs, the word, 375

D.

Cuneiform Inscriptions, the, deciphered by Burnouf, 172
— importance of the discovery of the inscriptions of Darius and Xerxes, 214
— progress in deciphering, 290
— letter from Sir H. Rawlinson, quoted, 290

D, origin of the letter, in forming English preterites, 240
Dacian language, the ancient, 125 note, 200 note
Dame, origin of the word, 233
Danish language, growth of the, 64, 173
Darius, claimed for himself an Aryan descent, 230
Dative case in Greek, 229
— in Chinese, 118 note
Daughter, origin of the word, 49
Decay, phonetic, one of the processes which comprise the growth of language, 42
— instances of phonetic decay, 43–48
Declension, most of the terminations of, demonstrative roots, 262
Della, del, origin of the Italian, 62
Democritus, his travels, 90
Dialect, what is meant by, 50
Dialects, Italian, 50, 52
— French, 50
— Modern Greek, 50
— Prussian, 51
— English, 52
— dialects the feeders rather than the channels of a literary language, 52, 63
— Grimm on the origin of dialects in general, 52
— difficulty in tracing the history of dialects, 53
— American dialects, 54
— Burmese, 56
— of the Ostiakes, 56
— Mongolian, 57
— Southern Africa, 57
— class dialects, 59
— unbounded resources of dialect, 64
— dialectic growth beyond the control of individuals, 67
Dictionary, Comparative, of Catherine the Great of Russia, 144
Did, origin of, as a preterite, 242
Diez, Professor, his 'Comparative Grammar of the Six Romance Dialects,' 161
Dionysius Thrax, the author of the first practical Greek grammar, 96

DIO

Dionysius of Halicarnassus, on the Pelasgi, 134 note
Diversion, etymology of, 44
Dorpat dialect of Kothounen, 331
Du, origin of the French, 67
Dual, the, first recognised by Zenodotus, 95
Dumareq, Rev. Daniel, his 'Comparative Vocabulary of Eastern Languages,' 144
Duret, Claude, his work on language, 132 note
Dutch language, work of Goropius written to prove that it was the language spoken in Paradise, 135
— age of Dutch, 182

E
EARL (the Norse Jarl), origin of the title, 293
Earth, guess of Philolaus as to its motion round the sun, 30
Edda, the two, 196, 197
— the name Edda, 199 note
Egypt, number of words in the ancient vocabulary of, 277
Egyptian language, family to which it is referable, 294
Elder, origin of the word, 235
Elements, constituent, of language, 260
English language, changes in the, since the translation of the Bible in 1611, 36
— pronunciations in Pope and Johnson's times, 37 note
— richness of the vocabulary of the dialects of, 52
— real sources of the English language, 62
— Prince L. Bonaparte's collection of English dialects, 63
— the English language Teutonic, 74
— fall of words derived from the most distant sources, 75
— proportion of Saxon to Norman words, 78
— tests proving the Teutonic origin of the English language, 80
— genitives in English, 110, 113
— nominatives and accusatives, 115
— origin of grammatical forms in the English language, 119
— number of words in the English language, 270
— number of words in Milton, Shakspeare, and the Old Testament, 275
— Ennius, 101
— his translations from Greek into Latin, 101

FIK

Eos, original meaning of the name, 12
Ephraem Syrus, 227 note
Epicharmus, his philosophy translated into Latin by Ennius, 101
Epicurus, doctrines of, embraced in Rome, 104
Erin, Pictet's derivation of the name, 254, 255 note
— Mr. Whitley Stokes's remarks on the word Erin, 255 note
Erysipyle, origin of the word, 270
Esths, or Esthonians, their language, 331
— dialects of, 331
Estienne, Henry, his grammatical labours anticipated by the Brahmans, 500 B.C., 43
— his work on language, 181 note
Ethiopic, or Abyssinian, origin of the, 293
Eudemus, on the Aryan race, 251
Eukeumatos of Messene, his astrologian work translated into Latin by Ennius, 101
Eulalia, Song of, age of the, 201
Euripides, first translated into Latin by Ennius, 101
Ewald, on the relation of the Turanian to the Aryan languages, 351
Exur-Veda, the, 159 note
Ezra, Chaldee fragments in the Book of, 268

F
FABIUS Pictor, his history of Rome in Greek, 100
Fa-hian, the Chinese pilgrim to India, his travels, 130
Families of languages, tests for reducing the principal dialects of Europe and Asia to certain, 176
Fatum, original meaning of the name, 11
Feeble, origin of the word, 122
Feini and the Brahman, story of, 156
Fez, origin of the French word, 122
Finnic class of languages, 328
— branches of Finnic, 329
— the 'Kalewala,' the Iliad of the Finns, 330
Finnic tribes, original seat of the, 328
— their language and literature, 330
— national feeling lately arisen, 330
Firdusi, language in which he wrote his 'Shahnameh,' 218
Fire-worshippers. See Parsis
Firuz Shah, translations from Sanskrit into Persian, made by order of, 153

422 INDEX.

FLA

Flaminius, his knowledge of Greek, 95
Flemish language and literature, 182
Fradum, the German *friede*; from it *fraie* and *diffrayer*, 122 note
French dialects, number of, 50
— laws of change in the French language, 67
— nominatives and accusatives, 118
— origin of grammatical terminations in, 238
— origin of the French future in *rai*, 238
Friesian, multitude of the dialects of, 51
— language and literature, 182
Fromage, origin of the French word, 122
Future, the, in French, 238
— in Latin, 239
— in Greek, 239
— in Chinese, 405
— in other languages, 239, 240

G AEDHELIC, 203
 Gaelic, 203
Galatia, foundation and language of, 204
Galla language of Africa, family to which it belongs, 294
Ganas, the, or lists of remarkable words in Samskrit, 114
Garo, formation of adjectives in, 110 note
Gaur, 127
Gâthâs, or songs of Zoroaster, 217
Gobelin, Count de, his 'Monde Primitif,' 140
— compared with Hervas, 140
Gees language, 222
Genitive case, the term used in India, 109
— terminations of the genitive in most cases identical with the derivative suffixes by which substantives are changed into adjectives, 109
— mode of forming the genitive in Chinese, 116 note
— formation of genitives in Latin, 222
Geometry, origin of the word, 8
German language, history of the, 181
Gipsies, language of the, 219
Glass, painted, before and since the Reformation. 10
Gordon, Captain, on the dialects of Harness, 56

GOR

Goropius, his work written to prove that Dutch was the language spoken in Paradise, 135
Gospel, origin of the word, 130
Gothic, a modern language, 131
— similarity between Gothic and Latin, 128
— class of languages to which Gothic belongs, 184
— number of roots in it, 276 note
Goths, the, and Bishop Ulfilas, 188
Grammar, the criterion of relationship in almost all languages, 79
— English grammar unmistakably of Teutonic origin, 80
— no trace of grammar in ancient Chinese, 80
— early achievements of the Brahmans in grammar, 68
— and the Greeks, 86
— origin of grammar, 66
— causes of the earnestness with which Greek grammar was taken up at Rome, 103
— the Hindû science of grammar, 114
— origin and history of Samskrit grammar, 114
— origin of grammatical forms, 119
— historical evidence, 120
— collateral evidence, 121
— genealogical classification, 123
— comparative value of grammar in the classification of languages, 174
— comparative grammar, 222
— Bopp's ' Comparative Grammar,' 222
— origin of grammatical forms, 223
— mode of tracing back the grammatical framework of the Aryan languages to original independent words, 240, 242
— result of Bopp's ' Comparative Grammar,' 242
— Aryan grammar, 244
— Turkish grammar, 221
Grammarians, the, at Rome, 89
Greek language, the, studied and cultivated by the barbarians Berosus, Menander, and Manetho, 90, 91
— critical study of ancient Greek at Alexandria, 93
— first practical Greek grammar, 96
— generally spoken at Rome, 97
— earnestness with which Greek grammar was taken up at Rome, 105, 106
— principles which governed the formation of adjectives and genitives, 110 note

GRE

Greek language, spread of the Greek grammar, 111
— genitives in Greek, 115
— the principle of classification never applied to speech by the Greeks, 122
— Greeks and Barbarians, 122
— Plato's notion of the origin of the Greek language, 125
— similarity between Greek and Sanskrit, 145
— affinity between Sanskrit and Greek, 161
— formation of the dative in Greek, 229
— the future in Greek, 239
— number of forms each verb in Greek yields, if conjugated through all its voices, tenses, &c. 283 *note*
Greek, modern, number of the dialects of, 50
Greeks, their speculations on languages, 84
— the Grammarians, 95
— reasons why the ancient Greeks never thought of learning a foreign language, 95
— first encouragement given by trade to interpreters, 92
— imaginary travels of Greek philosophers, 82 *note*
— the Greek use of the term Barbarian, 125
Gregory of Nyssa, St., his defence of St. Basil, 31 *note*
Grimm, on the origin of dialects in general, quoted, 52
— on the klikon of nomads, quoted, 62
— his 'Teutonic Grammar,' 171
Growth of language, 39, 59
— examination of the idea that man can change or improve language, 40
— causes of the growth of language, 41
Guichard, Estienne, his work on language, 132 *note*
Guslava. *See Parsis*

HALHED, his remarks on the affinity between Greek and Sanskrit, quoted, 162
— his 'Code of Gentoo Laws,' 162 *note*
Hamilton, Sir W., on the origin of the general and particular in language, 394 *note*
Harold Haarfager, King of Norway, his despotic rule and its consequences, 196, 197
Haru-spex, origin of the name, 270
Harun-al-Rashid, translations made from Sanskrit works at his court, 153

HOM

Haug, his labours in Zend, 217
Hausa, language of Africa, family to which it belongs, 294
Hebrew, idea of the fathers of the church that it was the primitive language of mankind, 132
— amount of learning and ingenuity wasted on this question, 133
— Leibniz, the first who really conquered this prejudice, 135
— first Hebrew Grammar and Dictionary of the Bible, 43 *note*
— number of roots in, 278
— idea of, 42 *note*
— ancient form of the, 292
— Aramean modifications of, 292
— swept away by Arabic, 272
Hekate, an old name of the moon, 12
'Heljand,' the, of the Low Germans, 182
Hellenic branch of the Indo-European family of languages, 203
Herat, origin of the name, 253
Hermippus, his translation of the works of Zoroaster into Greek, 92
Herodotus, his travels, 90
— on the Pelasgi, 124 *note*
Hervas, his reduction of the multitude of American dialects to eleven families, 53, 56
— his list of works published during the 16th century, on the science of language, 130 *note*
— account of him and of his labours, 139, 140
— compared with Gabelin, 140
— his discovery of the Malay and Polynesian family of speech, 142
Hickes, on the proportion of Saxon to Norman words in the English language, 72
Himyaritic inscriptions, 292
Hindustani, real origin of, 68
— the genitive and adjective in, 110 *note*
— Urdu-zabán, the proper name of Hindustani, 329
Hiouen-thsang, the Chinese pilgrim, his travels into India, 130
Hiram, fleet of, 203
History and language, connection between, 71
Hôkol, or yhôla, of Norway, 197
— Snorraed's collection of, 198
Hom-sing, the Chinese pilgrim to India, his travels, 130
Homer, critical study of, at Alexandria, 94, 93
— influence of the critical study of

on the development of grammatical terminology, 93
Homer, on the changes Latin had undergone in his time, 40
Hors, origin of the French word, 122
Houses, name for, in Sanskrit, and other Aryan languages, 245
Humanity, the word, not to be found in Plato or Aristotle, 127
Humboldt, Alex. von, on the limits of exact knowledge, quoted, 19
Humboldt, Wilhelm von, his patronage of Comparative Philology, 171
Hungarians, ancestors of the, 333
— language of the, 338
— its affinity to the Ugro-Finnic dialects, 333
Huron Indians, rapid changes in the dialects of the, 54
Hymian, origin of the word, 7

IBN-WAHSHIYYAH, the Chaldean, his Arabic translation of 'the Nabatean Agriculture,' 291
— account of him and his works, 291 note
Iceland, foundation of an aristocratic republic in, 197
— intellectual and literary activity of the people of, 197
— later history of, 197
Icelandic language, 195-197
Iconium, Turkish sultans of, 319
Ilahi religion of the Emperor Akbar, 134
Illumination of manuscripts, lost art of, 10
Illyrians, Greek and Roman writers on the race and language of the, 123 note
Illyrian language, the ancient, 200 and
— languages, 243
India, the Mufti Abdul-Kadir Maluk's general history of, 183 note
— origin of the name of India, 236
Indian philosophers, difficulty of admitting the influence of, on Greek philosophers, 89 note
Indies, East and West, historical meaning of the names, 236
Indo-European family of languages. See Aryan
Inflectional stage of language, 287
Instrumental, formation of the, in Chinese, 117 note, 337
Interjectional theory of roots, 323
Interpreters, first encouragement given to, by trade, 52

Iran, modern name of Persia, origin of the, 231
Iranic class of languages, 213
Irish language, 303
Iron, name for, in Sanskrit and Gothic, 243
Iron, the Os of the Caucasus calling themselves, 252
Italian dialects, number of, 40, 201
— general growth of, 50
— real sources of, 49
Italians, the, indebted to the Greeks for the very rudiments of civilisation, 23
Italic class of languages, 201
Italy, dialects spoken in, before the rise of Rome, 201
Its, as a possessive pronoun, introduction of, 38

JARL, the Norse, 253
Jerome, St., his opinion that Hebrew was the primitive language of mankind, 132
Jews, literary idiom of the, in the century preceding and following the Christian era, 288
— and from the fourth to the tenth centuries, 289
— their adoption of Arabic, 289
— their return to a kind of modernised Hebrew, 289
Jones, Sir William, his remarks on the affinity between Sanskrit and Greek, 162
Julien, M. Stanislas, his notes on the Chinese language, 114 note
Jupiter Vizarius or Vinictus, 7
Justinian, the Emperor, sends an embassy to the Turks, 314

KÂFIR, 127
'Kalewala,' the, the Iliad of the Finns, 330
Kalmüks, the, 308, 313
Kapchakian empire, the, 310
Kara-Kalpak tribes near Aral-Lake, 316
Karadan dialect of Finnic, 331
Karians, Greek authors on the, 124 note
Kempe, André, his notion of the languages spoken in Paradise, 133 note
Kepler, quoted, 128 note
Khi-ян, the Chinese pilgrim, his travels into India, 130
Kirgis tribe, the, 317
Kirgis Hordes, the three, 317

KIR

Kirgis-Kasak, tribe of the, 318
Kumüks, tribe of the, in the Caucasus, 318
Kuthami, the Nabatæan, his work on 'Nabatæan Agriculture,' 291
— period in which he lived, 291 note
Kymric, 203

LABAN, language of, 289

Lady, the word, 316 note
Language, science of, one of the physical sciences, 1, 22
— modern date of the science of, 3
— names of the science of, 4
— meaning of the science of, 4
— little it offers to the utilitarian spirit of our age, 10
— modern importance of the science of, in political and social questions, 12
— the barrier between man and brute, 18
— importance of the science of, 23
— realm of, 26
— the growth of, in contradistinction to the history of, 29
— Dr. Whewell on the classification of, 29 note
— examination of objections against the science of, as a physical science, 30
— considered as an invention of man, 30
— the science of, considered as an historical science, 32
— historical changes of, 33
— almost stationary amongst highly civilised nations, 36
— growth of, 39
— the idea that man can change or improve language examined, 40
— causes of the growth of, 41
— processes of the growth of :—
  1. phonetic decay, 42
  2. dialectical regeneration, 49
— laws of change in, 66
— futile attempts of single grammarians and purists to improve, 68
— connection between language and history, 71
— independent of historical events, 72
— no possibility of a mixed, 74
— the Empirical Stage in the historical progress of the science of, 82
— speculations of the Brahmans and Greeks, 82
— the classificatory stage of, 113

LAN

Language, empirical or formal grammar, 115
— genealogical classification of, 122
— Harens's catalogue of works published during the 16th century on the science of, 130 note
— Leibniz, 135 et seq.
— Hervas, 139
— Adelung, 143
— Catherine the Great, 144
— importance of the discovery of Sanskrit, 147, 173
— value of comparative grammar, 174
— glance at the modern history of language, 177
— distinction between the radical and formal elements of, 223
— constituent elements of, 260
— morphological classification, 286, 287
— the inflectional stage of, 299, 337
— the radical stage of language, 296
— the terminational stage, 299
— consideration of the problem of a common origin of languages, 339 et seq.
— former theories, 339
— proper method of inquiry, 340
— man and brute, faculties of, 343
— the difference between man and brute, 366, 367
— the inward power of which language is the outward sign and manifestation, 369
— universal ideas, 370
— general ideas and roots, 370
— the primum cognitum and primum appellatum, 388, 389
— knowing and naming, 393
— language and reason, 400
— sound and thought, 401
— natural selection of roots, 403
— nothing arbitrary in language, 407
— origin and confusion of tongues, 402, 403

Languages, number of known, 26
— teaching of foreign languages comparatively a modern invention, 85
— reason why the ancient Greeks never learned foreign languages, 85
— 'The Mountain of Languages,' 88
— geographical classification of, 170
— tree for reducing the principal dialects in Europe and Asia to certain families of languages, 173 et seq.
— genealogical classification not applicable to all, 178
— radical relationship, 180
— comparative grammar, 222

Languages, formal and radical elements of, 234
— all formal elements of language originally substantial, 237
— degrees of relationship of, 290
— all languages reducible in the end to roots, 295
Langue d'Oïl, ancient song in the, 201
Laps, or Laplanders, 331
— their habitat, 331
— their language, 331
Latin, what is meant by, 60
— changes in, according to Polybius, 60
— the old Salian poems, 60
— provincialisms of Cicero, 60, 61
— stagnation of Latin when it became the language of civilisation, 61
— Latin genitives, 113
— similarity between Gothic and Latin, 128
— genealogical relation of Latin to Greek, 178
— the future in Latin, 229
Leibnitz, the first to conquer the prejudice that Hebrew was the primitive language of mankind, 136
— and the first to apply the principle of inductive reasoning to the subject of languages, 136
— his letter to Peter the Great, quoted, 137
— his labours in the science of languages, 138
— his various studies, 138
— on the formation of thought and language, quoted, 263
Lewlaw, dialects of the Island of, 50
Lettic language, the, 204
Lewis, Sir G. Cornewall, his criticisms on the theory of Raynouard, 175
Linnæus, his system, although imperfect, important to science, 16
Literary languages, origin of, 58
— inevitable decay of, 60, 61
Lithuanian language, the, 204
— the oldest documents in, 204
Livius Andronicus, 100
— his translation of the Odyssey into Latin verse, 100
Livonians, dialect of the, 351
Locative, formation of the, in all the Aryan languages, 226
— in Chinese, 117 note, 226, 227
— in Latin, 226
Locke, John, on language as the barrier between man and brutes, quoted, 14
— on universal ideas, quoted, 309
— his opinion on the origin of languages, 31

Lord, origin of the word, 126, 216
Lord's Prayer, number of languages in which it was published by various authors in the 16th century, 131 note
Lucilius, his book on the reform of Latin orthography, 107
Lucina, a name of the moon, 13
Luna, origin of the name, 12
Lusatia, language of, 205
Lycurgus, his travels mythical, 89

MACEDONIANS, ancient authors on the, 194 note
Madam, origin of word, 254
Mago, the Carthaginian, his book in Punic on agriculture, 90 note
Man, ancient words for, 309
Man and brutes, faculties of, 362
— differences between man and brutes, 367
Man, Isle of, dialect of the, 203
Manchu tribes, speaking a Tungusic language, 309
— grammar of, 336
— imitative sounds in, 353 note
Maneths, his study and cultivation of the Greek language, 90
— his work on Egypt, 91
— his knowledge of hieroglyphics, 91
Manka, the Indian, his translations from Sanskrit into Persian, 132
Massu, idiom in which it was written, 339
Maulana Izzu-d-din Khalid Khani, his translations from Sanskrit into Persian, 133
Mène, origin of the French word, 49
Menander, his study and cultivation of the Greek language, 90
— his work on Phœnicia, 90
Mendalites, or Nazoreans, the 'Book of Adam' of the, 280
Ment, origin of the termination in French adverbs, 47
Mescherâks, tribe of the, their present settlements, 316
Milton, John, number of words used by, in his works, 278
Ming-ti, the Emperor of China, allows the introduction of Buddhism into his empire, 149
— sends officials to India to study the doctrines of Buddha, 149
Missionaries, their importance in elucidating the problem of the dialectical life of language, 53, 54
Mixobibos, a barbarian, the same as Welsh and Belech? 37

Moallakat, or 'suspended poems,' of the Arabs, 713
Moffat, Rev. Robert, on the dialects of Southern Africa, 37
Mohammed ben Musa, his translation of the Indian treatise on algebra into Arabic, 152
Monboddo, Lord, on language as the barrier between man and brutes, quoted, 16
— his 'Ancient Metaphysics,' quoted, 163 note, 164
Mongolian dialects, entering a new phase of grammatical life, 37
Mongolian class of languages, 309
— grammar of, 336
Mongols, their original seat, 309
— three classes of them, 309
— their conquests, 309
— dissolution of the empire, 311
— their present state, 312
— their language, 312
Moon, antiquity of the word, 6
— Rask name for the, 6 note
Moravia devastated by the Mongols, 311
Mortal, origin of the word, 399
Mark and Vary, distinction between, 40
Mythology, real nature of, 11, 245

NABATEANS, the, supposed to have been descendants of the Babylonians and Chaldeans, 291
— the work of Kuthami on 'Nabatean Agriculture,' 291
National languages, origin of, 54
Nature, immutability of, in all her works, 33
— Dr. Whewell, quoted, 33, 34
Nebuchadnezzar, his name stamped on all the bricks made during his reign, 290
Neo-Latin dialects, 291
Neurgica, the, of Constantinus Porphyrogeneta, 57 note
Nestorians of Syria, former and present condition of their language, 287 note
Nicopolis, battle of, 380
No and nay as used by Chaucer, 254
Nobili, Roberto de, 158
— his study of Sanskrit, 158
Nogai tribes, history of the, 315
Nomad languages, 302
— indispensable requirements of a nomad language, 304
— wealth of, 41
— nomadic tribes and their wars, 324
— their languages, 328

Nominalism and Realism, controversy between, in the middle ages, 12
Norman words in the English language, proportion of, to Saxon words, 76
Norway, poetry of, 197
— the Skald or guide, 197
— the two Eddas, 198-199
Norwegian language, stagnation of the, 64
Number of known languages, 26

OBSOLETE words and senses since the translation of the Bible in 1611, 36, 37
Olötes, or Kalmüks, the, 309, 313
Onomatopoeia, theory of, 372
Ophir of the Bible, 208
Optics, a physical science, 32 note
Origen, his opinion that Hebrew was the primitive language of mankind, 132
Origin of language, consideration of the problem of the common, 339 et seq.
Ormuzd, the god of the Zoroastrians, mentioned by Plato, 214
— discovery of the name Auramazda in the cuneiform inscriptions, 214
— origin of the name Auramazda or Ormuzd, 214
Os, the, of Ossethi, calling themselves Iron, 232
Oscan language and literature, the, 202
Ossetish language, the, 313, 313
Outlakes, dialects of the, 36
Oula, 304 note
Owl-glass, stories of, 270

PAINTING, an historical science, 32 note
Pâli, once the popular dialect of Bahar, 147
Panaetius the Stoic philosopher at Rome, 103
Pânini, Sanskrit grammar of, 114
Pantomime, the, and the King, story of, 385
Paolino de San Bartolomeo, Fra, first Sanskrit grammar published by, 145, 161
Paradise, languages supposed by various authors to have been spoken in, 135
Parsi, period when it was spoken in Persia, 215
Parsis or fire-worshippers, the ancient, 213
— their prosperous colony in Bombay, 213

Parsis, their various emigrations, 218 note
— their ancient language, 213, 219
Pastric race, the, 333
Patar, origin of the Latin word, 49
Pay, as, origin of the word, 122
Pedro, Padre, the missionary at Calicut, 187
Pehlevi, or Huzvaresh language, 218
Pelasgi, Herodotus on the, 124 note
— Dionysius of Halicarnassus on the, 124 note
Percussion, etymology of, 44
Perion, his work on language, 131 note
Persian tribes and language, 333
Permic branch of the Finnic class of languages, 332
— the name of Perm, 332
— the Permic tribes, 323
Persia, origin of the Turkman or Kisilbash of, 315
Persian language, 76
— influence of the, over the Turkish language, 77
— the ancient Persian language. See Zend, Zend-avesta
— subsequent history of Persian, 218, 219
Peshin, meaning of the word, 237
Philolaus, the Pythagorean, his guess on the motion of the earth round the sun, 20
Philology, comparative, science of, 22
— an historical science, 23
— aim of the science, 74
Phœnician, closely allied to Hebrew, 292
Plato, his notion of the origin of the Greek language, 125
— on Zoroaster, quoted, 214 note
Plautus, Greek words in the plays of, 100
— all his plays were adaptations of Greek originals, 100
Pleiades, the origin of the word, 7
Poland invaded by the Mongols, 311
Polish, oldest specimens of, 304
Polybius, on the changes Latin had undergone in his time, 60
Pons, Father, his report of the literary treasures of the Brahmans, 141
Pott, Professor, his 'Etymological Researches,' 171
— his advocacy of the polygenetic theory, 353 note
Prâkrit idioms, the, 187
Prâtiçâkhyas, the, of the Brahmans, 124
Priest, origin of the word, 130
Priscianus, influence of his grammatical work on later ages, 112

Protagoras, his attempts to improve the language of Homer, 40
Provençal, the daughter of Latin, 175
— not the mother of French, Italian, Spanish, and Portuguese, 173
— the earliest Provençal poem, 201
Prussian, the old, language and literature of, 305
Ptolemy, his system of astronomy, although wrong, important to science, 17
Ptolemy Philadelphus and the Septuagint, 92 note
Ptôsis, meaning of the word in the language of the Stoics, 108, 109
Publius Crassus, his knowledge of the Greek dialects, 103
Pukhto, the language of Afghanistan, 218
Pythagoras, his travels mythical, 90
Pyrrha, original meaning of the name, 12

QUATREMÈRE on the Ophir of the Bible, 210 note
Quincy, origin of the word, 398 note
Quintilian, on the changes Latin had undergone in his time, 60
— on the omission of the final s in Latin, 61 note

RADICAL relationship of languages, 180
Radicals. See Roots
Rae, Dr., on the rapid changes in language in small communities, 55 note
Rask, Erasmus, his studies of Zend, 171, 212
Raven, the word, 378
Raynouard, his labours in comparative grammar, 175
— criticism of his theory of the Langue Romane, 175
Realism and Nominalism, controversy between, in the middle ages, 72
Regeneration, dialectic, one of the processes which comprise the growth of language, 42
Respectable, origin of the word, 244
Reval dialect of Esthonian, 331
Rig-Veda, the, quoted, 32 note
Romance languages, their Latin origin, 174
— modifications of, 200
— their origin in the ancient Latin languages, 202
Romans, the Langue, 175
Romansch language of the Grisons, 200
— translation of the Bible into, 201 note

Romance language, lower, or Engha-
     line, 201 note
Romans, their use of the term Barbarian,
     126
Rome, Greek generally spoken at, 96
— influence of Greece on Rome, 97
— changes in the intellectual atmo-
     sphere of, caused by Greek civilisa-
     tion, 103, 104
— the religious life of Rome more
     Greek than Roman, 104
— expulsion of the Greek grammar-
     ians and philosophers from Rome,
     104, 105
— compromise between religion and
     philosophy, 105
— while interest excited by grammati-
     cal studies in Roman society, 107
Roots or radicals, 262
— classes of roots, primary, secondary,
     and tertiary, 273, 274
— demonstrative and predicative roots,
     279, 280
— how many forms of speech may
     be produced by the free combina-
     tion of these constituent elements,
     286
— all languages reducible in the end to
     roots, 298
— the radical stage of language, 298
— general ideas and roots, 370
— origin of roots, 371
— the bow-wow theory, 372
— the pooh-pooh theory, 392
— natural selection of roots, 400
Russia devastated by the Mongols, 211

SABIUS, a word not found in clas-
     sical Latin, 99 note
Sæmund, Sigfusson, his collection of
     songs in Icelandic, 193
Sagard, Gabriel, on the languages of the
     Hurons, 54
Salian poems, the, and later Latin, 80
Salotar, translation of his work on veter-
     inary medicine from Sanskrit into
     Persian, 153
Sanskrit, formation of adjectives in,
     110 note
— grammar, 114
— similarity between Greek and, 141
— importance of the discovery of, 147
— history of the language, 147
— doubts as to its age and authenticity
     examined, 148
— accounts given by writers of various
     nations who became acquainted with
     the language and literature of India,
     148, 149

Sanskrit, the Mahommedans in India and
     their translations of Sanskrit works
     into Arabic and Persian, 150
Sanskrit, European Missionaries, 157
— studies and works of Frederick
     Schlegel, 168
— importance of the discovery of, in
     the classification of languages, 174
— its genealogical relation to Greek and
     Latin, 175
— antiquity of, 201
— Iranic languages, relation to, 212
— formation of the locative in, 227
— number of roots in, 276
Saraya, 252
Sassanian dynasty, Persian language of
     the, 215
Saxon language, proportion of Saxon
     to Norman words in the English
     language, 78
Savage tribes, rapid changes which take
     place in the languages of, 33, 34
Scaliger, J. J., his 'Diatriba de Euro-
     pæorum Linguis,' 133 note
Scandinavian branch of the Teutonic
     class of languages, 195
— the East and West Scandinavian
     races, 194
Schlegel, Frederick, his Sanskrit studies,
     168
— his work 'On the Language and
     Wisdom of the Indians,' 168
— how his work was taken up in Ger-
     many, 170
— his view of the origin of language,
     224
Schlegel, August W. von, his 'Indische
     Bibliothek,' 171
— his criticism on the theory of Ray-
     nouard, 173
Sciences, uniformity in the history of
     most, 4
— the empirical stage, 5
— the necessity that science should
     answer some practical purpose, 9
— the classificatory stage, 13
— theoretical or metaphysical stage, 18
— impulses received by the physical
     sciences from the philosopher and
     poet, 19
— difference between physical and his-
     torical sciences, 22
Scipios, influence of the 'Cosmopolitan
     Club,' at the house of the, 104
Scythian words mentioned by Greek
     writers, 252
Semitic family of languages, 34
— study of, 130
— constituent elements of the, 294

Semitic languages, divisions of the Semitic family of speech, 287
— Aramaic class, 287
— Hebraic class, 288
— Arabic class, 292
— intimate relations of the three classes to each other, 293
— Berber dialects, 294
— the Semitic and Aryan, the only families of speech deserving that title, 294
— genealogical table, 412
Serere, the tribe, 283
Serapeum, the, and Ptolemy Philadelphus, 83 note
Serpent, origin of the word, 395
Shah, title of, 218, 330
Shakspeare, William, total number of words used by, in his plays, 278
Shiria, Tungusic tribes of, 305
— Turkic tribes settled in, 316
— dialects, 318
Sibylla, or Sibulla, meaning of the word, 99 note
Sibyls of Cumæ, oracles of the, written in Greek, 97
Sigfusson. See Sæmund
Sigismund, the Emperor, and the Bohemian schoolmaster, anecdote of, 50
Silesia invaded by the Mongols, 309
Sinhind, meaning of, 151 note
Sir, origin of the word, 234, 235
Siriane tribes, their habitat, 332
— their language, 332
Sister, origin of, 45
'Skalda,' the, of Snorri Sturluson, 198
Sclavonic tribes, their settlement in Russia, 200 note
— languages, properly so called, 203
Slovakian language, the, 205
Smith, Adam, his opinion on the origin of language, 31
— on the formation of thought and language, quoted, 289
Smith, Sydney, on the superiority of mankind over brutes, quoted, 34 ?
Snorri Sturluson, his prose Edda, 198
— his 'Heimskringla,' 198
— his 'Skalda,' 198
Solomon's fleet of Tharshish, 268
Sung-yun, the Chinese pilgrim to India, his travels, 150
Sound, small number of names formed by the imitation of, 342
Species, offshoots of the root, 367
Spoken, origin of the Latin, 371
Squirrel, origin of the name, 392
Stewart, Dugald, his opinion on the origin of language, 31

Stewart, Dugald, his doubts as to the age and authenticity of Sanskrit, 146
— his view of the affinity of Greek and Sanskrit, 147
— on the origin of language, quoted, 355
Stoics, philosophy of the, in Rome, 105
Strabo on the Barbarians, 128 note
Sturluson. See Snorri
Super, origin of the word, 381
Swedish language, growth of the, 64, 199
Synonymes, 128, 297 400
Syria, origin of the Turks of, 318
Syriac language, date of the translation of the Bible into the, 287
— meaning of Peshito, 287 note
— decline and present position of the language, 287

TALMUD of Jerusalem and that of Babylon, literary riches of the Jews in the, 285
Targums, language in which they were written, 289
— most celebrated of them, 288 note
'Tarikhul-Hind,' the, of Al Birûni, 152
Tatar tribes, 308
— terms caused by the name, 309
— the Golden Horde, 310
Tataric languages, 309
— sometimes used in the same sense as Turanian, 306
Tavastian dialect of Finnic, 321
Terminations, grammatical, Horne Tooke's remarks on, quoted, 361
Terminology, grammatical, of the Greeks and Hindus, coincidences between the, 113
Testament, the New, translated into Persian, 164
— Old, number of words in the, 274
Teutonic class of languages, 191
— the English language, a branch of, 71
Tharshish, Solomon's fleet of, 268
Themistocles, his acquaintance with the Persian language, 44
Thommerel, M., on the proportion Saxon words bear to those from classical and miscellaneous sources in the English language, 79
Thracians, ancient, authors on the, 124 note
Thunder, origin of the word, 380
Tiberius Gracchus, his knowledge of Greek, 39
Tiberius the Emperor, and the grammarians, anecdote of, 39

INDEX. 431

TIB

Tibetan language, how adjectives are formed in the, 116 note
Timur, Mongolian empire of, 312
Tooke, Horne, on grammatical terminations, quoted, 261
— his answer to the Interjectional theory of roots, 264
Torgod Mongols, the, 313
Trade first encouraged the profession of interpreters, 24
Tungusic idioms, new phase of grammatical life of the, 37
Tungusic class of languages, 305
— geographical limits of the, 306
— grammar of, 334
Turanian class of languages, 34
— origin of term Turanian, 248
— Turanian race, 253
— names mentioned by Greek writers, 253
— component parts of Turanian speech, 254
— class of languages, 300
— a terminational or agglutinative class of languages, 300, 303
— divisions of the Turanian class, 301
— the name Turanian, 303
— characteristic features of the Turanian languages, 301, 303
— account of the languages of the Turanian group, 307
— genealogical table, 313
Turkic class of languages, 318
— grammar, 321
— profuse system of conjugation, 336
Turkish language, influence of imported words over the whole native aspect of the, 76
— two classes of vowels in, 307
— ingenuity of Turkish grammar, 321
— its advance towards inflectional forms, 331
Turkman, or Kisil-bash, origin of the, of Persia, 315
Turks, history of the, 312
— origin of the Turks of Asia Minor and Syria, 318
— origin and progress of the Osmanlis, 319
— spread of the Osmanli dialect, 318, 319
Turner, Sharon, on the proportion of Norman to Saxon words in the English language, 72
Turvâsa, the Turanian, 250
Twenty, origin of the [illegible]

UGR

UGRIC branch of the Finnic class of languages, 343
Ulfilas, Bishop, notice of him and of his Gothic translation of the Bible, 180
Umbrian language and literature, 202
Upanishads, the, translated from Sanskrit into Persian by Dârâ, 137
— translated into French by Anquetil Duperron, 137
Uralic languages, 328
Uran'hæ tribes, on the Chulym, 316
Urdû-zabân, the proper name of Hindustani, 399
Usbeks, history of the, 315

V

VÂCH, the goddess of speech, her verses quoted from the Rig-Veda, 93 note
Varro, de Re Rust. on Mago's Carthaginian agricultural work, quoted, 95 note
— his work on the Latin language, 107
— appointed by Cæsar librarian to the Greek and Latin library in Rome, 108
Vasco da Gama; takes a missionary to Calicut, 157
Vedas, the, 114
— differences between the dialect of the Vedas and later Sanskrit, 114
— objections of the Brahmans to allow the Vedas to be translated, 135
— story of Fehl, 135
Verbs, formation of the terminations of, in the Aryan dialects, 330
— modern formations, 331
Vergilius, 7
Very and Much, distinctions between, 40
Vibhakti, in Sanskrit grammar, 114
Voguls, the, 328
Votiakes, idiom of the, 332
— habitat of the, 332
Vyâkarana, Sanskrit name for grammar, 114

W

WALLACHIAN language, the, 200 note
Welsh, 203
Wends, language of the, 206
Whewell, Dr., on the science of language, 28
Williams, M., on the affinity between Sanskrit and Greek, 184
Windic, or Slavonic, languages, 204
— divisions and subdivisions of, 204

432 INDEX.

Winishu, the, 204
Witsen, Nicholas, the Dutch traveller, his collection of words, 135 note

XAVIER, Francis, his organisation of the preaching of the Gospel in India, 157
— his gift of tongues, 156

YAKUTS, tribe of the, 316
— dialect of the, 317
Yea and Yes, as used by Chaucer, 233

ZEND, Rask's studies of, 171
— Burnouf's, 172
— Haug's, 217
Zend-avesta, the, 171
— translated into Greek, 92
— Anquetil Duperron's translation, 172, 213

Zend-avesta, Rask and Burnouf's labours, 171, 172, 213
— antiquity of, 172, 213
— the words Zend and Zend-avesta, 212 note
— authority of the Zend-avesta for the antiquity of the word Arya, 245
Zenodotus, his renovation of the Article before proper names in Homer, 92
— the first to recognise the Anti, 92
Zens, original meaning of the word, 12
Zoroaster, or Zarathustra, his writings (the Zend-avesta), translated into Greek, 92
— translated by Anquetil Duperron, 172
— his Gâthâs, or songs, 217
— age in which he lived, 217
— not the same as Jaradashti in the Veda, 217
Zoroastrians. See Parsis.
— original seat of the, 239

www.ingramcontent.com/pod-product-compliance
Lightning Source LLC
Chambersburg PA
CBHW051722300426
44115CB00007B/430